WOMEN'S STUDIES QUARTERLY
VOLUME 53   NUMBERS 1 & 2   SPRING/SUMMER 2025

An educational project of the Feminist Press at the City University of New York and York College, City University of New York, with support from the Center for the Study of Women and Society and the Center for the Humanities at the Graduate Center, City University of New York

EDITORS
Shereen Inayatulla, York College, City University of New York
Andie Silva, York College, City University of New York

EDITORIAL DIRECTORS
Dána-Ain Davis and Kendra Sullivan

GUEST EDITORS
Ángeles Donoso Macaya, Borough of Manhattan Community College and The Graduate Center, City University of New York
Kendra Sullivan, The Graduate Center, City University of New York

POETRY EDITORS
JP Howard
Melissa Castillo Planas
Coco Sofia Fitterman
Kahina Meziant
Grisel Y. Acosta

CREATIVE PROSE EDITORS
Keisha-Gaye Anderson
Anna Joy Springer

VISUAL ARTS EDITORS
Maya von Ziegesar
jah elyse sayers
Crystal Z. Campbell
Shebani Rao

EDITORIAL ASSISTANTS
jah elyse sayers
Maya von Ziegesar

SOCIAL MEDIA & EVENTS MANAGER
Juwon Jun

INTERNS
Hannah Salzer
Maya Shabazz-Williams
Isabella Pinkhasov
Jennifer Bae Zorn
Abrelle Lawson

EDITORS EMERITAE
Red Washburn 2020–2023 ▪ Brianne Waychoff 2020–2022 ▪ Natalie Havlin 2017–2020
Jillian M. Báez 2017–2020 ▪ Matt Brim 2014–2017 ▪ Cynthia Chris 2014–2017
Amy Herzog 2011–2014 ▪ Joe Rollins 2011–2014 ▪ Victoria Pitts-Taylor 2008–2011
Talia Schaffer 2008–2011 ▪ Cindi Katz 2004–2008 ▪ Nancy K. Miller 2004–2008
Diane Hope 2000–2004 ▪ Janet Zandy 1995–2000 ▪ Nancy Porter 1982–1992
Florence Howe 1972–1982; 1993–1994

The Feminist Press at the City University of New York
ART DIRECTOR
Drew Stevens

DEVELOPMENT COORDINATOR & MANAGING EDITOR
Rachel Page

WSQ: Women's Studies Quarterly, a peer-reviewed, theme-based journal, is published by the Feminist Press at the City University of New York.

COVER ART
Home in the Hand, photograph by Mónica Palma

WEBSITE
feministpress.org/wsq

EDITORIAL CORRESPONDENCE
WSQ: Women's Studies Quarterly, The Feminist Press at the City University of New York, The Graduate Center, 365 Fifth Avenue, Suite 5406, New York, NY 10016; wsqeditorial@gmail.com and wsqeditors@gmail.com.

PRINT SUBSCRIPTIONS
Subscribers in the United States: Individuals—$70 for 1 year; $175 for 3 years. Institutions—$99 for 1 year; $249 for 3 years. Subscribers outside the United States: Add $40 per year for delivery. To subscribe or change an address, contact *WSQ* Customer Service, The Feminist Press at the City University of New York, The Graduate Center, 365 Fifth Avenue, Suite 5406, New York, NY 10016; 212-817-7915; info@feministpress.org.

FORTHCOMING ISSUES
WSQ Body Matters, Shereen Inayatulla, York College, City University of New York, Andie Silva, York College and The Graduate Center, City University of New York
WSQ Chronic: Living with Chronic Illness, Nancy K. Miller, The Graduate Center, City University of New York, Tahneer Oksman, Marymount Manhattan College

RIGHTS & PERMISSIONS
Fred Courtright, The Permissions Company, 570-839-7477; permdude@eclipse.net.

SUBMISSION INFORMATION
For the most up-to-date guidelines, calls for papers, and information concerning forthcoming issues, write to wsqeditors@gmail.com or visit feministpress.org/wsq or womensstudiesquarterly.com.

ADVERTISING
For information on display-ad sizes, rates, exchanges, and schedules, please write to *WSQ* Marketing, The Feminist Press at the City University of New York, The Graduate Center, 365 Fifth Avenue, Suite 5406, New York, NY 10016; 212-817-7918; sales@feministpress.org.

ELECTRONIC ACCESS AND SUBSCRIPTIONS
Access to electronic databases containing backlist issues of *WSQ* may be purchased through JSTOR at www.jstor.org. Access to electronic databases containing current issues of *WSQ* may be purchased through Project MUSE at muse.jhu.edu, muse@muse.jhu.edu; and ProQuest at www.il.proquest.com, info@il.proquest.com. Individual electronic subscriptions for *WSQ* may also be purchased through Project MUSE.

Compilation copyright © 2025 by the Feminist Press at the City University of New York. Unless otherwise noted, copyright in the individual essays is held in the name of their authors.

ISSN: 0732-1562   ISBN: 978-1-55861-324-9 $30.00

EDITORIAL BOARD

Aneil Rallin, Independent Scholar
Ángeles Donoso Macaya, The Graduate Center, CUNY, and BMCC, CUNY
Anna Zeemont, SUNY Buffalo State
Carolina Martins Vieira, Oncoclinicas
Chelsey Carter, Yale University
Christina Chica, University of California, Los Angeles
Cindy Tekobbe, University of Illinois Chicago
Damayanti Banerjee, Colorado State University
Debarati Biswas, New York City College of Technology, CUNY
Emily Drabinski, Queens College, CUNY
Javiela Evangelista, New York City College of Technology, CUNY
Jennifer Dominique Jones, University of Michigan
Jina B. Kim, Smith College
K. Allison Hammer, Southern Illinois University
Kate Haffey, University of Mary Washington
Kate Ozment, California State Polytechnic University, Pomona
Katina L. Rogers, Inkcap Consulting
Kendra Krueger, ASRC Community SensorLab and The Graduate Center, CUNY
LaToya Lydia Sawyer, St. John's University
Mariahadessa Tallie, Brown University
Maria Rita Drumond Viana, Universidade Federal de Ouro Preto
Marisa Solomon, Barnard College
Meg Weeks, University of Florida
Meredith Powers, York College, CUNY
Michael T. MacDonald, University of Michigan–Dearborn
Michelle M. Wright, Emory University
Nessette Falu, University of Texas at Austin
Nina Sharma, Barnard College
N. Tulio Bermúdez Mejía, University of Chicago
Peace Medie, University of Bristol
Rashida L. Harrison, Michigan State University
Ravynn K. Stringfield, University of Richmond
Roopika Risam, Dartmouth College
Sawyer K. Kemp, Queens College, CUNY
Sean Grattan, Quincy University
Shaka McGlotten, Purchase College
Shana MacDonald, University of Waterloo
Shardé Chapman, University of Detroit Mercy
Shay-Akil McLean, Independent Scholar
Sherita V. Roundtree, Towson University
Simone Chess, Wayne State University
Soniya Munshi, Queens College, CUNY
Stephanie Troutman Robbins, University of Arizona
Tanisha Ford, The Graduate Center, CUNY
Vani Kannan, Emory University

ADVISORY BOARD

Allia Abdullah-Matta, LaGuardia Community College, CUNY
Alyson Cole, Queens College and The Graduate Center, CUNY
Amy Herzog, Queens College and The Graduate Center, CUNY
Barbara Shaw, Allegheny College
Claudia Sofia Garriga-López, California State University, Chico
Cristina Khan, Stony Brook University
Crystal A. Jackson, Arizona State University
Heather Hewett, SUNY New Paltz
Heather Love, University of Pennsylvania
Heather Rellihan, Anne Arundel Community College
Hsiao-Lan Hu, University of Detroit Mercy
Kimberly Williams Brown, Vassar College
Laura Westengard, New York City College of Technology, CUNY
L. Ayu Saraswati, University of Hawai`i, Manoa
Lili Shi, Kingsborough Community College, CUNY
Loretta LeMaster, Arizona State University
Matthew Richardson, University of California, Santa Barbara
Namulundah Florence, Brooklyn College
Ren-Yo Hwang, Mount Holyoke College
Robyn Spencer, Lehman College, CUNY
Rupal Oza, Hunter College, CUNY
Saadia Toor, College of Staten Island, CUNY
Sarah Chinn, Hunter College, CUNY
Terri Gordon, The New School
TJ Boisseau, Purdue University

Contents

9 **Editors' Note**
Shereen Inayatulla and Andie Silva

13 **Introduction: *No estamos a la intemperie*: Opening Up the House of Feminisms**
Ángeles Donoso Macaya and Kendra Sullivan

23 ***Homes, Houses, and Shelters***
Mónica Palma
Casa 1. Casa maleta (Luggage House)
Casa 2. Shelter para Cayetana (A Shelter for Cayetana)
Casa 3. Muros para practicar matemáticas (Walls to Practice Math)
Casa 4. Un estacionamiento (A Parking Garage)

SECTION I. **ARTICLES**

31 **How Can Eurasian Borderlands Reshape Transnational Feminism? A Critical Examination of Missing Geographies and Overlooked Genealogies**
Tatsiana Shchurko

53 **Where's This Child's Mother? Black Birthing as "Raw Materials" in Media**
Makeba Lavan

69 **Blackqueer Currere: A Method in Three Breaths**
Robert P. Robinson

91 **How Do You Solve a Problem Like Maria von Clapp? Drag Pedagogy and the Limits of DEI**
Nino Testa

115 **Otra vez el hielo: Exclusión epistémica de los feminismos en espacios académicos**
Fernanda Rojas-Müller, Ana Luisa Muñoz-García, y Kyuttzza Gómez-Guinart

135 **The Ice Again: Epistemic Exclusion of Feminisms in Academic Spaces**
Fernanda Rojas-Müller, Ana Luisa Muñoz-García, and Kyuttzza Gómez-Guinart (translated by Camila Valle)

155 **Trans-Uranic Intimacies on a Queer(er) Planet**
Daisy Atterbury

177 **Anti-Colonial Dreams and Their Resonant Afterlives: Facing the Ends of Man in Han Kang's *The Vegetarian***
Sunhay You

197 ***Homes, Houses, and Shelters***
Mónica Palma
Casa 5. Casa y alberca (House and Swimming Pool)
Casa 6. En esta escuela están permitidos los gatos (In This School Cats Are Welcome)

SECTION II. **POETRY**

201 **Lessons on (from, for, to) a Free Press: My Path to the Newsroom**
Jen Schneider

205 **Women on horses**
Virginia Gris

207 **Everything sold to women**
Virginia Gris

209 **surface tension**
Elizabeth Sine

213 **Art and War (Homer's Art)**
Onur Ayaz

217 **The Sea Is Not a Question of Power**
Issis Palomo Sánchez

223 **slick**
Destiny Crockett

SECTION III. **CREATIVE PROSE**

231 **Indigenous Reflections on Poethood**
Lois Beardslee

237 **Cartas a Fabián (Recién llegamos y ya nos queremos ir)**
Carolina Suárez Latorre

247 **Circle Home**
Camille Goodison

251 **Watery Eyes**
Saba Khan

261 **La Vorágine en Cuerpo**
Fátima Vélez

SECTION IV. **CLASSICS REVISITED**

271 **Cartas y recados de una militancia por la paz: Olga Poblete y Gabriela Mistral**
Javiera Manzi A.

279 **Letters and Recados of a Militancy for Peace: Olga Poblete and Gabriela Mistral**
Javiera Manzi A. (translated by Camila Valle)

SECTION V. **BOOK REVIEWS**

287 **Review of *Psychoanalysis Under Occupation: Practicing Resistance in Palestine* by Lara Sheehi and Stephen Sheehi**
Ghina Abi-Ghannam

295 **Review of *The Home as Laboratory: Finance, Housing, and Feminist Struggle* by Lucía Cavallero and Verónica Gago, translated by Liz Mason-Deese**
César Barros Arteaga

301 **Review of *Set Fear on Fire: The Feminist Call That Set the Americas Ablaze* by LASTESIS, translated by Camila Valle, and *Against Ageism: A Queer Manifesto* by Simon(e) van Saarloos**
Claudia Cabello Hutt

307 **Review of *Between Shadows and Noise: Sensation, Situatedness, and the Undisciplined* by Amber Jamilla Musser**
Kimberly Juanita Brown

309 **Review of *Disappearing Rooms: The Hidden Theaters of Immigration Law* by Michelle Castañeda, with illustrations by Molly Crabapple**
Anne McNevin

313 **Review of *Of Human Born: Fetal Lives, 1800–1950* by Caroline Arni, translated by Kate Sturge**
Googie Karrass

317 *Homes, Houses, and Shelters*
Mónica Palma
Casa 7. Museo de arte, entre (Art Museum, Please Enter)
Casa 8. Una panadería con patio trasero (A Baker's Shop with a Back Patio)

SECTION VI. ALERTS AND PROVOCATIONS

321 **Através da lente dos Orixás:
Repensando solidaridades feministas globais**
Djamila Ribeiro

329 **Through the Lens of the Orixás:
Rethinking Feminist and Global Solidarities**
Djamila Ribeiro

Editors' Note

Shereen Inayatulla and Andie Silva

WSQ is uniquely positioned as an American journal that releases, almost exclusively, special themed issues. When we began our editorship term in 2023, the editorial team shared many possible avenues for the journal's future. Dána-Ain Davis, one of the editorial directors of *WSQ*, floated the idea of an unthemed issue with a broad call for papers open to feminist scholarship traversing a range of subject matters and approaches. We found this idea exhilarating, and the proposal was met with much enthusiasm among the members of our editorial board. We are grateful to and awed by Kendra Sullivan (*WSQ*'s other editorial director) and Ángeles Donoso Macaya (BMCC and The Graduate Center, CUNY) for bringing their creative vision to this Open Call and shaping the issue before you today.

The response to the call for papers proved that our readership was equally energized by the idea of an unthemed issue; it garnered an overwhelming number of submissions. This unprecedented volume of work felt at once heartening and indicative of the urgent need for feminist venues that welcome an array of articles, poetry, short fiction, and visual art. Unfortunately, as the guest editors discuss in their introduction, many barriers remain that impede the effort to share feminist scholarship, particularly with regard to securing funding at all stages of the publication process, inviting meaningful language inclusivity, and protecting academic freedom. These barriers reveal the rift between feminist mission statements such as ours and the material constraints imposed by an institutional context. As a number of authors as well as the Alerts and Provocations contributor, Djamila Ribeiro, consider, American exceptionalism also plays a role in the voices amplified and ideas circulated within U.S.-based publications. And thus, from our vantage point as general editors, this issue presented a humbling opportunity to reconsider our routines, reassess our process, learn from our limitations, and envision transformation.

This issue contains pieces composed in both their original language and in translation, underscoring the value of translanguaging within feminist knowledges but also scholarly production on a broader scale. We are incredibly grateful to Ángeles and Kendra for their tireless commitment to inclusivity. Yet we are sobered by the reality that translanguaging labor in the world of publishing—while invaluable to intellectual production and the exchange of ideas—demands resources and compensation not typically available to smaller-scale venues such as *WSQ*. We began this project with an earnest desire: a bilingual call for papers inviting bilingual submissions, and we were ambitious in our expectations of how our small-scale operation could respond.

Understandably, a bilingual call necessitates the availability of bilingual editorial team members prepared to answer queries or handle general email correspondence; likewise, bilingual submissions must be met with a process in place for bilingual copyediting and proofreading. With our dearth of resources, we struggled to cover all the tasks at hand and often relied on select members of the editorial team to wear multiple hats for the issue to remain on schedule. All publications (and print in particular) rely on production schedules to ensure timely turnarounds between submission and publication. Yet these timelines can expose the myriad pressures and constraints imposed by institutional mechanisms. In these moments of contradiction—of racing breathlessly to keep up with our own ambitions—we were reminded that much of this effort to stretch beyond our means inevitably falls to individuals already navigating layers of burden, already tasked with competing responsibilities. The challenges also underscore the ways in which feminist labor, and specifically feminist scholarship in the U.S., are often imprisoned by the strictures of monolingual anglocentric chauvinism. We are never surprised by this reality but feel distressed and indignant nonetheless.

As Kendra and Ángeles discuss in their introduction to this issue, our Open Call also faced an unexpected challenge with regards to peer review. Along with the guest editors, we did not foresee how gatekeeping, even when unintended, could manifest throughout the review and selection process. As feminist reviewers of feminist work, many of us are trained to approach contributors in earnest, as peers, by providing feedback with common questions in mind: Does this work meet the style and theme of the journal? Does it attend to conversations in the field while offering a significant contribution? Ideally, the resulting feedback can also communicate an awareness of the inevitable subjectivity that comes with such assessments. But these questions occlude the actual human interactions involved in meaningful peer support, mutual mentorship, and a baseline criteria of care. Ángeles and Kendra ask: "What processes, resources, and principles are needed so feminist peer review can materialize and thrive, so it is possible to accompany the writing process more holistically without reproducing the violence and the harms that seem embedded in the traditional double-blind peer-review process?" Extending their question, we add: How might we accomplish this when the work of peer review implies some level of gatekeeping in its underlying premise that there are "insiders" who hold the power to allow "outsiders" in? How can we rethink feminist peer review (and, more broadly, the labor of feminist journals) by prioritizing equity, mutual support, and shared knowledge?

The lessons gleaned during the production of this issue are not disconnected from broader sociopolitical conditions that demand we press on with "business as usual" in times of unacceptable colonial destruction, relentless violence, and attempts to eliminate fundamental human rights. The current living and working conditions are surreal; we cannot bend to ongoing demands that we compartmentalize daily horrors in order to complete our tasks. Instead, we are moved to strategize resistance through publications such as *WSQ*.

We know there are (and have always been) creative solutions to dismantling the barriers that dilute or distort feminist endeavors. The interventions we value rely upon collaboration and the deliberate recentering of our ideals and purpose. So, to begin, we invite readers to join us in acting upon the suggestions Kendra and Ángeles offer for transforming our practice of peer review. We take their reflections as a call to reexamine our principles in the face of an ever-ominous political landscape operating nationally and globally. This is also an optimal moment to act in homage to the ever-beloved Nikki Giovanni and Dorothy Allison, whose incredible legacies teach us to write with empathy and tell our stories, refusing to be silenced, dismissed, buried. We are eager to collaborate with our readers, contributors, and future coeditors on ushering more "open call" issues into existence, and in doing so, opening ourselves to possibilities as of yet unimagined.

As always, we are taking a moment to name the members of our exceptional *WSQ* team in a note of heartfelt gratitude. Thank you to our incomparable editorial assistants, Maya von Ziegesar and jah elyse sayers, who uphold the day-to-day activities of the journal with energy, elegance, and care. Thanks also to our wonderful fall 2024 intern from Queens College, Isabella Pinkhasov, and our brilliant graduate interns, Hannah Salzer, Maya Shabazz-Williams, and Jennifer Bae Zorn. Hannah, Maya, and Jennifer play a key role in helping us grow new spaces for *WSQ*, including our e-newsletter and forthcoming digital archive. We are continually grateful to Margot Atwell and Rachel Page at Feminist Press for their leadership and expertise, and to Jeanne Thornton and Lucia Brown for the patience and precision they bring to supporting *WSQ* events. We'd like to thank our magnificent editorial directors, Kendra Sullivan (Center for the Humanities) and Dána-Ain Davis (Center for the Study of Women and Society), for helping us shape and manage the labor of this journal with unwavering compassion. Endless gratitude to the *WSQ* editorial board and to the poetry, creative prose, and visual arts editors for their incredible labor and insights during the process of accepting submissions and beyond. Finally, many thanks to Juwon Jun and Sampson Starkweather (Center for the Humanities) for helping to amplify and celebrate the work published in *WSQ*.

Shereen Inayatulla
Professor of English
York College, CUNY

Andie Silva
Associate Professor of English
York College, CUNY

Introduction: *No estamos a la intemperie*: Opening Up the House of Feminisms

Ángeles Donoso Macaya and Kendra Sullivan

When we began to develop our Open Call issue, we found inspiration in the image-concept of feminisms as a madriguera—a den, a hole, a burrow—which Argentine feminist thinker Verónica Gago offers in her prologue to Carolina Meloni's book *Feminismos transfronterizos* (2021, 7). The burrow is a porous refuge; its many openings and holes enable nonhierarchical ways of entering, engaging with, and departing from.

This seemed an eloquent image as a starting point; it captured the impetus underpinning the Open Call. Hence the title of the Open Call: *No estamos a la intemperie* (we are not in the open). However, given the context(s) in which we were/are writing—manufactured crisis everywhere: a housing crisis in NYC aggravated by the misadministration of Eric Adams, who has put the blame on necessary spending after an "unprecedented influx" of asylum seekers (New York City Comptroller 2024); a manufactured humanitarian crisis on the southern border of the United States and in many other borders (Morales 2018); a manufactured famine and a genocide in Palestine that seems to have no end and that has already lasted for more than a year (B'Tselem 2024)—we ask, what does it mean to be able to pause to give oneself the time and the space to think and write? How can one formulate thoughts, rehearse ideas, amid such widespread precariousness—amid a genocide? Can we say, "No estamos a la intemperie," given the lethal conditions under which thousands of people are forced to survive daily?

We think we can as long as this clause, more than an affirmation, is read and understood as a rehearsal—the rehearsal of a possibility, of a horizon.

We mean the kind of horizons that *also* materialize daily in NYC as well as in many other places and corners of the world, the worldings that an ecology of practices—mutual aid projects, Gaza solidarity encampments, and many other initiatives—have enabled and set in motion, and continue doing so, despite all.

This is why in this issue we center Escuelita Santuario, the weekly art workshop that artist Mónica Palma facilitated for children in Bay Ridge, Brooklyn. While their parents filled out asylum paperwork, the children imagined and manifested cardboard houses.

Their artworks annex in practical, imaginal, and conceptual ways other sanctuary and migrant solidarity initiatives devised by community members, as well as, more broadly, the multinodal work of the activist-scholars in this issue trying to write or organize *into*—literally burrow *into*—the everyday emergency of the present in order to break ground and build foundations that better support societal resistance and its cousin, environmental resurgence.

We are moved—no, motivated—by the dedication and imagination of the children who participated in Escuelita Santuario, by their playfulness and creativity, by their will to make home despite everything, wherever they are, in whatever situation they find themselves. In Mónica's accompanying text, we learn that as often as not, the children were building their shelters for each other—their siblings and friends, both present and absent. This tracks for us, too.

"Home" has to be built *for* something bigger than the individual body or exclusionary community. Shelter is a social desire—achieved, if at all, socially through some combination of glass, brick, mortar, stone, and the will to co-construct belonging in spite of unsafety on behalf of the collective body. Such shelters are gestures that protect against isolation. How do we conceive of and construct belonging during times of violent conflict, organized neglect, and social and environmental breakdown? How do we conceive and construct a house of feminisms?

While celebrating the Halloween and Día de los Muertos season in New York City, a six-year-old reminds us that the veil is thin between the city and spirit world. He says it is a good time to talk to our ancestors. During times of near-total planetary discord such as we are living in and through, the social safety net is similarly thin. We can see right through it. We can see others slip right through it. It is a good time to see who is a la intemperie:

who is out in the open. It is a good time to ask: How can we bring everyone in? We find, sadly, we cannot answer that question, even at the scale of a special issue.

It is in and through this era of massive, unscripted slippage between the inside and outside that the children build their dream homes. They build homes out of recycling collected by Mónica on the Upper West Side of Manhattan, one of the world's most affluent neighborhoods. When we look at the homes they built, terms like *ad hoc, at-hand, handmade, just-in-time*, and *temporary* come to mind. But so do words like *heartful, indomitable*, and *belonging against all odds*.

Some of their homes come with handles, and Mónica writes that they are luggage homes—homes as suitcases, maletas, or valijas. The children's responses to their plight are generative, poetic, and at the same time very strategic and concrete. Their ideal houses have material form: strong walls, windows, and doors that open, enabling the flow of air and the strength of hope, and close, fabricating protections that honor inherent human vulnerabilities. They have handles and wheels. Because. The makeshift cities they knit into neighborhoods suggest a context and a past both common and specific that survives the violence of conflict and displacement. They conjure a somewhere to settle without recapitulating to the usual patterns of colonial settlement. They offer a collective design led by children amply supported by adults who believe in the authority and autonomy of their collaborators, no matter their age, education, or access to power, privilege, and platform. The sculptures remind us that all children are artists, agents of their own experience, and architects of the pasts they inhabit, the presents they have inherited, and the futures they will bring into being.

The Escuelita Santuario project also connects us to the architectural imaginings of June Jordan, a onetime CUNY professor who collaborated with R. Buckminster Fuller, the "philosopher of shelter," to reimagine Harlem. Jordan worked with Fuller to research an architectural horizon that would allow Harlem residents to outmaneuver urban development and renewal plans that were thinly masked efforts to exile Black communities from their social centers. Likewise, in her young adult novel *His Own Where* (1971), Jordan narrates a season in the life of a young person whose father has been hit by a car. A life cut short by badly designed highways bisecting Black neighborhoods in NYC. The "man-child," as Sapphire calls him in the introduction to the reprint published by Feminist Press (2010), manages his life and household alone until he meets Angela, with whom he rebuilds his home's interior and, later, a graveyard, in the architectural image of joyful resistance. Before she wrote the book, Jordan described it in a letter to Matilda Welter as the story of a child who draws the city differently. She imagines:

> A boy who conceives an elaborate plan for a New City and then presents this plan as a writing assignment to his teacher. ("What a lovely imagination you have, Reggie.") Then presents the plan to his parents/father: "That's a fine fantasy, you have there." Then shows it to his friends: "You some kind of a nut? Where you going to put the cars, man?" Thing is, Reggie is not dreaming: His New City is a place and a way of living that he wants to happen, right away, for real. . . .
>
> The story, his plan, would present many facets of what I take as essentials to humane environment. It could be called: A Pad is a Place or His Own Where. (Jordan 1969, quoted in Fish 2019, 196–214)

Jordan's projects help us remember ancient and rehearse new ways of acknowledging children as historical actors with the capacity to remake the world out of cardboard, tape, and paint.

Syrian architect Marwa al-Sabouni offers insight into how humans might build enduring peace out of rubble: "We cannot imagine our dream home without engaging with reality: we must ask ourselves, of which materials should it be built, what kind of stone, wood or mortar? We cannot begin to design it without imagining its location and picturing its surroundings" (2021, 10). We don't want to stretch the metaphor too much, but if feminisms are a porous house rebuilt in equal parts from the radical imaginary and from the rubble of the patriarchy, so is *WSQ*.

With this Open Call issue, we sought to open *WSQ* to voices, perspectives, and problems that may have been previously ignored or left out in the open—a la intemperie. We wanted to give material form to the openness of the Open Call by expanding the boundaries horizontally. Our Open Call asked: "Who is missing from *WSQ*'s discourse and how can the journal remove barriers to those already actively reworlding feminisms?"

The metrics we formulated as editors for the peer-review process was part of this rehearsal—our (naive?) attempt to counter the rigidity and the weight (the burden?) of the peer-review process.

The metrics asked:

— Is it written by an extramural scholar (defined as an individual advancing theory outside of institutional support structures) or an emerging scholar (defined as an individual with less than two journal articles or chapters, no more than one monograph, graduate students, non-tenure-track professors, postdoctoral fellows, and contingent faculty)?
— Is it written from an underrepresented standpoint and/or does it speak to and from the experiences and perspectives of frontline intellectuals?
— Does it expand or constellate feminist geographies and solidarities?
— Does it foreground creativity, community, and collaboration as intrinsic to knowledge process, practice, and product?
— Does it increase equity or redistribute power in demonstrable ways?
— Is it timely and urgent?
— Is it engaged with, does it depart from, or does it build upon feminist legacies?

We thought we could do it, that we could stretch the possible just a bit. We thought that we could open *WSQ*, this wonderful house of feminisms, so that other voices could enter; yet pretty soon we realized we would not be able to live up to our own expectations as editors. Two people might hold up a tent, but a temporary home will never supplant the need for housing, hospitals, and schools.

The Open Call Process
We received over eighty article submissions before the submission deadline. There were submissions on an array of topics, from Black birth to breath to death, from the U.S. legal system's culpability for impacts of the HIV/AIDS crisis on Black women and families to the socio-spatial symptoms, contours, and habits of settler colonialism. There were amazingly insightful and important papers on the National Police Archives in Guatemala, women oncologists in positions of power, Indigenous femicide in what is commonly referred to as Canada, the quiet resistance of nail salon workers, and the invisibilized lives of university sex workers.

Because we still needed to abide by the editorial guidelines and the peer-review process, we had to cut the amount of articles down to twenty—not only would it have been materially impossible for us coeditors to find peer reviewers for every single submission, but also we knew that, even if we did, we would not be able to publish eighty articles in one single issue. This was, perhaps, the first humbling / "mmmmmm ... ok" moment.

After the first round of peer reviews was complete, another humbling / "mmmmmm ... ok" moment. While all reviewers offered generous and thorough feedback, only some reviewers followed the metrics we set forth in their evaluations. Many defaulted to the metrics of their own field(s) or area(s) of expertise. The problem of disciplinary specialization, and the difficulty of finding readers who have the skills, tools, and support necessary to transcend specialization, affects all inter- and intradisciplinary projects, but it is especially a problem when trying to outmaneuver barriers to participation that might look or feel like "quality control" when in reality they reflect internalized gatekeeping. The reviews made us doubt our own capacities as readers and evaluators working purposively outside of any bounded disciplinary milieu, a la intemperie. We heard: This article does not meet the standard or quality level of *WSQ* (what is that standard? we ask); this author does not know how to write an academic article (is there only one acceptable way of writing academic articles? we ask); this article has structural issues; this one lacks a literature review; and so on. This is not to criticize reviewers, who are straight-up amazing activists, scholars, and administrators making big strides in their fields and in the lives of emerging feminist scholars. This is to call for greater discussion around the merits and habits of anonymous peer review as anti-egalitarian: as being unfit for the cultivation of more inclusive feminisms.

After we digested these reviews and responses, we tried to guide the authors in the revision process. We had to let go of some of the articles we had chosen in that first round. After the second review round, we had to reject a few other articles. We ended up with seven articles—less than 10 percent of what we initially received. To us, all of this felt like a failure, an abdication. However, we did not have the resources needed—above all, the time—to provide meaningful accompaniment and guidance to the authors in the revision process.

So much for this Open Call! An Open Call we had initially envisioned as "a mechanism to ensure feminists who have been missing from the field and feminist discourse gain entry into the house of feminisms." Yes, undoubtedly many peers felt invited to enter la madriguera, the house of feminisms— numerous authors indicated in their cover letters that they had felt inspired and moved by the Call. But then, prospective authors and guest coeditors, we all found ourselves facing up the insurmountable tower (or lost in the rabbit hole?) that is the peer-review process.

So, what the Open Call process taught us—or, better said, what it made us remember, because we learned this lesson from Audre Lorde, another CUNY educator—is that you can't dismantle existing barriers and disciplinary habits (academia's inertia) with the tools—or in the houses—of the master. We actually need to step outside, and like Mónica Palma, like June Jordan, invite others to imagine other kinds of shelter.

For a *WSQ* open call to work effectively as a "nonexclusionary framework," it would need to rely on (or work with) feminist forms of peer reviewing. So, we ask, what does feminist peer reviewing look like? What processes, resources, and principles are needed so feminist peer review can materialize and thrive, so it is possible to accompany the writing process more holistically without reproducing the violence and the harms that seem embedded in the traditional double-blind peer-review process?

We can say that we felt inadequate in our capacity to assess what good writing or good scholarship look like after we received the peer reviewers' reports. We can also say we failed as coeditors in that we were not able to ensure that all prospective authors felt welcomed, seen, and heard in this porous house—as we indicated, in numbers, of the over eighty submissions we originally received, only seven made it to the final table of contents.

We can say we experienced and learned about failure; and this learning process has been truly generative.

We can say, following Jack Halberstam in *The Queer Art of Failure*, that failure is "a refusal of mastery" (2011, 11). In *Unthinking Mastery*, Julietta Singh revisits Halberstam's ideas; we echo her reading. There, Singh offers, "the undoing of masterful subjectivities can be located precisely in mastery's disappointments, in understanding failure as a 'refusal of mastery'" (2018, 175). This reading casts light into our own refusal to master the peer-review process. Who gets to decide what counts and what does not count as an "academic article"? In a way, after the whole process, we come to understand, following Singh, that "our ways of 'inhabiting structures of knowing' are ways that obscure and legitimize the masterful fracturing of particular bodies, spaces and things" (175).

When we refuse mastery, we already are a la intemperie, in a way—we are left to our own devices. Among these devices, we offer a situated reading of the correspondence between Chilean writers Gabriela Mistral and Olga Poblete, "two friends, intellectuals, and peace activists who in the mid-twentieth century strengthened the horizons of feminist emancipation with a materialist and anti-imperialist conception of peace," as Javiera Manzi A. writes in her Classics Revisited piece. Also, the work of feminist scholars, writers, and thinkers who penned their contributions in Spanish or Portuguese. Offering their work in their original language alongside an English translation is a minor gesture that continues the work started by fellow *WSQ* guest coeditors to counter the lack of English translations of feminist voices from the Global South—particularly of Black feminist voices, as Djamila Ribeiro argues in her Alerts and Provocations piece.

Besides these commissioned pieces, the list of books reviews that we carefully curated to offer a wider range of problematics, methods, and analytics, and the poems and creative prose that are a staple of *WSQ*—as they are for us in life—the works and topics that we present in this Open Call issue include transnational feminisms that surface new geographies and genealogies; representations of Black maternity in popular media; an emerging curriculum for understanding Black and queer experience; drag pedagogy in a conservative state; the hegemony of English feminisms and novel pathways to publication and circulation of vast and vital feminist strategies that hold no truck with English; deep readings of vegetarianism as resistance to the colonial state and corporeal subjection of othered bodies in fiction; and the afterlives of uranium resonating with the lingering possibility of a queerness that seeps into every aspect of nature and culture.

We close our brief introduction by extending our deepest gratitude to *WSQ* general editors Shereen Inayatulla and Andie Silva, our colleagues and accomplices, and to editorial assistant Maya von Ziegesar for her relentless work and constant guidance. We also thank Rachel Page, jah elyse sayers, Feminist Press, and the Center for the Humanities for their essential support.

Ángeles Donoso Macaya is an immigrant feminist scholar, educator, and writer from Santiago, Chile, based in New York. She is professor of Latin American visual studies in the PhD program in Latin American, Iberian, and Latino Cultures at the CUNY Graduate Center, and professor of Spanish and Latin American literatures and cultures at BMCC. Her research and writing spans Latin American and Caribbean photography theory and history, counter-archival production, human rights activism, documentary film, (trans)feminisms in the Southern Cone, and public humanities scholarship. She is the author of *The Insubordination of Photography/La insubordinación de la fotografía* (University of Florida Press, 2020; Metales Pesados, 2021) and the autobiographical essay *Lanallwe* (Tusquets, 2023), and coauthor, along with photographer Paz Errázuriz, of *archivo imperfecto* (Metales Pesados, 2023). Between 2020 and 2023, Ángeles was faculty lead of the Mellon Seminar on Public Engagement and Collaborative Research

Archives in Common: Migrant Practices/Knowledges/Memory, a project developed in collaboration with La Morada, an undocumented family–owned Oaxacan restaurant in the South Bronx. Ángeles is member of the Social Text Collective and cofounder of the activist research collective somoslacélula, which creates video-essays that respond to pressing matters.

Kendra Sullivan is a poet, a public artist, and an activist scholar. She is director of the Center for the Humanities at the CUNY Graduate Center, where she led the Andrew W. Mellon Seminar on Public Engagement and Collaborative Research from 2014 to 2024. She is a codirector of the NYC Climate Justice Hub, the publisher of *Lost & Found: The CUNY Poetics Document Initiative,* and a co-editorial director of *Women's Studies Quarterly*. Kendra has produced public art addressing water access and equity issues in cities around the world and has published her writing on art, environment, and engagement widely—her most recent op-ed in *City Limits* calls on civic leaders to help make CUNY the climate justice university of New York. She is the cofounder of the Sunview Luncheonette, a cooperative arts venue in Greenpoint, Brooklyn, and a member of Mare Liberum, an eco-art collective. Her books include *Zero Point Dream Poems* (Doublecross Press) and *Reps* (Ugly Duckling Presse).

Works Cited

B'Tselem: The Israeli Information Center for Human Rights in the Occupied Territories. 2024. "Manufacturing Famine: Israel Is Committing the War Crime of Starvation in the Gaza Strip." https://www.btselem.org/publications/202404_manufacturing_famine.

Fish, Amy. 2019. "Dreaming 'for Real': June Jordan's *His Own Where* as Youth History." *The Lion and the Unicorn* 43 (2): 196–214. https://dx.doi.org/10.1353/uni.2019.0019.

Gago, Verónica. 2021. Prologue to *Feminismos Transfronterizos: Mestizas, Abyectas y Perras,* by Carolina Meloni. Madrid: Kaótica Libros.

Halberstam, Jack. 2011. *The Queer Art of Failure*. Durham: Duke University Press.

Morales, Maria Cristina. 2018. "The Manufacturing of the US-Mexico Border Crisis." In *The Oxford Handbook of Migration Crises*, edited by Cecilia Menjívar, Marie Ruiz, and Immanuel Ness. London: Oxford University Press. https://doi.org/10.1093/oxfordhb/9780190856908.013.40.

New York City Comptroller. 2024. "Asylum Seeker Staffing Contract Comparison and Review." https://comptroller.nyc.gov/reports/asylum-seeker-staffing-contract-comparison-and-review/.

al-Sabouni, Marwa. 2021. *Building for Hope*. London: Thames & Hudson.

Singh, Julietta. 2018. *Unthinking Mastery: Dehumanism and Decolonial Entanglements*. Durham: Duke University Press.

Homes, Houses, and Shelters

Mónica Palma

In the middle of the week, I walk on the streets looking for cardboard; each neighborhood's recycled bundles look different. In Crown Heights, Brooklyn, where I live, I mainly see produce boxes stained with vegetable juice and neatly packed by grocers, but one afternoon, I found an impeccable box filled with three beautiful, corrugated layers. Soho in Manhattan has the cleanest and newest trash at a particular time of the afternoon.

At the Good Shepherd Lutheran Church Immigration Legal Clinic in Bay Ridge, Brooklyn, a group of two to six volunteers, me included, work with a group of children, making art while the adults fill out forms to apply for asylum. Single mothers, aunts and grandmothers, cousins, and all kinds of family configurations come to the clinic from places like Venezuela, Honduras, Colombia, and Ecuador, and some single men in groups arriving from Congo and Senegal. Most of them come seeking help in their application for asylum, but the clinic also tries to be an environment of community and companionship.

I brought in the cardboard I'd collected. That Thursday, as usual, we had children of different ages, starting from two years old. Almost in unison, as if intuitively, the children started to build miniature homes and fantastical playgrounds. A few weeks before, the children had been making cartonera books, so most were already familiar with the material. The preverbal children used a few essential words and many body gestures to narrate their constructions, while the older kids narrated their intentions with lots of detail. A child whose name I sadly don't remember (many children come only for one to two sessions) came with her two-year-old sister to make a construction and, looking rushed and energetic, told me that she also wanted to make a shelter for the little one. The first constructions made by a group of young children, ages two to six, were about playgrounds; as they glued and painted shapes, slides, and swings, they made sounds like wooosh, yooohooo, and weeee.

The activity of building homes and shelters was initiated by the children. In the Reggio Emilia educational approach, this is referred to as a "child-centered" curriculum; it consists of tuning in to children's actions, stories, and interests with the aim of fostering activities that are relevant to their circumstances. Many of the designs ended up being portable, foldable, or having wheels. The children's capacity to express their current reality was profoundly moving.

Mónica Palma is a multidiciplinary artist and art educator. She was born in Mexico City and currently lives and works in Brooklyn, New York. She is an adjunct lecturer at Lehman College.

Casa maleta (*Luggage House*), 2024. Photograph by Mónica Palma.

Only a week after the family's arrival to NYC, three sisters and one brother worked on this house. The youngest of the sisters was around seven years old, and the others around twelve and fourteen—the brother was fourteen or fifteen. I always thought that the older girls looked like twins, the same hair length and style, same height, and similar facial expressions.

When they worked on their project, the floor was our table; the materials were roughly organized on the edges of the room. At the end of the session, the children showed me that the house had walls that elevated and enclosed the construction. There was a handle too, at the top of the structure, like purses and bags have. One of the older girls looked at me, excited, and said: It's a luggage house! It looked to me that in that precise moment, she realized that their house was also a suitcase, a maleta, a valija, but maybe since the beginning, the four of them had this in mind.

Shelter para Cayetana (*A Shelter for Cayetana*), 2024. Photograph by Mónica Palma.

The girl is nine years old and wears her hair long. In the few sessions that I've seen her, it's clear that she loves materials. She is always rushing to make something; she is kind, soft-spoken, and speaks with a lisp. She has eczema on her neck and arms. She always comes with her toddler sister, Cayetana, a determined two-year-old. (I feel embarrassed for not learning all the children's names, I feel I'm being unfair to them). During the house-making session, Cayetana's sister decided to make a shelter for the little one. The legal clinic was about to close, but she was committed to finishing her construction. When she finished it, she brought it to Cayetana like it was Día de Reyes and said: Here is your shelter, Caye.

Muros para practicar matemáticas (*Walls to Practice Math*), 2024.
Photograph by Mónica Palma.

Two young boys worked together in the construction of this house. From our cardboard pile, they picked a set of cardboard cell dividers, those used to ship wine and ketchup bottles; the two of them tried hard to push the blue paint inside of the walls. While working, I spotted them doodling on the walls of their tiny house, but then I realized that they were practicing math; doing some basic additions and subtractions. One was a year older and was teaching math to his younger brother. Maybe because the floor of the atrium became a tiny city under construction, I saw the two boys practicing math in the walls of an actual town.

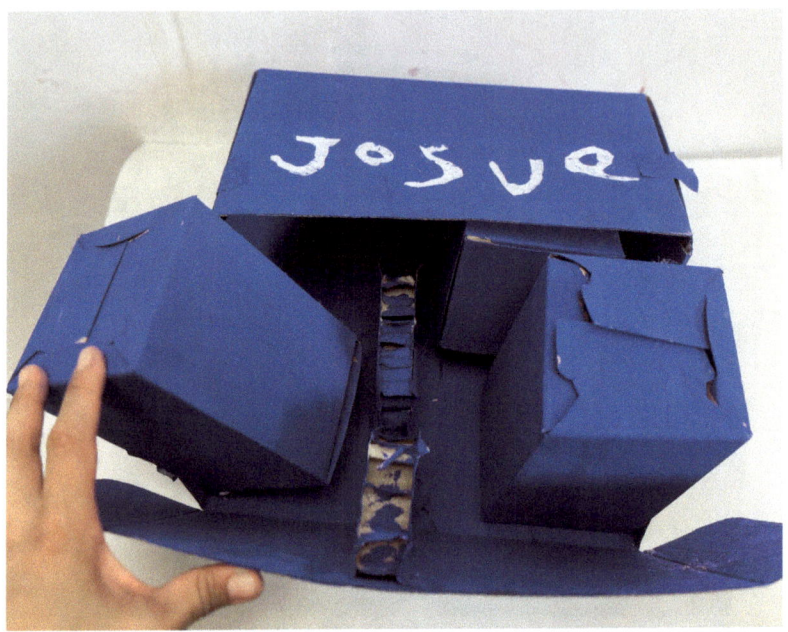

Un estacionamiento (*A Parking Garage*), 2024. Photograph by Mónica Palma.

This house is a parking garage. I remembered that when other volunteers and I saw the dynamism in the house, we were amazed. The structure is made of units, and when the parking garage closes, the construction folds, and everything fits perfectly inside. Everything is blue, and that effort takes time. Inside, there is a car with two wheels that needs to exit in reverse to fit. This project reminds me of the casa maleta, of living-places that fold and are movable and portable.

SECTION I. **ARTICLES**

How Can Eurasian Borderlands Reshape Transnational Feminism? A Critical Examination of Missing Geographies and Overlooked Genealogies

Tatsiana Shchurko

Abstract: This paper critically examines the marginalization of Eurasian perspectives within transnational feminist studies, arguing that the omission of former state-socialist geographies limits feminist engagement with global power dynamics, imperialism, and coloniality. It highlights the importance of integrating insights from Eurasian borderlands, shaped by Russian and other imperial formations, to expand feminist analyses of state violence, neoliberalism, and resistance. Drawing from historical connections and contemporary challenges, the paper advocates for reimagining transnational feminism through geographically diverse and epistemically inclusive frameworks. By addressing gaps in scholarship and fostering solidarities that transcend U.S.-centric narratives, the paper underscores the urgency of incorporating Eurasian feminist contributions to deepen the understanding of imperial crises and global struggles against oppression. **Keywords:** Eurasia, transnational feminism, Cold War, imperialism, feminist methodologies, solidarity

In 2016, I moved to the U.S. to pursue a PhD in Women's, Gender, and Sexuality Studies, building on my work as a queer feminist scholar and activist in Belarus. My PhD work expanded my interest in how feminist movements connect across geographies, particularly within the power dynamics of empires. I became intrigued by the historical links between U.S. Black activists and the Soviet Eurasian borderlands. I examined how these connections, alongside Eurasia's complex history of imperialism and authoritarianism, could challenge and enrich transnational feminist frameworks. However, I encountered epistemic gaps when trying to position Eurasia within U.S.-centric transnational feminist frameworks, prompting me to question why Eurasia is often overlooked. Highlighting Eurasia and amplifying its perspectives became both a challenge to U.S.-centric feminist thought and a search for new pathways of solidarity between oppressed communities.

Posing a Problem
Despite its roots in the work of scholars of color like Chandra Talpade Mohanty, Inderpal Grewal, Elora Halim Chowdhury, and Richa Nagar, U.S.-centric narratives still dominate transnational feminist inquiries. Feminist scholarship from the Eurasian borderlands is often relegated to "area studies," which prioritizes Western knowledge and reduces local scholars to "native informants" (Donovan 2023; Doolotkeldieva and Ortmann 2024; Marat and Aisarina 2021). Eurasia is frequently imagined as an isolated cultural landscape, excluding its relevance to key transnational issues such as migration, capitalism, racism, and global sexual economies (Hock and Allas 2018; Kaczmarska and Ortmann 2021). This narrow view of Eurasia reinforces the dominance of the U.S. as the sole imperial power, even within critical feminist discourses, and overlooks the diversity of feminist thought outside the U.S.—a concern raised by U.S. scholars themselves (Fernandes 2013; Kaplan and Grewal 2002). I focus on U.S. feminist narratives for two reasons: First, because they shape much of transnational feminist discourses, especially in critiquing imperialism, yet fail to account for Eurasian experiences and hinder broader solidarity networks; and second, to challenge U.S. exceptionalism and consider Euro-American imperialisms as part of the global imperial landscape. This exceptionalism, justified by the focus on "which empire is the strongest," explains the lack of proper analysis of other empires, like Russia, leaving oppressed populations without support.

The dominance of U.S.-centric perspectives is not just theoretical—it is palpable in everyday feminist spaces. One anecdote highlights this issue well: At a U.S. feminist conference, I attended a presentation on Kurdish women political prisoners in Turkey. During the Q&A, an audience member shifted the conversation by blaming the U.S. for global carceral systems. While this critique was partly valid, it overlooked other imperial and authoritarian powers, like Russia and Turkey, that also uphold oppressive systems independently of the U.S. This moment highlighted a recurring issue: U.S.-centric views often dominate discussions of imperialism, sidelining other contexts, particularly Eurasia, where authoritarianism and carcerality are also on the rise. This incident underscored the need to broaden transnational feminist frameworks beyond U.S.-centric interpretations of imperialism and repression, as the Eurasian borderlands, I believe, have much to offer. Reflecting on this, I realized the goal is not to fit into dominant narratives but to reimagine transnational feminisms as spaces for diverse, cross-geographic dialogues that reflect varying power dynamics and entanglements between imperial forces. As a scholar and activist from the Eurasian borderlands, navigating the U.S. feminist landscape, I explore not just whether but how the Eurasian borderlands are transnational (Kuzhabekova 2020). How do they reshape feminist inquiries, and what contributions do these overlooked landscapes offer? While I am not the first to ask these questions (e.g., Nachescu 2019; Nowicka 1995; Tlostanova et al. 2019), I seek to contribute to the conversation by highlighting the insights Eurasia brings to transnational feminist inquiries.

In *Signs*, Jennifer Suchland (2011) posed the provocative question "Is Postsocialism Transnational?" She highlighted the exclusion of former state-socialist Eurasia from transnational feminist studies and challenged the outdated Cold War–era division of the world into three geopolitical blocs. Suchland's critique reflects a broader issue within transnational feminism, which often focuses on first-/third- and first-/second-world relations, reducing Eurasia to Russian megapolises while overlooking its diverse populations, colonial histories, and subaltern experiences (see also Marciniak 2006; Tlostanova 2010). Scholars from the Eurasian borderlands have long contested this exclusion, arguing that Eurocentric and postcolonial frameworks fail to fully capture the region's complex histories and imperial legacies (for more recent inquiries, see Burlyuk and Musliu 2023; Marat 2021; Tsymbalyuk 2022). Yet critical scholarship from Eurasia remains marginalized in Western transnational feminist discourse, raising ongoing concerns about its erasure (Koobak 2020; Kulawik 2020; Tsymbalyuk 2023). In this essay, I argue that the persistent erasure of Eurasian feminist thought has broader consequences: It limits our understanding of global geopolitics, imperial crises, colonial and racial violence, global sexual economies, and other interconnected issues. It also hinders the formation of meaningful transnational collaborations, reinforcing the dominance of imperial powers like the U.S. and Russia.

I developed this critical perspective through my research recognizing Eurasian borderlands as active contributors to the global landscape. My work examines how U.S. Black activists viewed the Eurasian borderlands not just as a backdrop but as vital interlocutors and explores the relevance of these historical connections amid today's imperial crises. I expanded postsocialist feminist methodology to explore complex relationships with the past, particularly the ties between anti-colonial and anti-capitalist movements (Atanasoski and Vora 2018; Shih 2012). Transnational feminist studies, as conceptualized in the U.S. after the Cold War, have often overlooked Eurasia's role in anti-colonial efforts, as evidenced by the scarcity of publications engaging with anti-colonial feminisms in Eurasian borderlands (Tlostanova 2012). This scarcity mirrors broader critiques by U.S. scholars who note that, despite the influence of U.S. Black and Indigenous feminisms on transnational frameworks, both remain underrepresented, alongside Eurasian feminisms (Das 2023; Nash 2019). Building on this, my research seeks to recover hidden genealogies of transnational feminist thought by highlighting the intersecting oppressions and imperialisms U.S. Black women have engaged with in dialogue with the Eurasian borderlands.

Drawing on my research, this paper critiques the politics of knowledge production that contribute to the erasure of the Eurasian borderlands in transnational feminist scholarship. It challenges dominant geographical and temporal frameworks that overlook Eurasia's complex global entanglements. By exploring the historical and potential contributions of the Eurasian borderlands, the paper highlights their relevance to understanding imperialism, racism, capitalism, and state authoritarianism, among other issues. I argue that recognizing these contributions is crucial for building transnational feminist networks capable of addressing today's imperial crises.

Eurasian Borderlands: Rethinking Feminist Geographies

The term "transnational feminism" is used in various ways, but it consistently involves geographical considerations to address power imbalances between the Global North and South, which are rooted in colonial histories, economic disparities, and cultural dynamics (Carty and Mohanty 2015; Desai 2015). Ella Shohat (2001) critiqued Eurocentric global feminism for its "reductive identity practice" (1269) and "additive/sponge approach" (1271), which simply incorporates "other" cultures into existing Western feminist frameworks. She called for a relational feminism that recognizes global interconnections shaped by geopolitics and imperial powers (see also Tambe and Thayer 2021). Shohat argued that transnational feminism must move beyond Euro-American frameworks, which overlook the agency and struggles of women in the Global South. Similarly, Janet Conway (2008) suggested "geographies of transnational feminisms" as "a network of spatial connectivity" linking the experiences, struggles, and politics of poor women across vast distances while honoring their differences and local contexts (222). Transnational feminisms, thus, challenge dominant frameworks by centering the knowledge produced by racialized women in the Global South, shaped by colonialism and imperialism. However, despite its critical stance, transnational feminist inquiry often remains bound to the Anglophone West and its former colonies, overlooking regions like the Eurasian borderlands. This geographic boundedness is central to my research interests.

In this article, I use the term "Eurasian borderlands" to refer geographically to territories that were once under state-socialist rule during the Cold War, including East Europe, the Baltics, Siberia, Central Asia, the Caucasus, the Far East, and the North. Drawing on the work of Madina Tlostanova (2010), I highlight spaces and communities at the periphery or in the borderlands, shaped by multiple imperial formations, especially Russian and Soviet ones. It is important to note that Tlostanova develops her ideas about borderlands by relying on the works of Gloria Anzaldúa, a U.S. queer Chicana poet, writer, and feminist theorist. Historically, "Eurasia" has been used by European and Russian powers to assert control over Asian territories (Bassin et al. 2015) and has more recently been co-opted by Russian right-wing factions to justify territorial claims (Kassymbekova and Marat 2022). My usage of this term, approached with caution, focuses specifically on the regions impacted by Russian imperialism, among other empires. The Eurasian borderlands embody diverse yet interconnected experiences of subalternity. Therefore, beyond a mere geographical descriptor, this term serves as a coalitional concept too, linking borderland communities across vast regions. Scholars such as Botakoz Kassymbekova and Aminat Chokobaeva (2021) argue that, for example, examining Soviet legacies in Central Asia alongside those in other Eurasian borderlands illuminates the imperial and racializing strategies of the Soviet state. Furthermore, connecting Soviet Central Asia with other Eurasian borderlands enables comparisons of Soviet rule to other illiberal regimes that relied on imperial discourses and expansion (494).

Engaging with the Eurasian borderlands complicates theories of imperialism by demonstrating how racism, modernity, and colonialism extend beyond the Western hemisphere (Grabowska 2012). Borderlands reflect the experience of living under the influence of diverse imperial formations—reinforcing an unjust global order—alongside competing narratives and cultures, none of which are limited to the West (Tlostanova 2010). For instance, East Europe has long been influenced by competing empires—Russian, Ottoman, and Habsburg (Parvulescu and Boatcă 2022; Sonevytsky 2022). For example, Lesia Pahulich (2024) highlights how anti-Roma violence in East Europe, including Ukraine, stems from racial logics shaped and mediated by multiple imperial powers. Likewise, Central Asia has served as a zone of influence for Russian, British, and Chinese powers (Salimjan 2024; Tlostanova 2010). This perspective on the complexity of the Eurasian context also reveals how Indigenous communities in Russia continue to endure settler colonial oppression (Ulturgasheva 2023), while post-decolonization Africa, the Middle East, and Asia became battlegrounds for competing empires, including Russia (Al-Shami 2018; Ndlovu-Gatsheni 2015; Starodubtsev 2023). Despite their differences, empires share interconnected logics of suppression, extraction, and expansion, often supporting one another and exchanging colonial technologies.

The Russian invasion of Ukraine exemplifies how misunderstanding the Eurasian borderlands hinders thoughtful engagement with imperial legacies and forging solidarity networks. Many feminists from the West and Global South respond to the war without considering local contexts, histories, or the voices of those directly affected by Russian aggression. Transnational feminist debates often become polarized: some criticize Russia's imperialism while ignoring Western interventions, while others blame the U.S. and NATO for global conflicts, justifying Russia's actions as rightful retaliation—albeit at Ukraine's expense. Both perspectives tend to deny Ukraine and its people agency (Hendl et al. 2023). Moreover, many high-ranking feminist journals and media outlets in Europe and the U.S. showed a significant absence of interest in this issue (Graff 2022, 60). For instance, Agnieszka Graff (2022) notes that the AtGender Conference in Milan in spring 2022, the largest academic feminist conference in Europe, made no mention of the war, nor did the organizers invite any Ukrainian feminists as speakers: "In fact, one of the keynotes, Jasbir Puar, suggested in her lecture that Ukraine should not be supported, because NATO is instrumentalizing LGBTQ rights in its propaganda" (59). Although Puar later apologized, her apology was not included in the conference recording, and a promised statement of solidarity never materialized (59). Similarly, I myself attended the 2023 NWSA conference, organized a year after the full-scale invasion, which lacked panels or papers discussing Ukraine—a trend from previous years. Despite ongoing U.S. military support for Ukraine raising concerns among U.S. feminists about increased militarization, there were no dedicated discussions on the topic. Graff concludes that Western feminists have not only failed to use their privilege to support Ukraine on the transnational scene but also "exerted pressure in the opposite direction" (60). Harmful statements that derail attention from Russian imperialism and promote "abstract pacifism" prompted feminists from Ukraine to write a manifesto declaring their "right to resist" imperial power and calling for transnational solidarity (Feminist Initiative Group 2022).

It is unsurprising that many issues provoked by the war remain largely unaddressed by transnational feminist scholarship outside the region. For example, despite sanctions, transnational flows of weapons and resources to and from Russia persist (Baczynska 2023). Europe's commendable acceptance of Ukrainian refugees, while significant, does not challenge its violent migration policies that continue to exclude people from the Eurasian borderlands and the Global South (Grupa Granica 2022). People of color fleeing Ukraine, including Ukrainian citizens, face racial profiling and discrimination in Europe (European Network Against Racism 2022; European Roma Rights Centre 2023). Furthermore, the movement of migrants, conscripts, refugees, and dissidents to and from Russia—particularly those from communities historically colonized by Russia—underscores the complexities of imperial power. Transnational feminist scholars from the region highlight these overlapping dispossessions caused by both Russian and European imperialisms, with a focus on the Eurasian borderlands (Hendl 2022). Engaging more deeply with this emerging scholarship could offer new insights into gender, warfare, militarism, and imperialism and their effects on the global landscape.

The failure to understand the war and its associated imperial relations reflects how geographic boundedness leads to epistemic erasures and limitations in existing theories of imperialism. The feminist oversight of Eurasian geographies obscures significant global interconnections and diverse forms of interdependency and vulnerability. In this context, Barbara Smith, a U.S. Black feminist and socialist, presented another perspective on transnational feminist politics during a *Democracy Now!* discussion (2023) on the Russian-Ukrainian war. As a cofounder of the Combahee River Collective and coauthor of "A Black Feminist Statement," she emphasized that global solidarity is central to Black feminist politics. Smith argued that Black feminists must engage with the war in Ukraine, and her decision to join the Ukraine Solidarity Network reflects her commitment to combating all forms of oppression. She condemned the Russian invasion as an imperial act, expressed solidarity with the Ukrainian people, and sought to decenter U.S. exceptionalism, which often portrays the U.S. as the sole superpower (see also Samudzi 2022).

Decentering U.S. imperialism reveals the complexity of the global landscape and challenges Western-dominated understandings of various forms of oppression. For example, Central Asian scholars Kassymbekova and Chokobaeva (2021) reveal how a focus on Soviet and Russian imperialisms can disrupt conventional notions of "modernity," "development," and "colonialism." They criticize Western narratives that portray the Soviet state as the primary agent of "emancipation" and "development," despite its often harmful and indifferent policies toward Central Asian Indigenous populations (486). These narratives overlook the dynamism of these communities and the intellectual and political alternatives that existed before the Russian conquest. Kassymbekova and Chokobaeva highlight numerous instances of disenfranchisement and marginalization caused by Soviet officials and their settler colonial practices, which emphasized progress while downplaying the violent and exploitative aspects of Soviet rule. Likewise, many scholars from the region advocate for a deeper understanding of non-Western Eurasian experiences and their contributions to global politics, given regional trajectories of authoritarianism, poverty, colonialism, and geopolitical marginalization (Donovan 2024; Hendl et al. 2023; Marat 2021; Marat and Aisarina 2021).

Tamar Koplatadze (2019) also critiques the uncritical application of postcolonial theory to Russia, which tends to focus primarily on ethnic Russians while neglecting the diverse Eurasian borderlands and their inhabitants affected by imperial rule. This approach not only allows Russia to obscure its colonial past and present (see also Kassymbekova and Marat 2022), but it also remolds postcolonial theory in surprising ways. Many influential works erroneously categorize Russian identity as "postcolonial," "internally colonized," or "subaltern" (473). This misclassification denies the imperial status of Russian colonialism while ignoring its violent racial politics (see also Mogilner 2013; Shahrani 1993; Tlostanova 2010). "Placing Russia in a subaltern position without paying attention to the country's racial politics," as Koplatadze notes, "shifts the focus away from the ex-Soviet republics, the voices of whose peoples are unheard or slow in emerging"

(476). Similarly, Miglena Todorova (2021) examines the interconnected local and global forces driving racialization, socialist state policies, and Eurocentric Marxist and Leninist ideologies in Bulgaria, raising questions about capitalism and its entanglements with state socialism.

In this sense, Eurasian theorizations of imperialism challenge narrow understandings of the concept and insist on moving beyond the "either-or" approach, advocating for a focus on global interrelations and entanglements. Engaging with Eurasian borderlands can contribute to developing theories of global imperialism, especially regarding how crises provoked by imperial formations manifest in growing authoritarianism, militarism, and imperial expansion both domestically and globally. Eurasian borderlands share commonalities with regions affected by multiple imperial formations, such as Syria and Iran, and are actively fostering non-Western south-to-south/east-to-south collaborations (e.g., see Lykke et al. 2024; South/South Movement n.d.; Ukraine-Palestine Solidarity Group 2023). These solidarities challenge existing knowledge-production frameworks that often require the West as a mediator in transnational feminist exchanges.

A notable example is also the creation of the RUTA Association for Central, South-Eastern, and Eastern European, Baltic, Caucasus, Central, and Northern Asian Studies in Global Conversation in 2024 (Hosaka and Schmidt 2024). RUTA centers on the knowledge, scholarly traditions, and expertise of scholars, artists, and social justice advocates in these regions, promoting critical research on ongoing imperial and colonial legacies that shape their societies. Eurasian borderlands have historically been analyzed or understood from perspectives that impose external control or authority. They were surrounded by negative stereotypes and hierarchical narratives, which portray them as backward and dependent. Instead, RUTA aims to foster conversations and highlight knowledge rooted in the regions' rich cultures, social justice movements, creativity, intellectual heritage, solidarity, and resistance. This is just one example of how Eurasian epistemologies are steadily constructing alternative geographies of transnational feminisms, positioning the regions in dynamic relationships with oppressed and marginalized communities worldwide. This work continues the legacies of past relations obscured by the formal end of the Cold War and its linear temporality, which portrayed the region as existing in a state of limbo, devoid of agency and radical politics—a topic I will discuss further in the next section.

Origin Stories and the Ascendance of Liberalism

In *Black Feminism Reimagined* (2019), Jennifer Nash reconnects transnationalism and intersectionality, distinguishing between origin stories and genealogies, thereby challenging the temporal dimensions of transnational feminist inquiry. Origin stories posit a singular historical moment and specific texts as foundational to a concept, while genealogies, as Nash explains, trace how concepts emerge from multiple traditions or how different theoretical traditions engage with the same concept in diverse ways (39). Drawing on Nash's work, I suggest that U.S. transnational feminists often focus on origin stories of transnational feminism, particularly emphasizing two key aspects: the transformative era of the 1990s and the experiences of Global South women. However, I argue that these narratives oversimplify the complex historical processes and intellectual traditions shaping the global landscape. They tend to reinforce specific body politics, focusing on particular marginalized groups while overlooking the nuances of their marginality—such as how, for example, Russian imperialism shapes the Global South. These stories erase experiences of imperial violence not stemming from Western empires. Nash (2019) challenges us to consider "which bodies transnationalism does not, or even refuses to, describe" (98). Engaging with Suchland's work, Nash highlights how the "second world" remains untheorized within transnational feminist studies, revealing the hidden racial politics behind the invisibility of certain locations and bodies (98). The racial and colonial violence experienced by former state-socialist Eurasia, for instance, does not fit neatly within the body politics of much of transnational feminist inquiry.

The collapse of the Soviet Union was not merely a backdrop to globalization and the rise of the U.S. as a global superpower and promoter of liberal capitalism. Russia continues to assert global influence, sustaining extractive economies much like the U.S., with operations extending into various regions of the Global South. Within Russia, racialized populations perform extensive manual labor, including domestic work, construction, farming, and mining. Indigenous lands in Siberia and the North are exploited for resource extraction, leading to environmental damage, Indigenous impoverishment, and the disruption of traditional ways of life. These resources, however, are critical to the global economy and local contexts alike. Despite this, issues occurring in the Eurasian borderlands are often viewed as regionally specific, disconnected from the broader global landscape. For a long time, authoritarianism was considered a hallmark of Eurasian totalitarianism and seen as an inherent feature of the region, attributed to its socialist legacies and perceived incompatibility with capitalism (Graff 2022, 61). However, the rise of right-wing populism, including in the U.S., shows that these processes—capitalism and authoritarianism—are intertwined, with right-wing groups building transnational networks across geographies. Russian nationalist formations, for instance, have a long history of collaborating with similar groups in the U.S. and supporting authoritarianisms both within Eurasian borderlands and beyond (Wegren 2024). Viewing the rise of conservatism in Eurasia as part of global dynamics can reveal its ties to the broader development of imperialism as a global condition. The neglect of such complex inquiries is largely shaped by post–Cold War temporality, which has significantly influenced transnational feminist scholarship.

For example, the collection *Transnational Feminist Itineraries* (2021), edited by Ashwini Tambe and Millie Thayer, offers both "provocations about the current state of transnational feminism" and a historical perspective on its activism (6). The editors explore the genealogies and trajectories of transnational feminist thought, defining it as "a distinct moment within a longer history of cross-border women's activism" (14), with roots in the early 1990s. The collection elaborates that this period was marked by "worldwide social upheaval" and "changing historical conditions" such as the restructuring of industrial production, globalization of financial capital, and market and media liberalization (2). By the early 2000s, the editors note, feminists faced a growing right-wing resurgence in international venues like the United Nations, once supportive of their advocacy (25). Alliances of right-wing states and religious forces began to dominate debates, threatening to undo earlier feminist gains and even erase terms like "gender," which had been key to challenging essentialist and oppressive ideas (25). It is important to add here that the collapse of the Soviet Union and the reconfiguration of Cold War dynamics have contributed to shaping this evolving global landscape. As Suchland (2011) highlights:

> Ironically, it is precisely the end of the Cold War that has brought about so many of the practices and challenges of globalization that are of concern to feminist scholars. Yet the former state-socialist space falls between the cracks—between the predominant discussion about neoliberalism that opposes the first and third worlds (or the global North and South) and between the racialized discussions of orientalism that oppose the West and the non-West. (853)

The collapse of the Soviet Union and the reshaping of Cold War geopolitics paved the way for the ascendance of liberalism and racial capitalism, which in turn fueled the growth of right-wing populism and new forms of authoritarianism on the global scale (Atanasoski and Vora 2018; Pahulich 2023). The collection acknowledges the rise of authoritarianism and the "rightward political tilt" in countries like Britain, India, Brazil, Turkey, Israel, and Russia (Tambe and Thayer 2021, 8). Yet, it lacks articles addressing the Eurasian borderlands, including how Russia's nationalist resurgence has both local and global implications. This perspective aligns, for example, with Inderpal Grewal's discussions in the collection on right-wing populism and corruption during the Trump administration. Therefore, exploring right-wing resurgence and authoritarianism in the Eurasian borderlands could complicate our understanding of imperial crises, capitalism, and liberalism.

The collection also examines gender and feminist education programs; women's social mobilization in India, Mexico, and Brazil; and how states and nationalisms shape feminist politics. The Eurasian borderlands could certainly contribute to this inquiry. The scholarship on anti-gender mobilizations has a rich history, particularly in East Europe. East European academics and activists warned about the growing threat of right-wing populism and its attacks on education and reproductive and sexual politics amid virulent economic pressures. They highlighted how U.S. right-wing forces found support in the East European context.

For example, Katja Kahlina (2022) focuses on the World Congress of Families (WCF), established by members of the influential U.S. Christian Right in the mid-1990s. She illuminates how "in the context of transnational anti-gender mobilization, former state-socialist countries, including Russia, have come to be regarded as valuable role models for their Western counterparts" (1). WCF members have testified to the importance of collaboration between U.S. Christian Right members and their Russian counterparts since its inception; some even suggest that the idea for the WCF emerged during a trip to Russia. Kahlina argues that this connection forms a key part of "a new civilizationalist imaginary" based on the notion of a common Christian civilization threatened by contemporary liberal politics of gender and sexuality (1). This example demonstrates how the Eurasian borderlands not only contribute to scholarship on anti-gender movements but also enhance our understanding of the roots and dynamics of emerging organizations and political movements (see also Korolczuk and Graff 2018; Kováts 2017).

Eurasian borderlands scholarship emphasizes global entanglements and their implications, truly embodying the relational ethos of transnational feminist studies. Furthermore, it reveals new antiauthoritarian practices emerging from communities affected by the complex landscapes of imperialism, authoritarianism, and global capitalism. For instance, Diana T. Kudaibergen's recent book, *The Kazakh Spring* (2024), illuminates resistance practices countering one of the most resilient authoritarian regimes, inspiring mass protests in 2022. Similarly, scholars from Belarus analyze the 2020 antiauthoritarian uprisings, sparking new discussions on feminist ethics of care and vulnerability (Stebur 2021), while also addressing the entanglements of authoritarianism, imperialism, and neoliberalism in Belarus (Artiukh 2022; Vozyanov 2021). These issues are intertwined with the rise of police violence and state repression, creating avenues for broad transnational solidarity, what I discuss in more details elsewhere (Shchurko 2022).

Eurasian borderlands feminist mobilization responds to the complex environments of neoliberalism, state repression, and ongoing imperialism, highlighting global entanglements across contexts (Sultanalieva 2023). Similar to scholars in Tambe and Thayer's collection (2021), researchers from Eurasia document the rise of carcerality and policing throughout the region (Marat 2018), as well as anti-migration policies that perpetuate unequal power dynamics between imperial centers and so-called former colonies. For instance, the influx of migrants from Central Asia into Moscow and St. Petersburg has led to increasing violence against them (Marat 2009), while laborers from East Europe face overexploitation in West European countries (Hrycak 2011; Parvulescu 2014). These migration patterns reveal ongoing racial and sexual violence that upholds imperial claims. The patterns of migration from the Eurasian borderlands speak to the violent practices of capitalism, exposing its racial and colonial logics, and complicate its entanglements with imperialism and authoritarianism (Liu 2023).

Furthermore, neoliberalization is often viewed as a remedy for the Soviet past that obscures the ongoing actions of both historical and contemporary imperial powers, provokes the rise of right-wing forces, and stifles anti-capitalist critiques (Koobak and Marling 2024). This mirrors trends in the U.S., where there are particularly virulent attacks on education and anti-capitalist social movements (Burden-Stelly 2023). Scholars have noted that the institutionalization of feminist studies coincided with the co-opting of difference and a disavowal of radical roots in favor of liberal diversity

(Coogan-Gehr 2011; Nash 2019). For instance, this neglect of radical roots has created a division between Black feminist studies and transnational feminism. Jennifer Nash (2021) questions the assumption that intersectionality and transnationalism are separate frameworks, emphasizing that Black women practiced "intersectional transnationalism" long before these terms were divided (38). She calls for a reimagined narrative in women's studies, positioning Black feminism at the forefront (38). Nash (2019) asks "what it might mean to tell a different story about women's studies' histories and its key analytics, and for black feminism to be at the vanguard of this different kind of telling" (83). Similarly, Julie R. Enszer and Agatha Beins (2018) challenge the binary of "international/transnational," critiquing how transnational feminist narratives often overlook specific internationalist histories that defy a simplistic "U.S./non-U.S." or "women of color versus third world women" dichotomy. They explore how engaging with figures like Audre Lorde, Frances Beal, and Linda Burnham as transnational, diasporic subjects opens up spaces to consider the overlapping subjectivities of third-world women and women of color (39).

These perspectives on occluded histories are particularly important, as transnational feminist narratives have emerged from past socialist movements with deep connections to the Eurasian borderlands. The homogenization of socialist practices as Eurocentric and corrupted overlooks the rich plurality of socialist praxis in Eurasia and the Global South, perpetuating the status quo of liberal Western modernity and racial capitalism. Scholars and activists from the region challenge this exclusion by highlighting historical interconnections between the Eurasian borderlands and the Global South that fostered alternative anti-capitalist practices (Grabowska 2017). The writings of Black internationalist women reveal these transnational connections between the U.S. and Eurasia, illuminating potential affinities for contemporary movements, as I explore in my research project (see also Todorova 2018).

After the collapse of the Soviet Union, U.S. and Global South socialist feminists have not only distanced themselves from Eurasian genealogies but have also overlooked the socialist foundations of past anti-racist and anti-colonial movements in feminist scholarship. Transnational feminist histories frequently ignore the legacies of socialist feminisms and internationalist praxis (Bonfiglioli and Ghodsee 2020; Buyendelgeriyn 2008; Jelača and Lugarić 2018). For instance, the *Transnational Feminist Itineraries* collection outlines cross-border activism and internationalism that predate the emergence of transnational feminism in the 1990s. However, it misses significant practices of anti-colonial internationalism, such as Black feminist internationalism, Afro–Asian solidarity, and Third Worldism. Although the collection highlights a shift from individual political rights to collective social and economic entitlements in the internationalist movements of the 1970s (Tambe and Thayer 2021, 23), it does not acknowledge the crucial role of communist and socialist women from the Global South in driving this change. The dissolution of the Soviet Union and the ensuing post–Cold War geopolitics severely disrupted these infrastructures, creating challenging conditions for feminist scholars, writers, and activists. As the editors observe, "activists far less often meet face-to-face, coordinate campaigns across borders, or engage in networks as actively as they once did" (26). Thus, the collapse of the Soviet Union has had significant material and epistemic consequences for feminism, influencing which perspectives gain prominence and determining whose works are deemed classics in feminist theory. In formerly state-socialist Eurasia, the dissolution of the Soviet Union marked the beginning of gender studies, often dominated by white Western theories, which marginalized the contributions of Black, Indigenous, and women of color methodologies. Nevertheless, this landscape is evolving, showcasing vibrant knowledge production rooted in local contexts and in dialogue with marginalized and Global South epistemologies, both historically and currently.

Conclusions

The analysis presented in this paper highlights the intricate entanglements of the Eurasian borderlands within transnational frameworks, revealing their critical contributions to feminist discourse on imperialism, state violence, neoliberalism, capitalism, and resistance. While the scope of this study is not exhaustive, it underscores the necessity of incorporating diverse regional perspectives into the broader conversation on feminist scholarship. The identified gaps in existing literature are particularly significant for Eurasian feminists. For scholars from outside the region, these gaps serve as vital considerations when examining global power dynamics. However, for feminists within Eurasia, they illuminate the pressing need for a deeper understanding of how gender and sexuality intersect with imperial occupation, settler colonial extraction, and the multifaceted nature of resistance. Predominantly shaped by Western academic frameworks, the discourse surrounding gender and sexuality in the region often fails to account for the complexities of local contexts and the historical legacies of colonialism. Engaging in transnational feminist inquiry not only broadens our comprehension of these dynamics but also reveals how the coloniality of gender and sexuality continues to be an ongoing project within the region. This coloniality is intricately linked to the labor of women and gender-expansive individuals from diverse backgrounds within the Eurasian borderlands. As we move forward, it is imperative that scholars actively engage with these issues, recognizing the vital contributions of Eurasian feminists to the global feminist movement. By centering these perspectives, we can foster a more nuanced understanding of transnational feminist frameworks and their implications for global struggles against oppression. This approach not only enriches feminist scholarship but also fortifies the connections between diverse movements for justice.

Tatsiana Shchurko is a queer feminist researcher and activist from Belarus specializing in transnational feminist theorizing. She holds a PhD from the Ohio State University, where she also held a postdoctoral ACLS Fellowship. Currently, she is an assistant professor of instruction in the Department of Women's, Gender, and Sexuality Studies at the University of South Florida. Her book project investigates the relationship between U.S. Black feminist internationalism and Eurasian knowledge production. She can be reached at shchurkot@usf.edu.

Works Cited

Al-Shami, Leila. 2018. "The 'Anti-Imperialism' of Idiots." *Leila's blog*, April 14. https://leilashami.wordpress.com/2018/04/14/the-anti-imperialism-of-idiots/.

Artiukh, Volodymyr. 2022. "The Political Logic of Russia's Imperialism." *LeftEast*, July 4. https://lefteast.org/political-logic-of-russias-imperialism.

Atanasoski, Neda, and Kalindi Vora. 2018. "Postsocialist Politics and the Ends of Revolution." *Social Identities* 24 (2): 139–54.

Baczynska, Gabriela. 2023. "EU Keeps on Doing Business with Russia Despite Sanctions." *Reuters*, March 29. https://www.reuters.com/world/europe/eu-keeps-doing-business-with-russia-despite-sanctions-2023-03-29/.

Bassin, Mark, Glebov Sergeĭ, and Laruelle Marlène, eds. 2015. *Between Europe and Asia: The Origins, Theories, and Legacies of Russian Eurasianism*. Pittsburgh: University of Pittsburgh Press.

Bonfiglioli, Chiara, and Kristen Ghodsee. 2020. "Vanishing Act: Global Socialist Feminism as the 'Missing Other' of Transnational Feminism—A Response to Tlostanova, Thapar-Björkert and Koobak (2019)." *Feminist Review* 126 (1): 168–72.

Burden-Stelly, Charisse. 2023. *Black Scare / Red Scare*. University of Chicago Press.
Burlyuk, Olga, and Vjosa Musliu. 2023. "The Responsibility to Remain Silent? On the Politics of Knowledge Production, Expertise and (Self-)Reflection in Russia's War Against Ukraine." *Journal of International Relations and Development*, no. 26, 605–18.
Buyendelgeriyn, Manduhai. 2008. "Post-Post-Transition Theories: Walking on Multiple Paths." *Annual Review of Anthropology*, no. 37, 235–50.
Carty, Linda, and Chandra Talpade Mohanty. 2015. "Mapping Transnational Feminist Engagements: Neoliberalism and the Politics of Solidarity." In *The Oxford Handbook of Transnational Feminist Movements*, edited by Rawwida Baksh and Wendy Harcourt, 82–115. Oxford University Press.
Conway, Janet. 2008. "Geographies of Transnational Feminisms: The Politics of Place and Scale in the World March of Women." *Social Politics* 15 (2): 207–31.
Coogan-Gehr, Kelly. 2011. *The Geopolitics of the Cold War and Narratives of Inclusion: Excavating a Feminist Archive*. Palgrave Macmillan.
Das, Devaleena. 2023. "What Transnational Feminism Has Not Disrupted Yet: Toward a Quilted Epistemology." *Meridians* 22 (2): 240–66.
Democracy Now! 2023. "Can Peace in Ukraine Be Achieved Without War? Extended Debate Between Medea Benjamin and Barbara Smith." October 11. https://www.democracynow.org/2023/10/11/can_peace_in_ukraine_be_achieved.
Desai, Manisha. 2015. "Critical Cartography, Theories, and Praxis of Transnational Feminisms." In *The Oxford Handbook of Transnational Feminist Movements*, edited by Rawwida Baksh and Wendy Harcourt, 116–30. Oxford University Press.
Donovan, Victoria. 2023. "Against Academic 'Resourcification': Collaboration as Delinking from Extractivist 'Area Studies' Paradigms." *Canadian Slavonic Papers* 65 (2): 163–73.
Donovan, Victoria. 2024. "On Decolonial Shelters, or What to Do with Problematic Scholarly Inheritances?" *Forum for Modern Language Studies* 60 (3): 385–90.
Doolotkeldieva, Asel, and Stefanie Ortmann. 2024. "Between Local and Global Political Economies of Knowledge Production: The Emergence of Central Asian Area Studies." *International Studies Review* 26 (1): 7–10.
Enszer, Julie R., and Agatha Beins. 2018. "Inter- and Transnational Feminist Theory and Practice in *Triple Jeopardy* and *Conditions*." *Women's Studies* 47 (1): 21–43.
European Network Against Racism. 2022. "Press Release: Racist Double-Standards Persist at EU/Ukraine Borders and Beyond." March 30. https://www.enar-eu.org/racism-borders-eu-ukraine/.

European Roma Rights Centre. 2023. "War in Ukraine: ERRC Monitoring Report Confirms Discrimination Against Romani Refugees." February 28. https://www.errc.org/press-releases/war-in-ukraine-errc-monitoring-report-confirms-discrimination-against-romani-refugees.

Feminist Initiative Group. 2022. "'The Right to Resist': A Feminist Manifesto." *Commons*, July 7. https://commons.com.ua/en/right-resist-feminist-manifesto/.

Fernandes, Leela. 2013. *Transnational Feminism in the United States*. New York University Press.

Grabowska, Magdalena. 2012. "Bringing the Second World In: Conservative Revolution(s), Socialist Legacies, and Transnational Silences in the Trajectories of Polish Feminism." *Signs* 37 (2): 385–411.

Grabowska, Magdalena. 2017. "Beyond the 'Development' Paradigm: State Socialist Women's Activism, Transnationalism, and the 'Long Sixties.'" In *Women's Activism and "Second Wave" Feminism*, edited by Barbara Molony and Jennifer Nelson, 147–72. Bloomsbury Academic.

Graff, Agnieszka. 2022. "Solidarity with Ukraine; or, Why East-West Still Matters to Feminism." *Gender Studies* 26 (1): 57–61.

Grupa Granica. 2022. "Building Solidarity Against Poland's Two-Faced Refugee Policy." *Roar*, April 3. https://roarmag.org/essays/poland-belarus-refugees-border.

Hendl, Tereza. 2022. "Towards Accounting for Russian Imperialism and Building Meaningful Transnational Feminist Solidarity with Ukraine." *Gender Studies* 26 (1): 62–93.

Hendl, Tereza, Olga Burlyuk, Mila O'Sullivan, and Aizada Arystanbek. 2023. "(En)Countering Epistemic Imperialism: A Critique of 'Westsplaining' and Coloniality in Dominant Debates on Russia's Invasion of Ukraine." *Contemporary Security Policy*, December 4. https://doi.org/10.1080/13523260.2023.2288468.

Hock, Beata, and Anu Allas, eds. 2018. *Globalizing East European Art Histories*. Routledge, Taylor & Francis Group.

Hosaka, Sanshiro, and Anselm Schmidt. 2024. "A New Tradition: First RUTA Conference in Wartime Ukraine." *Substack*, October 3. https://substack.com/home/post/p-149762184.

Hrycak, Alexandra. 2011. "Women as Migrants on the Margins of the European Union." In *Mapping Difference*, edited by Marian J. Rubchak, 47–64. Berghahn Books.

Jelača, Dijana, and Danijela Lugarić. 2018. "The 'Radiant Future' of Spatial and Temporal Dis/Orientations." In *The Future of (Post)Socialism: Eastern European Perspectives*, edited by John Frederick Bailyn, Dijana Jelača, and Danijela Lugarić, 1–16. State University of New York Press.

Kaczmarska, Katarzyna, and Stefanie Ortmann. 2021. "IR Theory and Area Studies: A Plea for Displaced Knowledge About International Politics." *Journal of International Relations and Development* 24 (4): 820–47.

Kahlina, Katja. 2022. "Learning from 'The East': Transnational Anti-Gender Mobilizations and the East/West Divide." *Culture Wars Papers*, no. 21. https://www.illiberalism.org/wp-content/uploads/2022/10/Culture-Wars-papers-no.-21-October-2022.pdf.

Kaplan, Caren, and Inderpal Grewal. 2002. "Transnational Practices and Interdisciplinary Feminist Scholarship: Refiguring Women's and Gender Studies." In *Women's Studies on Its Own*, edited by Robyn Wiegman, 66–81. Duke University Press.

Kassymbekova, Botakoz, and Aminat Chokobaeva. 2021. "On Writing Soviet History of Central Asia: Frameworks, Challenges, Prospects." *Central Asian Survey* 40 (4): 483–503.

Kassymbekova, Botakoz, and Erica Marat. 2022. "Time to Question Russia's Imperial Innocence." PONARS Eurasia Policy Memo No. 771. https://www.ponarseurasia.org/time-to-question-russias-imperial-innocence/.

Koobak, Redi. 2020. "Determined Disidentifications Reframing the Limits of the Field Imaginary of Feminist Studies." In *Borderlands in European Gender Studies*, edited by Teresa Kulawik and Zhanna Kravchenko, 170–87. Routledge.

Koobak, Redi, and Raili Marling. 2024. "Transnational and Decolonial Feminist Insights into the Neoliberalization of Estonian Academia." *Studia Litteraria et Historica*, no. 12. https://doi.org/10.11649/slh.3094.

Koplatadze, Tamar. 2019. "Theorising Russian Postcolonial Studies." *Postcolonial Studies* 22 (4): 469–89.

Korolczuk, Elżbieta, and Agnieszka Graff. 2018. "Gender as 'Ebola from Brussels': The Anticolonial Frame and the Rise of Illiberal Populism." *Signs* 43 (4): 797–821.

Kováts, Eszter. 2017. "The Emergence of Powerful Anti-Gender Movements in Europe and the Crisis of Liberal Democracy." In *Gender and Far Right Politics in Europe*, edited by Michaela Köttig, Renate Bitzan, and Andrea Petö, 175–89. Palgrave Macmillan.

Kudaibergen, Diana T. 2024. *The Kazakh Spring: Digital Activism and the Challenge to Dictatorship*. Cambridge University Press.

Kulawik, Teresa. 2020. "Introduction: European Borderlands and Topographies of Transnational Feminism." In *Borderlands in European Gender Studies*, edited by Teresa Kulawik and Zhanna Kravchenko, 1–38. Routledge.

Kuzhabekova, Aliya. 2020. "Invisibilizing Eurasia: How North-South Dichotomization Marginalizes Post-Soviet Scholars in International

Research Collaborations." *Journal of Studies in International Education* 24 (1): 113–30.

Liu, Petrus. 2023. *The Specter of Materialism: Queer Theory and Marxism in the Age of the Beijing Consensus*. Duke University Press.

Lykke, Nina, Redi Koobak, Petra Bakos, Swati Arora, and Kharnita Mohamed, eds. 2024. *Pluriversal Conversations on Transnational Feminisms: And Words Collide from a Place*. Routledge.

Marat, Erica. 2009. *Labor Migration in Central Asia: Implications of the Global Economic Crisis*. Washington, D.C.: Central Asia–Caucasus Institute / Silk Road Studies Program.

Marat, Erica. 2018. "Mimicking 'Broken Windows' Policing in Post-Soviet Cities: Expanding Social Control in Uncertain Times." *Policing and Society* 29 (9): 1005–21.

Marat, Erica. 2021. "Introduction: 30 Years of Central Asian Studies—The Best Is Yet to Come." *Central Asian Survey* 40 (4): 477–82.

Marat, Erica, and Zhibek Aisarina. 2021. "Towards a More Equal Field in Central Asia Research." *Open Democracy*, January 8. https://www.opendemocracy.net/en/odr/towards-more-equal-field-central-asia-research/.

Marciniak, Katarzyna. 2006. *Alienhood: Citizenship, Exile, and the Logic of Difference*. University of Minnesota Press.

Mogilner, Marina. 2013. *Homo Imperii: A History of Physical Anthropology in Russia*. University of Nebraska Press.

Nachescu, Voichita. 2019. "Unclassifiable Outsiders: Eastern European Women, Transnational Whiteness, and Solidarity." In *Narratives of Marginalized Identities in Higher Education*, edited by Santosh Khadka, Joanna Davis-McElligatt, and Keith Dorwick, 188–200. Routledge.

Nash, Jennifer C. 2019. *Black Feminism Reimagined: After Intersectionality*. Duke University Press.

Nash, Jennifer C. 2021. "Beyond Antagonism: Rethinking Intersectionality, Transnationalism, and the Women's Studies Academic Job Market." In *Transnational Feminist Itineraries: Situating Theory and Activist Practices*, edited by Ashwini Tambe and Millie Thayer. Duke University Press.

Ndlovu-Gatsheni, Sabelo J. 2015. "Genealogies of Coloniality and Implications for Africa's Development." *Africa Development* 40 (3): 13–40.

Nowicka, Wanda. 1995. "Statement from the Non-Region." Statement made at the Fourth World Conference of Women, Beijing, September 13.

Pahulich, Lesia. 2023. "Postsocialist Queer Critique: Anti-Roma Violence and the Reconfiguration of the Commons in Ukraine." PhD diss., Ohio State University.

Pahulich, Lesia. 2024. "Entangled Imperialisms, Coloniality, and the Racialization of Roma in East Europe." Paper presented at The RUTA

Association Annual Conference, "Re(Kn)Own: Region(s) from Within," June 27–30, Uzhhorod, Ukraine.

Parvulescu, Anca. 2014. *The Traffic in Women's Work: East European Migration and the Making of Europe*. Chicago: University of Chicago Press.

Parvulescu, Anca, and Manuela Boatcă. 2022. *Creolizing the Modern: Transylvania Across Empires*. Cornell University Press.

Salimjan, Guldana. 2024. "Green Colonialism in China: Socialist Legacy and Kazakh Dispossession." *The Funambulist*, August 21, 66–71.

Samudzi, Zoé. 2022. "Journey from 'The Center of the World': On U.S. Exceptionalism and Disgust." *The Funambulist*, April 13. https://thefunambulist.net/magazine/decentering-the-us/journey-from-the-center-of-the-world-on-u-s-exceptionalism-and-disgust.

Shahrani, Nazif. 1993. "Central Asia and the Challenge of the Soviet Legacy." *Central Asian Survey* 12 (2): 123–35.

Shchurko, Tatsiana. 2022. "From Belarus to Black Lives Matter: Rethinking Protests in Belarus Through a Transnational Feminist Perspective." *Intersections* 8 (4): 25–41.

Shih, Shu-mei. 2012. "Is the *Post* in Postsocialism the *Post* in Posthumanism?" *Social Text* [no. 110] 30 (1): 27–50.

Shohat, Ella. 2001. "Area Studies, Transnationalism, and the Feminist Production of Knowledge." *Signs* 26 (4): 1269–72.

Sonevytsky, Maria. 2022. "What Is Ukraine? Notes on Epistemic Imperialism." *Topos*, no. 2, 21–30.

South/South Movement. n.d. "Global Souths as Knowing Otherwise?" Accessed November 21, 2024. https://www.southsouthmovement.org/about-us/.

Starodubtsev, Vladyslav. 2023. "Africa and the War in Ukraine: Russian Money, Wagner Group, and Grassroots Solidarity." *Commons*, May 31. https://commons.com.ua/en/afrika-rosijskij-imperializm-ta-vijna-v-ukrayini/.

Stebur, Antonina. 2021. "The Body Is an Instrument of Struggle and a Source of Hope." *tranzit.at*, September 28. https://at.tranzit.org/en/news/0/2021-09-28/the-body-is-an-instrument-of-struggle-and-a-source-of-hope.

Suchland, Jennifer. 2011. "Is Postsocialism Transnational?" *Signs* 36 (4): 837–62.

Sultanalieva, Syinat. 2023. *"Nomadity of Being" in Central Asia: Narratives of Kyrgyzstani Women's Rights Activists*. Palgrave Macmillan.

Tambe, Ashwini, and Millie Thayer, eds. 2021. *Transnational Feminist Itineraries*. Duke University Press.

Tlostanova, Madina. 2010. *Gender Epistemologies and Eurasian Borderlands*. Palgrave Macmillan.

Tlostanova, Madina. 2012. "Non-European Soviet Ex-Colonies and the Coloniality of Gender; or, How to Unlearn Western Feminism in Eurasian

Borderlands." In *Learning to Unlearn: Decolonial Reflections from Eurasia and the Americas*, by Madina V. Tlostanova and Walter D. Mignolo, 122–49. Columbus: Ohio State University Press.

Tlostanova, Madina, Suruchi Thapar-Björkert, and Redi Koobak. 2019. "The Postsocialist 'Missing Other' of Transnational Feminism?" *Feminist Review* 121 (1): 81–7.

Todorova, Miglena S. 2018. "Race and Women of Color in Socialist/Postsocialist Transnational Feminisms in Central and Southeastern Europe." *Meridians* 16 (1): 114–41.

Todorova, Miglena S. 2021. *Unequal Under Socialism: Race, Women, and Transnationalism in Bulgaria*. University of Toronto Press.

Tsymbalyuk, Darya. 2022. "Academia Must Recentre Embodied and Uncomfortable Knowledge." *Nature Human Behaviour*, no. 6, 758–59.

Tsymbalyuk, Darya. 2023. "What My Body Taught Me About Being a Scholar of Ukraine and from Ukraine in Times of Russia's War of Aggression." *Journal of International Relations and Development*, no. 26, 698–709.

Ukraine-Palestine Solidarity Group. 2023. "Ukrainian Letter of Solidarity with Palestinian People." *Commons*, November 2. https://commons.com.ua/en/ukrayinskij-list-solidarnosti/.

Ulturgasheva, Olga. 2023. "Gender in Decolonial Indigenous Perspective." In *The Cambridge Handbook of the Anthropology of Gender and Sexuality*, edited by Cecilia McCallum, Silvia Posocco, and Martin Fotta, 370–94. Cambridge University Press.

Vozyanov, Andrey. 2021. "Grassroots Sociology, Data Hierarchies, and the Challenges of Posing Relevant Questions in and About Belarus." *Status Research Project*, December 10. http://statusproject.net/grassroots-sociology.

Wegren, Stephen K. 2024. "Russia's Support for Authoritarian Regimes Through Food Trade." *Post-Communist Economies* 36 (6): 672–94.

Where's This Child's Mother? Black Birthing as "Raw Materials" in Media

Makeba Lavan

Abstract: Drawing on Black/feminist concepts from scholars such as bell hooks, Hortense Spillers, and Cheryl L. Harris, this article critically examines the role of media institutions in perpetuating and reinforcing dominant power structures. Across genre, media serves as a tool for maintaining hegemonic whiteness. Through an analysis of three media texts—*Orphan Black*, *The Baby-Sitters Club*, and *Marry Me*—I analyze the disturbing media trend of the deliberate erasure of Black mothering across genre. In each of these works, mixed-race children are used as a proxy for diversity without actually providing the corresponding cultural context. In this way, these texts highlight the failure of what Kristin Warner calls "plastic representation." Ultimately, the article underscores the need for greater diversity and equity in all levels of media creation. **Keywords:** Black mothering, race bending, plastic representation, hegemonic whiteness, media studies, cultural studies

I watch a lot of television. Regardless, I did not expect to write an article about the erasure of Black mothers in television shows and films. The three media texts I write about are programs I watched for a variety of reasons. I love science fiction shows and binge-watched *Orphan Black* as soon as it hit a streaming service. Nostalgia for one of my favorite childhood book series caused me to excitedly watch *The Baby-Sitters Club*, and boredom led me to *Marry Me*, which at the time was the latest movie starring Jennifer Lopez in a zany marriage-focused romantic comedy. After watching these programs, a disturbing trend emerged: Black women were written for the purpose of birthing children who are raised and shaped solely by white families.

To be clear, I am not suggesting this is the case with every media text. However, it is one of the current trends among media aimed at the "general population," or dominant culture, in a hollow gesture toward representation. Visual media shapes our perception of people and cultures. bell hooks makes it plain: "There is a direct and abiding connection between the maintenance of white supremacist patriarchy in this society and the institutionalization via mass media of specific images, representations of race, *of blackness that support and maintain the oppression, exploitation, and overall domination of all black people*" (hooks 1992, 2; emphasis mine). The Black birthing women mentioned in this article leave behind children who may mourn their absence but are nevertheless not granted any access to Blackness or Black culture. In *Orphan Black, The Baby-Sitters Club,* and *Marry Me*, there is no blending of families or culture, only a triumph over what Ebony Elizabeth Thomas calls "the Dark Other" (2019, 5). Through their children and their own embodied Blackness, the women gesture at diversity while maintaining the hegemonic experience of whiteness as universal.

Similarly, Hortense Spillers writes that "the women's movement and the Black movement have always been in tandem, but what I saw happening was *Black people being treated as a kind of raw material*. That the history of Black people was something you could use as a note of inspiration but it was never anything that had anything to do with you" (Spillers et al. 2007, 300–301; emphasis mine). While Spillers speaks specifically about the theoretical frameworks undergirding feminism and the fight for Black lives and rights, I also find this to be true in terms of media representation. Media that prominently features Black people is overly concerned with the worst of American history, overwhelmingly casting Black actors as enslaved people on forced-labor camps (plantations sound too romantic for what happened there), servants, or comedic sidekicks with no interiority. We are inspiration for non-Black people. They can feel empowered and sympathetic about what we have *overcome in the past.*

And often, within television shows and movies, Black suffering and death are used to move the story forward, with Black people centered only as ghosts or cogs in the machine. This is certainly true in the three pieces of media I analyze in this article, where the central theme is the specter of the Black mother sacrificed on an otherwise pristine altar of whiteness. These Black women are written into white worlds built around their roles as walking wombs, the "raw material" from which families are built, because of them and despite them. They are killed off for sympathy (*Orphan Black, The Baby-Sitters Club*) or remain inexplicably alive and still absent (*Marry Me*).

Ultimately, the ideological foundation of societal domination includes media. Therefore, what we see on television and on movie screens will mostly reflect and confirm stereotypes and presumed ideals that uphold hegemonic whiteness. The following media selections are examples that highlight the ways in which the erasure of Black mothers and Black mothering has appeared across three different genres: science fiction, young adult, and romantic comedy. *Orphan Black*, *The Baby-Sitters Club*, and *Marry Me* present Black women as surrogates for white life; these shows and movie depict a refusal to engage with Black cultural interiority, instead settling for limp overtures toward skin-deep representation.

Orphan Black (2013–2017) is a fast-paced Canadian science fiction thriller about a woman who discovers that she is one of many clones. The show's claim to fame is that all of the clones are thrillingly portrayed by one actor, Tatiana Maslany. In an attempt to discover their origins, the clones uncover a massive eugenics-based cult called Neolution that is hell-bent on achieving self-directed human evolution. Neolution is financially supported through a maze of shell corporations with shadowy leadership and deeply immoral practices. One of those practices is targeting poor Black women and convincing them to be surrogates in exchange for resources. These dark-skinned Black women with natural hair (Kendra has a short afro and Amelia has long locs) are integral to the show's plot development. Alongside a heartless assassin, who is also dark-skinned, with close-cropped hair, they are the only Black women with speaking roles, however brief, on the five-season-long show.

We meet Amelia in season 1, episode 9. At twenty-two, Amelia (whose name literally means "hardworking") agrees to be a surrogate in exchange for housing and financial support in London. Amelia makes this decision purely for economic reasons as an immigrant to a new country in need of financial stability. Her backstory highlights the ways many Black women and women of color are vulnerable to economic exploitation, a fact so ingrained in our cultural fabric that the show's writers explicitly state this as a reason that the Black women become surrogates. Unfortunately for Amelia, Neolution scientists tricked her into carrying genetically engineered embryos destined to become paragons of human evolution. Regarding eugenics, we know that "the arrangement of human reproduction in order to increase the proportion of characteristics regarded as desirable (or to reduce the proportion regarded as undesirable) within a population or the species as a whole" can only produce bigoted outcomes in an imperialist, white supremacist, capitalist patriarchy (*Oxford English Dictionary* 2023). Therefore, it becomes painfully clear that the image of these Black women birthing and caring for white babies echoes Black women's plight during enslavement.

African/Black women were forced to birth babies who were deemed property, used to increase enslavers' net worth and influence. As Dorothy Roberts writes, enslavement "marked Black women from the beginning as subjects whose decisions about reproduction should be subject to social regulation rather than to their own will" (Roberts 1999). Using Black women as creators of property and expanders of wealth was fundamental to this country's economic, social, and ideological foundations.

One of the most horrific twists of the show is that the clones are literally patented. Their embryos, their bodies, and their children are the actual property of Neolution. In addition to the chattel-slavery link, given our current real-world battle around women's/birthing people's fertility and body autonomy, including in vitro fertilization (IVF), the show sends some bleak messages. The clones are enslaved to Neolution, and the series is an ongoing, humanizing quest for their freedom. On the other hand, the Black women on the show are poor and disenfranchised, because in the afterlives of (chattel) enslavement, the willful refusal to imagine Black women existing and thriving as fully realized, outside of what they can provide to white people and oppressive institutions, is still far more common than it should be. Therefore, these characters exist solely to humanize the white protagonists.

In this way, Amelia and Kendra are "raw material," not mothers. It is by design that all the perfect genetically modified babies advertised at BrightBorn are white. Black and Brown babies are not even part of the conversation regarding this self-directed evolution. White babies are shown as a triumph of eugenics and also as a cautionary tale, sympathetic victims of eugenics' high cost. Children are quite literally the future, and in *Orphan Black*, that future is white.

In this way, as Ebony Elizabeth Thomas writes, "for many readers, viewers, and fans of color . . . to participate in the fantastic is to watch yourself be slain. . . . To watch a science fiction film is to learn that you have no future . . . very often, when you appear on the page or on the screen, you are a slave, a servant, or a prostitute—even your very body is not your own. If you have words, your speech serves only to support the narrative, never to subvert it" (2019, 4). I also believed that Black people and people of color were simply absent or incidental to "the English language fantasy tradition." Now, as a grown woman who is trained to analyze and close-read, I have noticed the haunting of the Dark Other, the Africanist Other's presence (Morrison

1992), in all these seemingly innocuous, "universal" texts (Thomas 2019, 5). And with *Orphan Black*, the violence and haunting play out against the Black women, who are reduced to medical experiments, walking wombs, and facilitators of emotional catharsis for the white protagonists.

Fleeing captivity, Amelia gives birth to the clones and surrenders Sarah to the state and Helena to a church, which is unfortunately another cult. Almost thirty years later, the white woman who raised Sarah brings her to meet Amelia so she can get answers about her past. Upon first meeting, Amelia tells Sarah, "I'm not what you expected, I'm sure." Clearly, the show's writers expect that Amelia's Blackness, particularly given her role as Sarah and Helena's "birth mother," will shock and thrill the audience. In this moment, Amelia becomes an audience surrogate, saying the quiet part out loud. Sarah replies, "I kind of gave up expecting." Sarah's capacity to be shocked is tempered by the knowledge that she is a clone. However, Sarah's twin sister Helena, who has been driven mad by the cult in which she was raised, laughs derisively and asks how Amelia could possibly be their birth mother. Here Helena also becomes an audience surrogate, making it safe for the audience to titter in disbelief and derision.

Prior to this point in the narrative, Helena and Sarah were shocked to learn that they were clones, a thing that should not be possible. Now, they are just as shocked to discover that they were gestated in the womb of a Black woman, again, a thing that should not be possible. It is as Jared Sexton expounds: "In a world structured by the twin axioms of white superiority and black inferiority, of white existence and black *nonexistence*, a world structured by a negative categorical imperative—'above all, don't be black'—in this world, the zero degree of world transformation is the turn toward blackness, a turn toward the shame, as it were, that resides in the idea that 'I am thought of as less than human'" (2012; emphasis mine). In a fictional world built to tell the story of a group of clones who band together to take down the corporation that owns them, Blackness remains the bigger horror. As a Black woman stepping into this "world-that-never-was," it was a slap in the face, a dousing of cold water, that the plot twist regarding the white twin clones' birth had a Black woman at the center, who exists simply to drive the emotional catharsis of said white clones. This unimaginative catharsis comes at the expense of the Black character's life in a brutal murder by one of the children she gestated and gave up everything to protect.

Shock value aside, we know next to nothing about Amelia. We learn nothing of her life, including where she is actually from. Before meeting Sarah, she mentions fleeing Cape Town, South Africa. She is a one-dimensional character who lacks interiority. In the end, she is written as nothing more than a reproductive tool for racist eugenics practices. Amelia's sole purpose rests in what she can provide for the white protagonists. Aside from that, she is *nonexistent*.

However, given that she was a twenty-two-year-old surrogate and almost thirty years have passed, we can speculate that Amelia may have been part of the Windrush generation: Black people from Caribbean countries who emigrated to the United Kingdom to help alleviate the post–World War II labor shortage. This particular migration story culminated seventy years later with forcible removals and the withdrawal of the UK from the European Union in hopes of closing borders. The Windrush generation's migration cannot be explored without its imperial connection. Amelia "could be understood as symbolically enacting the third, long-postponed and final leg of the historic process of unequal exchange known as 'the triangular trade'" (Hall 2017). She was brought to London to labor, solely. Aside from this, we learn nothing of Amelia's family, or the kind of life she has managed to create outside of the clone conflict.

Since Amelia's comically short story arc occurs in season 1, it becomes foundational to the show that poor Black women are reduced to walking wombs who labor for this eugenics project. This is also the case with Kendra, the other Black woman who is paid to carry a genetically altered child. She gives birth to a blind white baby. Because BrightBorn considers blindness a defect, Kendra goes on the run with the baby, leaving her own biological Black child with family. Kendra's name means "prophetess" or "knowing," which is fitting, because it was her video of company scientists euthanizing a white baby with severe birth defects that helped tank BrightBorn. In the end, BrightBorn captures Kendra off-screen. We never find out what happened to her or the baby. Kendra appears in one episode for about ten minutes, and her capture is simply mentioned in a later conversation. Her character was written solely to place blame for BrightBorn's unsavory eugenicist practices on another nonwhite woman, Evie Cho, the figurehead for the company, while providing some sort of justice and closure for the clones (*Orphan Black* 2016).

Amelia did not even exist on the show long enough for Sarah to develop any type of bond with her. Her death, therefore, is only met with the pain of a relationship that will never be and answers that Sarah may never discover. Like so many Black women on television, Amelia's character is a catalyst for the white protagonist's emotional catharsis and growth. As she watches Amelia die, Sarah tearfully tells Helena, "You killed someone I've been dreaming about my whole life" (*Orphan Black* 2013). After just a few scant scenes across two episodes, Amelia is violently killed by Helena, the other clone she gestated. Her death at the hands of a child she carried is especially heinous and holds echoes of the forced-labor camps' cyclical cruelty. Black women would nourish white babies from their own breasts, raising them only to have those babies visit unspeakable acts of violence upon them. And just like so many generations of enslaved Black women, there can be no emancipation for Amelia or Kendra. The show, like all examples in this article, creates a world that continues to reaffirm hegemonic whiteness. Black women can only be facilitators of bright, white futures. Black children, and eventually Blackness, will not even exist.

The term "race bending" was created to describe fan disappointment about the whitewashing of characters in the live-action film adaptation of *Avatar: The Last Airbender*. The website racebending.com defines race bending as "situations where a media content creator (movie studio, publisher, etc.) has changed the race or ethnicity of a character," and notes that "this long-standing Hollywood practice has historically been used to discriminate against people of color." The original use of the term shed light on the common practice of white actors being cast in roles who were originally meant for people of color. Today, the term is also used when describing a canonically white character that is recast as nonwhite. In fact, we can posit that race bending is "part of a long history of racial masquerade that can work both to destabilize the fixity of identity, as well as to shore up racialized hegemonic power structures" (Lopez 2011). Both of these arguments ring true for the Netflix adaptation of *The Baby-Sitters Club*.

In the original book series, Mary Anne Spier is described as a white preteen with brown hair. The Netflix series adaptation is a nostalgia-infused young adult series aimed at an intergenerational audience. In it, Mary Anne is recast as a biracial girl with a white dad and a Black mother. Her mother, Alma, died of cancer when Mary Anne was a baby; therefore, Mary Anne has no memory of her. She is being raised by her white father in the affluent (white) town of Stoneybrook, Connecticut. We do not see Mary Anne interacting with other members of Alma's family. Mary Anne's cultural connections to Blackness died with Alma, who becomes a specter, visible only in her child, no longer needed after the child is produced. In an interview about these decisions to race-bend some of the characters, series author Ann M. Martin states, "We wanted to stay true to the original series, but make it even more diverse"; she goes on to say that the original book series and the series adaptation is "about celebrating differences" (Nahas 2020). This is how many shows are doing diversity: casting a mixed-race child as "proof" of a diverse family structure they do not actually have to show but merely hint at.

Regardless of this supposed goal of "celebrating difference," Mary Anne's cultural expression bears no difference to the other white characters. In fact, in one scene, Mary Anne and her father, Richard, have dinner with fellow babysitter Dawn and her mother, Sharon. Sharon serves vegan tacos as an ode to both their Latina heritage and their Californian health-obsessed lifestyle. Here, it is imperative to note that the Schafers are simply described nebulously as Latino-American, no specific country of origin is given. In the scene, Dawn complains that the seitan "lacks heat," and Richard states that Sharon cooked it with his palate in mind. This is, of course, a play on the stereotype that white people mostly eat bland food and the "spicy Latin cuisine" would overwhelm Richard. Huffing playfully, Dawn grabs the hot sauce and douses her taco. Mary Anne insists that she can take the heat, so Dawn douses hers as well. After taking a bite, it becomes clear that Mary Anne cannot tolerate hot sauce, and she feverishly requests milk. The low tolerance for spice aligns Mary Anne's tastes, and therefore her cultural identity, solely with that of her white father. It seems as if the show wants to make it clear that Mary Anne's mixed-race identity is only skin-deep. After all, "adolescents do not develop identity in isolation, but within their embedding in various social contexts" (Schachner et al. 2017).

These are all deliberate choices regarding Mary Anne's race-bent characterization. None of the original *Baby-Sitters Club* characters are Black. Therefore, someone made the decision to race-bend Mary Anne, specifically, and to have her raised by a white dad and not a Black one. It is important to note that Mary Anne's mother dies when she is a baby in the original book series as well. But unlike the book series, we do not see or hear members of either side of Mary Anne's family, white or Black. We never see any grandparents, aunts and uncles, or siblings. It is quite odd to know that her mother died when Mary Anne was a baby and not see any other kinship connections to her Black family. It is also peculiar that Richard's family does not appear to be lending support to the single father. The lack of effort to situate Mary Anne within a mix of both Black and white cultural contexts means that her character is a perfect example of plastic representation, which "can be understood as a combination of synthetic elements put together and shaped to look like meaningful imagery, but which can only approximate depth and substance because ultimately it is hollow and cannot survive close scrutiny." Mary Anne's race-bent character perfectly illustrates a type of "minority visibility," a visual diversity that is only skin-deep (Warner 2017, 35). The decision to cast Mary Anne as a mixed-race child with no Black family is especially confusing because in the book series, Mary Anne learns that when she was a baby, her father, drowning in grief, sent her to live with her maternal grandparents for a time (Martin 1992). In that very same book, we learn that Mary Anne's mother, Alma, wrote her a letter before she died. Therefore, the source material already provided a solution to maintain kinship with her Black family members. Why does that plotline cease to matter now that the character is Black?

This is the danger with race bending. When you change the race of a character, you must consider the cultural context in which the new character resides. These choices, whether consciously made or no, support a cultural hegemony of whiteness. It is assumed that because her Black mother is dead, her father is not responsible for facilitating the connections. Therefore, this is not simply an issue of representation. Often, when a character's race is changed from white, everything else about the fictional world stays the same. This reinforces the comforting lie that racism is a problem of the past, even as the nonwhite character is utterly stripped of their cultural heritage. It also feeds into the dangerous idea that white stories are culturally universal. In this way, we literally see the generational whitening of a familial structure. The Black cultural connections are not severed, they never existed in the first place.

By erasing Black people and eventually Black culture in visual media, the dominant culture attempts to establish fictional futures where we do not exist. Even more importantly, they manufacture consent to make this vision possible in real life as well. The reluctance to practice racially and culturally informed storytelling is completely undergirded by the belief that nonwhite people's stories, particularly Black stories, are unrelatable to white audiences and therefore not worth telling or watching, despite numbers that say otherwise. According to a study commissioned by McKinsey and Company, a global management consulting firm, "in 2019, the top films with Black leads were distributed in 30 percent fewer international markets on average—yet they earned nearly the same global box-office sales as films with white leads and earned more than those films on a per-market basis"

(Dunn et al. 2021). True diversity is profitable and expands the imagination, regardless of the lies we are told.

Currently, we live in a society where (mostly white) gatekeepers of entertainment maintain a firm grip on the number of nonwhite stories that are allowed to be made. In fact, 87 percent of TV executives and 92 percent of film executives are white, hugely disproportionate numbers given that the 2020 census places white people at just 60 percent of the U.S. population. These executives often exist in echo chambers, surrounded by other white people with similar experiences, and are reticent to share resources with "untested, niche" markets. By contrast, less than 6 percent of the writers, directors, and producers of US-produced films are Black (Dunn et al. 2021).

Nonwhite representation is tightly controlled and usually told from a white person's perspective regardless. These statistics and the reasons they exist renders the missing Black mother trend in media very concerning. Mothering is nurturing. And for too long we have been inundated with denigrating images of Black nonmothering that cement the foundational dehumanizing beliefs that the dominant culture holds and continues to perpetuate about the Black family. Dr. Phillipe Copeland has coined the term "white replacement paranoia" to describe this often subconscious adherence to the ideology of white replacement theory (2023). Thus, in these wide-reaching stories, it is utterly expected (though no less disappointing) that the trend of removing Black mothers, and ultimately Black culture, is thought of as progress, as positive representation.

With Jennifer Lopez and *Marry Me*, art may imitate life. Jennifer Lopez's anti-Blackness has been documented for decades. Therefore, it makes sense that this Hallmark-type movie pays lip service to diversity while rendering the Black mother an afterthought in the quest to create the perfect nuclear family. *Marry Me* is a 2022 film adaptation of a graphic novel series created and written by Bobby Crosby. Jennifer Lopez and Owen Wilson star in the film. Owen Wilson's character, a math teacher named Charlie, has a twelve-year-old daughter, Lou, who is mixed-race. Charlie, alongside his best friend, takes Lou to a concert that is supposed to culminate in a televised wedding of two pop stars. When Kat, a Latina pop star whose crossover appeal rivals Lopez's herself, finds out her fiancé is cheating on her moments before their nuptials in front of tens of thousands of fans, she is bereft. Desperate, she decides to take a chance and looks out into the crowd to see Charlie, holding his best friend's sign that says, "marry me." In a twenty-first-century update of the marriage plot, a truly resplendent Kat decides to marry Charlie at that very moment. Charlie then leaves his preteen daughter in the crowd with said best friend as he goes onto the stadium's stage to marry a famous woman, a stranger, on television.

This scene is supposed to be romantic and not an indictment of Charlie's egregiously irresponsible parenting. In fact, we are led to believe that Charlie's terrible decision is Lou's unnamed Black mother's fault, because she remarried and brings Lou on adventures such as cave diving with her new husband. Charlie only attends Kat's concert in an effort to be more spontaneous and fun. The whole time I watched this story unfold, I wondered, where is this child's Black mother? We never see a conversation between the parents regarding the dangers of his rash decision to publicly marry a very famous celebrity and the effect it could have on Lou. Further, we do not even see Lou's mother until about halfway into the movie. In fact, the first time I watched the film, I assumed she was dead.

However, unlike *Orphan Black* and *The Baby-Sitters Club*, Lou's mother is very much alive and actively parenting. When Lou's mother finally appears, she picks Lou up from school, smiles at Charlie, and walks away. Her lack of on-screen mothering seems nonsensical unless one knows the historical context regarding the treatment of Black women and Black mothers in our society. When it comes to history and Black mothering, Dorothy Roberts writes, "if an enslaved woman was fortunate enough to keep her children with her, she was deprived of the opportunity to nurture them" (Roberts 1999). The only motherly nurturing we witness on-screen is between Jennifer Lopez's character (Kat) and Lou. That is a deliberate choice, one steeped in anti-Blackness.

Similar to the plastic representation of race-bent Mary Anne, choices that reinscribe hegemonic whiteness were made in this screenplay. The film's writers do not give the child's mother, a Black woman, any speaking lines whatsoever. We do not see this Black mother engaging in any sort of mothering. The action she performs outside of the school is one of any caretaker, impersonal or otherwise. At that moment, she could be the nanny who performs her duties with silence and a smile. The writers of this movie made the choice to keep this Black mother alive, unlike other shows and movies with Black moms, so it makes no sense that we do not see her being active in her child's life, especially when her co-parent makes such rash and potentially dangerous life decisions. It begs the questions: Why cast a mixed-race child at all, particularly one who is Black and white? What does this say about the ways that Black mothering is portrayed in the media? How is that portrayal a mirror of our society? Why is this woman, this Black mother, not given a name?

These dehumanizing choices are compounded by the number of significant moments that occur in the film, moments that a mother with joint custody would usually appear for. Kat is there instead. She is there to teach Lou and her class mnemonic devices for math. Kat encourages and supports Lou at the math competition. Kat spends quality family time with Lou and Charlie at home. The movie is less interested in telling the story of a blended family than it is in telling a nontraditional boy-meets-girl love story. Ultimately, one must wonder: Why include a child at all? It only serves to make Owen Wilson's character look irresponsible, a truly bad parent. Why complicate the story with children and terrible parenting that is never acknowledged and, in fact, not even painted as such? Perhaps Charlie's faulty parenting and the Black mother's absence provides Jennifer Lopez's character, Kat, with the role of a sympathetic mother figure, the one that Kat's character desperately needs to begin looking and caring outside herself and her brand. This movie creates a familial fantasy in which a non-Black woman saves a mixed-race child from the abandonment of her Black and largely absent mother. The message could not be clearer.

In fact, the story comes full circle by ending with a picture of Lou, Charlie, and Kat on the living room table, an insidious callback to the one picture we see of Lou's unnamed mother in the beginning of the film. The Black mother has been left in the past, and the picture-perfect family can move forward into the future. In fact, because she does not have a speaking role, the Black woman who portrays Lou's mother is not even credited on IMDB. I could not even find her name. For all intents and purposes, she does not exist. Even in the Ebert review of the movie, Wilson is described as a "single father" (Minow 2022). And while he is a father who is currently unpartnered, the label infers that he is raising Lou on his own. The character's silence in the movie is made more poignant and sinister by the actor's erasure in real life.

It must also be noted that Jennifer Lopez is an executive producer for the film. The movie's baffling decisions regarding Lou's Black mother are compounded and complicated by Jennifer Lopez's anti-Blackness. *The New York Times* once described Jennifer Lopez as a "one woman entertainment empire" (Kennedy 2002), whose current net worth is allegedly hundreds of millions of dollars. She has been a celebrity for around thirty years. In that time, Lopez climbed the ranks from backup dancer (Fly Girl) on the groundbreaking Black sketch show *In Living Color* to trading on her South Bronx "Jenny from the Block" persona, and its proximity to Blackness, on her way to crossover superstardom. Her most famous songs are allegedly ghost-sung by Black R&B and soul singers, including Ashanti and legendary soul group DeBarge's sole female sibling, Shawnyette Harrell. She also casually sprinkled the N-word in one of her more "urban" hits.

On July 12, 2016, less than a week after Black Lives Matter protested the state-sponsored murder of Philando Castile, Lopez tweeted a picture of her and Lin-Manuel Miranda promoting their song "Love Make the World Go Round," which they dedicated to the victims of the Pulse nightclub shooting. In the tweet, she used the white rage–inspired hashtag #AllLivesMatter. Of course, the tweet was promptly deleted after a deluge of disappointed fans replied asking if she knew the true meaning and history behind the hashtag.

Most recently, she rekindled her romance with Ben Affleck, with whom she is credited for the first celebrity portmanteau, "Bennifer." The pair married at one of Ben's homes, a mansion specifically designed to replicate a forced-labor camp (plantation), known as "The Big House." The wedding took place in 2022, the same year that *Marry Me* was released. Ben Affleck has owned the Georgia property since 2003 and tried to sell it after his infamous "Finding Your Roots" episode that revealed ancestors on Affleck's maternal side enslaved people near this very property. At the time, Affleck wielded his A-list stardom and white privilege to suppress the discovery, leading to the program's suspension (NPR 2015).

Just like these real-world examples, the movie provides excellent examples for what Cheryl Harris names as the three most enduring functions of whiteness: the right to use and enjoyment, the absolute right to exclude, and the reputation and status property. Harris notes that since whiteness is also a commodity, it can be "experienced and deployed as a resource" (1993, 1734–36). Celebrity privilege is akin to white privilege. Both groups have valuable resources: power in the forms of financial wealth, parasocial relationships, whiteness, or all three. Both trade in exclusivity and the power to exclude. And we certainly see that exclusion play out in *Marry Me* where Jennifer Lopez's character, Kat, steps seamlessly into the mothering role, whittling the unnamed, silent Black mother into the shadowy role of a smiling surrogate and domestic.

In his essay "Old and New Identities, Old and New Ethnicities," Stuart Hall writes, "Hegemony is not the disappearance or destruction of difference. It is the construction of a collective will through difference. It is the articulation of differences which do not disappear" (2019, 79). The silent, disappeared Black mothers in these examples are laden with the historical residue of a world built on chattel slavery that violently maintains a foundation of imperialist, white supremacist, capitalist patriarchy. Time does not equal progress; progress does not occur passively, and progress is not linear. In the case of the examples included in this article, we must eschew hollow, plastic progress narratives in favor of actual progress (media and otherwise) led by minoritized populations. Moya Bailey, in her book *Misogynoir Transformed*, writes, "Black feminist theory clearly articulates the power of the image to serve the hegemony of 'white supremacist capitalist patriarchy' by controlling the way society views marginalized groups and how we view ourselves" (2021, 2). Therefore, it remains important to note that the fight for representation is not simply to see people like oneself on television. It is a fight to be confirmed within the cultural landscape, a visual confirmation that one's own culture exists, matters, and deserves to be seen.

This article began with my attempt to watch the aforementioned media programs for simple enjoyment. However, there is no such thing as mindless watching when it comes to media. Whether acknowledged or not, we absorb the implicit and explicit messages propagated in television shows and movies. They inscribe and reinscribe our ideologies with each viewing. Therefore, we must be critical of the media we absorb. When we watch, we have to ask ourselves: How do the narratives of what we are being shown fit in with our lived reality? This article is meant to help others notice one of the narratives being aggressively pushed in media. It is also a starting point for critiquing what rules and rubrics we follow as we proclaim that media is diverse or representative.

The elimination of the Black mother in these texts effectively annihilates the need for deep, nuanced depictions of Black life, Black culture. Ultimately, they are sinister reminders that despite half-hearted attempts at plastic diversity, mainstream media remains committed to keeping visual media as white as possible while maintaining that whiteness is the universal experience or, at least, the only point of view that matters. Visual media shows us that racism is not a passive endeavor. It permeates all our entertainment outlets and institutions, which provides fodder for real-world bigotry. Therefore, media representations are extremely important to the lived experience. Art imitates life and vice versa, for better or worse.

Makeba Lavan received her PhD from the Department of English at The Graduate Center, CUNY. Currently, she is an assistant professor of English at Grinnell College. Her research focuses on (African) American studies, Afrofuturism/speculative fiction, and popular culture. Lavan has been published in *Radical Teacher*, *Africology: The Journal of Pan African Studies*, and *Modern Language Studies*. As part of Lost and Found: The CUNY Poetics Document Initiative, she coedited *"Realizing the Dream of a Black University" & Other Writings*, a collaborative publication of Toni Cade Bambara's teaching materials from CUNY and Spelman College. She can be reached at lavanmak@grinnell.edu.

Works Cited

The Baby-Sitters Club. 2020–2021. Netflix.
Bailey, Moya. 2021. *Misogynoir Transformed: Black Women's Digital Resistance*. New York University Press.
Coiro, Kat, dir. 2022. *Marry Me*. Universal.
Copeland, Phillipe. 2023. "Fear of a Black Hobbit." *Word in Black*, February 2. https://wordinblack.com/2023/02/fear-of-a-black-hobbit/.
Dunn, Jonathan, Sheldon Lyn, Nony Onyeador, and Ammanuel Zegeye. 2021. "Black Representation in Film and TV: The Challenges and Impact of Increasing Diversity." McKinsey & Company, March 11. https://www.mckinsey.com/featured-insights/diversity-and-inclusion/black-representation-in-film-and-tv-the-challenges-and-impact-of-increasing-diversity.
Hall, Stuart. 2017. *Familiar Stranger: A Life Between Two Islands*. Edited by Bill Schwarz. Duke University Press.
Hall, Stuart. 2019. "Old and New Identities, Old and New Ethnicities." In *Identity and Diaspora*, edited by David Morley. Vol. 2 of *Essential Essays*. Duke University Press.
Harris, Cheryl I. 1993. "Whiteness as Property." *Harvard Law Review* 106 (8): 1707–91.
hooks, bell. 1992. *Black Looks: Race and Representation*. South End Press.
Kennedy, Dana. 2002. "Holiday Movies: Homegirl, Working Woman, Empire Builder." *New York Times*, November 3. https://www.nytimes.com/2002/11/03/movies/holiday-movies-homegirl-working-woman-empire-builder.html.
Lopez, Lori Kido. 2011. "Fan Activists and the Politics of Race in *The Last Airbender*." *International Journal of Cultural Studies* 15 (5): 431–45.
Martin, Ann M. 1992. *Mary Anne and the Secret in the Attic*. Scholastic Paperbacks.
Minow, Nell. 2022. "Marry Me." *RogerEbert.com*, February 11. https://www.rogerebert.com/reviews/marry-me-movie-review-2022.

Morrison, Toni. 1992. *Playing in the Dark: Whiteness and the Literary Imagination*. Harvard University Press.

Nahas, Aili. 2020. "The Baby-Sitters Club Author Ann M. Martin Is 'Proud' of Netflix's Diverse Spin on Series," *People*. https://people.com/tv/the-baby-sitters-club-author-is-proud-of-netflix-diverse-spin-on-the-series/.

NPR. 2015. "After Ben Affleck Scandal, PBS Postpones 'Finding Your Roots.'" June 25. https://www.npr.org/sections/thetwo-way/2015/06/25/417455657/after-ben-affleck-scandal-pbs-postpones-finding-your-roots.

Orphan Black. 2013. "Endless Forms Most Beautiful." *Prime Video*. June 1.

Orphan Black. 2016. "The Mitigation of Competition." *Prime Video*. June 9.

Oxford English Dictionary (*OED*). 2023. "eugenics (n.)." July. https://doi.org/10.1093/OED/9281777902.

Roberts, Dorothy. 1999. *Killing the Black Body: Race, Reproduction, and the Meaning of Liberty*. Vintage.

Schachner, M. K., F. J. R. van de Vijver, and P. Noack. 2017. "Contextual Conditions for Acculturation and Adjustment of Adolescent Immigrants—Integrating Theory and Findings." *Online Readings in Psychology and Culture* 8 (1). https://doi.org/10.9707/2307-0919.1142.

Sexton, Jared. 2012. "Ante-Anti-Blackness: Afterthoughts." *Lateral*, no. 1. https://csalateral.org/issue/1/ante-anti-blackness-afterthoughts-sexton/.

Spillers, Hortense, Saidiya Hartman, Farah Jasmine Griffin, Shelly Eversley, and Jennifer L. Morgan. 2007. "'Whatcha Gonna Do?': Revisiting 'Mama's Baby, Papa's Maybe: An American Grammar Book': A Conversation with Hortense Spillers, Saidiya Hartman, Farah Jasmine Griffin, Shelly Eversley, and Jennifer L. Morgan." *Women's Studies Quarterly* 35 (1–2) : 299–309.

Thomas, Ebony Elizabeth. 2019. *The Dark Fantastic: Race and the Imagination from Harry Potter to the Hunger Games*. New York University Press.

Warner, Kristen J. 2017. "In the Time of Plastic Representation." *Film Quarterly* 71 (2): 32–37.

Blackqueer Currere: A Method in Three Breaths

Robert P. Robinson

Abstract: *Currere* comes from the Latin infinitive for *curriculum*. Recognizing the need for intersectional curriculum inquiry, Denise Taliaferro-Baszile coined critical race/feminist currere. This paper employs currere to focus on the experiences and theorizing of Blackqueer educators and students. It outlines the term, explores specific works that inform the approach, critically examines the author's positionality, and analyzes moments in which he employed the method. It ends with a call for researchers interested in this inquiry both within and beyond the meta-discipline of education. **Keywords:** Blackqueer studies, curriculum studies, Black education, self-inquiry, currere

It's been months since I've written a solid "midnight essay." It is in these late hours that my soul is forced into conversation—I dream in real time here. As painful as it can be at times, I prefer this writing to any form of writing. I hug younger and future me at once.
　　　　　　　　　—tweeted by me at 12:43 a.m. on May 3, 2022

In a previous essay, I discuss the form of writing I call "midnight essays." The term was coined by my bestie, Tony, to describe this deeply personal writing that I often do in the midnight hours—the space between days—a liminal space of spiritual, intellectual, and creative possibility (Robinson 2024). While the midnight essay is my favorite, it lives under the larger umbrella of autobiography. I write to know the self—often the self in relationship to others, but in this form, rarely the self in explicit relationship to institutions or systems of power. In 2020, while in my first semester as a freshly minted PhD, I began to look at a different form of self-inquiry we all know as autoethnography. In fact, less than a year later, I coauthored one public apology to my students about my own practices of antiblackness in the classroom and solo-authored an essay about my journey as a Black visiting professor in a predominately white Iowa town after the horrific murder of a Black man. Both essays of self-inquiry examine the specific institutions and the broader white supremacist foundations of education as an (capital "I") Institution. While midnight essays provided an opportunity for me to explore my becoming as a long-closeted Blackqueer cis-man educator, autoethnography helped me to interrogate my triumphs, failures, and concessions as an educator. Through knowing the ever-becoming self as subject-object, oppressor-oppressed, and liberator-liberated—among many other identities between and beyond the binaries—I was able to see the contexts that fostered both reproductions of social inequity and liberatory praxis.

The type of writing I discuss is by no means new. This paper, in some ways, is an homage to those historical versions of critical autoethnography with a specific focus on educational inquiry. Though many disciplines have dismissed education as an unserious or less rigorous metadiscipline, I think it is important to note how many of the Black intellectuals we admire spoke to, from, and through discourses and subfields of educational thought. Anna Julia Cooper, Ida B. Wells, Alain Locke, W. E. B. Du Bois, Mary Church Terrell, and Carter G. Woodson—to name a handful—were all educators who provided foundations into Black intellectual thought in education (Bay 2009; Du Bois [1899] 2015; Du Bois [1903] 1994; Grant et al. 2016; James 1997; McDuffie 2011). While I can spend pages on the need to position Black intellectual thought in education within the canon of serious Black study, I will leave that for a different essay. What I will argue is that Black critical autoethnography is an important tool in educational thought, and Black feminist scholars have noted this both within and beyond educational theory (Boylorn 2008, 2016; Boylorn and Orbe 2014; Dillard 2016; Slay 2022).

Recognizing the strength of this form of critical thought, I call for a specific form of introspective inquiry that examines intersections of race, gender, and sexuality to unearth pathways to educational thought, which also informs pedagogical practice: Blackqueer currere. In this paper, I will outline the term, explore specific works that inform the approach, critically examine my own positionality, and analyze moments in which I employed the method of inquiry. The hope is to both name the narrative inquiry method and provide examples for researchers interested in this form of memoir and autoethnographic inquiry both within and beyond the meta-discipline of education.

Currere

While I was in graduate school, I learned about currere. Imagine critical autoethnography in the educational context; this essentially captures much of its definition. I say "much" because currere also argues the biographical as evidence. Currere comes from the Latin infinitive for curriculum: "to run the course: Thus *currere* refers to the existential experience of institutional structures. The method of *currere* is a strategy devised to disclose experience, so that we may see more of it and see more clearly" (Pinar et al. 1995). Under this definition, this form of inquiry looks at life course in conversation with institutions for the purposes of a deepened understanding and potential liberatory praxis in education. I would argue, then, that currere is a form of critical autoethnography that focuses on "the life course" in conversation with curriculum, pedagogy, curriculum theory, and education. While currere and autoethnographic inquiry broadly have been critiqued for overindulgence of the self or an untrustworthiness of the self as evidence—a fair argument—we must also recognize that well-respected versions of such inquiry have long existed in educational discourse. In Black American history specifically, we need only to look to *Narrative of the Life of Frederick Douglass* (Douglass [1845] 2002), *Incidents in the Life of a Slave Girl* (Jacobs [1861] 2016), *The Souls of Black Folks* (Du Bois [1903] 1994), or *Mis-Education of the Negro* (Woodson 1933) to see how the self has been used in conversation with institutions and other forms of data to paint a picture of both oppressive structures and possible pathways to liberation. In the aforementioned texts, the authors share personal narratives to unpack the very institutions they seek to dismantle: enslavement, racism, and racist education.

Blackqueer Pedagogy

In her 2011 article "Body of Knowledge: Black Queer Feminist Pedagogy, Praxis, and Embodied Text," Mel Michelle Lewis employs autoethnographic narrative to discuss the body as a site of Blackqueer possibility in the classroom. Looking specifically at her identity as a Black lesbian professor in women's studies classrooms, she asserts,

> As we explore these intersectional ideas, I use my own complex and multiple identities as an example. My body is an illustration, a site of knowledge; this makes me deliberately vulnerable. I can not refuse to be vulnerable while encouraging students to take risks without establishing a classroom climate that remains a location for coercive power. (Clark 2005, 267; quoted in Lewis 2011, 55)

Lewis draws from arguments in *Black Queer Studies: A Critical Anthology* to elucidate that the body is also curriculum—a site of knowledge to highlight individual identities and their relationship to systems of power and oppression. She directly cites Bryant Keith Alexander's chapter, which states, "I am more interested in the notion of speaking about issues of sexuality, outing oneself, and positioning one's acknowledged gay body in the classroom. I am interested in constructing the *material fact* of the black gay body as subtext to the material content of the classroom" (Alexander 2005, 250). From these renderings, we see the body, the perspectives, and the lived experiences of Blackqueer folks implicitly and explicitly supporting the traditional texts of the classroom. The pedagogy itself refers to the body as curriculum within the classroom, but their methods of reflection mirror those of currere: critical reflection of their educational experiences. Self-as-text and self-as-evidence, in this sense, is concerned with how Blackqueer educators show up in the classroom, specifically in the higher education context, and how they reflect on those experiences.

The late bell hooks cautions us in *Talking Back: Thinking Feminist, Thinking Black* against the dangers of oversimplifying "the personal is political." As part of the feminist ethos, the phrase was supposed to allude to a liberatory consciousness wherein politics, politicization, and the self were mutually shaping forces. Moreover, in her reflection, she notes, "This slogan had such power because it insisted on the primacy of the personal, not in a narcissistic way, but in its implied naming of the self as a site for politicization, which was in this society a very radical challenge to notions of self and identity" (1989, 105). She later clarifies,

> Feminist critiques of identity politics which call attention to the way it undermines feminist movement should not deny the importance of naming and giving voice to one's experience. It must be continually stressed that this is only part of the process of politicization, one which must be linked to

education for critical consciousness that teaches about structures of domination and how they function. (109)

Ultimately, hooks is arguing for a sort of massaging of the interplay between the personal and political that sees identity in relationship to collective powers of critical consciousness speaking truth to interlocking systems of domination. The personal is important, but not to the degree that it completely evades the larger extensions to the world beyond. Lewis and Alexander similarly argue that the self as text becomes both an extension of and response to the contexts of the classroom, the texts in the course, and the larger questions of race, class, gender, sexuality. While both authors are *out*, neither suggest that this is a necessary prerequisite for Blackqueer pedagogies—"through our conviction and the *material fact* of our [B]lack gay bodies in the classroom, which always already signals a teachable moment." These texts are all important to the degree that each of the authors engages in the act of currere through their Blackqueer and feminist positionalities and reflections on their educational practice. In doing so, they leverage Blackqueer experiences and politics as identity, inquiry, and pedagogical praxis. Again, the pedagogy is the act of recognizing the Blackqueer body as part of the teaching practice. Currere is the exercise of critically reflecting on the educational experience through their positionality.

Critical Race and Feminist Currere

While the aforementioned Pinar piece on currere opens up the conversation to the practice more broadly, the explicit discussion on race and gender or interlocking systems is missing from the conversation. Recognizing this phenomenon, curriculum scholar Denise Taliaferro-Baszile extends the conversation through the practice. Claiming boldly, "All work is autobiographical. That is, we all bring our sorted histories, hopes, and desires to the project of curriculum theory, hooking onto familiar stories and creating new ones," she solidifies the need to read herself and experiences into white and heteropatriarchal texts and contexts (Taliaferro-Baszile 2010, 486). Drawing on the traditions of Anna Julia Cooper, Mary Church Terrell, and Fannie Jackson Coppin, she argues for the need to understand curriculum as a racial text, "but more to the point, to understand the racial self as a curricular construction" (486). She references an "Ellisonian self" à la Charles Mills to discuss the question of invisibility in terms of race, by employing the parabolic storytelling style of Derrick Bell, who often theorized through his character Geneva Crenshaw (Bell 1987, 1992). In a conversation with an imaginary woman, Taliaferro-Baszile further takes this question of the self into the discussion of her specific positionality, asserting, "I think gender is absolutely, if implicitly, influencing my process of theorizing. I cannot think as anyone other than a Black woman, a self that I am perhaps projecting onto my analysis in a way that actually subsumes the question of maleness" (490). With the (spoiler alert) *aha* realization that the imaginary woman is indeed herself, she recognizes that the constructed self in Blackness, especially as it pertains to Black women, is as much a self-recognition as it is an affirmation to the personal and political identity of Black women—not as *the* voice but as one of many voices within the collective *I* for the purposes of reading Black folks, and especially Black women, into educational discourse.

Picking up on this conversation a half decade later, Taliaferro-Baszile further questions, "If we understand education as a journey toward self-understanding, then the critical and reoccurring question (perhaps in different forms) is who am I?" (Taliaferro-Baszile 2015, 2). She further outlines the demands of currere:

> (1) remember and reflect on his/her past educational experiences, (2) contemplate desires and fantasies of the future, (3) consider the impact of both the past and future on the shape of the present, and (4) synthesize thinking across these moments as a way to purposefully engage one's learning in the present. (2)

She advances critical race and feminist currere as

> a desire to both understand and to free oneself from the confines of oppressive ways of knowing and being.... It is a process through which women of color, and perhaps other people too, can wrestle with the epistemological dimensions of domination; that is to say that the projects of domination (in terms of race, gender, class, sexuality, and more) are most intractable when those who are being dominated cannot think, cannot imagine, cannot be outside of ways of knowing, being, and doing that have brought about the situation of domination in the first place. (3)

Currere, as a process of making sense or meaning through reflexive inquiry, asks the writer-thinker to explore questions of the self in relationship to histories, politics, and various practices. This is essentially an element of critical autoethnography, broadly speaking. In her work, Taliaferro-Baszile takes it a step further to argue that the self must do that specifically through positions and institutions of power as they tie to curriculum theory. She draws from the trifecta of curriculum theory, critical race theory, and Black feminist theory to ask important questions of power and privilege through this meaning-making project. In the end, she argues that it is autobiographical like other forms of self-inquiry but much more concerned with the ongoing project of self-actualization and "decolonization of the mind" (7). Currere, then, is the act of critical self-inquiry and reflection with an attention to ways to theorize education on the personal, interpersonal, and structural levels.

While Denise Taliaferro-Baszile names gender and sexuality within this argument, the articulation of sexuality and gender through a queer theorization is absent from the discussion. I say this not as a critique but as an opportunity to add to the conversation. With our growing sense of the distinctions between gender and sexuality and what queerness means in this regard, I think it is important for Blackqueer scholars to take up her praxis of currere with a specific emphasis on the feminist call for the personal and political alongside the queer call to recognize queerness as an act of being and doing (Sawyer 2022). Opting for a way to practice currere with this specific intentionality, I would like to take up the method of Blackqueer currere: critical self-inquiry with an attention to one's educational journey as a site of research, personal growth, and renewed focus on educational praxis.

But Wait—Who Are You?

I think it is important to unpack the question of identity here, as I am exploring a form of inquiry that is an affirmation of both my identity and those in the communities I inhabit, even as it is a way to interrogate hegemonic ways of knowing, being, and doing. I identify as a Blackqueer man. More specifically, I am a Black cis gay man from working-class Baptecostal and non-denom roots. I was born and raised in California, but New York has my heart. I often discuss how I was raised by women of color feminists . . . not exactly, though. I was born into a very Christian home, but my intellectual coming of age in undergraduate school was very much facilitated by the 1980s and 1990s work of important BIPOC feminist thinkers. As an English major and ethnic American literatures minor (cross between ethnic studies, women's studies, and English), I read Toni Morrison, bell hooks, Cherríe Moraga, Audre Lorde, Gloria Anzaldúa, Jewelle Gomez, and Beverly Daniel Tatum. Alice Walker and Harriet Jacobs helped me to gain

Black literacy and literary consciousness, and Lorna Dee Cervantes named "that nagging preoccupation with the feeling of not being good enough" (Cervantes 1982). June Jordan taught me, "I am not wrong; wrong is not my name" (Jordan [2005] 2023). While the heteropatriarchal framings of my church life kept me in the closet, Black feminism showed me the way out.

Though this romanticized retelling might be cute, I must also acknowledge that as a cis man, I still benefit from the privileges of cisheteropatriarchy. My active work to fight these systems does not preclude me from doing the internal work to see ways that my behaviors connected to earlier socialization must undergo the same critique I have of the institutions that reinforced them. While bell hooks argues that a feminist politics can be shared among us all (hooks [2000] 2015), I also recognize the important call from foundational Black radical feminists that cis men might not be able to speak to this experience without femme or womyn interiority. Moreover, as a member of a privileged gender category, I must be careful not to take up an authoritative position in the discourse of feminism (hooks 1989). Mindful of this, I advance Blackqueer currere as theory, method, and praxis directly owed to feminist consciousness and questions that explore race, class, gender, sexuality, geography, imperialism, and carcerality—questions that we face as Blackqueer folks both within and beyond the classroom. Critical race and feminist currere speaks to some of these questions already; Blackqueer currere narrows the focus by exploring the specific educational experiences of Blackqueer people as students and educators.

A Reflection of Practice
In 2021 I formed an undergraduate research team to examine Blackqueer artists' and intellectuals' contributions to education. For ten weeks, we met, shared texts, and investigated individual research topics. In the fall of 2022, I expanded the project with a graduate course entitled Blackqueer Lives & Pedagogies. From the independent study and course, I realized that I needed to name the forms of autoethnography and currere, and I urged students to do so in their research and analysis. In the initial study with undergrads, I recognized how the students often saw themselves and their prospective selves in their interactions with their chosen historical figures. The one non-Black person of color noted his positionality and simultaneously saw himself as an ally who taught his family and friends about a Black woman's work he had only just encountered that summer. As I was forewarned, the

graduate course was more non-Black than Black, but I was comforted by the amount of honesty we as Black folks felt in the space. Nevertheless, we held an affinity session the second-to-last day, to open space for deeper conversation. Those conversations pushed me to consider a form of currere that named this interpersonal and deeply personal experience and that opened the door for this type of written reflection.

A Method in Three Breaths

When I finally decided to come out publicly, I spoke to one of my long-term advisors from undergrad. She encouraged me to read Tim'm West's *Red Dirt Revival: A Poetic Memoir in 6 Breaths* (West 2002) to unpack questions of Blackness, queerness, desire, and voice. This was such an important text to me, as it spoke directly to my experiences as a Blackqueer man from struggle foundations. I borrow the concept of breaths here. Whereas West uses the breaths to connote poetic themes in his work, I employ "breaths" as a signal to three separate moments in which I practiced currere.

Vignette 1

My academic career jump-started when I was in first grade. At one of my brother's games, I stood next to my dad and his friend, who also happened to be my brother's Little League coach.

"Hey, Rob. When you gone be on the field?" Coach Black asked.

"Never!" I squeaked.

"What do you want to play?"

"I don't wanna play any sports. Not even golf!"

Both men laughed synchronously. When the laughing eased, my dad came to my defense: "He likes to read. This one's gonna be my scholar."

I was encouraged by my father's words, yet I had no idea how prophetic they would become.

Though comforting that day, his proclamation could not save me from the subsequent sports conversations. Each year, I endured the ridicule. As the sixth of seven children—the fifth of six boys—I had a major sports legacy to follow. Rejecting it was dangerous for multiple reasons. Nearly all the other Black boys in my poor and working-class neighborhood played at least one sport. People teased me for being the outsider. I was in Mrs. Thompson's class. She was a wonderfully proud Black woman who managed high expectations with high support. By this year, I had a reputation for being a great reader and writer: a progression I owe to my mother and sister, who read to me and taught me how to read. One moment a student was reading aloud, and with my whole chest, I sighed and pronounced the word for her. Mrs. Thompson stopped me: "EXCUSE US, Mr. R.; not all of us are as intelligent as you." The heat burned behind my ears. It was at once a compliment, humbling check, and sadly, an added support for and critique of the struggling student. I apologized and shut up the rest of the period.

A few days later, Ronald, one of the two Black boys white substitutes always confused me for (we looked nothing alike) came up behind me as we descended the stairs to lunch. "Hello Mr. R., you intelligent faggot." I knew enough about the term at the time to feel all the markers of assault. This, too, became a part of my complicated relationship to academics, between schooling, education, and the process of becoming.

As time progressed and my parents divorced, my father could accept that I was not an athlete, but I could never come out; homosexuality was utterly sinful. I was different. I was not supposed to love learning. I was not supposed to be gay. I was not supposed to be me. Nevertheless, my existence was a slow and painful act of defiance that allowed me to empathize with my students.

Analysis 1

The vignette outlined an early awareness of difference, and the epithet from my peer was a part of my queer consciousness. While school was the site in which I learned so much about human existence, this encounter introduced a new dynamic—one that associated the peer social space as dangerous terrain. I was socialized into a new realm of masculine performance for my own sense of safety. The hidden curriculum of the playground, lunch line, and cafeteria presented the need for new defenses (Apple 2018).

Shamari K. Reid unpacks these types of questions of safety and becoming in his work with queer and trans youth. Drawing on Roderick Ferguson's "Queer of Color Critique" (2018), Reid focuses the discussion on education to highlight the "negative experiences of Black LGBTQ+ youth" (Reid 2022). This is an important contribution to analyze intersectional research within the field. In my own reflections above, I recognize the desire for otherwise possibilities (Crawley 2016; Robinson 2021) in education. This same work of exploring otherwise possibilities was the hope of helping Blackqueer youth feel a sense of safety and belonging amidst the very antiblack, anti-trans, and anti-queer terrain in schools. My experience is situated within the 1990s, but these forms of linguistic and physical violence persist thirty years later.

Blackqueer currere in this context paints a specific scene of a particular period, but as with all forms of self-inquiry, it draws us into the need for representation beyond sheer numbers and toward liberatory ends. Pairing my schooling experience with the curriculum of the home, I outline the very real traps that render Blackqueer youth both invisible and hypervisible at home, religious institutions, and schools. In my reflection I locate my desire for a safe space in childhood and how this hope undergirded my own teaching and classroom spaces when I became a K–12 educator (Taliaferro-Baszile 2015, 2). Whereas queer of color critique offers a lens to analyze education, Blackqueer currere employs the method specifically for Blackqueer folks to unpack their educational experiences: an attempt at a type of specificity of experience (Ferguson 2018).

Vignette 2

Normativity is a useful lens for examining my questions of identity and pedagogy. As a teacher of color, I built my classes on the foundation of social justice and ethnic studies. I strategically chose texts that discussed race, class, gender, sexual orientation, and ability. We even had lengthy discussions about Butler's (1990; 2007) interrogation of heteronormativity and performativity. Because I was engaging in this work, I thought I was a hotshot pedagogue on the path of co-constructing a minirevolution with my fellow marginalized students. At the exact same time, I was deeply closeted, only out to a handful of people I swore to secrecy. In class, I stood tall on my elaborately decorated soapbox and passed it around, so that students could live and speak their truths freely—and yet I denied myself the opportunity to engage in my own truth. Early on, I learned from my fundamentalist father that same-sex attraction was utterly sinful—wrong. I applied this assessment to my life, using the rubric to invalidate my own existence. My students' truths about themselves were valid, but mine weren't. In many ways, I envied them.

… The deficit model I applied to my own life was not explicit in my lessons or discussions, but it definitely manifested itself in my writing assessment. Internally, I carried the struggle between the margins and the center—hegemony and resistance; surely it appeared elsewhere in my practice. What if I spent more time embracing the strengths of student writing instead of establishing a series of wrongs based on a limited notion of normal? What if I had found the courage to live my truth much earlier? (Robinson 2020)

Analysis 2

This was an excerpt from an essay I wrote about the keyword "normativity." The more I wrote, the more I was confronted with the limitations of my praxis. Though I did not name the student directly, I reached out to him to ask permission and apologized for some of the ways I responded with such intensity. His response was, "No problem, Mr. Rob. You still the GOAT." It was comforting to receive, but I think it made me also think about the concept of the closet and what that means in teaching.

I think sharing the essay and discussing it also allowed me to further complicate the compulsory nature of "coming out." In a Foucauldian sense, the experience feels like a confession (Foucault [1978] 1990). Regardless of the explicit or implicit nature, my sexual and political identities loomed like the specter in the classroom community, often felt even if never expressed (Sedgwick [1990] 2008). These questions of this *need* to *out* oneself are established by heteronormative discourse, even as they are a part of queer liberatory processes, and thus the tension I faced as an educator. Whether or not I was out, I was sure I was queer, and I always spoke about liberation across contexts. At the same time, the same forces that kept me closeted also hindered the extent to which I could model what a liberated person looked like. In later conversations, I was affirmed in what I thought to be true: some could feel me holding my breath. How beautiful it would have been to breathe together.

When I began teaching college, I found myriad ways to claim my identities. Sometimes it was the first day when we did introductions. Other days, it was through a discussion about queer teachers in the classroom. Just the other day, when I was challenging a white student who felt a sense of moral high ground because he seemed angrier than everyone else in the room, I said, "We are a BIPOC classroom; hell, I'm a Blackqueer man, they are— we are always angry." I was able to find my voice in that moment because I had unlocked it through my reflections of identity and practice. And while I caution against identity as the end-all-be-all of political consciousness-raising, political organizing, or critical engagement, I also frequently disrupt white advocacy that positions white allies as moral or political authorities in the lives of the people they claim to support (hooks 1989, 42–48). Experience, too, is important to politicization, and currere aims to help us uncover such experience as we theorize. Those of us who are in the margins of the margins must occupy more space in our pedagogy, research, and action to further such learning experiences for BIPOC students and the white students in the room.

Vignette 3

When I was an adjunct in my alma mater, I taught a graduate course entitled Blackqueer Lives & Pedagogies, emphasizing "Blackqueer" as one word to solidify an intersectional framing. The course dedicated the first weeks to playing with Blackqueer and feminist theories of teaching, and the subsequent weeks honing in on primary and secondary sources around the featured historical figures. It was through this course that I also emphasized the process of currere. I was curious about the ways in which students were engaging with the material and what the content, questions, and discussions meant for the reshaping of their politics—especially for the Blackqueer students in the room.

That semester, I was a tenure-track full-time academic counselor with one first-year seminar, in a course called Education & Justice, with a second overflow course at the graduate school. Our graduate conversations were so rich, partly because the bulk of the room were folks who had engaged in several years of K–12 teaching. We opened sessions with breathing, check-ins, and reflection questions. I would do some light framing, and then the students who facilitated for the day were tasked with guiding us through the readings. In this room of graduate students, teachers, and education scholars, we did so much. Even amidst the mixed racial company, I made clear arguments about the need for Black interiority and highlighted the importance of Black feminist practice. We wrestled with the question of Blackqueer embodiment as sacrifice. We questioned the ethics of posthumously outing a person. Sessions used the lives, curricula, and pedagogical approaches of folks like James Baldwin, Audre Lorde, and June Jordan to help us reflect on our own pedagogy, and we were honest about where we were and how we showed up each week. This class was as healing for me as (according to student evaluations) it was for the students. I was reminded of how in the Black radical tradition in education, our freedom consistently creates opportunities for other folks to get free, and for those of us who sit at multiple axes of difference—especially Blackqueer femmes and women—this liberation highlights a creative resistance with universal implications (Taylor 2017).

In our second-to-last session, a pair of students—one of whom was Black—orchestrated our final formal session in affinity-group style: Black students, non-Black POC, and white folks. In the Black affinity group, we responded to the question "Can everyone/anyone ethically use Blackqueer pedagogy?" It was an intense discussion, but we ultimately said, "No"—harkening back to our discussions of "for-us-by-us" and the need for Black interiority. Even when I tried to make a concession about "influenced by" or "inspired by" for non-Black scholars, we recognized that it still maintained a feeling of extraction devoid of Black embodiment and experience.

Analysis 3

The Blackqueer Lives course was very much the drive for this paper. I think the entire experience, as with most pedagogy courses, was extremely metacognitive. I was a Blackqueer educator, looking at Blackqueer figures' contributions to our understanding of pedagogy, curriculum, and the self. In reflecting on my experience as a Blackqueer educator in this course, I was able to tease out what it meant for students to explore their own positionalities. For the white students, the space helped them to investigate queerness across race, class, gender, and internationalism. For students of color, it meant drawing parallels of the same institutions of power, even as they recognized the specificity of their respective experiences of race and gender. For Blackqueer folks, especially lesbian, nonbinary, and femme folks in the room, it was an acknowledgment of multiple pieces of their identity and politics in conversation with structural dynamics. The most significant highlight was the intersection of race, class, gender, and queerness and how the discourse helped each of us find a potential pathway to liberation.

The reflection also highlights the direct connections to Blackqueerness and pedagogy. By leveraging texts that speak to these phenomena, I made my politics explicit and opened doors for students to explore their positionality in relationship to the course content, themes, and epistemological foundations. At the same time, I must note that I primarily focused on U.S. contexts and largely U.S.-rendered conceptualizations of Blackness and antiblack struggle.

There is also the trickiness of analyzing Black solidarities and teetering on essentialism. We could have looked more deeply at how Blackness is varied, even if we saw the connections in our readings. The students' insistence on identifying the need for a Blackqueer interiority was important, even if it caused discomfort in the room. In her twenty-year-old collection of essays entitled *The Black Interior*, Elizabeth Alexander asserts, "The black interior is a metaphysical space beyond the black public everyday toward power and wild imagination that black people ourselves know we possess but need to be reminded of and know" (2004, x). It is the space we need outside of the white gaze. When I created the course, I knew white students and non-Black folks of color would be present, but I ultimately created it for the Black students. The affinity group, then, offered the space for candor that all of us secretly yearned for that term. Within the class discussions, I would make multiple Black references, speaking to the whole class but whispering to Black students.

Just weeks before the semester, I had witnessed this phenomenon in *A Strange Loop* on Broadway. The room was primarily composed of non-Black patrons, but there were a number of jokes meant just for Black folks, and especially Blackqueer folks raised in the church. My Black friends and I yelped at scenes that our non-Black members awkwardly chuckled at or silently pondered over. This, too, happened in class with explicit mention of the power of Black interiority. We spoke as if non-Black students were not in the room, but in the specific Black affinity space, we focused on the power of that positionality with shared queer politics. This practice explored the fullness of a Blackqueer pedagogy (not to be confused with Blackqueer currere—the research approach) and the shared power of student and teacher to reflect on culturally and politically relevant realities within an academic space (Lewis 2011). We dreamt together in real time based on our past reflections. The currere example I provided engaged in a metadiscourse of practice (thinking about our thinking and then my reflection of that thinking). And perhaps this dynamic speaks to the need for a currere that addresses an embodied practice and reflexive praxis that does the same: engages Black folks in a reflexive process for cocreated learning and knowledge-building (Alexander 2005). Furthermore, this discussion highlights Taliaferro-Baszile's approach of considering the impact of the past and future and of synthesizing across moments to engage the present.

Still, I spoke about Blackness largely within a U.S. context; in spaces where I have experienced a diversity of Blackness (Caribbean, African, Afro-Latinx contexts), we recognize the similarities and differences of cultures, with attention to the overwhelming elements of antiblackness. This, too, should be further explored for future Blackqueer scholars who take up this form of narrative inquiry and analysis beyond U.S. conceptions of Blackness in education.

Push It to the Limit

As with all forms of inquiry, we risk the dangers of oversimplification, overgeneralizing the world of the individual. One person's articulation of their experience is not supposed to substitute for the whole. This is especially important to consider when we note that *Blackness* can be and has been used as a diasporic word for those of us connected to the African diaspora. In addition, as folks inculcated in the academy, we risk the dangers of looking into our work with too much self-aggrandizement, too limiting an analysis, or too much self-critique. (My vignettes have not sufficiently critiqued the class politics of my own working poor experiences—an added but important dimension in articulations of gender and sexuality.) These are all valid points. As with many forms of qualitative inquiry—or potentially all inquiry, for that matter—these limitations can be true for data interpretation as a whole. Yes, even numbers and "brute facts" are subject to historical, political, and power-based dynamics and the biases associated with them.

Furthermore, to make the argument for the self as a site of knowledge is to also add a data point to, or provide an interpretation for, what we see in the larger discourse of experience and phenomena. The articulations of the self and myriad microhistories are meant to elucidate the complexities of human experiences. Currere is meant to do the same. It differs to the degree that it is not merely a question of research and evidence; it is also a snapshot into the life processes of becoming as we explore the self as learner, teacher, researcher, and activist. It is a critical reflexive approach to inform pedagogical framing, intrapersonal exploration (and sometimes healing), and interpersonal guidance.

We must also contend with the argument that identity is not fixed. In the processes of becoming, none of us is the same at any two moments. Just as Black approaches to critical thought are not monolithic, especially within the fields of gender studies and queer studies (Barker 2016; Olufemi 2020), our approaches to the self must also recognize these experiences as data points of a particular time—necessarily placed in conversation with the contexts of the moment and multiple voices of the time. I take up Blackqueer currere from a U.S. perspective, but this same approach can help other scholars and scholar-practitioners of the diaspora to more closely reflect on the diversity of Blackness and queerness internationally. With a focus on critical consciousness of one's positionality (especially as a Blackqueer person) in educational contexts, the process of currere can uncover the teachable moments within and beyond the classroom. Identity politics become murky terrain when identity is the sole driving force. When those markers help us to see the series of systems that operate across spaces, we are better able to recognize the interlocking nature of these systems and the compounded affects they have on Blackqueer people as educators, students, and scholars.

Blackqueer currere is not for all scholars; the name conveys the communities it aims to speak from, to, and with. Critical race theory (CRT) speaks to race broadly with the attention to the history of the Civil Rights Movement (Capper 2015; Ladson-Billings and Tate 1995). BlackCrit focuses on the specific racialized experiences of Black people (Dumas and ross, 2016). LatCrit has extended CRT with a focus on the experiences of Latinx peoples (Delgado Bernal 2002, 2020). Jotería pedagogy looks at teaching approaches through feminist, trans, and queer contexts with LatCrit underpinnings (Alvarez 2014; Caraves 2020). Critical race and feminist currere forwards a focus on race and gender through the method of educational autoethnography (Taliaferro-Baszile 2015). Queer currere takes up a similar charge, as it employs queer narrative theory to disrupt "normative" discourse in autobiography (Sawyer 2022). Blackqueer currere, then, further narrows the narrative lens on Blackqueer experiences by using the specific attention on the educational experiences and the paired structural analysis and critique of Blackqueer people. Currere itself "redefines curriculum: no longer course objectives or test outcomes, but complicated conversation among those studying the world through academic knowledge" (Pinar 2019, 52). Like other forms of currere, Blackqueer currere is a method of inquiry even as it is connected to the lengthier existential practice of understanding the ever-evolving self as Blackqueer subject(s). I am not vying for a monolithic or static Blackness; instead, I argue that Blackqueer experiences in education—in their variety and complexity—matter. The more each of us chart our "life course" in ways that help us more clearly see educational tensions and possibilities, the more clearly we can chart new liberatory futures in education.

So Why Blackqueer Currere?
The aforementioned three approaches to currere do not capture the entire range of possibility, but they do introduce multiple ways of recognizing the power of reflection and story in our articulations of educational theory and practice.

In the first vignette, we see the personal educational journey as an impetus for educational practice later. Existing at the axes of Black, gay, and working class, I taught and teach from a place acknowledging the experiences of students in the classroom and their ways of knowing, being, experiencing the room. Identity here becomes less about leveraging the elements of oppression in some form of competition and more about expanding capacity to recognize interlocking systems and the possibility of liberation through solidarity. This ties directly to the aims of the Combahee River Collective (1977), bell hooks (1989), Patricia Hill Collins (1990), and Kimberlé Crenshaw (1991) and their articulations of intersectionality as a confrontation of interlocking systems of domination and oppression.

The second vignette speaks to the questions and complications of the closet and what it represents. Given the conditions of locality and region, school dynamics, personal and familial dynamics, and the like, I speak to the constraints of the closet, the dichotomous framing of sexuality, and the closet's metaphorical inhibitions in my own educational praxis (Sedgwick [1990] 2008). I locate the embedded contradiction. Recognizing the freedom with too many constraints, I imagine a world where my whole Black-ass, queer-ass, nerd-hood-ass self could model a liberatory consciousness and being that helped even more students to do the same.

The third vignette recounts my teaching practices as of late. Exploring my role as educator, educator of educators, and researcher within and beyond education, I had to speak to the importance of Black interiority (Alexander 2004) within multiracial spaces, even as I took on feminist praxis as a cis man. The paradox of this reflection and practice is not lost on me as I write this piece. What I saw in this classroom was a space of generative possibility: the body, experience, reflection, aesthetics, histories, biographies, autobiographies, and joint storytelling and meaning-making as sites of liberatory possibility. Leveraging the dreams of "a room of one's own" (Woolf [1929] 2015) and what Blackqueer thinker Ashon Crawley refers to as "otherwise possibilities" (2016), our space looked into the histories, theories, and worlds of Black futurity—Blackqueer futurity as revolutionary space. As a cis man, my goal is not to be the authority on this method. *Blackness*, *queerness*, and *Blackqueer folks* are expansive categories. On the contrary, my goal is to open the discussion through this method, so that folks can tease at it further. By exploring *queer* as who we are, the ways we disrupt, and how we support our communities, we encourage narratives with articulations of trans-ness, gender expansiveness, ace-ness, and how all these identities also intersect with the structures of racial capitalism, colonialism, ableism, nationalism, and xenophobia (Taliaferro-Baszile 2015; Caraves 2020; Sawyer 2022). I have charged newer scholars to excavate their own worlds with even more specific attention to the intersectional spaces they occupy and structural spaces they speak and write to.

In our hopes and dreams of Blackqueer worlds (especially in education) that provide liberatory possibilities for all of us, we continue to tell our stories of struggle, of joy, of questions, fears, love, community, failure, beauty, learning, teaching, and building. Let this entry conversation into Blackqueer currere—the charge to locate critical Blackqueer educational narratives—be the celebration of what was, what could have been, and what can be.

Robert P. Robinson is an assistant professor of Africana Studies at John Jay College and doctoral faculty in the Departments of Urban Education, Africana Studies, and Interactive Technology & Pedagogy at The Graduate Center, CUNY. Prior to higher education, he was a K–12 educator and mentor for eleven years. His broad research and teaching focus on the Black freedom movement, Black education history, Blackqueer studies, digital humanities, history of education, and curriculum studies. His forthcoming book project is a history of the Black Panther Party's Oakland Community School as a site for understanding Black self-determination, the shift in mainstream curriculum and pedagogy, and the Black radical imagination in education. He can be reached at rrobinson@jjay.cuny.edu.

Works Cited

Alexander, Bryant Keith. 2005. "Embracing the Teachable Moment: The Black Gay Body in the Classroom as Embodied Text." In *Black Queer Studies: A Critical Anthology*, edited by E. Patrick Johnson and Mae G. Henderson. Duke University Press.

Alexander, Elizabeth. 2004. *The Black Interior*. Graywolf Press.

Alvarez, Eddy Francisco, Jr. 2014. "Jotería Pedagogy, SWAPA, and Sandovalian Approaches to Liberation." *Aztlán* 39 (1): 215–27. https://doi.org/10.1525/azt.2014.39.1.215.

Apple, Michael W. 2018. *Ideology and Curriculum*. 4th ed. Routledge.

Barker, Meg-John. 2016. *Queer: A Graphic History*. Icon Books.

Bay, Mia. 2009. *To Tell the Truth Freely: The Life of Ida B. Wells*. Hill and Wang.

Bell, Derrick. 1987. *And We Are Not Saved: The Elusive Quest for Racial Justice*. Basic Books.

Bell, Derrick. 1992. *Faces at the Bottom of the Well: The Permanence of Racism*. Basic Books.

Boylorn, Robin M. 2008. "As Seen on TV: An Autoethnographic Reflection on Race and Reality Television." *Critical Studies in Media Communication* 25 (4): 413–33. https://doi.org/10.1080/15295030802327758.

Boylorn, Robin M. 2016. "On Being at Home with Myself: Blackgirl Autoethnography as Research Praxis." *International Review of Qualitative Research* 9 (1): 44–58. https://doi.org/10.1525/irqr.2016.9.1.44.

Boylorn, Robin M., and Mark P. Orbe, eds. 2014. *Critical Autoethnography: Intersecting Cultural Identities in Everyday Life*. Left Coast Press.

Butler, Judith. 1990. *Gender Trouble: Feminism and the Subversion of Identity*. Routledge.

Butler, Judith. 2007. Interview. YouTube. Posted February 23, 2007, by Stef. Trans. https://youtu.be/DLnv322X4tY?si=WvyBlXmZGKaJ5gsF.

Caraves, Jack. 2020. "Centering the 'T': Envisioning a Trans Jotería Pedagogy." *Association of Mexican American Educators Journal* 14 (2): 104–23. https://doi.org/10.24974/amae.14.2.364.

Cervantes, Lorna Dee. 1982. "Poem for the Young White Man Who Asked Me How I, an Intelligent, Well-Read Person, Could Believe in the War Between Races." In *Emplumada*. University of Pittsburgh Press.

Clark, Keith. 2005. "Are We Family? Pedagogy and the Race for Queerness." In *Black Queer Studies: A Critical Anthology*, edited by E. Patrick Johnson and Mae G. Henderson. Duke University Press.

Combahee River Collective. 1977. *The Combahee River Collective Statement*. http://circuitous.org/scraps/combahee.html.

Crawley, Ashon T. 2016. *Blackpentecostal Breath: The Aesthetics of Possibility*. Fordham University Press.

Crenshaw, Kimberlé. 1991. "Mapping the Margins: Intersectionality, Identity Politics, and Violence Against Women of Color." *Stanford Law Review* 43 (6): 1241–99.

Delgado Bernal, Dolores. 2002. "Critical Race Theory, Latino Critical Theory, and Critical Raced-Gendered Epistemologies: Recognizing Students of Color as Holders and Creators of Knowledge." *Qualitative Inquiry* 8 (1): 105–26. https://doi.org/10.1177/107780040200800107.

Delgado Bernal, Dolores. 2020. "Disrupting Epistemological Boundaries: Reflections on Feminista Methodological and Pedagogical Interventions." *Aztlán* 45 (1): 155–69. https://doi.org/10.1525/azt.2020.45.1.155.

Dillard, Cynthia B. 2016. "Towards an Education That (Re)members: Centering Identity, Race, and Spirituality in Education." *Tikkun* 31 (4): 50–54. https://doi.org/10.1215/08879982-3676900.

Douglass, Frederick. (1845) 2002. *Narrative of the Life of Frederick Douglass: An American Slave, Written by Himself*. 2nd ed. Bedford/St. Martin's.

Du Bois, W. E. B. (1899) 2015. "A Negro Schoolmaster in the South." *The Atlantic*, January 1899. https://www.theatlantic.com/magazine/archive/1899/01/a-negro-schoolmaster-in-the-south/400028/.

Du Bois, W. E. B. (1903) 1994. *The Souls of Black Folk*. Dover.
Dumas, Michael J., and kihana miraya ross. 2016. "'Be Real Black for Me': Imagining BlackCrit in Education." *Urban Education* 51 (4): 415–42. https://doi.org/10.1177/0042085916628611.
Ferguson, Roderick A. 2018. "Queer of Color Critique." In *Oxford Research Encyclopedia of Literature*. March 28. https://doi.org/10.1093/acrefore/9780190201098.013.33.
Foucault, Michel. (1978) 1990. *The History of Sexuality, Vol. 1: An Introduction*. Vintage.
Grant, Carl A., Keffrelyn D. Brown, and Anthony L. Brown. 2016. *Black Intellectual Thought in Education: The Missing Traditions of Anna Julia Cooper, Carter G. Woodson, and Alain LeRoy Locke*. Routledge.
Hill Collins, Patricia. 1990. *Black Feminist Thought: Knowledge, Consciousness, and the Politics of Empowerment*. Unwin Hyman.
hooks, bell. 1989. *Talking Back: Thinking Feminist, Thinking Black*. South End Press.
hooks, bell. (2000) 2015. *Feminism Is for Everybody: Passionate Politics*. 2nd ed. Routledge.
Jacobs, Harriet. (1861) 2016. *Incidents in the Life of a Slave Girl*. Open Road.
James, Joy. 1997. *Transcending the Talented Tenth: Black Leaders and American Intellectuals*. Routledge.
Jordan, June. (2005) 2023. "Poem About My Rights." *Poetry* 223 (2): 171–78.
Ladson-Billings, Gloria, and William F. Tate. 1995. "Toward a Critical Race Theory of Education." *Teachers College Record* 97 (1): 47–68.
Lewis, Mel Michelle. 2011. "Body of Knowledge: Black Queer Feminist Pedagogy, Praxis, and Embodied Text." *Journal of Lesbian Studies* 15 (1): 49–57. https://doi.org/10.1080/10894160.2010.508411.
McDuffie, Erik S. 2011. *Sojourning for Freedom: Black Women, American Communism, and the Making of Black Left Feminism*. Duke University Press.
Olufemi, Lola. 2020. *Feminism, Interrupted: Disrupting Power*. Pluto Press.
Pinar, William F. 2019. "Currere." In *Key Concepts in Curriculum Studies: Perspectives on the Fundamentals*, edited by Judy Wearing, Marcea Ingersoll, Christopher DeLuca, Benjamin Bolden, Holly Ogden, and Theodore Michael Christou. Routledge.
Pinar, William F., William M. Reynolds, Patrick Slattery, and Peter M. Taubman. 1995. *Understanding Curriculum: An Introduction to the Study of Historical and Contemporary Curriculum Discourses*. Peter Lang.
Reid, Shamari. 2022. "Exploring the Agency of Black LGBTQ+ Youth in Schools and in NYC's Ballroom Culture." *Teachers College Record* 124 (6): 92–117. https://doi.org/10.1177/01614681221111072.

Robinson, Robert P. 2020. "A New Diagnosis: Rethinking Normativity." In *Key Concepts in Curriculum Studies: Perspectives on the Fundamentals*, edited by Judy Wearing, Marcea Ingersoll, Christopher DeLuca, Benjamin Bolden, Holly Ogden, and Theodore Michael Christou. Routledge.

Robinson, Robert P. 2021. "Teaching Black Lives Amidst Black Death: Reflections from a Black Visiting Professor." *Journal of Effective Teaching in Higher Education* 4 (2): 99–117. https://doi.org/10.36021/jethe.v4i2.200.

Robinson, Robert P. 2024. "To the Famous Jett Jackson: A Midnight Essay on Black Possibility." *Killens Review of Arts & Letters* (Spring): 22–26.

Sawyer, Richard D. 2022. "Queer Narrative Theory and Currere: Thoughts Toward Queering Currere as a Method of Queer (Curricular) Self-Study." *Journal of Curriculum Theorizing* 37 (1): 23–38.

Sedgwick, Eve Kosofsky. (1990) 2008. *Epistemology of the Closet*. Updated with a new preface. University of California Press.

Slay, ZaDonna M. 2022. "Unmasking My Truth: Autoethnography of Psychological Stress as a Black Woman in the Academy." *Journal of Black Studies* 54 (1): 3–22. https://doi.org/10.1177/00219347221134280.

Taliaferro-Baszile, Denise. 2010. "In Ellisonian Eyes, What Is Curriculum Theory?" In *Curriculum Studies Handbook: The Next Moment*, edited by Erik Malewski. Routledge.

Taliaferro-Baszile, Denise. 2015. "Critical Race / Feminist Currere." In *The SAGE Guide to Curriculum in Education*, edited by Ming Fang He, Brian D. Schultz, and William H. Schubert. SAGE Publications.

Taylor, Keeanga-Yamahtta. 2017. *How We Get Free: Black Feminism and the Combahee River Collective*. Haymarket Books.

West, Tim'm. 2002. *Red Dirt Revival: A Poetic Memoir in 6 Breaths*. Poz'Trophy Pub.

Woodson, Carter Godwin. 1933. *The Mis-Education of the Negro*. Alexander Street Press.

Woolf, Virginia. (1929) 2015. *A Room of One's Own*. Wiley Blackwell.

How Do You Solve a Problem Like Maria von Clapp? Drag Pedagogy and the Limits of DEI

Nino Testa

Abstract: In this article, I argue that drag pedagogy, both in the women's, gender, and sexuality studies classroom and in student affairs and activities, reveals the limits of current neoliberal university formulations of diversity, equity, and inclusion during the current backlash against "gender ideology." My drag persona (Maria von Clapp) and I reflect on our experiences developing drag initiatives and curriculum at a private primarily white institution (PWI) in Texas, including a 2019 Drag Story Hour event that was canceled by the university and the university's refusal to respond to an anti-queer harassment campaign targeting these initiatives. Drag is a critical performance practice that can illuminate structural inequities and help students develop queer feminist praxis outside of neoliberal diversity, equity, and inclusion (DEI) discourse. **Keywords:** drag, pedagogy, DEI, diversity, queer, university

We have a lot to learn from drag. The urgency of drag's pedagogical potential is evident at this political moment as anti-queer forces in the United States, in the form of state legislatures, right-wing provocateurs, and white supremacist organizations, are coalescing to criminalize drag performance, harass drag venues and artists, defund public libraries, outlaw gender-affirming care, and ban critical theories from being taught at any level of education. Judith Butler argues that this movement's "opposition to [gender ideology], along with the defense of the family (against any challenge to heteronormativity) and the nation (against any challenge to its racial purity), is linked with a eugenics that belongs to the history and present of fascism" (Butler 2024, 52). The stakes of this "anti-gender ideology movement" are high, both for the individuals who experience physical and emotional violence as part of its project and for the institutions that traffic in its logics. Drag, an important site of political contestation for this movement, is more than a "distraction," as some of its well-intentioned defenders have claimed in the wake of criminalization efforts (Squirrell and Davey 2023). Careful attention to the ways that institutions encounter and respond to drag can reveal the workings of power across diverse geographies.

In this article, my teacherly drag persona, Maria von Clapp (*Hello, there!*), will help me to reflect on one such institutional encounter, in the form of five years of drag pedagogy (classroom curricula, performances, workshops, events, and initiatives), which we developed with campus and community partners at Texas Christian University, a private, non–religiously affiliated (*The name throws people off!*) predominately white institution in Texas. These curricular and cocurricular initiatives have faced ongoing attacks, but in 2023 were the target of a widespread anti-queer and anti-drag harassment campaign. Deploying Sara Ahmed's theory of diversity work as "brick wall," Roderick Ferguson's theories of the neoliberal university, and Butler's recent work unpacking the discourse of the transnational anti–gender ideology movement, I argue that drag pedagogy reveals the limits of diversity, equity, and inclusion (DEI) language on American college campuses today. Next, I use my class and programming experiences—from my positionality as a gay, cis white man at this conservative, primarily white institution (PWI)—as an example of how drag can be deployed as a critical pedagogical practice. In a moment of heightened political attack, drag pedagogy also reminds us of the fundamental tools we have at our disposal to carve out space for queer learning, creativity, and community. (*But first, let's talk about why I am here . . .*)

Drag Voice as Method

In the interview "Lessons in Drag," Kareem Khubchandani utilizes an innovative narrative method—a conversation between themself and their drag persona, LaWhore Vagistan—to describe their drag pedagogy. By conversing with their drag persona, Khubchandani rehearses the very mechanisms that allow drag to bring dominant values, norms, and ways of being into relief, challenging and trivializing their totalizing logics (Khubchandani 2015). K. Bradford's equally creative essay "Grease Cowboy Fever; or, The Making of Johnny T." unfolds as a "mix of theory, memoir, and performance narrative" grounded in gender theory and is punctuated by snarky commentary and crude puns offered by Bradford's titular drag king persona, set off in italics (Bradford 2002, 15). (*Oh, I like that idea very much. Thank you, Johnny T., for this clever little device! And by the way, reader, when I speak, I speak both to you and to Nino. Do try to keep up with the context clues.*) LaWhore's and Johnny T.'s casual asides bring Khubchandani's and Bradford's respective scholarly analysis into the realm of the performance itself, underscoring the critical work done in and by drag. Khubchandani and Bradford introduce *drag voice as method*, a creative spin on autoethnography where the queer ways of knowing and being embodied in their drag performances show up as quips, witty retorts, and indecorous asides. (*A few of my favorite things, indeed.*)

As these scholars and their drag personas suggest, drag offers analysis through breach of decorum (Khubchandani 2015, 285; Bradford 2002, 16). Simply put, drag personas tend to say things that we might not otherwise say. Drag superstar Sasha Velour summarizes this framework in a recent interview: "'The drag way' is about radical honesty, dramatized through complete over-the-top fantasy" (*Them* 2023). Thematizing this colloquial truth in scholarship about drag is a generative hermeneutic. I employ drag voice as analytical method specifically to highlight the gaps between official university DEI discourse and the queer experiences that fail to fall under the supposedly inclusive banner of DEI. Ahmed warns against facile analysis of institutional language and challenges us to look beyond the veneer of "diversity." She argues that thinking through diversity work by focusing on official statements would be to "miss the point by making [institutional obfuscation] the point" (Ahmed 2012, 6). Education scholars Harper Keenan and Lil Miss Hot Mess demonstrate how drag can help us do this vital analytical work: "A common drag performance trope [is redirecting] away from what's said on the surface and towards the subtle nods and zingers that gesture at what is happening between the lines" (Keenan and Lil Miss Hot Mess 2020, 448). Because official DEI language tends to translate complex systems of oppression into corporate HR lingo, allowing Maria to speak back in this essay is a way of reading institutional logics, in all of the queer valences that the term *reading* invokes. (*I am quite happy to be here, dearie, but no one allows Maria to speak. She does this all on her own.*) As Maria and I will explore in this essay, the erasures, canceled events, and failed projects that constitute queer life on campus can be kept alive as queer history and pedagogy for those who find themselves hitting Sara Ahmed's proverbial "brick wall" of diversity work.

Diversity Work and Institutional Life

The "brick wall" is, for Ahmed, a way of envisioning the experience of "doing" diversity work at the university: "The wall gives physical form to what a number of practitioners describe as 'institutional inertia,' the lack of an institutional will to change" (Ahmed 2012, 26). Markers of "diversity," like the now ubiquitous language of "DEI" and "inclusive excellence," might appear to be in tension with the lived experience of those who think of themselves as engaged in the work of diversity on campus, but, Ahmed argues, that tension is the point: "the managerial focus on diversity works to individuate differences and conceal the continuation of systematic inequalities within universities" (53). (*And every few years it's a different set of terms, isn't it? Multiculturalism ... social justice ... diversity ... DEI ... inclusive excellence. ... I have confidence that in one more committee, they'll get where they are going. Heaven bless them.*) Roderick Ferguson understands the neoliberal university as organized around "an ideological offensive against the redistributive demands of progressive student movements, demands for a downward redistribution of social resources" (2017, 116), an offensive that is masked by the veneer of DEI. (*Oh, I see: the flashy talk of diversity is a bit of shell game, isn't it? The neoliberal university asks us to "Look over there!"—to quote the great Jaida Essence Hall.*)

Ferguson frames these institutional practices and discourses as *neoliberal* insofar as the "administrative university unmarks and reabsorbs difference" (2012, 213). This powerful maneuver allows universities to prioritize marketing and communications over redistribution of resources, while obfuscating the experiences of marginalized people on campus. For Ferguson, the commodification of difference that was hastened by the managerial impulse of the university is directly tied to the university's capital investments within a globalized economy. Ferguson describes "power as emanating from capital's encampment within the university and its culmination in administrative arrangements within university settings" (2012, 211). The work of DEI, then, is not simply about branding to attract a more diverse student body, as official university statements might suggest, but is a legitimizing strategy to further the neoliberal corporatization of the university. This process has produced an administrative class with the supposed "managerial and economic profile appropriate for the contemporary moment of globalization" (Ferguson 2012, 211), where "capital and the academy have to work through and with difference in the global moment if they can claim any integrity at all" (225–26). (*Institutions are wily things, indeed! They almost had me fooled, but I think I've caught on now. Very smart, Maria, very smart!*)

Both Ahmed and Ferguson center their arguments on the incorporation and management of racial diversity into university structures but also see LGBTQ "inclusion" as frequently participating in the racialized neoliberal project of diversity work, or what Ahmed calls a "technology for reproducing whiteness" (Ahmed 2012, 151). Ahmed describes the way "respectable differences," or positive representations of diversity within institutional life, such as Pride celebrations, can easily be used to reify structural inequalities and white supremacy (2012, 151). Ferguson locates this dynamic in a long history of white-led assimilationist LGBT organizing whose political aims steered normative gays toward incorporation into institutional and national logics when such inclusion would sync up with the "interest politics in liberal capitalist nation-states" (Ferguson 2012, 217). As the work of Ahmed and Ferguson demonstrates, these interest politics fully dictate the incorporation or exclusion (or both) of particular racialized narratives of LGBTQ life within the university.

While these critiques of whitewashed LGBTQ inclusion ring true for many of us, we should also pay attention to the workings of institutions when even banal iterations of LGBTQ "diversity" are positioned as dangerous and are disqualified from incorporation into the neoliberal project of DEI. What constitutes "respectable difference" is a moving target and varies widely across geographies and institutions. The public attacks of the so-called anti–gender ideology movement have heightened institutional aversion to public supports for LGBTQ people in places like Texas, revealing the hollowness of DEI as a campus project; even nominal public support for queer people becomes unspeakable in the face of what Butler calls a global movement that pursues "the restoration of a patriarchal dreamorder" (Butler 2024, 15). According to Butler, anti-queer political actors "insist that [LGBTQ+ communities] and their political demands are destructive forces. ... In effect, they rename the object of destruction as its cause, engaging in a contemporary form of fascist rebranding" (2024, 55). (*I know a thing or two about dealing with fascists. One must cut off their engine before they start revving up, mustn't one?*)

For such a movement, even neoliberal expressions of "Pride," rainbows, and nondiscrimination statements become a form of radical political speech, a maneuver that Butler identifies as itself a complex if "wrongheaded or prepolitical [response] to neoliberalism, the powers of global financial institutions, the continuing legacies of colonial power" (2024, 70). Like the corporate Pride lingo that is pulled from the shelves at the first sign of anti-queer hostility, even minimal signs of queer affirmation become liabilities for neoliberal institutions that rely on the purveyors of the anti–gender ideology movement for connection to capital. (*Universities may use the "slap a rainbow on it" method to distract from the structural inequalities and racism on which they operate, but they will tear that rainbow down just as fast if it threatens their branding, won't they?*)

Hitting the Brick Wall

At my former institution, for example, with an enormous apparatus for DEI, including a university-wide DEI strategic plan, an Office of Diversity & Inclusion, and even a newly created Chief Inclusion Officer position, one might imagine that a clear and distinct vision for LGBTQ life on campus would be easily discerned and felt by LGBTQ people. A video touting the university's winning of the Heed Award for Diversity in 2019 includes LGBTQ iconography like a rainbow and an equality sign, suggesting that LGBTQ inclusion is a part of the university's DEI mission (TCU 2019). More concretely, the university's nondiscrimination policy includes "sexual orientation, gender, gender identity, gender expression" ("Notice of Nondiscrimination" 2022). The university's painstakingly developed strategic plan for Diversity & Inclusion includes goals like the following: "Bolster curriculum, training and other academic initiatives that promote an understanding of diversity, equity and inclusion" and "promote a campus environment that is welcoming for all and free of bias" ("Strategic Plan" 2022). (*How do these official statements measure up, I wonder?*)

Ahmed reminds us that "statements of commitment are non-performatives: they do not bring about the effects they name" (2012, 17). Here is an example of the failure of DEI to take so much as minimal institutional risk on behalf of queer people: Upon realizing that historic gay rights activist and labor organizer Morris Kight graduated from TCU in 1942, I collaborated with a partner from TCU's Marketing and Communications team to write a website profile of this important figure for Pride month in 2021. Kight not only organized the first Gay Pride Parade in the world, Los Angeles's Christopher Street West in 1970, he helped start nearly every LGBTQ+ organization in Southern California, including what is now called the Los Angeles LGBT Center, the largest such support center in the world. (*Wow—do you mean to tell me that the* founder of Pride, *an annually celebrated commemoration of the Stonewall uprisings that takes place* all over the world, *graduated from* our *university? How remarkable! Can you imagine what it would mean to queer students to learn this?*) This low-stakes project was in clear alignment with the university's stated strategic plan for DEI. (*Yes, what a wonderful DEI opportunity. Low-hanging fruit, as it were.*) However, the story was unceremoniously nixed just days before it was set to be shared, with no official justification for the cancellation, but unofficial confirmation that it was deemed too controversial. (*I guess starting a social movement that is celebrated annually across the globe isn't exactly noteworthy, when you think about it. Perhaps if he could throw a football?*)

In some ways, this project itself could have been deemed a neoliberal DEI tactic, "celebrating" diversity on the university's webpage. (*Indeed, we second-guessed our own participation for that reason! "Doing Diversity Work" can really test the limits of your theoretical and political commitments, can't it?*) But the institution's politics are such that even this sort of mundane celebration of a notable figure in gay history was deemed too queer. At another institution or in another time or location, we might easily imagine this "celebrating a famous white gay" tactic as participating in the sort of diversity whitewashing described by Ahmed and Ferguson, centering a "gay white hero" to distract from the structural racism or anti-queerness on campus. But in the face of a rabid "anti-gender ideology movement," such a move quickly loses its political utility for the institution, whose happy-go-lucky DEI discourse is revealed, once again, to have been an empty promise. Ahmed argues: "Organizations can be considered as modes of attention: what is attended to can be thought of as what is valued; attention is how some things come into view (and other things do not)" (2012, 30). When we look for messages of value, then, we need to pay special attention to what isn't there. (*A difficult task, indeed! Like searching for ghosts with a flashlight.*)

The Morris Kight incident was not the only time a queer program or initiative had been canceled on campus, and fear of anti-queer backlash is not new. In 2009, the Office of Residence Life was planning to launch a new system of Living Learning Communities, where students with shared interests or values might live together in a hall and form intentional communities. One of these was to be a space for students interested in affirming community for LGBTQ+ students. After some negative press from Fox News, the chancellor decided to cancel not just the LGBTQ+–themed housing unit, but all the Living Learning Communities, citing concerns that the project was "splitting students up instead of uniting them" (KHOU Staff 2009). This cancellation, which occurred eight years before my arrival on campus, had an enormous chilling effect on LGBTQ programs. The incident was brought up at every turn and at countless DEI committee meetings as a cautionary tale about the limits of LGBTQ inclusion initiatives on campus. (*A cancellation has ripple effects, you see. The thing that never was is with us still.*) Even after the formation of a so-called Gender Resource Office (*Interesting name for an LGBTQ+ resource on campus. No lesbian, gay, bisexual, transgender, or queer people to be found in the title. I wonder why that is? Ghosts with a flashlight!*), new ideas for queer programming have been routinely met with hushed reminders of the Living Learning Community incident. A "brick wall," to use Ahmed's term. The absence has afterlives, stifling queer thought and creativity. If someone proposes a large-scale, public-facing LGBTQ program, they can count on someone invoking the LLC incident. (*Just as sure as I know that a drag king performing a George Michael song is wearing tearaway pants. They won't fool me, but I love it every time!*)

On another occasion, in an effort to develop campus understanding of drag as a critical performance practice, I planned a multicomponent Critical Drag Residency in 2019, which was to feature guest lectures, performances, workshops, and a Drag Story Hour, featuring one of the cofounders of this program, Michelle Tea. (*And a performance by moi. I was ready to read my favorite books from Dolly Parton's* Imagination Library. *Talk about drag queens reading to children!*) We created elaborate learning objectives that tied the event directly to university DEI goals and produced a detailed one-sheet explaining our process and partnerships, and even citing relevant research on the value of gender-affirming programming for youth at a time when Texas led the nation in murders of transgender people (McGaughy 2019). (*This is all very thorough just to play dress up! You seem to have covered all your bases. What could possibly go wrong?*)

We were speaking the language of institutional DEI goals to carve out space for our program on a normative campus and to insist that queer people are integral to campus life, as the DEI goals themselves, ostensibly, suggest. Weeks before the event was set to take place, we were informed that university leadership was canceling the Drag Story Hour event. We were given a slew of anti-queer justifications for the cancellation, centered on the "inappropriateness" of drag in the presence of children (several years before this anti-drag discourse would take center stage in state politics). (*Of the many hurtful things that were said, this one, from a senior administrator at my university, is a direct quote, dear children: "If we are going to do all of this DEI work, we aren't going to start with drag queens." "Well, well, well, of course not," I replied. "No one ever gets to the drag queens, so we have to get to ourselves."*)

As a mere amateur drag queen in a non-tenure-track, instructional staff position, I was in no position to fight the cancellation on my own. I will admit that I felt equal parts rage and embarrassment at hearing the reasons for the cancellation. (*Perhaps you should have taken the advice you give so freely to your students and done some organizing on campus? A teachable moment indeed.*) What the cancellation reveals, to quote Ahmed, is the "paradoxical condition that is a life situation for many diversity practitioners. Having an institutional aim to make diversity a goal can even be a sign that diversity is *not* an institutional goal" (2012, 22). The cancellation also serves as a powerful tool for teaching drag history and queer history more broadly. (*Ah yes, here is queer history: the event that is canceled, the program that is erased, the possibilities for being in the world that are trampled before they can take shape. Take note, children: queer history is as much about what you* don't *see as what you do see.*) For example, by creating and sharing digital timelines of drag history and queer history at my institution that include these canceled initiatives (and the anti-queer justifications for their cancellations), we helped to keep them as part of the public record instead of letting them fade from memory. These timelines appear on our department website, and faculty (myself included) regularly incorporate them in their teaching, taking seriously Ahmed's call for attention to erasures, cancellations, and absences in the institutional archive.

Hoping to regain the momentum that was lost, and to thwart the kind of programmatic censorship we had experienced, I developed a class for Women and Gender Studies called The Queer Art of Drag. A class, after all, could not be so easily canceled by a university. Nor could the contents of my curriculum be easily censored by my institution. (*Although, as I recently learned, this will not stop people from trying.*) I was inspired by Khubchandani's course Critical Drag at Tufts University, where students learn about drag while developing their own critical drag personas. I launched The Queer Art of Drag virtually in spring 2021 at a time when student need for community, connection, and creative outlet could not have been higher. As Keenan and Lil Miss Hot Mess write, "drag is an imaginative and creative process. It is grounded in building character, both in the sense of constructing a persona and in better understanding one's own relations to others" (2020, 454). The course offered a space for beleaguered students to vent their frustrations, share their passions, and build community while separated by COVID. That April, we hosted a post-vaccine, masked, hybrid drag show featuring student video drag performances—which they conceptualized, filmed, and edited as their final project—and live performances by local drag performers, who had spent the year mostly unable to perform. (*After a year in isolation, I shed a tear at the gorgeous and emotional performance of local burlesque artist Tulla Moore: She manipulated full-body-length silk fans, illuminated in blue and purple stage lights, to the ballad portion of "Bohemian Rhapsody." Not a night I shall soon forget.*)

After offering the course for three years, the right-wing clickbait machine finally caught wind (likely as a result of my speaking to public news outlets about the attacks on drag performance in Texas and beyond), and in June of 2023, coverage by *Fox News*, Turning Point USA, *Campus Reform*, and *The Daily Mail* (among many others) led to an explosion of hateful and bigoted anti-queer phone calls and emails directed toward me, my department, and my university. The comments and social media postings about me and my class were scary and overwhelming; framed in a kind of clerical fascism, they accused me of violence against children, encouraged me to self-harm, and demanded that I be fired, insisting that there was no place for trans people or drag performers in public life. As Butler argues, in the logic of the anti–gender ideology movement, "the allegations of indoctrination and pedophilia tend to blur, based on the belief, and the fear, that to take in an idea is to be subject to unwanted penetration" (2024, 101). The accusation that curriculum (even university curriculum) is a form of sexual violence against children is part of a fascist strategy to make queer and trans inclusion in social life "unsayable, unreadable, and unthinkable" (Butler 2024, 99). This project of unspeakability makes actual violence against queer and trans people, including children, invisible and illegible.

When I tried to speak to university leaders about my experience and ask for basic safety measures and support (such as having my teaching schedule and location removed from public view), I felt that I was the problem (to use Ahmed's term), instead of the victim of a relentless harassment campaign for the DEI-related work I have done on campus; my requests were denied. The incident culminated in the Texas Republican Party sending out a fundraising email targeting my class (*The email went to every registered Republican in the state of Texas? How many people could that be?*). A member of our board of trustees, who is also a sitting Republican member of the U.S. House of Representatives, disparaged the class in the press and vowed to use his role on the board to fight the "woke agenda." After these comments, I received a threat of violence that resulted in action by TCU police. Butler reminds us that the specific "attack on 'woke' is animated by a psychosocial fantasy that the loss of patriarchal, heteronormative, and white supremacist social orders is an unbearable one, tantamount to social death and, at times, physical danger" (2024, 110–11) and that "once installed in the phantasmatic scene as dangerous actors, [woke indoctrinators] must be stopped by any means necessary, including violent ones" (111); so, it is no surprise that such a threat of violence occurred so soon after a prominent political and university leader invoked the anti-"woke" framework against me.

Knowing how hurt LGBTQ students were by ongoing university silence, concerned faculty demanded that the university make a public statement of support for LGBTQ people and LGBTQ studies on campus (Gonzalez 2023), but, to date, the trustee's comments are the only public university response to the anti-queer harassment campaign. Much other ugliness occurred (targeted harassment by Turning Point USA against both me and a staff colleague; a university leader publicly accusing me of using my students as political pawns and not caring about their safety; attempts to censor my pedagogical practices in the classroom), but one experience is particularly illustrative of the ways that queerness was positioned in the wake of these events and in relation to DEI: In 2023, colleagues nominated me for the university's DEI award, and I became a second-time finalist, presumably for my LGBTQ programming, curriculum, and initiatives. At an August 2023 celebratory campus event honoring finalists and listing their accomplishments, no university leadership mentioned the words *drag*, *queer*, or *LGBTQ* in reference to my work, while my fabulous colleagues had their specific initiatives, accomplishments, and contributions listed in detail. I was lauded for my work "streamlining advising" in my department, quite literally erasing drag and queerness from the work of DEI. (*Fear not, children. I showed up in full Maria regalia at the university's Welcome Back luncheon, where the DEI award winner was named, mere days before a statewide ban on drag in the presence of minors was set to take place. I didn't win the award, but I had a good time losing. Besides which, I knew they'd see, I have confidence in me! We have our ways, don't we?*)

The experience of anti-queer violence and harassment against me—a cis, gay, white man—must be understood in the context of racialized anti-trans violence in the state of Texas (Transgender Law Center 2024). Even as I feared for my safety and the safety of my students (who were often themselves queer and trans students of color), throughout this experience, I had institutionalized privilege, fortified by my whiteness and the whiteness of TCU, which would have registered physical harm against me as more meaningful and newsworthy than the many recent deaths of trans women of color in North Texas, which are accepted as inevitable or inconsequential. For instance, Muhlaysia Booker's filmed assault and subsequent murder in Dallas in the spring of 2019 was just months before the cancellation of our Drag Story Hour event and was cited in our program materials about the importance of gender-affirming programming at a time of great loss for the trans community (Donaghue 2021). We tried to connect the censorship of our event with the climate that normalizes and erases violence against trans women of color in our community and were met with confused stares by administrators who don't see the work of the university as connected to these systems of anti-trans violence.

The censorship and harassment that I experienced obviously do not compare to Booker's horrific murder; what I mean to point out is how the privilege that insulated me and my institution is bound up with these local experiences of racialized anti-trans violence and death in establishing a local vocabulary of acceptability and inevitability across a range of violent experiences. As we know, the violent fantasies of the gender binary actually work to (re)produce race and colonial power. (*Oh, once the anti-woke brigade got ahold of our syllabus, they really hated seeing the short essay "The Gender Binary Is a Tool of White Supremacy," didn't they? But if they had read, actually read, the article, no lies would have been detected, as the children say*) (Marshall 2020).

Drag, with its irreverent rejection of normative ways of being, presents a problem for the otherwise efficient mechanisms of the neoliberal university that "cannibalize difference and its potential for rupture" (Ferguson 2012, 213). (*I guess we are sort of hard to chew up and spit out as "diversity," aren't we?*) The delicate balance of "doing" diversity work on campus while articulating these institutional logics can turn people into problems for institutions. As Ahmed writes in *Living a Feminist Life*, "When you expose a problem, you pose a problem" (2017, 37). Maria von Clapp poses a problem. She challenges official DEI language and dares the university to prove their statements are true, but she does not fall under the banner of DEI. Neoliberal university frameworks for DEI do not include drag performers. (*As I was told in no uncertain terms!*) That is to say, they do not include queer ways of being. This gives drag a unique vantage point from which to interpret and critique normative institutional practices.

The Pedagogical Potential of Drag

Keenan and Lil Miss Hot Mess define drag pedagogy as a queer framework that moves beyond "vocabulary lessons and the token inclusion of LGBT heroes" (*Hello, Morris Kight!*) that we might associate with LGBTQ inclusive curriculum (Keenan and Lil Miss Hot Mess 2020, 443). Instead, drag pedagogy creates space for communities of learners "to engage deeper understandings of queer cultures and envision new modes of being together" (443). Uninterested in neoliberal logics of representation and inclusion, drag pedagogy asks us to radically reimagine the world and our place in it: "drag pedagogy offers one model for learning not simply about queer lives, but how to *live queerly*" (444). Drag pedagogy can illuminate and lay bare the gap between official DEI discourse and the experiences of queer people on campus. It can also provide students a space to think outside of the neoliberal logics that organize contemporary university life.

When I began formulating a teacherly drag persona, I started with the queer teacher who inspired me most when I was a kid. (*A reasonable strategy. For somewhere in your youth or childhood, you must have done something gay.*) As Wayne Koestenbaum famously wrote, "Julie Andrews prepared me for ... homosexuality" (Koestenbaum 2001, 11). (*So funny! But Dame Andrews is known for being so wholesome, virtuous, and pure, isn't she? How might she have prepared someone for the debaucherous and antisocial life of a homosexual?*) Brett Farmer notes that Andrews's image does not appear, at first glance, to possess any of the qualities that typically lead to diva worship (such as camp, searing wit, personal trauma, or melodrama), but has, nonetheless, inspired many queer authors and artists (Farmer 2007, 144). Farmer locates queer affinities for Andrews in what he considers the most salient feature of the diva, "transformational empowerment" (145). The most compelling pedagogical strategies that Andrews's characters employ is the ability to swoop in and show students that they have all the tools they need possess to transform themselves and their world.

As Farmer argues, "under the diva's melodic tutelage, the children ... undertake a profoundly therapeutic process of enfranchisement, transcending various incapacities to embrace a renewed and expansive vision of self. Even, daresay, of queer self" (147). Perhaps what makes this reading of such an iconic figure so compelling to so many queer people is the productive tension between finding a place for ourselves in a wholesome learning community, where, so often, such a space is denied to us (*Oh, yes, you had some rough times in school, didn't you? A story for another time.*), and the queer desire to dismantle the hallowed texts of the cisheteropatriachy. (*Ahhh— this is why those hate-filled online comments about your class said that I was "perverting" the family values of the* Sound of Music *with that gonorrhea pun in my name! As if destigmatizing STIs isn't a vital part of education. Well, I also just like to clap to get my students' attention. They should get their minds out of the gutter.*) You'll find no banking model of education in these Julie Andrews films (*The banks don't serve the Banks children very well, do they?*); instead, the iconic teachers Andrews portrays center the knowledge, skills, and values of each learner (*A regular, Paulo Fairy Godmother!*) (Freire 2000).

Like the beloved characters who inspired her, Maria von Clapp encourages her students to see the world queerly—that is, to articulate the ways that gender norms and neoliberal logics cause them harm and to find creative, joyful ways to center curiosity and community. Maria von Trapp, Mary Poppins, and Eliza Doolittle (*Julie Andrews was in the Broadway show, not the film, of course!*) can't singlehandedly stop Nazis or end the violence of capitalism in one fell swoop, but they curate active learning opportunities where students might cultivate joy in simple moments (*Raindrops on roses, and whiskers on kittens!*), value community over capital (*Feed the birds, tuppence a bag!*), prioritize pleasure (*I could have danced all night!*), develop praxis (*Just a spoon full of sugar helps the medicine go down!*), speak truth to power (*Just you wait, Henry Higgins!*), emphasize the power of storytelling (*High on a hill lies the lonely goatherd!*), delight in nonsense (*Supercalifragilisticexpialidocious!*), and celebrate the transformational possibilities of collaborative learning (*When you know the notes to sing, you can sing most anything!*). They do this while reworking the taken-for-granted power dynamics between teacher/student (*Henry has far more to learn than Eliza, if you ask me*), adult/child (*Maria beat those mischievous children at their own game, after all*), and stranger/friend (*A queer one, that Mary Poppins is*).

The genesis of my drag initiatives was listening to students and letting their needs steer my imagination. (*Just as the needs of the von Trapp children steered Maria toward those hideous curtain garments.*) While the student organization Spectrum has organized a semiannual drag show since 2008, the success of the show was dependent on current student leadership, which can change dramatically from year to year. The annual show was anchored by professional performers from North Texas, but when organizers tried to encourage student participation, they had varying levels of success. When I joined the planning committee in 2019, I tried to secure student performers through Women and Gender Studies and tended to get some variation of these two responses: "Absolutely not" or "I'm interested . . . but I've never done drag! How could I ever get it together to perform later this semester?" It occurred to me that students who offered the second response had quite a good point. I, myself, had never performed in drag before, and here I was trying to convince eighteen-year-olds at a conservative PWI to get onstage in front of their peers in bedazzled costumes (*And who would do the bedazzling?*) and elaborate makeup (*Despite protests to the contrary, we do* not *wake up like this!*) to lip-sync a Britney Spears song. How could I expect students to take this risk if I was not willing to do the same?

I told interested students that I would perform too and would be happy to support the development of their numbers. (*Silly girl—this is like Mother Superior presuming to teach her postulants how to tango.*) At the crux of this dilemma—wanting to encourage and support student participation in the drag show and having never done drag myself—Maria von Clapp was born. Maria isn't the most polished drag queen in town; she is a simple mountain girl. (*Sounds like an excuse for our rudimentary makeup skills, if you ask me.*) She is also a queer teacher. She does not position herself as an authority but, rather, learns alongside her students, taking risks, exposing her own ignorance, and learning to inhabit a place of vulnerability instead of mastery. (*And there's an excuse for messing up our choreo.*)

(*The von Clapp children—that's what I call my students, of course—have taken this little class and made it all their own!*) It's one thing to say that every student in a classroom contributes to knowledge production; it's quite another to have your students show you how to fix your contouring. (*You know what they say: when you become a teacher, by your pupils you'll be taught! Oh wait . . . this one's from that rather racist show,* The King and I, *isn't it? Well, here is a moment of learning for us all: the things we love must be critiqued and need not always be recuperated. Phewy to Anna and her maternalistic colonialism!*) It's one thing to encourage active learning in the classroom; it's quite another to ask students to understand drag by developing their own drag personas (*Many thanks to Auntie LaWhore for this invention. Let's be honest, Dr., you would not have gotten very far without her example!*). It is one thing to talk to students about the violence of cultural appropriation; it is quite another to ask them to determine the ethics of their own performance and to hold themselves and each other accountable for the choices that they make. (*If you have to ask whether it's "okay" for you to perform that song, dearie . . . it probably isn't.*) In this collaborative learning space, we each examined our unique positionalities based on race, gender, sexuality, and ability as we crafted our personas and performances in community. We asked challenging questions about which archives we should access for inspiration, how diverse audiences would experience our performances, and how to position ourselves in relation to drag histories. (*I am quite aware that stodgy old white musicals are not everyone's cup of tea; my drag cannot be someone else's drag, and their drag cannot be mine. The whys and wherefores are where the best learning takes place!*)

We begin the semester learning about drag ethics and the importance of drag to queer community. We learn about the powerful history of drag as a survival strategy for queer and trans people, especially people of color, throughout the twentieth century, as they faced criminalization, harassment, violence, and familial dispossession, realities that queer and trans people continue to face today. Drag is one of the ways queer people have responded to and thrived in the face of these violent realities. What became painfully clear in the university's failed response to the harassment campaign I outlined above was that they could not conceive of drag as part of DEI; but more than that, that they could not understand why drag and LGBTQ history, culture, identity, and experience, more broadly, were integrally tied to race and racism, making no space for the queer students of color—including Black and Indigenous students—who they claimed to be supporting in their DEI initiatives. These students of color found the class and drag programs on campus to be especially powerful spaces of community formation, which comes as no surprise, since contemporary drag in queer communities can trace its history to the survival strategies of people like William Dorsey Swann, a formerly enslaved person who threw elaborate drag balls for Black participants in the D.C. area (Joseph n.d.); the Black and brown street queens of Stonewall; and the Harlem ball culture famously represented in the film *Paris Is Burning*. (*Perhaps your school's fancy administrators would know this history if they had actually taken your class or attended the fabulous ball history program organized by queer and trans BIPOC students on campus.*)

As I taught this course in the spring of 2023, the Texas legislature had introduced 140 anti-LGBTQ bills, some of which sought to criminalize both gender-affirming care for trans children and the performance of drag in the presence of children. Several of these bills became law. When students asked, "How can this be happening in 2023?," drag pedagogy reminded us that it has *always* been happening and that we have the tools to respond to it and thrive despite it. That semester, we learned about the history of "manless"

Figure 1. Going to the Chapel: Maria von Clapp stages a "Manless/Womanless Wedding" with the von Clapp Children at TCU's Annual Night of Drag, 2023. Photograph by Josh Folan. Image courtesy of Nino Testa.

and "womanless" weddings, traditions across the U.S. South where presumably straight and cis white people would gather in low-tech drag and stage elaborate wedding rituals as community-building events, sometimes with minstrel performances, reifying gender norms and white supremacy (Friend 2009, 221). The earliest record of such an event at our own institution was in 1904, at the same time that a so-called cross-dressing ordinance criminalized drag performance for queer and trans people in our city (*Manless Wedding* 1904). (*Goodness. Some things truly never change.*) For our spring 2023 class drag performance, we staged a manless/womanless wedding of our own. Performing songs, from "Chapel of Love" to "Single Ladies," we traced shifting norms around romance, marriage, race, and gender, teaching our community about a century-old hypocrisy, and insisting on the right of queer students to express themselves (figure 1).

While learning about the long history of drag, we also consider what drag can reveal about gender. As Alana Kumbier argues, drag is a "social technology that challenges discourses and practices which perpetuate the 'naturality' of binary systems of gender and sexuality" (2002, 193). Drag offers students a chance to explore how their own gendered sense of self manifests through a series of social and material technologies to which we each have varying levels of access (which is to say, that these technologies are laden with power dynamics). Finding new ways to deploy technologies of gender can bring into relief the mundane ways in which particular gender expressions can be naturalized and socially rewarded while others are policed. Khubchandani describes how the process of showing drag's component parts demonstrates these queer ways of approaching gender, by showing students how Dr. Khubchandani "becomes" LaWhore Vagistan (Khubchandani 2015, 290). Invoking Butler's iconic and contested invocation of drag as revealing the citational practices and appeals to authority of all gender (*but especially those we might call cisgender, whose authority is taken as, well, authoritative!*), Khubchandani reminds us that "performativity is not only about describing clothing, makeup, and hair, but also bodily comportment and kinesthetics" (290). Asking students to move, speak, and otherwise embody their personas, drag pedagogy gives students space to explore the gendered readings and misreadings that we engage in every day.

(*And you don't need to teach an entire class on drag to learn all this, dearies! Sometimes, while Dr. Testa is prattling on, I try this: I have my students watch Stromae's "Tous les Mêmes" or some other gender-expansive performance and ask them to each select* one *movement or motion that embodies a particular norm, idea, or belief about gender. They find the fun, and snap! The analysis is a game. They talk about how cis men are allowed to take up more space and expose their bodies. How cis women must move softly and cover up or face harsh judgments. How trans and nonbinary people are policed no matter what they do. They talk about how race complicates these binary understandings of gender appropriateness. But they don't tell* me, *they show* me *by dancing. Words! Words! Words! I'm so sick of words! Don't talk of gender,* show me, *I say. Then, we stand in a circle and do each motion in sequence, making our own little gender dance.*) As Keenan and Lil Miss Hot Mess write, "drag helps us better understand dominant culture by transforming its constitutive elements" (2020, 453). Turning gender norms into parody invokes the queer art of camp, trivializing the traditions, customs, and norms of the cisheteropatriarchy that demonizes queerness. (*The macho moves and misogynistic gestures sure do look silly when we do them together in our classroom.*)

Keenan and Lil Miss Hot Mess ask: "What if we took play, defiance, and imagination seriously as norms of knowledge production?" (2020, 443). Maria answers this call by asking students to lip-sync to their favorite song in class, caricature and theatricalize the oppressive norms that organize their lives on campus, and create an elaborate drag persona that can be deployed not just on a stage but in moments of uncertainty, discomfort, or even violence. While some students from the class go on to continue performing in drag, those who never perform again cite their drag persona as their own personal Sasha Fierce, a confident, sexy, and empowered alter ego who is ready to face moments that would typically cause stress or anxiety in their daily lives. Many have cited the class as the first time they were able to explore their gender identity and expression in a meaningful way on campus. More than one student has broken down in tears at the end of the semester, noting that the class was the first place they felt queer community.

In this sense, critical drag pedagogy—which utilizes drag as a form of social critique and queer world-making—has a clear learning outcome: to help students envision themselves as empowered in an increasingly terrifying and apocalyptic world of viruses, white supremacy, anti-queerness, and climate change. (*Not all drag does this, of course. We talk about normative drag, minstrelsy, and colonial drag in class as well.*) Student projects for this class defy racial respectability politics, resist the racist border policies and environmental degradation of our state, theatricalize the process of queer community-building, mock the normative culture of Greek life on campus, reclaim sexual desire for survivors of sexual violence, and more. (*So much more. I wish I could share their drag names and performances here with you . . . they are so brilliant. But, you know, IRB . . .*) One live group performance by students at the 2024 show (to the tune of Elton John's "I'm Still Standing") thematized and responded to the 2023 anti-queer harassment campaign and was a powerful act of student performance as protest. (*And it was accompanied by some very impressive LGBTQ student activism on campus that year! I guess the children were feeling mobilized!*) Our final group number in 2024 celebrated the transformation of each von Clapp child into their persona when they were gifted a magical item from Maria's bag of "favorite things," reminding us all that when we face violence, we have queer and feminist tools to help us survive and thrive. Each of the von Clapp children positions themselves in relation to the larger power dynamics that have been vexing them and speaks back powerfully, offering a model to the audience for how they might do the same (*Answering Auntie LaWhore's call to "conjure* new worlds through the body" and "flaunt irreverence for colonial forms" [Khubchandani 2023, 180]. What? You didn't think a drag queen knew how to cite?)

Conclusion

To write a piece on drag pedagogy grounded in my experience at a wealthy PWI has its limits. For one, drag is expensive. (*As Dolly Parton says, "It takes a lot of money to look this cheap." You can't assume that everyone can find funds for their students to buy wigs, heels, and rhinestones!*) While I argue that drag pedagogy, ultimately, falls outside of neoliberal DEI discourse, my work was generously supported by individuals who do DEI work on campus (including my own department, partners in student affairs and activities, and a grant from the Office of Diversity & Inclusion), despite other institutional resistance that I outline in this article. The wealth of the institution fully shaped the possibilities of my pedagogy. As Matt Brim argues in *Poor Queer Studies*, the field of queer studies "cannot be separated from the large-scale institutional production of racialized class stratification" (2020, 3). Brim calls us to do more than acknowledge class privilege and immoral distributions of wealth; he calls for a structural sharing of resources and a "dynamic movement between centers and margins," which he calls "queer ferrying" (199). For my course, this call to "enact queer pedagogies as cross-class pedagogies" (199) has looked like compensating local drag performers for their expertise in the classroom, offering free drag pedagogy workshops and talks in community spaces, and even making space for community members to participate fully as part of the class. Critiques of DEI discourse can themselves reveal class-, race-, and geography-based disparities. This is especially true as I write this article and state legislatures continue to pass bills that dismantle DEI infrastructure and critical studies at public universities, including in Texas. My argument is meant neither as universalizing gesture nor as attempt to gloss over the enormous institutional privilege I have to do the work that I outline, even as I did so in the face of threats of violence and high-profile attacks on my pedagogy and personal character; instead, I hope these experiences and reflections shed light on how drag pedagogy might resist the neoliberal logics that we all encounter, differently situated as we are across diverse institutional affiliations, geographies, and positionalities.

Drag can offer powerful tools to help us resist the neoliberal circularity of DEI discourse on campus; drag pedagogy underscores how these tools are readily available to us in our daily lives. Drag pedagogy transcends the classroom; in fact, it turns the club, the Pride parade, the campus, the Story Hour, the Insta post, and even the house of worship into a classroom, reminding us of the expansive possibilities of our bodies and our spirits in the face of the mundane, the bureaucratic, and the hostile. (*I must thank the next drag performer I see. What a* gift *they are. What a* treasure.) Teaching and learning with Maria von Clapp has been a pure joy. Despite canceled events, opposition to drag shows and initiatives, a coordinated harassment campaign, and even a threat of violence, she has helped students claim their own space, explore their own genders, and develop queer ways of being on a normative campus. Maria stays with me when I am in my professor drag, reminding me how to center the needs of my students, open myself up to the learning that happens in my classroom, and model queer praxis in a world that can make us all feel so disempowered (Scudera 2015). Maria teaches us a better way to think through and against the neoliberal, anti-queer logics of DEI discourse and to build queer community in the process. (*When the dog bites, when the bee stings, when I'm feeling sad, I simply remember* my students in drag, *and then I don't feel so bad!*)

Nino Testa is a visiting scholar at the Women's Institute at Chatham University in Pittsburgh. He is coeditor with Catherine Evans of the upcoming collection *Iconic: Drag Celebrity and Queer Community* from University of Delaware Press. He can be reached at n.testa@chatham.edu.

Works Cited

Ahmed, Sara. 2012. *On Being Included: Racism and Diversity in Institutional Life*. Duke University Press.

Ahmed, Sara. 2017. *Living a Feminist Life*. Duke University Press.

Bradford, K. 2002. "Grease Cowboy Fever; or, The Making of Johnny T." *Journal of Homosexuality* 43 (3–4): 15–30.

Brim, Matt. 2020. *Poor Queer Studies: Confronting Elitism in the University*. Duke University Press.

Butler, Judith. 2024. *Who's Afraid of Gender?* Farrar, Straus, and Giroux.

Donaghue, Erin. 2021. "Muhlaysia Booker Case: Man Convicted in Videotaped Assault of Transgender Woman Who Was Later Found Slain." *CBS News*, May 7. https://www.cbsnews.com/news/muhlaysia-booker-case-man-convicted-in-videotaped-assault-of-transgender-woman-who-was-later-found-slain/.

Farmer, Brett. 2007. "Julie Andrews Made Me Gay." *Camera Obscura* 22 (2): 144–53. https://doi.org/10.1215/02705346-2007-007.

Ferguson, Roderick. 2012. *The Reorder of Things: The University and Its Pedagogies of Minority Difference*. University of Minnesota Press.

Ferguson, Roderick. 2017. *We Demand: The University and Student Protests*. University of California Press.

Freire, Paulo. 2000. *Pedagogy of the Oppressed*. 30th anniv. ed. Continuum Press.

Friend, Craig Thompson. 2009. "The Womanless Wedding: Masculinity, Cross-Dressing and Gender Inversions in the Modern South." In *Southern Masculinity: Perspectives on Manhood in the South Since Reconstruction*, edited by Craig Thompson Friend, 219–45. University of Georgia Press.

Gonzalez, Ella. 2023. "Over 200 People Sign Faculty Petition in Support of LGBTQ Campus Community." *TCU360*, October 13. https://tcu360.com/2023/10/13/over-200-signatures-sign-faculty-petition-in-support-of-lgbtq-campus-community/.

Joseph, Channing Gerard. n.d. "Historical Research and Discoveries." *Channing Joseph* (blog). Accessed April 1, 2023. https://www.channingjoseph.com/elements/discoveries.html.

Keenan, Harper, and Lil Miss Hot Mess. 2020. "Drag Pedagogy: The Playful Practice of Queer Imagination in Early Childhood." *Curriculum Inquiry* 50 (5): 440–61.

KHOU Staff. 2009. "TCU Shelves Plan for Gay-Themed Housing." KHOU, October 26. https://www.khou.com/article/news/tcu-shelves-plan-for-gay-themed-housing/285-342779356.

Khubchandani, Kareem. 2015. "Lessons in Drag: An Interview with LaWhore Vagistan." *Theatre Topics* 25 (3): 285–94.

Khubchandani, Kareem. 2023. *Decolonize Drag*. OR Books.

Koestenbaum, Wayne. 2001. *The Queen's Throat: Opera, Homosexuality, and the Mystery of Desire*. De Capo Press.

Kumbier, Alana. 2002. "One Body, Some Genders: Drag Performances and Technologies." *Journal of Homosexuality* 43 (3–4): 191–200.

Manless Wedding. 1904. JPEG image of photo. *TCU Digital Repository*. Texas Christian University. https://repository.tcu.edu/handle/116099117/3735.

Marshall, Kravitz. 2020. "The Gender Binary Is a Tool of White Supremacy." *Medium*. July 14, 2020. https://aninjusticemag.com/the-gender-binary-is-a-tool-of-white-supremacy-db89d0bc9044.

McGaughy, Lauren. 2019. "Texas Leads the Nation in Transgender Murders. After the Latest Attack, the Dallas Trans Community Asks Why." *Dallas News*, October 2, 2019. https://www.dallasnews.com/news/2019/09/30/texas-leads-nation-transgender-murders-according-national-lgbtq-organization/.

"Notice of Nondiscrimination." 2022. *Texas Christian University*. October 28. https://www.tcu.edu/compliance/notice-of-nondiscrimination.

Scudera, Dominick. 2015. "The Professor Is a Drag Queen." *Chronicle of Higher Education*, November 30. https://www.chronicle.com/article/the-professor-is-a-drag-queen/.

Squirrell, Tim, and Jacob Davey. 2023. *A Year of Hate: Understanding Threats and Harassment Targeting Drag Shows and the LGBTQ+ Community*. Institute for Strategic Dialogue. https://www.isdglobal.org/wp-content/uploads/2023/06/Understanding-Threats-and-Harassment-Targeting-Drag-Shows-and-the-LGBTQ-Community.pdf.

"Strategic Plan: About Diversity & Inclusion at TCU." 2022. *Strategic Plan*. Texas Christian University. Accessed November 16, 2024. https://www.tcu.edu/diversity-inclusion/about/strategic-plan.php.

TCU. 2019. "TCU Diversity, Equity and Inclusion: Learn More About TCU's Exciting Achievement and Our Continued Efforts in Diversity, Inclusion and Equity." *Facebook*. April 25. https://www.facebook.com/TCUTexasChristianUniversity/videos/tcu-diversity-equity-and-inclusion/606858199820819/.

Them. 2023. "Survival, Glamorously." *Instagram*. April 7. https://www.instagram.com/reel/CqwKsZnA1Yd/?igshid=YmMyMTA2M2Y.

Transgender Law Center. 2024. "Regional Reports—Texas—Transgender Law Center." June 26. https://transgenderlawcenter.org/regional-reports-texas/.

Otra vez el hielo: Exclusión epistémica de los feminismos en espacios académicos

Fernanda Rojas-Müller, Ana Luisa Muñoz-García y Kyuttzza Gómez-Guinart

---

Resumen: En este artículo nos preguntamos por las condiciones materiales que posibilitan la creación de conocimientos feministas, sus avances y marginaciones entretejidas en una academia neoliberal, racista y heterocispatriarcal. A partir de un estudio sobre género y conocimientos desde una perspectiva feminista (2021–2024), este artículo elabora un relato colectivo de investigadoras/es sobre exclusión epistémica del género y los feminismos en los espacios académicos chileno y argentino. El relato, narrado en primera persona y construido desde las citas de las y los investigadores en temas de género y feminismo, transita entre lo individual y lo colectivo, situando las problemáticas de género en lo político para materializar deslocalizadamente las formas de exclusión epistémica. Esta se expresa en vulneraciones directas sobre las personas, pero también se aloja en dimensiones estructurales, por ejemplo, la imposibilidad de transversalizar curricularmente la perspectiva de género, dificultades para conseguir financiamiento o asociar estas perspectivas negativamente con el activismo. En medio de la avanzada de las ultraderechas internacionalmente, es urgente dialogar sobre el estatus epistémico de los conocimientos feministas en la academia. **Palabras clave:** exclusión epistémica, feminismos, género, academia, conocimiento

---

Otra vez el hielo

Abre el correo. Hay un nuevo mail en su bandeja de entrada. "Están regalando las notas en el extranjero". Queda helada. Se arrepiente de haberle contado orgullosa que le había ido muy bien en la primera tanda de trabajos. Su cuerpo la lleva al recuerdo de la vez en que, unos años antes, cometió el error de mostrarle su tesis sobre mujer e historia. "Debería titularse 'mujeres', no 'mujer'". Sintió rabia, sobre todo porque tenía razón.

No le contó que se graduó con distinción. No lo iba a entender. "Tú que pareces ser una chica inteligente ¿por qué te vas a dedicar a esto si te puedes dedicar a otras cosas?" Menos puede decirle que es feminista, contarle en qué trabaja, a qué dedica su tiempo, qué lee y qué se pregunta. Sabe que va a ser visto "como una cuestión activista o como una cuestión poco seria". Opta por hablar de "género", esa "especie de rótulo que con todas sus dificultades se presenta como más científico que decir 'soy feminista'". Las feministas son las que marchan, gritan y protestan. La academia y el activismo son dos cosas separadas.

Unos años después, de vuelta en el culo del mundo, su cuerpo revivirá varias veces el hielo de ese correo. Lo repasará mentalmente. Sentirá rabia y pena. En parte, se resignará. "¿Qué pasa? ¿[Eres] lesbiana? ¿Estás enojada con los varones?" Aprende a disimular. Sus "proyectos de investigación van a tener que blindarse". En paralelo, activará, luchará por instalar temas que le parecen vitales, irá a las actividades a las que la invitan sus estudiantes, se desafiará con lecturas y proyectos, escribirá, irá a congresos, publicará, producirá, producirá, producirá, producirá. Será la más productiva en una academia neoliberal. Como otras, además, se hará cargo del trabajo reproductivo y doméstico de su facultad, ese para el que otros -casi siempre hombres- asumen que tiene más habilidades. Ese que sabe no es sino otra forma de sumarle obstáculos a su carrera.

Una parte de sí está cansada de pelear, de que sea siempre tan difícil, de sentirse habitando un margen, de tener miedo, de sentirse minimizada, de ser "la loca, la rara". Una parte de sí se cansa de la batalla constante. Siempre el peor horario, el curso optativo que más o menos te dejan hacer, "como una carga anexa, como una extensión de la militancia para seguir poniendo estos temas". Siempre tantas reuniones. Tener que hacer "mucho esfuerzo en las discusiones, en las negociaciones, en las estrategias, en las argumentaciones". Piensa en compañeras a las que han ignorado, a las que han vetado de hacer clases, a las que han echado. Siente el hielo de esa "marginalidad horrorosa". Lleva años "casi predicando, 'oiga sí, estoy haciendo esto, sí esto es investigación'" para que llegue un colega a invitarla a su curso "media horita a explicar lo que es la perspectiva de género". Media horita. La perspectiva de género.

En la fila para comprar café escucha a unas colegas decir que con los movimientos estudiantiles feministas y la entrada del activismo a la academia ya se superó el tema. Nuevamente el hielo en el cuerpo. Son hitos importantes, qué duda cabe. Permitieron "modificar la importancia que tiene el género en la institucionalidad de las universidades". Pero ¿de ahí a superado? Se acuerda de esa jefa que le dijo que "pasó la moda, ya nadie quiere tomar los temas de género".

Cómo va a estar superado, piensa, si todavía hay áreas del conocimiento donde el género no entra, donde quien trabaja género es bicho raro, donde se le pregunta si de verdad lo que investiga es economía o derecho o historia o filosofía o lo que sea. Cómo se va a haber superado si todavía no hay legitimidad, si "todavía no tenemos derecho a estar". Piensa en esos estudiantes que alguna vez tuvieron la audacia de decirle que activar, hacer, estudiar, investigar género, bien, "pero en el ámbito universitario no, la ciencia es otra cosa, la producción de conocimiento tiene que ir por otro contenido". "Como si el género fuera un tema más que se puede poner o sacar".

Suena la notificación del calendario en su celular. Le recuerda que tiene otra reunión. Cruza el patio hacia la oficina de su superior. Su cabeza no deja de rumiar. "Ahora es mal visto no ser feminista", pero los cambios "no son tan radicales". Seguimos en los márgenes. Piensa cómo ella misma lo devaluó en su momento. Cómo eventualmente también se dio cuenta de que no era una locura suya "sino que realmente es una línea de investigación seria, sistemática, que tiene determinados antecedentes y que también tiene una producción específica". Piensa también en lo que escuchaba decir a sus pares, a todas las que hoy -enhorabuena- se declaran feministas. Piensa, orgullosa, cómo entre muchas y en muchas partes, a pesar de todo, "han ido corriendo los límites de lo posible" y sonríe.

La hacen pasar a la oficina. Su superior le dice que *lamentablemente* no será la encargada de la comisión de género de la facultad. "El cargo se lo dieron a un hombre que no trabaja género, que ni siquiera sabe lo que es, que todavía piensa que es el material del que se hace su ropa".

Otra vez el hielo.

Introducción

El relato con el que abrimos este texto fue construido a partir de entrevistas realizadas entre los años 2021 y 2022 a 25 académicas y académicos que trabajan temas de género en Chile (13) y en Argentina (12), como parte de un proyecto (todavía en curso) sobre políticas de conocimiento y género en Educación Superior. En un contexto donde los movimientos feministas durante los últimos años han impactado fuertemente las agendas de los Estados y, especialmente, las de los sistemas educativos, el proyecto liderado por una de las autoras busca indagar qué conocimientos sobre género y feminismos se utilizan para informar a las políticas de género en Educación Superior y de qué manera están permeando las universidades. Creemos en la urgencia de esta investigación en un presente de consolidación de ideologías radicales de derecha en el mundo y en Latinoamérica. Argentina, con la elección y promulgación de Javier Milei como Presidente, ha sufrido la eliminación de instituciones vigilantes de los derechos humanos y democratizadoras del conocimiento. En el caso de Chile, José Antonio Kast pasó a la segunda vuelta presidencial el 2021 con un programa que prometía eliminar el Ministerio de la Mujer y Equidad de Género, entre otras medidas.

Con este contexto en nuestros cuerpos, el relato inicial invita a profundizar cómo se ha excluido el conocimiento feminista en el ámbito académico chileno y argentino. Para ello, nos enfocamos en desentramar tres nudos: la historicidad del trabajo académico feminista; el impacto material y afectivo de la exclusión epistémica en las trayectorias laborales de académicos/as; y la lucha por la validación del conocimiento feminista o de género.

En lo que sigue, organizamos este artículo de la siguiente manera. Primero, proponemos la producción de relatos ficcionales como herramienta novedosa para indagar las materializaciones de un fenómeno de interés, en este caso, la exclusión del conocimiento feminista en ámbitos académicos. Segundo, describimos los rasgos de un contexto académico neoliberal que promueve la exclusión tanto de estos conocimientos como de quienes los producen. Tercero, introducimos el concepto de exclusión epistémica. Cuarto, generamos un diálogo entre el relato y la literatura para tirar de los tres nudos mencionados. Finalmente, insistimos en deslizarnos a través de propuestas neomaterialistas y feministas para resistir las interpelaciones de "investigación poco seria" con las que hostigan a los conocimientos feministas y de género en ámbitos académicos latinoamericanos. Hacerlo es un acto reivindicativo de quienes, desde la academia, ponemos nuestros cuerpos al servicio de los derechos, las libertades y la justicia.

Urgencias y resistencias feministas frente a la ultraderecha
Los movimientos feministas han sido fundamentales para entender el contexto de esta investigación y manuscrito. Tanto Chile como Argentina han vivido procesos en los últimos diez años que han producido impactos importantes en las universidades y en la investigación, agitados por movimientos herederos de una larga historia feminista en ambos países.

En Chile, el llamado Mayo Feminista se tomó la agenda política y mediática el 2018 (de Fina Gonzalez y Figueroa Vidal 2019) y marcó un hito en el debate público al concentrar las demandas de las estudiantes en las diversas violencias a las que eran sometidas en las instituciones de educación superior y exigir a las autoridades atender y resolver casos de violencia y acoso sexual (Schuster et al. 2019). Así, inspirado en la historia de las movilizaciones estudiantiles previas en Chile, la conmoción feminista internacional del #MeToo (Williams, Singh y Mezey 2019) y el #NiUnaMenos en Argentina (Forstenzer 2019), las estudiantes ocuparon universidades, liceos y calles con demandas feministas. La discusión excedió los muros de las instituciones y se trasladó a la política pública mediante diversas iniciativas. Desde entonces, se han publicado documentos tanto gubernamentales como institucionales, políticas, programas y leyes en temáticas de género en Educación Superior (Silva Hope et al. 2024). Un hito importante fue la promulgación de la Ley 21.369 en 2019, que promueve políticas integrales que tienen por objetivo la prevención, investigación y sanción del acoso, las violencias y la discriminación por razón de género. Esta ley, impulsada por la Red de Investigadoras, ha significado que hoy más del 90% de las universidades tengan una política integral para abordar la violencia, protocolos y/o direcciones o unidades de género. Esto, sin embargo, no ha estado exento de resistencias y una agenda anti-género que ha impactado la libertad académica y ha supuesto el acoso a investigadoras feministas, por ejemplo, mediante solicitudes a diferentes universidades de listados de académicas que enseñen o investiguen sobre "ideología de género" por parte de congresistas del Partido Republicano (de derecha radical).

En Argentina, las protestas feministas que irrumpieron durante la década pasada con el movimiento #NiUnaMenos forman parte de los movimientos sociales permanentes del país (Lenguita 2021). El movimiento de 2015 posicionó demandas públicas en contra de la violencia machista haciendo visible un problema sistémico. Dentro de los logros de los movimientos feministas de la última década se encuentra la visibilización de discursos sobre los cuerpos que van más allá de lo binario (Abbate 2018), la legalización del aborto en 2018 (Acosta 2020) y la elaboración de protocolos contra las violencias (Trebisacce y Dulbecco 2021), entre otros. En diciembre de 2018 se sanciona la Ley 27.499, conocida como Ley Micaela, que establece, en su primer artículo, la obligatoriedad de la capacitación sobre temáticas de género y violencia contra las mujeres para toda persona que trabaje en el ámbito público de los tres poderes del Estado. En la implementación de esta ley ha tenido una labor importante la Red Interuniversitaria de Género (RUGE), particularmente en el diseño y desarrollo de políticas institucionales que contribuyan a erradicar las desigualdades de género y las violencias en todo el sistema universitario (Torlucci, Cruz y Vasquez Laba 2023).

Al momento de escribir este manuscrito, un presidente que se autodenomina radical libertario cerró el Ministerio de Mujeres, Género y de Diversidad y el de Educación y Ciencia, Tecnología e Innovación, entre otros. Además, congeló para el 2024 el presupuesto para investigación y becas doctorales. Más aún, desde su campaña ha atacado los movimientos feministas y las políticas de género, repudiando efusivamente las políticas de igualdad, prohibiendo el lenguaje inclusivo (CNN 2024) y cerrando el Instituto Nacional contra la Discriminación, la Xenofobia y el Racismo por ser considerado un organismo que "no sirve absolutamente para nada" con funcionarios de "dudosa idoneidad" (Meganoticias 2024).

El contexto de avances y resistencias en temas de género y feminismos que describimos nos permite comprender la posicionalidad de los estudios de género y feministas en los espacios universitarios. Por una parte, existe una avanzada de políticas, programas, cursos, investigación, entre otros, que da respuesta a demandas masivas, pero, por otro lado, una resistencia que, si bien pareciera no ser masiva aún, pone en tela de juicio el avance de derechos y espacios conquistados. La exclusión epistémica navega en este vaivén que sitúa a estos conocimientos en el umbral de la academia (Muñoz-García y Trebisacce 2024).

El relato como plataforma teórico-metodológica

Las historias que se entraman en el relato fueron recogidas mediante entrevistas semiestructuradas realizadas[1] entre agosto del 2021 y mayo del 2022 a académicos/as en Chile y Argentina. Se abordaron tópicos como las trayectorias de trabajo, el diagnóstico de la investigación y la construcción de políticas en torno a género y conocimiento en cada país.

El primer paso para alejarnos de las ideas de representación (Lather 2000) y de codificación (MacLure 2013; St. Pierre y Jackson 2014) en la investigación fue "dialogar con la data". Dichas ideas sustentan una de las formas tradicionales de análisis en las investigaciones cualitativas: la necesidad de "localizar la voz" o "dar voz". Nos preguntamos, entonces, qué significa "dar voz" en un escenario donde "dialogar con la data" implica reencontrarnos con nosotras mismas en medio de nuestras prácticas de creación de conocimiento, formación e historia. ¿A quién/es dimos voz? ¿Y cómo representamos esa voz? (Mazzei 2013). Primordialmente a partir de estas interrogantes, elegimos el camino de construir una narrativa inaugural donde se realiza una voz colectiva que señala comunalidades, divergencias y resistencias transversalizables. Esto permite ofrecer otro punto de partida analítico para evadir los vínculos artificialmente fragmentados entre investigadores-datos-participantes-teoría, usualmente poco cuestionados (Mazzei 2013; Mazzei y Jackson 2017; St. Pierre 2018). Íntegramente, este texto es apenas un "agenciamiento colectivo de enunciación, de actos y de enunciados, transformaciones incorporales que se atribuyen a los cuerpos" (Deleuze y Guattari 2002, 11).

Soltamos el control completo sobre la búsqueda de códigos, categorías y su saturación en las entrevistas. Nos dejamos afectar por sus choques, perforaciones y heridas; por sus escapes agentivos de supervivencia académica y humana. El relato sobre el fenómeno de "exclusión epistémica" emergió entre confluencias transversales a las entrevistas y a nuestras prácticas como hacedoras de conocimiento y transgredió las directrices del análisis crítico del discurso. Tomando como metodología referente la producción narrativa (Balasch y Montenegro 2003), usamos como disparadores las propias experiencias de exclusión experimentadas por las autoras, actualizadas en las repercusiones afectivo-corporales emergidas de sus intra-acciones (Barad 2007) con la data. No obstante, en algunas de sus partes, el relato es fiel a citas textuales de las entrevistas (con comillas). De este modo, es precisamente esa posibilidad de encarnación de lo múltiple lo que permite su potencia y la identificación de otras personas, más allá de las autoras y entrevistadas, con el relato. Siguiendo a Lipton (2020), existe un deslizamiento entre las historias individuales y las colectivas que no debe interpretarse como una homogeneización de la categoría o identidad de "mujer" que ignore otras diferencias. Más bien, la historia de diversas mujeres y hombres tiene el potencial de revelar los poderes estructurales e institucionales que crean y perpetúan una miríada de desigualdades de género, raza e injusticias sociales (Lipton 2020), en este caso, en dos mundos académicos.

Exclusión epistémica

Existen diferentes formas de nombrar lo que en este artículo denominamos exclusión epistémica. En general, la literatura coincide en atribuir la génesis de esta conceptualización al trabajo de Miranda Fricker sobre la "injusticia epistémica". Fricker (2007) introdujo el concepto para referirse al fenómeno de experimentar, como sujeto epistémico, las desventajas de encontrarse en una relación subordinada por prejuicios de identidad (género, etnia u otros). Según la autora, las injusticias epistémicas surgen de la distribución desigual de reconocimiento y respeto hacia ciertos conocimientos. En este sentido, permea las relaciones de poder dentro de las universidades y las políticas gubernamentales (Blackmore 2022).

Desde que fuera acuñado, el concepto de injusticia epistémica ha estado sujeto a críticas y reformulaciones. Entre ellas destacan los cuestionamientos al foco individual de la teorización, que invitan a ampliar la reflexión al carácter estructural de la injusticia epistémica (López Cardona 2022). En esta línea, Kristie Dotson (2014) opta por hablar de "opresión epistémica" para hacer referencia a la exclusión epistémica persistente que obstaculiza la propia contribución a la producción de conocimientos. La exclusión epistémica, a su vez, se entiende como una infracción injustificada de la agencia epistémica de las y los conocedores. Por último, la agencia epistémica refiere a la capacidad de utilizar persuasivamente recursos epistémicos compartidos dentro de una comunidad dada de conocimiento para participar en la producción de este y, si es necesario, en la revisión de esos mismos recursos (Dotson 2014).

Settles y colegas (2020) teorizan e investigan empíricamente la exclusión epistémica y la entienden como una forma de deslegitimación académica arraigada en prejuicios disciplinarios sobre qué tipos de investigación son valorados, así como prejuicios basados en la identidad social contra individuos de grupos marginados. Puede tener un efecto desproporcionadamente negativo en mujeres y el profesorado de color debido a estereotipos negativos sobre su competencia y su probabilidad de participar en investigaciones fuera de la corriente disciplinaria principal (Settles et al. 2021). En este sentido, refleja tanto un sesgo interpersonal como la opresión estructural (Settles et al. 2020).

En resumen, la exclusión epistémica propone que ciertas corporalidades "en los márgenes", es decir, fuera del centro disciplinario, se ven desproporcionadamente perjudicadas por estándares de desempeño presentados como ostensiblemente objetivos y neutrales (Settles et al. 2021). Esto tiene consecuencias para su contratación, retención y promoción en las universidades. La exclusión epistémica refleja el discurso y las afirmaciones dominantes que definen la investigación "rigurosa" y "legítima", y a las/os investigadoras/os creíbles dentro de una disciplina (Settles et al. 2020). De este modo, actúa como una forma de control e impide que ciertas personas, particularmente de grupos marginados, sean valoradas como conocedores legítimos y creíbles.

Debatiendo algunas formas de exclusión epistémica del conocimiento feminista

En esta sección nos proponemos un diálogo entre el relato que abre este texto y la literatura sobre exclusión epistémica para articular tres nudos: la historicidad que permea el trabajo de los y las académicas entrevistadas; el impacto material y afectivo de la exclusión en sus trayectorias laborales y sus posibilidades epistémicas; y la lucha por la validación del conocimiento feminista o de género.

Los estudios de género y feministas en Latinoamérica tienen la particularidad de haberse originado -y fortalecido- a la par con los movimientos de mujeres o feministas en contextos de dictaduras y autoritarismo (Carosio 2019; Valdés 2007). Así, desde su origen, la investigación y la militancia feminista han estado intrínsecamente relacionadas (Carosio 2019). Según Pereira (2015), este compromiso declarado de las académicas feministas por articular la investigación académica y la acción política ha sido invocado por otros académicos como prueba (entre otras) de que su trabajo no podía, y no debía, tomarse en serio como erudición "propiamente dicha". Los estudios feministas y de género, históricamente, han sido afectados por prejuicios disciplinarios sobre qué tipo de investigación es valorada (Settles et al. 2020).

En el caso chileno, la producción de conocimiento sobre estos temas tiene un origen en los movimientos sociales antes que en los espacios académicos. Las feministas se hicieron académicas después, desde la militancia, en los años 70–80 (Valdés 2007). En los años 90, con el avance de las políticas públicas sobre género e hitos clave como los acuerdos internacionales de CEDAW y Beijing, se pasa a una búsqueda de equidad e igualdad de oportunidades donde prima un interés en conocimientos de tipo instrumental-tecnológico. Luego, ya en la década de los 2000 comienza a emerger con más fuerza el debate en torno a la diferencia y la diversidad con miradas teóricas diferentes que proponen, entre otras, distinguir entre sexo y género desde la crítica cultural (Valdés 2007). En el caso argentino, existieron diversos grupos feministas y de mujeres en la década de los 60 y comienzo de los 70, en plena dictadura (Carosio 2019). Ya en los 80, la Facultad de Psicología de la Universidad de Buenos Aires abrió el ciclo de una Carrera Interdisciplinaria de Estudios de la Mujer (Carosio 2019). A partir de los 90, se crearon iniciativas en diversas universidades y desde entonces se han ido desarrollando estudios feministas, de género y de las mujeres en diversas universidades, que se concentran mayoritariamente en investigación y formación de posgrado (Carosio 2019). En la actualidad los estudios de género están notoriamente instalados en universidades en cada país (Valdés 2007), sobre todo en los estudios de posgrado (Carosio 2019), pero no necesariamente han permeado las otras disciplinas científicas ni la formación profesional más allá de cursos optativos en carreras sociales (Valdés 2007).

El relato permite entrever que en ambos países la construcción de conocimiento feminista y de género en la academia se encuentra profundamente interpelado por los movimientos estudiantiles feministas de la última década. La historicidad de la producción de conocimientos feministas y de género aparece en el relato marcada por la idea de un *antes* y un *después*. El *antes* está asociado, generalmente, a las experiencias de exclusión más fuertes de la producción propia o de enfrentamientos más duros con temas de validación y financiamiento de la producción del conocimiento.

En el *después* aparece un halo de mayor valoración, de menos exclusión marcado principalmente por la presencia de temáticas de género o feministas en un estatus distinto, debido en gran medida a la presión de los movimientos feministas estudiantiles. A partir de estos hitos la institucionalidad de las universidades (no todas) se abre a incorporar temas de género y a crear políticas e iniciativas institucionales para abordar la violencia de género. Pero se trata de un después con gusto amargo, porque ahí, detrás de la supuesta aceptación e importancia de los estudios de género y de los feminismos, se oculta la desconfianza, la exclusión, la duda, el peligro, el miedo. Se trata de un después marcado por formas más sutiles de devaluación y con ello de exclusión de los conocimientos feministas, que todavía tienen que camuflarse o son relegados a un plano más bien discursivo o de nicho, muy vinculado (negativamente) al activismo, como una forma de exclusión arraigada en prejuicios disciplinarios sobre qué tipos de investigación son valorados, pero también basada en prejuicios respecto de la identidad social de quien realiza la investigación (Settles et al. 2020). El conocimiento feminista y de género es excluido -antes y después- en función de quiénes lo realizan (asociadas a un activismo mal visto) y de qué estudian (erudición poco rigurosa e ilegítima, en parte por quienes la realizan también). Por lo mismo, aún no es posible transversalizar dicho conocimiento en el currículo de las carreras. Se trata de un reconocimiento parcial (Pereira 2012), que todavía no es considerado conocimiento propiamente académico (Pereira 2015).

Tanto en el ámbito chileno como en el argentino, como parte de esta historicidad, está la instalación del uso de la categoría "género". Según Tarducci (2010), se trata de un concepto creado por el feminismo como parte del lenguaje que todo grupo revolucionario crea en su actuar. El uso de género ha sido bastante teorizado (Pereira 2012), pero a la luz del relato y de la historicidad de la instalación de los estudios feministas y de género, la pregunta que se hace Tarducci (2010) nos parece fundamental: ¿Lo empleamos como concepto intelectual aséptico o como una herramienta política, como un motor del cambio señalando las relaciones de poder que implica? Según Valdés (2007), en el caso chileno, la transición a usar el concepto de género desde los 90 hasta la actualidad ha sido criticado por instalarse como una categoría usualmente despolitizada y desvinculada de los movimientos feministas. No obstante, el relato -y la pregunta de Tarducci (2010)- también nos invitan a pensar que se trata de una herramienta política, de una estrategia. Como otros "antes y después" que emergen en el relato, parece ser que en la actualidad en ambos contextos se estaría abriendo la posibilidad de hablar más directamente de feminismo, aunque todavía para muchas disimular o camuflarse sigue siendo una estrategia de supervivencia clave.

El cruce del relato con la literatura también permite dar cuenta del impacto material y afectivo de la exclusión epistémica en las trayectorias laborales y en las posibilidades de construcción de conocimiento. A pesar del antes y el después referido anteriormente, persiste la sensación de devaluación del quehacer académico. Interesante en este punto es que este no se presenta siempre como una vulneración directa y explícita a las personas, sino como violencia sutil. Esta se caracteriza por no ser fácil de percibir, identificar y nombrar puesto que se realiza mediante prácticas que parecieran no tener la intención de causar daño (Castelao-Huerta 2022). Así, el relato arroja luces de que la exclusión epistémica experimentada por las "personas de género" (Henderson 2019) de este estudio es una forma de violencia, a veces, sutil o "de pasillo" (Pereira 2012).

Además, el relato permite visualizar que la exclusión epistémica parece más bien alojada en lo estructural, ya sea en la imposibilidad de transversalizar la perspectiva de género, donde los cursos siguen siendo optativos y la investigación se construye en los umbrales de la academia (Muñoz-García y Trebisacce, 2024). Pero también se expresa en las dificultades para conseguir financiamiento y construir una trayectoria académica en estos temas, contrario a lo que reporta Pereira (2015, 2017) para el caso de Portugal.

El relato también da cuenta del cansancio y la fatiga que produce la lucha contra la exclusión epistémica. Esto se agrava en el marco de una academia neoliberal y generizada, con formas de organización de larga data que agudizan desventajas específicas que afectan a las académicas y se basan en la división sexual del trabajo académico (Mandiola, Ríos y Varas 2019), por ejemplo, como muestra el relato, relegándolas a los trabajos considerados "de cuidado" y alejándolas de las posiciones de liderazgo. La situación descrita afecta de sobremanera a las "personas de género", un constructo que se sustenta en la precariedad y la inestabilidad tanto de los conocimientos como de las condiciones de empleo (Henderson 2019). Precisamente se trata de un grupo, como otros en los márgenes, sobre el cual la exclusión epistémica tiene un efecto desproporcionadamente negativo (Settles et al. 2021). En este escenario, una estrategia de supervivencia para muchas es recurrir aún más a "blindarse" detrás de la productividad neoliberal. Lo anterior revela una trampa interesante que posibilita una existencia de ser y hacer feminismos en la academia en clave neoliberal (Mandiola, 2024).[2]

Sin embargo, como ilumina el relato, paralelo al refugio en la productividad neoliberal está el trabajo activista. Este trabajo revitaliza, pero, a la vez, genera círculos recursivos que tributan más aún al cansancio: por un lado, para poder activar tranquilamente, hay que ser aún más productiva, pero, a la vez, invertir tiempo en activar deja menos tiempo para esa producción (Pereira 2016). Por otro lado, el activismo aumenta el cuestionamiento al conocimiento producido por estas personas, lo que implica aún más trabajo de negociación sobre su estatus epistémico (Pereira 2016) y aumenta el agotamiento. En este contexto también aparece la invocación regular, en diferentes sitios o situaciones y por parte de diferentes personas (colegas, superiores e incluso estudiantes, como muestra el relato), de la creencia de que el activismo equivale a una contaminación inaceptable de la práctica académica (socavando el valor y el rigor de las reivindicaciones de conocimiento) (Pereira 2015).

Todo esto da lugar a lo que Pereira (2019) llama una atmósfera enfermiza, un estado compartido de agotamiento y alienación que no es una experiencia individual. Se trata de un clima que enferma a todos y todas, aunque puede afectar a unas personas más que otras dependiendo de condiciones de trabajo, temperamento o generación (Pereira 2019). Henderson (2019) en su trabajo da cuenta de que varias "personas de género" afirmaron sentirse aisladas y solas, inadaptadas en sus departamentos. Según la autora, las consecuencias de este aislamiento incluyen la falta de comunidad y de compromiso crítico, pero también pueden llevarlas a abandonar por completo el mundo académico. De este modo, la exclusión epistémica que sufren las personas de género del relato actúa como una forma de control que impide que sean valoradas como conocedoras legítimas y creíbles.

Finalmente, la exclusión epistémica convive con la constante tensión sobre su validación y legitimación y las formas de hacer y ser en ese conocimiento. Desde las epistemologías feministas existe un largo debate sobre la marginalidad del conocimiento feminista en los espacios académicos y las complejidades de posicionarlo como un conocimiento validado y legitimado teniendo que responder a estructuras de credibilidad y legitimidad del conocimiento imitando estructuras de poder y orden social sin someterlas a cuestionamiento (Fricker 2007). Se trata de prácticas "que operan como estrategias de legitimación del orden disciplinario y masculino vigente" (Ríos, Mandiola y Varas 2017). Lo anterior nos invita a preguntarnos sobre las prácticas y materialidades que entretejen su exclusión (Maffía 2006) y que posicionan a determinadas investigadoras como "conocedoras putativas" en las universidades, a quienes se las ve participando sin ser legitimadas como conocedoras (Code 2014). En este sentido, como señala Code (2014), la marginalidad del conocimiento tiene muchos vértices. Significa no solo ser excluida como conocedora, sino también la negación de la credibilidad de procesos y prácticas epistémicas para construir conocimientos, y entre otras, la desacreditación en el marco de una determinada fórmula hegemónica o conjunto de directrices para lo que cuenta como conocimiento genuino. Algo relevante que aparece en el relato es que aunque puede parecer que estos aspectos operan de forma aislada en algunos casos, a menudo se superponen o se entrelazan para silenciar, ignorar o desacreditar ciertas voces y puntos de vista (Tuana y Sullivan 2007). Por lo tanto, una construcción de conocimiento responsable y ética implica reflexionar sobre nuestras decisiones de qué conocimientos consideramos posibles, pero al mismo tiempo, a quiénes visibilizamos en esas decisiones (Grasswick 2011).

Aperturas feministas neo-materialistas para incubar conocimientos en resistencia

El artículo muestra la utilidad de la exclusión epistémica para vigilar críticamente cómo se estratifican y sedimentan los modos de construcción de conocimiento. Nuestras enunciaciones sólo especifican y pertenecen a contextos específicos, y son, por tanto, escasamente estables y trascendentes. A cambio, nuestra decisión metodológica de contar una historia para inaugurar este texto fertiliza otros senderos para resistir haciendo conocimiento feminista latinoamericano, uno que usualmente ha estado en el umbral de la academia (Muñoz-García y Trebisacce 2024).

Precisamente, contar historias y dejarnos llevar hilando sus vaivenes ficcionales destaca como método y modalidad fundamental del quehacer crítico feminista y es punto de partida para imaginar nuevas racionalidades y éticas (Davies y Gannon 2006; Bhavnani y Haraway 1994). Por lo tanto, el uso empírico de historias –derivadas y no de experiencias o biografías individualizables– se instala como estrategia clave para hacer conocimiento objetivamente situado (Beniscelli-Contreras y Gómez-Guinart 2023; Haraway 1995). Esto exige un compromiso epistémico ineludible: insistir en métodos que den cuenta de las complejidades de los fenómenos e, igualmente, se mantengan sensibles a las derivas de sus materializaciones y modos de re/producción. Así, el método de contar y crear historias es suscitar rebeldías e incomodidades, cambios súbitos o ínfimos desplazamientos nacidos desde lo íntimamente probable, y/o de nuevas fuerzas potencialmente vinculables a otras ya en insurrección (Davies y Gannon 2006; Stengers 2018; Haraway 2019; Osgood y Robinson 2019).

Sin temor a equivocarnos, el ponderar estas ranuras onto-epistémicas no niega otros esfuerzos reparatorios socioeconómicos o de corte cultural. Los activismos feministas y antirracistas han demostrado que la capacidad de trenzar historias funciona como intersticio micropolítico restaurador de cuerpos arruinados por violencias segregativas de toda índole (Anzaldúa 2015; Sharma y Nijjar 2018). Ensayar este método en arenas académicas inmersas en contextos de profundas desigualdades significa hacerse cargo del hecho de que algunos cuerpos no tendrán la opción de renunciar a las calles e intenciona encaminarnos hacia balances estratégicos entre luchas macropolíticas y batallas micropolíticas (Gandarias 2019; Ziga 2014). Encontrar formas de entregar poder a voces colectivas estimula la articulación de creatividades en la elaboración de teorías hábiles para puentear presentes fallidos y porvenires aparentemente imposibles sin sentarse a esperar certezas positivistas o reconciliaciones dialécticas (Braidotti 2022; Grossberg 2012). En definitiva, siempre resultará esperanzador aventurarse en investigaciones críticas que espanten los pesimismos del presente para dar la bienvenida a lo emergente. Tal y como apunta Grossberg (2012, 116): "Precisamente porque el presente no tenía que ser como es, el futuro puede ir hacia otro lugar que aquel donde parece dirigirse". Pareciera esta una clara invitación a favor de la justicia epistémica.

Fernanda Rojas-Müller es estudiante del doctorado en antropología de la Pontificia Universidad Católica de Chile y magíster en estudios de género por la London School of Economics and Political Science. Se especializa en temas de género y masculinidades. Tiene experiencia en investigación, docencia y comunicaciones. Su email es frojasmuller@uc.cl y su ORCID es https://orcid.org/0000-0003-2111-8502.

Ana Luisa Muñoz-García es profesora asociada de la facultad de educación de la Pontificia Universidad Católica de Chile, académica y feminista. Su investigación se ha enfocado en educación, políticas de conocimiento, feminismos, género e internacionalización. Su email es aumunoz@uc.cl y su ORCID es http://orcid.org/0000-0001-5639-2777.

Kyuttzza Gómez-Guinart es candidata a doctora en educación por la Pontificia Universidad Católica de Chile, magíster en educación por la misma universidad y psicóloga por la Universidad de La Habana. Sus intereses e investigación, ambos antirracistas, se dirigen hacia la producción de conocimiento crítico en ciencias sociales desde los nuevos materialismos y las epistemologías queer y feministas. Su email es kgomez3@uc.cl y su ORCID es https://orcid.org/0000-0002-0456-6824.

Agradecimientos
Este artículo es resultado del proyecto ANID/FONDECYT/REGULAR 1210477, "Mapeando la construcción de conocimiento desde una perspectiva de género."

Notas
1. Las entrevistas fueron grabadas y transcritas resguardando el anonimato de las y los participantes. Luego fueron leídas por las tres autoras y dialogadas en varias reuniones, que a su vez fueron grabadas y transcritas como data de investigación.
2. Agradecer la discusión vibrante y apasionada de Marcela Mandiola, Catalina Trebisacce, Gabriela Bard Wigdor, Vir Cano y Hillary Hiner para abrir tensiones necesarias sobre la cooptación neoliberal de los feminismos en las universidades y el uso de estrategias neoliberales para existir y construir conocimiento feminista.

Trabajos citados

Acosta, Marina. 2020. "Activismo Feminista en Instagram. El caso de la campaña nacional por el derecho al aborto legal, seguro y gratuito en Argentina." *Perspectivas de la comunicación* 13 (1): 29–46.

Abbate, Florencia. 2018. "Procesos de subjetivación feminista en las movilizaciones #NiUnaMenos en Argentina." *Letras Femeninas* 43 (2): 147–158.

Anzaldúa, Gloria. 2015. "Light in the Dark/Luz." En *Lo Oscuro: Rewriting Identity, Spirituality, Reality,* editado por Ana Louise Keating. Duke University Press.

Bacevic, Jana. 2023. "Epistemic Injustice and Epistemic Positioning: Towards an Intersectional Political Economy." *Current Sociology* 71 (6): 1122–1140.

Balasch, Marcel y Marisela Montenegro. 2003. "Una propuesta metodológica desde la epistemología de los conocimientos situados: las producciones narrativas." *Encuentros en psicología social* 1 (3): 44–48.

Barad, Karen. 2007. *Meeting the Universe Halfway: Quantum Physics and the Entanglement of Matter and Meaning.* Durham-London: Duke University Press.

Beniscelli-Contreras, L. y K. Gómez-Guinart. 2023. "Erotic Pedagogy Towards a Desiring Conviviality: A Visual Collective Biography Joining Island and Continent." *Globalisation, Societies and Education* 21 (4): 450–468. https://doi.org/10.1080/14767724.2023.2241200.

Blackmore, Jill. 2022. "Governing Knowledge in the Entrepreneurial University: A Feminist Account of Structural, Cultural and Political Epistemic Injustice." *Critical Studies in Education* 63 (5): 622–638.

Braidotti, Rosi. 2022. "The Virtual as Affirmative Praxis: A Neo-Materialist Approach." *Humanities* 11 (3): 1–13.

Carosio, Alba. 2019. "Sin disociar la investigación de la lucha: feminismos militantes en la academia latinoamericana y caribeña." *CS* 29: 139–162.

Castelao-Huerta, Isaura. 2022. "Recelos y envidias: violencias sutiles de género en la academia neoliberalizada." *Debate Feminista* 65: 1–34.

Code, Lorraine. 2014. "Ignorance, Injustice and the Politics of Knowledge." *Australian Feminist Studies* 29 (80): 148–160.

CNN. 2024. "El Gobierno de Javier Milei prohíbe el uso del lenguaje inclusivo en documentos oficiales en Argentina." Publicado en CNN, 27 de febrero.

Davies, Bronwyn y Susanne Gannon. 2006. *Doing Collective Biography: Investigating the Production of Subjectivity.* Maidenhead: Open University Press.

Deleuze, Gilles y Félix Guattari. 2002. *Mil Mesetas. Capitalismo y Esquizofrenia.* 5a. ed. Valencia: Pre-Textos.

de Fina Gonzalez, Débora y Francisca Figueroa Vidal. 2019. "Nuevos 'campos de acción política' feminista: una mirada a las recientes movilizaciones en Chile." *Revista Punto Género* 11 (julio): 51–72.

Dotson, Kristie. 2014. "Conceptualizing Epistemic Oppression." *Social Epistemology* 28 (2): 115–138.

Fricker, Miranda. 2007. *Epistemic Injustice: Power and Ethics in Knowing*. Oxford: Oxford University Press.

Forstenzer, Nicole. 2019. "Feminismos en el Chile post-dictadura: hegemonías y marginalidades." *Revista Punto Género* 11 (julio): 34–50.

Gandarias, Itziar. 2019. "Resistir desde la vulnerabilidad: narrativas de mujeres subsaharianas sobre su tránsito hacia Europa." *Papeles del CEIC* 1: 1–18.

Grasswick, Heidi. 2011. "Introduction: Feminist Epistemology and Philosophy of Science in the Twenty-First Century." En *Feminist Epistemology and Philosophy of Science: Power in Knowledge,* editado por Heidi Grasswick. Londres: Springer.

Grossberg, Lawrence. 2012. *Estudios culturales en tiempo futuro: cómo es el trabajo intelectual que requiere el mundo de hoy*. Buenos Aires: Siglo XXI Editores.

Haraway, Donna. 1995. "Conocimientos situados: la cuestión científica en el feminismo y el privilegio de la perspectiva parcial." En *Ciencia, cyborgs y mujeres: la reinvención de la naturaleza*. España: Cátedra.

Haraway, Donna. 2019. *Seguir con el problema: generar parentesco en Chthuluceno*. Bilbao: Consonni.

Henderson, Emily. 2019. "On Being the 'Gender Person' in an Academic Department: Constructions, Configurations and Implications." *Journal of Gender Studies* 28 (6): 730–742.

Bhavnani, Kum-Kum y Donna Haraway. 1994. "Shifting the Subject: A Conversation between Kum-Kum Bhavnani and Donna Haraway, 12 April 1993, Santa Cruz, California." *Feminism & Psychology* 4 (1): 19–39.

Lather, Patti. 2000. "Against Empathy, Voice and Authenticity." En *Voice in Qualitative Inquiry: Challenging Conventional, Interpretive, and Critical Conceptions in Qualitative Research,* editado por Alecia Jackson y Lisa Mazzei. Londres: Routledge.

Lenguita, Paula. 2021. "Rebelión de las pibas: trazos de una memoria feminista en Argentina." *Ventana* 6 (54): 48–73.

Lipton, Briony. 2020. *Academic Women in Neoliberal Times*. 1ra. ed. Springer International Publishing.

López Cardona, Diana. 2022. "Injusticias epistémicas y colonialidad del poder: aportes para pensar la descolonialidad desde América Latina." *Estudios de Filosofía* 66: 79–96.

MacLure, Maggie. 2013. "Researching Without Representation? Language and Materiality in Post-Qualitative Methodology." *International Journal of*

Qualitative Studies in Education 26 (6): 658–667. https://doi.org/10.1080/09518398.2013.788755.

Maffía, Diana. 2006. "El vínculo crítico entre género y ciencia." *Clepsydra* 5: 37–57.

Mandiola, Marcela, Nicolás Ríos, y Alejandro Varas. 2019. "'Hay un tema que no hemos conversado': la cassata como organización académica generizada en las universidades chilenas." *Pensamiento Educativo* 56 (1): 1–16.

Mandiola, Marcela. 2024. "Feminismos Neoliberales y la Agenda de Género en Chile." En *Feminismos en el Umbral de la Academia*, editado por Ana Luisa Muñoz-García y Catalina Trebisacce Marchand, 139–170. 1ra. ed. Santiago: Ediciones UC.

Mazzei, Lisa. 2013. "Materialist Mappings of Knowing in Being: Researchers Constituted in the Production of Knowledge." *Gender and Education* 25 (6): 776–785.

Mazzei, Lisa y Alecia Jackson. 2017. "Voice in the Agentic Assemblage." *Educational Philosophy and Theory* 49 (11): 1090–1098.

Meganoticias. 2024. "'No sirve absolutamente para nada': Gobierno argentino cierra Instituto contra Discriminación, Xenofobia y Racismo." *Meganoticias*, 22 de febrero.

Miranda Leibe, L. y Beatriz Roque López. 2020. "El mayo estudiantil feminista de 2018 en la Pontificia Universidad Católica de Chile: 'La revolución es nuestra.'" *Educación y Educadores* 23 (1): 89–102.

Muñoz-Garcia, A. L. y C. Trebisacce Marchand. 2024. "La Insistencia de los Feminismos." En *Feminismos en el Umbral de la Academia*, editado por A. L. Muñoz-Garcia y C. Trebisacce Marchand, 21–55. Santiago: Ediciones UC.

Osgood, Jayne y Kerry Robinson. 2019. *Feminists Researching Gendered Childhoods: Generative Entanglements*. Bloomsbury Academic.

Pereira, Maria do Mar. 2012. "'Feminist Theory Is Proper Knowledge, but …': The Status of Feminist Scholarship in the Academy." *Feminist Theory* 13 (3): 283–303.

Pereira, Maria do Mar. 2015. "Higher Education Cutbacks and the Reshaping of Epistemic Hierarchies: An Ethnography of the Case of Feminist Scholarship." *Sociology* 49 (2): 287–304.

Pereira, Maria do Mar. 2016. "Struggling within and beyond the Performative University: Articulating Activism and Work in an 'Academia without Walls.'" *Women's Studies International Forum* 54: 100–110.

Pereira, Maria do Mar. 2017. *Power, Knowledge and Feminist Scholarship*. Routledge.

Pereira, Maria do Mar. 2019. "'You Can Feel the Exhaustion in the Air around You': The Mood of Contemporary Universities and Its Impact on Feminist Scholarship." *Ex Aequo* 39: 171–186.

Schuster, Sofía, Antonia Santos, Lucía Miranda, Beatriz Roque, Javiera Arce-Riffo y Evelyne Medel. 2019. "Una mirada al movimiento feminista en Chile del año 2018: hitos, agenda y desafíos." *Iberoamericana* 19 (72): 223–246.

Settles, Isis H., Leah R. Warner, NiCole T. Buchanan y Martinque K. Jones. 2020. "Understanding Psychology's Resistance to Intersectionality Theory Using a Framework of Epistemic Exclusion and Invisibility." *Journal of Social Issues* 76 (4): 796–813.

Settles, Isis, Martinque Jones, NiCole Buchanan y Kristie Dotson. 2021. "Epistemic Exclusion: Scholar(Ly) Devaluation That Marginalizes Faculty of Color." *Journal of Diversity in Higher Education* 14 (4): 493–507.

Sharma, Sanjaym y Nijjar Jasbinder. 2018. "The Racialized Surveillant Assemblage: Islam and the Fear of Terrorism." *Popular Communication* 16 (1): 72–85.

Stengers, Isabelle. 2018. *Another Science Is Possible. A Manifesto for Slow Science*. Cambridge: Polity Press.

Silva Hope, M., A. L. Muñoz-Garcia y L. Medina Morales. 2024. "Unmothering the Conversation on Gender in Academia." *Journal of Women and Gender in Higher Education* 17 (2): 79–99. https://doi.org/10.1080/26379112.2024.2308676.

St. Pierre, Elizabeth y Alecia Jackson. 2014. "Qualitative Data Analysis After Coding." *Qualitative Inquiry* 20 (6): 715–719.

St. Pierre, Elizabeth. 2018. "Writing Post Qualitative Inquiry." *Qualitative Inquiry* 24 (9): 603–608.

Tarducci, Mónica. 2010. "La profesora feminista como agente de transformación." En *Aproximaciones críticas a las prácticas teórico-políticas del feminismo latinoamericano*, editado por Yuderkys Espinosa Miñoso, 1a ed. Buenos Aires: En la Frontera.

Tuana, Nancy y Shannon Sullivan. 2007. *Race and Epistemologies of Ignorance*. Albany, NY: State University of New York Press.

Trebisacce, Catalina y Paloma Dulbecco. 2021. "Feminismos universitarios en la elaboración de los protocolos contra las violencias (2014-2019)." En *RUGE: El género en las Universidades*, editado por Ana Martin, 69–95. Ciudad Autónoma de Buenos Aires: RUGE-CIN.

Torlucci, Sandra, Verónica Cruz y Vanesa Vasquez-Laba. 2023. "Género y universidades: ¿dónde nos encontramos?." En *RUGE. La formación de formadorxs en género en las universidades*, editado por Paula Torricella, María Flor Gianfrini y Candela Luquet, 5–16. Buenos Aires: RUGE-CIN.

Valdés, Teresa. 2007. "Estudios de género: una mirada evaluativa desde el Cono Sur." En *Género, mujeres y saberes en América Latina: entre el movimiento social, la academia y el Estado*, editado por Luz Gabriela Arango y Yolanda

Puyana. Bogotá: Universidad Nacional de Colombia.
Williams, Jamillah, Lisa Singh y Naomi Mezey. 2019. "#MeToo as Catalyst: A Glimpse into 21st Century Activism." *University of Chicago Legal Forum* 22.
Ziga, Itziar. 2014. "¿El corto verano del transfeminismo?" En *Transfeminismos: Epistemes, fricciones y flujos*. Txalaparta.

The Ice Again: Epistemic Exclusion of Feminisms in Academic Spaces

Fernanda Rojas-Müller, Ana Luisa Muñoz-García, and Kyuttzza Gómez-Guinart

Translated by Camila Valle

Abstract: In this essay, we ask ourselves about the material conditions that enable the creation of feminist knowledge, its advances and marginalizations interwoven in neoliberal, racist, and heterocispatriarchal academia. Based on a study of gender and knowledge from a feminist perspective (2021–24), this article elaborates a collective account from researchers on the epistemic exclusion of gender and feminisms in Chilean and Argentinian academic spaces. This account, narrated in the first person and constructed out of quotations from researchers of gender and feminism, moves between the individual and the collective, politicizing gender issues to concretize the forms of epistemic exclusion in a delocalized way. Not only is this exclusion manifested in direct violations against people, but it is also structurally located, such as in the impossibility of mainstreaming frameworks of gender into curricula and in the difficulties of obtaining funding or negatively associating these perspectives with activism. Amid the international advance of the far right, it is urgent to discuss the epistemic status of feminist knowledge in academia. **Keywords:** epistemic exclusion, feminisms, gender, academia, knowledge

The Ice Again

She opens her email. There's a new email in her inbox. "They're inflating grades abroad." She freezes. Regrets having proudly shared that she had done very well on the first batch of assignments. Her body brings her back to the time, a few years earlier, when she had made the mistake of showing her thesis on women and history. "It should be titled *women*, not *woman*." She felt rage, especially because he was right.

She didn't tell him that she graduated with honors. He wouldn't understand. "You seem like such a smart girl, why would you dedicate yourself to this when you could be doing other things?" Much less could she tell him that she is a feminist, what kind of work she does, what she spends her time on, what she reads, and what she asks herself. She knows it will be seen "as an activist issue or an unserious issue." She chooses instead to talk about "gender," that "kind of label that, even with all its difficulties, presents itself as more scientific than saying 'I'm a feminist.'" Feminists are those who march, shout, and protest. Academia and activism are two separate things.

A few years later, back at the end of the world, her body will relive, several times over, the coldness of that email. She'll go over it in her mind. She'll feel rage and sorrow. Partly, she'll give up. "What's wrong? Are you a lesbian? Are you angry at men?" She learns to *conceal*. Her "research projects are going to have to be shielded." At the same time, she will mobilize, she will fight to establish topics that seem vital to her, she will go to the events her students invite her to, she will challenge herself with readings and projects, she will write, she will go to conferences, she will publish, she will produce, produce, produce, produce. She will be the most productive worker in neoliberal academia. Like others, she will also take charge of the reproductive and domestic work of her department, the kind for which others—almost always men—assume she is better equipped. The kind she knows is nothing but another way of adding obstacles to her career.

A part of her is tired of fighting, of it always being so difficult, of feeling like she lives on the margins, of being afraid, of feeling belittled, of being "the crazy one, the weird one." A part of her is tired of the constant battle. Always the worst schedule, the elective that they more or less let you have, "like an additional load, an extension of activism to continue raising these issues." Always so many meetings. Having to "try so hard in discussions, in negotiations, in strategies, in argumentation." She thinks of colleagues who have been ignored, who have been banned from teaching, who have been thrown out. She feels the ice of that "horrific marginality." She has spent years "almost declaring, 'yes, I am doing this; yes, this is research,'" only for a colleague to invite her to one of his classes "for half an hour to explain the framework of gender." Half an hour. *THE* framework of gender.

In line to buy coffee, she hears some colleagues say that, with the feminist student movements and the entry of activism into academia, the issue has been overcome. Once again, ice in her body. These are, undoubtedly, important achievements. They "shifted the importance given to gender in the institutionality of universities." But, overcome? She remembers that boss who told her that "it's out of fashion now, nobody wants to take up gender issues anymore."

How can it be overcome, she thinks, if there are still areas of knowledge where gender cannot enter, where those who work on gender are freaks, where they are asked if what they really research is economics or law or history or philosophy or whatever. How can it be overcome if there is still no legitimacy, if "we still do not have the right to be here." She thinks of those students who once had the audacity to tell her that mobilizing, doing, studying, researching gender is fine, "but not in the university environment, science is something else, the production of knowledge has to happen through other content." "As if gender were just another topic that can be added or removed."

The calendar notification on her phone goes off. She has another meeting. She crosses the courtyard to her boss's office. She can't stop going over it all in her head. "Now it's frowned upon not to be a feminist," but the changes "are not so radical." We are still on the margins. She thinks about how she herself devalued it at the time. How she eventually realized that it wasn't her own madness, "that it really is a serious, systematic area of research, with its own specific history and knowledge production." She thinks, too, about what she has heard her peers say, all those who today—congratulations—declare themselves feminists. She thinks, proudly, how, despite everything, among many and in many places, "they have been pushing the limits of what is possible," and she smiles.

She is ushered into the office. Her boss tells her that, *unfortunately*, she will not be in charge of the department's gender commission. "The position was given to a man who does not work on gender, who does not even know what it is, who still thinks it is the material from which his clothes are made."

The ice again.

Introduction

The story with which we begin this text was constructed from interviews conducted between 2021 and 2022 with twenty-five academics who work on gender issues in Chile (13) and Argentina (12), as part of a (still ongoing) project on the politics and policies of knowledge and gender in higher education. At a time where feminist movements in recent years have strongly shaped government agendas, especially those of educational systems, the project, led by one of the authors of this piece, investigates what knowledge about gender and feminisms informs gender policies in higher education and how these gender policies are permeating universities. We believe in the urgency of this research as right-wing ideologies consolidate around the world and in Latin America. With the election and inauguration of Javier Milei as president, Argentina has suffered the elimination of institutions that monitor human rights and democratize knowledge. In Chile, José Antonio Kast made it to the second round of the presidential election in 2021 with a platform that promised to eliminate the Ministry of Women and Gender Equality, among other measures.

With this context in our bodies, the initial account invites us to delve deeper into how feminist knowledge has been excluded in the Chilean and Argentinian academic sphere. To do so, we focus on untangling three knots: the historicity of feminist academic work, the material and affective impact of epistemic exclusion on the career paths of academics, and the struggle for the validation of feminist or gender knowledge.

We have organized this essay as follows. First, we propose the production of fictional stories as an original tool to investigate the actualization of a phenomenon of interest; in this case, the exclusion of feminist knowledge in academic settings. Second, we describe the features of a neoliberal academic context that promotes the exclusion of both this knowledge and those who produce it. Third, we introduce the concept of epistemic exclusion. Fourth, we generate a dialogue between the story and the literature to pull at the three aforementioned knots. Finally, we insist on slipping through neomaterialist and feminist proposals to resist the interpellations of "unserious research" with which feminist and gender knowledge is harassed in Latin American academic settings. Doing so is an act of vindication by those of us who, from the academy, put our bodies at the service of rights, freedoms, and justice.

Feminist Emergencies and Resistances in the Face of the Far Right

Feminist movements have been fundamental to understanding the context of this research and text. In the last ten years, Chile and Argentina have undergone processes that have shaped universities and research in important ways, stirred by movements inherited from long feminist histories in both countries.

In Chile, what was dubbed the Feminist May took over the political and media agenda in 2018 (de Fina Gonzalez and Figueroa Vidal 2019). It marked a milestone in the public debate, with students focusing their demands on the various forms of violence they were subjected to in institutions of higher education and calling on authorities to address and resolve cases of sexual violence and harassment (Schuster et al. 2019). Thus, inspired by the history of previous student mobilizations in Chile, the international feminist upheaval of #MeToo (Williams et al. 2019), and #NiUnaMenos in 2015 in Argentina (Forstenzer 2019), students occupied universities, high schools, and streets with feminist demands. Discussions went beyond the walls of institutions and moved into public policy through various initiatives. Since then, governmental and institutional documents, policies, programs, and laws on gender issues in higher education have been published and initiated (Silva Hope et al. 2024). An important achievement was the enactment of Law 21.369 in 2019, which promotes comprehensive policies aimed at preventing, investigating, and punishing gendered harassment, violence, and discrimination. This law, pushed forward by the Network of Women Researchers, has meant that today more than 90 percent of universities have in place comprehensive policies to address violence, gender protocols and/or directions or modules. This, however, has not been without backlash and an anti-gender agenda that has impacted academic freedom and led to the harassment of feminist researchers, including, for example, through requests to different universities for lists of academics who teach or conduct research on "gender ideology" by congresspeople from the right-wing Republican Party of Chile.

In Argentina, the feminist protests that erupted in the last decade with the #NiUnaMenos movement are part of the country's permanent social movements (Lenguita 2021). The 2015 movement put forward public demands against sexist violence, making visible a systemic problem. Among the achievements of the feminist movements of the last decade is the bringing to light of discourses about bodies beyond the gender binary (Abbate 2018), the legalization of abortion in 2018 (Acosta 2020), and the development of protocols against violence (Trebisacce and Dulbecco 2021), among others. In December 2018, Law 27.499, known as the Micaela Law, was passed, which mandates, in its first article, training on gender issues and violence against women for anyone working in the public sphere of the three branches of government. The Interuniversity Gender Network (RUGE) has played an important role in the implementation of this law, particularly in the design and development of institutional policies that contribute to eradicating gender inequalities and violence in the university system (Torlucci et al. 2023).

At the time of writing this essay, a president who calls himself a radical libertarian has closed the Ministry of Women, Gender, and Diversity and the Ministry of Education and Science, Technology, and Innovation, among others. He also froze the 2024 budget for research and doctoral scholarships. Furthermore, since the beginning of his campaign, he has attacked feminist movements and gender-based policies, effusively repudiating policies of equality, prohibiting inclusive language (CNN 2024), and closing the National Institute Against Discrimination, Xenophobia, and Racism, calling it an "absolutely useless" organization staffed by officials of "dubious aptitude" (Meganoticias 2024).

The context of advances and resistance in issues of gender and feminism that we describe allows us to understand the positionality of gender and feminist studies in university spaces. On the one hand, there is headway being made in policies, programs, courses, research, and more that respond to mass demands, but on the other hand, there is a pushback that, though it does not yet seem to be massive, calls into question the advancement of rights and spaces won. Epistemic exclusion navigates this back-and-forth that places this knowledge on the threshold of academia (Muñoz-García and Trebisacce Marchand 2024).

Narration as a Theoretical-Methodological Platform

The stories woven into this retelling were collected through semi-structured interviews[1] conducted between August 2021 and May 2022 with academics in Chile and Argentina. Topics addressed included work trajectories, research assessments, and the development of policies around gender and knowledge in each country.

The first step in moving away from the ideas of representation (Lather 2000) and codification (MacLure 2013; St. Pierre and Jackson 2014) in the research was to enter into a "dialogue with the data." These ideas support one of the traditional forms of analysis in qualitative research: the need to "locate the voice" or "give voice." We then ask ourselves: What does it mean to "give voice" in a scenario where "dialoguing with the data" implies reconnecting with ourselves in the midst of our practices of knowledge creation, training, and history? To whom did we give voice? And how do we represent that voice? (Mazzei 2013). Based primarily on these questions, we chose to construct an inaugural narrative through a collective voice that points out commonalities, divergences, and transversable resistances. This allows us to offer another analytical starting point to avoid the artificially fragmented links between researchers-data-participants-theory, which are often unquestioned (Mazzei 2013; Mazzei and Jackson 2017; St. Pierre 2018). In its entirety, this text is nothing more than a "collective assemblage of enunciation, of acts and of statements, incorporeal transformations that are attributed to bodies" (Deleuze and Guattari 2002, 11).

We let go of the need to search for codes, categories, and their saturation in the interviews. We let ourselves be affected by their shocks, perforations, and wounds; by their agentive escapes of academic and human survival. The story of the phenomenon of "epistemic exclusion" emerged between confluences transversal to the interviews and to our practices as knowledge creators, and transgressed the guidelines of critical discourse analysis. Taking narrative production as a methodological model (Balasch and Montenegro 2003), we used the authors' own experiences of exclusion as impetus, updated in the affective-corporal results of their intra-actions (Barad 2007) with the data. However, in some parts, the narrative is faithful to textual quotations from the interviews (in quotation marks). It is precisely this possibility of embodying multiplicity that allows for its power and the identification of other people, beyond the authors and interviewees, with the story. Following Lipton (2020), there is a slippage between individual and collective stories that should not be interpreted as a homogenization of the category or identity of "woman" that ignores other differences. Rather, the stories of diverse women and men have the potential to reveal the structural and institutional powers that create and perpetuate a myriad of gender, racial, and social inequalities and injustices (Lipton 2020), in this case, in two academic worlds.

Epistemic Exclusion

There are different ways of naming what we call epistemic exclusion in this piece. In general, the literature agrees in attributing the genesis of this conceptualization to Miranda Fricker's work on "epistemic injustice." Fricker (2007) introduced the concept to refer to the phenomenon of experiencing, as an epistemic subject, the disadvantages of finding oneself in a subordinate relationship due to prejudice based on identity (gender, ethnicity, and others). According to the author, epistemic injustices arise from the unequal distribution of recognition and respect for certain knowledge. In this sense, epistemic injustice permeates power relations within universities and government policies (Blackmore 2022).

Since it was first coined, the concept of epistemic injustice has been subject to criticism and reformulation. Among these, the most notable are questions about the individual focus of theorization, which invite us to broaden our reflection to the structural nature of epistemic injustice (López Cardona 2022). Along these lines, Kristie Dotson (2014) chooses to speak of "epistemic oppression" to refer to the persistent epistemic exclusion that hinders one's own contribution to the production of knowledge. Epistemic exclusion, in turn, is understood as an unjustified infringement of the epistemic agency of knowers. Finally, epistemic agency refers to the ability to persuasively use shared epistemic resources within a given knowledge community to participate in the production of knowledge and, if necessary, in the revision of those same resources (Dotson 2014).

Settles and colleagues (2020) theorize and empirically investigate epistemic exclusion, understanding it as a form of academic delegitimization rooted in disciplinary biases about what types of research are valued, as well as identity-based biases against individuals from marginalized groups. It can have a disproportionately negative effect on women and faculty of color due to negative stereotypes about their competence and likelihood to engage in research outside the disciplinary mainstream (Settles et al. 2021). In this sense, it reflects both interpersonal bias and structural oppression (Settles et al. 2020).

In short, epistemic exclusion proposes that certain corporalities "at the margins"—that is, outside the disciplinary center—are disproportionately disadvantaged by performance standards presented as ostensibly objective and neutral (Settles et al. 2021). This has implications for their hiring, retention, and promotion in universities. Epistemic exclusion reflects the dominant discourse and claims that define "rigorous" and "legitimate" research and credible researchers within a discipline (Settles et al. 2020). In doing so, it acts as a form of gatekeeping and prevents certain individuals, particularly those from marginalized groups, from being valued as legitimate and credible knowers.

Debating Some Forms of Epistemic Exclusion of Feminist Knowledge
In this section we propose a dialogue between the narrative—which opens this text—and the literature on epistemic exclusion to articulate three nodes: the historicity that permeates the work of the academics interviewed, the material and affective impact of exclusion on their careers and their epistemic possibilities, and the struggle for the validation of feminist or gender knowledge.

Gender and feminist studies in Latin America have the particularity of having originated—and been strengthened—alongside women's or feminist movements in contexts of dictatorships and authoritarianism (Carosio 2019; Valdés 2007). Thus, since their origin, feminist research and activism have been intrinsically related (Carosio 2019). According to Pereira (2015), this declared commitment of feminist scholars to articulating academic research and political action has been invoked by other scholars as proof (among other things) that their work could not, and should not, be taken seriously as "proper" scholarship. Feminist and gender studies have historically been affected by disciplinary biases about what types of research are valued (Settles et al. 2020).

In the Chilean case, the production of knowledge on these issues has its origins in social movements rather than in academic spaces. Feminists became academics later, through activism, in the 1970s and '80s (Valdés 2007). In the 1990s, with the advancement of public policies on gender and key milestones such as the international Convention on the Elimination of All Forms of Discrimination Against Women and the Beijing Declaration and Platform for Action, there was a shift toward seeking equity and equal opportunities where an interest in instrumental-technological knowledge prevailed. Then, in the 2000s, the debate around difference and diversity began to emerge with greater force and with different theoretical perspectives, including proposals, for instance, to distinguish between sex and gender through a framework of cultural critique (Valdés 2007). In the Argentinian case, there were various feminist and women's groups in the 1960s and early '70s, in the midst of the dictatorship (Carosio 2019). Already in the 1980s, the Department of Psychology of the University of Buenos Aires had inaugurated an interdisciplinary degree in Women's Studies (Carosio 2019). Beginning in the 1990s, initiatives were created in various universities, and since then, feminist, gender, and women's studies have been developed in various universities, mainly centered around research and postgraduate training (Carosio 2019). Currently, gender studies have been established in universities in each country (Valdés 2007), especially in postgraduate studies (Carosio 2019), but they have not necessarily permeated other scientific disciplines or professional training beyond elective courses in the social sciences (Valdés 2007).

This retelling allows us to see that, in both countries, the construction of feminist and gender knowledge in academia is deeply linked to the feminist student movements of the last decade. The historicity of the production of feminist and gender knowledge is marked in the narrative by the idea of a *before* and an *after*. The *before* is generally associated with the strongest experiences of exclusion from one's own production or the toughest confrontations with issues of valorization and financing of the production of knowledge.

In the *after*, there appears a halo of greater appreciation, of less exclusion, characterized mainly by the different standing of gender or feminist topics, due in large part to the pressure of feminist student movements. From these achievements, the institutionality of universities (though not all of them) opens up to incorporate gender issues and to create institutional policies and initiatives to address gendered violence. But it is an after with a bitter taste, because behind the supposed acceptance and importance of gender studies and feminism lies distrust, exclusion, doubt, danger, fear. It is an after marked by more subtle forms of devaluation, and thus exclusion, of feminist knowledge, which still has to be camouflaged or it is relegated to a discursive or niche level, closely (and negatively) linked to activism. It is a form of exclusion rooted not only in disciplinary prejudices about what types of research are valued, but also in prejudices regarding the social identities of those who undertake this research (Settles et al. 2020). Feminist and gender knowledge is excluded—before and after—depending on who carries it out (associated with a frowned-upon activism) and what they study (unrigorous and illegitimate scholarship). For this reason, it is not yet possible to mainstream such knowledge into university curricula. It is a partial recognition (Pereira 2012), which is not yet considered properly academic knowledge (Pereira 2015).

In both the Chilean and Argentinian contexts, part of this historicity is the establishment and generalization of the category of "gender." According to Tarducci (2010), gender is a concept created by feminism as part of the language that every revolutionary group creates in its actions. The use of gender has been theorized quite a bit (Pereira 2012), but in light of the story and the historicity of the formation of feminist and gender studies, the question that Tarducci (2010) asks seems fundamental to us: Are we using it as an aseptic intellectual concept or as a political tool, as a driver of change, pointing out the power relations that it implies? According to Valdés (2007), in the Chilean case, the transition to using the concept of gender from the 1990s to the present has been criticized for entrenching itself as a category usually depoliticized and disconnected from feminist movements. However, the narrative—and Tarducci's question (2010)—also invites us to think of it as a political tool, a strategy. Like other "before and afters" that emerge in the story, it seems that in both contexts the possibility of speaking more directly about feminism is now opening up, although for many understatement or camouflage is still a key survival strategy.

The intersection of this retelling with the literature also allows us to account for the material and affective impact of epistemic exclusion on career paths and the possibilities of knowledge production. Despite the aforementioned before and after, the feeling of devaluation of academic work persists. Interestingly, this is not always presented as a direct and explicit violation of people, but rather as subtle violence. Subtle violence is characterized by being hard to perceive, identify, and name, and carried out through practices that do not seem to intend harm (Castelao-Huerta 2022). Thus, the narrative sheds light on how the epistemic exclusion experienced by "gender people" (Henderson 2019) in this study is a form of—sometimes subtle or "hallway" (Pereira 2012)—violence.

Furthermore, the report allows us to see that epistemic exclusion is housed in the structural, whether that be the impossibility of mainstreaming the perspective of gender, the optional nature of courses, or research carried out on the doorsteps of academia (Muñoz-García and Trebisacce Marchand 2024). But it is also expressed in the difficulty of obtaining funding and building an academic career in these topics, contrary to what Pereira (2015, 2017) reports in the case of Portugal.

The narrative also describes the weariness and fatigue of the struggle against epistemic exclusion. This is aggravated in the context of a neoliberal and gendered academy with long-standing forms of organization that exacerbate specific disadvantages that affect women academics and are based on the sexual division of academic labor (Mandiola et al. 2019), such as their relegation to what are considered "care" work jobs and their being distanced from leadership positions. The situation greatly affects "gender people," a construct based on the precariousness and instability of both knowledge and employment conditions (Henderson 2019). This is a group, like others on the margins, on which epistemic exclusion has a disproportionately negative effect (Settles et al. 2021). In this scenario, a survival strategy for many is to resort even more to "shielding" themselves behind neoliberal productivity. This reveals an interesting trap that enables the being and doing of feminisms in the academy in neoliberal code (Mandiola 2024).[2]

However, as the account illuminates, parallel to the refuge of neoliberal productivity is activist work. This work revitalizes, but at the same time generates recursive circles that contribute even more to fatigue: On the one hand, in order to mobilize, one must be even more productive, even though investing time in activism leaves less time for that production (Pereira 2016). On the other hand, activism increases the questioning of the knowledge produced by these people, which implies even more work negotiating their epistemic status (Pereira 2016) and further exhaustion. In this context, the regular invocation, in different places or situations and by different people (colleagues, bosses, even students), of the belief that activism amounts to an unacceptable contamination of academic practice (undermining the value and rigor of knowledge claims) also emerges (Pereira 2015).

All of this gives rise to what Pereira (2019) calls an unhealthy atmosphere, a shared state of exhaustion and alienation that is not just an individual experience. It is a climate that makes everyone sick, though it may affect some people more than others depending on working conditions, temperament, or generation (Pereira 2019). In her work, Henderson (2019) reports that several "gender people" claim to feel isolated and alone, misfits in their departments. According to the author, the consequences of this isolation include a lack of community and critical engagement, and even the decision to abandon the academic world altogether. In this way, the epistemic exclusion that gender people suffer acts as a form of control that prevents them from being valued as legitimate and credible experts.

Finally, epistemic exclusion coexists with the constant tension over its validation and legitimization and the ways of doing and being in that knowledge. From the perspective of feminist epistemologies there is a long debate about the marginality of feminist knowledge in academic spaces and the complexities of positioning it as valued and legitimized knowledge, thus having to respond to structures of credibility and legitimacy, and imitating structures of power and social order without questioning them (Fricker 2007). These are practices "that operate as strategies of legitimization of the current disciplinary and masculine order" (Ríos, Mandiola and Varas 2017). This invites us to ask ourselves about the practices and materialities that weave their exclusion (Maffía 2006) and that position certain researchers as "putative experts" in universities, while others are seen as participating without being legitimized as experts (Code 2014). In this sense, as Code (2014) points out, the marginality of knowledge has many vertices. It means not only being excluded as a knower, but also the denial of the credibility of epistemic processes and practices for constructing knowledge, discrediting them within the framework of a certain hegemonic formula or set of guidelines for what counts as genuine knowledge. Although these aspects may seem to operate in isolation in some cases, in the narrative they often appear to overlap or intertwine to silence, ignore, or discredit certain voices and points of view (Tuana and Sullivan 2007). Therefore, a responsible and ethical construction of knowledge implies reflecting on our decisions about what knowledge we consider possible and, at the same time, who we make visible in those decisions (Grasswick 2011).

Neo-Materialist Feminist Openings to Incubate Knowledge in Resistance
This essay shows the usefulness of epistemic exclusion to critically monitor how the modes of knowledge construction are stratified and sedimented. Our pronouncements only specify and pertain to specific contexts, and are therefore scarcely stable and transcendent. In return, our methodological decision to begin this piece with a narrative retelling fertilizes other paths, inspiring others to resist by making Latin American feminist knowledge—knowledge that has often been relegated to the doorstep of academia (Muñoz-García and Trebisacce Marchand 2024).

Storytelling and letting ourselves be carried away by fictional twists and turns stands out as a fundamental method and modality of feminist critical work and is a starting point for imagining new rationalities and ethics (Davies and Gannon 2006; Bhavnani and Haraway 1994). Therefore, the empirical use of narrative—both derived from and not derived from individualized experiences or biographies—is established as a key strategy for creating objectively situated knowledge (Beniscelli-Contreras and Gómez-Guinart 2023; Haraway 1995). This demands an unavoidable epistemic commitment: insisting on methods that account for the complexities of phenomena and also remain sensitive to the drifts of their materializations and modes of re/production. Thus, the method of telling and creating stories aims to provoke rebellions and discomforts, sudden changes or tiny displacements born from the intimately probable and/or from new forces potentially linked to others already in insurrection (Davies and Gannon 2006; Stengers 2018; Haraway 2019; Osgood and Robinson 2019).

Without fear of being wrong, considering these onto-epistemic gaps does not deny other socioeconomic or cultural reparative efforts. Feminist and antiracist activism has shown that the ability to weave narratives works as a micropolitical interstice that restores bodies ruined by segregationist violence of all kinds (Anzaldúa 2015; Sharma and Nijjar 2018). Testing this method in academic arenas immersed in contexts of profound inequality means taking charge of the fact that some bodies will not have the option of leaving the streets and intends to lead us toward strategic balances between macropolitical struggles and micropolitical battles (Gandarias 2019; Ziga 2014). Finding ways to empower collective voices stimulates creativity in the elaboration of theories that are able to bridge failed presents and seemingly impossible futures without sitting around waiting for positivist certainties or dialectical reconciliations (Braidotti 2022; Grossberg 2012). Ultimately, it will always be hopeful to venture into critical research that dispels the pessimism of the present in order to welcome the emerging. As Grossberg writes (Grossberg 2012, 116), "precisely because the present did not have to be as it is, the future can go somewhere other than where it seems to be headed." It is a clear invitation in favor of epistemic justice.

Fernanda Rojas-Müller is a PhD student in anthropology at the Pontificia Universidad Católica de Chile and holds a master's degree in gender studies from the London School of Economics and Political Science. She specializes in gender issues from an intersectional perspective. She has experience in formal and informal education, and has worked in the fields of communications and research. She can be reached at frojasmuller@uc.cl and https://orcid.org/0000-0003-2111-8502.

Ana Luisa Muñoz-García is associate professor at the Faculty of Education of the Pontificia Universidad Católica de Chile. She is an academic and feminist. The focus of her research work has been education, knowledge policies, feminisms and gender, and internationalization. She can be reached at aumunoz@uc.cl and http://orcid.org/0000-0001-5639-2777.

Kyuttzza Gómez-Guinart is a psychologist master and doctoral candidate in education at the Pontificia Universidad Católica de Chile. Her interests and research, with anti-racist purposes, are directed toward the production of critical knowledge in social sciences from new materialisms and queer-feminist epistemologies. She can be reached at kgomez3@uc.cl and https://orcid.org/0000-0002-0456-6824.

Acknowledgments

This article is a result of the ANID/FONDECYT/REGULAR 1210477 project "Mapping Knowledge Construction from a Gender Perspective."

Notes

1. The interviews were recorded and transcribed, safeguarding the anonymity of the participants. They were then read by the three authors and discussed in several meetings, which in turn were recorded and transcribed as research data.
2. We would like to thank Marcela Mandiola, Catalina Trebisacce, Gabriela Bard Wigdor, Vir Cano, and Hillary Hiner for the vibrant and passionate discussions that opened up necessary tensions about the neoliberal cooptation of feminisms in universities and the use of neoliberal strategies to exist and build feminist knowledge.

Works Cited

Abbate, Florencia. 2018. "Procesos de subjetivación feminista en las movilizaciones #NiUnaMenos en Argentina." *Letras Femeninas* 43 (2): 147–58.

Acosta, Marina. 2020. "Activismo Feminista en Instagram. El caso de la campaña nacional por el derecho al aborto legal, seguro y gratuito en Argentina." *Perspectivas de la comunicación* 13 (1): 29–46.

Anzaldúa, Gloria. 2015. "Light in the Dark/Luz." In *Lo Oscuro: Rewriting Identity, Spirituality, Reality,* edited by Ana Louise Keating. Duke University Press.

Bacevic, Jana. 2023. "Epistemic Injustice and Epistemic Positioning: Towards an Intersectional Political Economy." *Current Sociology* 71 (6): 1122–40.

Balasch, Marcel, and Marisela Montenegro. 2003. "Una propuesta metodológica desde la epistemología de los conocimientos situados: las producciones narrativas." *Encuentros en psicología social* 1 (3): 44–48.

Barad, Karen. 2007. *Meeting the Universe Halfway: Quantum Physics and the Entanglement of Matter and Meaning.* Durham-London: Duke University Press.

Beniscelli-Contreras, L., and K. Gómez-Guinart. 2023. "Erotic Pedagogy Towards a Desiring Conviviality: A Visual Collective Biography Joining Island and Continent." *Globalisation, Societies and Education* 21 (4): 450–468. https://doi.org/10.1080/14767724.2023.2241200.

Bhavnani, Kum-Kum, and Donna Haraway. 1994. "Shifting the Subject: A Conversation Between Kum-Kum Bhavnani and Donna Haraway, 12 April 1993, Santa Cruz, California." *Feminism & Psychology* 4 (1): 19–39.

Blackmore, Jill. 2022. "Governing Knowledge in the Entrepreneurial University: A Feminist Account of Structural, Cultural and Political Epistemic Injustice." *Critical Studies in Education* 63 (5): 622–38.

Braidotti, Rosi. 2022. "The Virtual as Affirmative Praxis: A Neo-Materialist Approach." *Humanities* 11 (3): 1–13.

Carosio, Alba. 2019. "Sin disociar la investigación de la lucha: feminismos militantes en la academia latinoamericana y caribeña." *CS* 29: 139–62.

Castelao-Huerta, Isaura. 2022. "Recelos y envidias: violencias sutiles de género en la academia neoliberalizada." *Debate Feminista* 65: 1–34.

CNN. 2024. "El Gobierno de Javier Milei prohíbe el uso del lenguaje inclusivo en documentos oficiales en Argentina." CNN, February 27.

Code, Lorraine. 2014. "Ignorance, Injustice and the Politics of Knowledge." *Australian Feminist Studies* 29 (80): 148–60.

Davies, Bronwyn, and Susanne Gannon. 2006. *Doing Collective Biography: Investigating the Production of Subjectivity.* Maidenhead: Open University Press.

Deleuze, Gilles, and Félix Guattari. 2002. *Mil Mesetas. Capitalismo y Esquizofrenia.* 5th ed. Valencia: Pre-Textos.

de Fina Gonzalez, Débora, and Francisca Figueroa Vidal. 2019. "Nuevos 'campos de acción política' feminista: una mirada a las recientes movilizaciones en Chile." *Revista Punto Género* 11 (July): 51–72.

Dotson, Kristie. 2014. "Conceptualizing Epistemic Oppression." *Social Epistemology* 28 (2): 115–38.

Forstenzer, Nicole. 2019. "Feminismos en el Chile post-dictadura: hegemonías y marginalidades." *Revista Punto Género* 11 (July): 34–50.

Fricker, Miranda. 2007. *Epistemic Injustice: Power and Ethics in Knowing.* Oxford: Oxford University Press.

Gandarias, Itziar. 2019. "Resistir desde la vulnerabilidad: narrativas de mujeres subsaharianas sobre su tránsito hacia Europa." *Papeles del CEIC* 1: 1–18.

Grasswick, Heidi. 2011. "Introduction: Feminist Epistemology and Philosophy of Science in the Twenty-First Century." In *Feminist Epistemology and Philosophy of Science: Power in Knowledge*, edited by Heidi Grasswick. London: Springer.

Grossberg, Lawrence. 2012. *Estudios culturales en tiempo futuro: cómo es el trabajo intelectual que requiere el mundo de hoy.* Buenos Aires: Siglo XXI Editores.

Haraway, Donna. 1995. "Conocimientos situados: la cuestión científica en el feminismo y el privilegio de la perspectiva parcial." In *Ciencia, cyborgs y mujeres: la reinvención de la naturaleza.* Spain: Cátedra.

Haraway, Donna. 2019. *Seguir con el problema: generar parentesco en Chthuluceno.* Bilbao: Consonni.

Henderson, Emily. 2019. "On Being the 'Gender Person' in an Academic Department: Constructions, Configurations and Implications." *Journal of Gender Studies* 28 (6): 730–42.

Lather, Patti. 2000. "Against Empathy, Voice and Authenticity." In *Voice in Qualitative Inquiry: Challenging Conventional, Interpretive, and Critical Conceptions in Qualitative Research,* edited by Alecia Jackson and Lisa Mazzei. London: Routledge.

Lenguita, Paula. 2021. "Rebelión de las pibas: trazos de una memoria feminista en Argentina." *Ventana* 6 (54): 48–73.

Lipton, Briony. 2020. *Academic Women in Neoliberal Times.* 1st ed. Springer International Publishing.

López Cardona, Diana. 2022. "Injusticias epistémicas y colonialidad del poder: aportes para pensar la descolonialidad desde América Latina." *Estudios de Filosofía* 66: 79–96.

MacLure, Maggie. 2013. "Researching Without Representation? Language and Materiality in Post-Qualitative Methodology." *International Journal of Qualitative Studies in Education* 26 (6): 658–67. https://doi.org/10.1080/09518398.2013.788755.

Maffía, Diana. 2006. "El vínculo crítico entre género y ciencia." *Clepsydra* 5: 37–57.

Mandiola, Marcela. 2024. "Feminismos Neoliberales y la Agenda de Género en Chile." In *Feminismos en el Umbral de la Academia,* edited by Ana Luisa Muñoz García and Catalina Trebisacce Marchand, 139–70. 1st ed. Santiago: Ediciones UC.

Mandiola, Marcela, Nicolás Ríos, and Alejandro Varas. 2019. "'Hay un tema que no hemos conversado': la cassata como organización académica generizada en las universidades chilenas." *Pensamiento Educativo* 56 (1): 1–16.

Mazzei, Lisa. 2013. "Materialist Mappings of Knowing in Being: Researchers Constituted in the Production of Knowledge." *Gender and Education* 25 (6): 776–85.

Mazzei, Lisa, and Alecia Jackson. 2017. "Voice in the Agentic Assemblage." *Educational Philosophy and Theory* 49 (11): 1090–98.

Meganoticias. 2024. "'No sirve absolutamente para nada': Gobierno argentino cierra Instituto contra Discriminación, Xenofobia y Racismo." *Meganoticias,* February 22.

Miranda Leibe, L., and Beatriz Roque López. 2020. "El mayo estudiantil feminista de 2018 en la Pontificia Universidad Católica de Chile: 'La revolución es nuestra.'" *Educación y Educadores* 23 (1): 89–102.

Muñoz-Garcia, A. L., and Trebisacce Marchand, C. 2024. "La Insistencia de los Feminismos." In *Feminismos en el Umbral de la Academia,* edited by A. L.

Muñoz-Garcia and C. Trebisacce Marchand, 21–55. Santiago: Ediciones UC.

Osgood, Jayne, and Kerry Robinson. 2019. *Feminists Researching Gendered Childhoods: Generative Entanglements*. Bloomsbury Academic.

Pereira, Maria do Mar. 2012. "'Feminist Theory Is Proper Knowledge, but…': The Status of Feminist Scholarship in the Academy." *Feminist Theory* 13 (3): 283–303.

Pereira, Maria do Mar. 2015. "Higher Education Cutbacks and the Reshaping of Epistemic Hierarchies: An Ethnography of the Case of Feminist Scholarship." *Sociology* 49 (2): 287–304.

Pereira, Maria do Mar. 2016. "Struggling Within and Beyond the Performative University: Articulating Activism and Work in an 'Academia Without Walls.'" *Women's Studies International Forum* 54: 100–10.

Pereira, Maria do Mar. 2017. *Power, Knowledge and Feminist Scholarship*. Routledge.

Pereira, Maria do Mar. 2019. "'You Can Feel the Exhaustion in the Air Around You': The Mood of Contemporary Universities and Its Impact on Feminist Scholarship." *Ex Aequo* 39: 171–86.

Schuster, Sofía, Antonia Santos, Lucía Miranda, Beatriz Roque, Javiera Arce-Riffo, and Evelyne Medel. 2019. "Una mirada al movimiento feminista en Chile del año 2018: Hitos, agenda y desafíos." *Iberoamericana* 19 (72): 223–46.

Settles, Isis H., Leah R. Warner, NiCole T. Buchanan, and Martinque K. Jones. 2020. "Understanding Psychology's Resistance to Intersectionality Theory Using a Framework of Epistemic Exclusion and Invisibility." *Journal of Social Issues* 76 (4): 796–813.

Settles, Isis, Martinque Jones, NiCole Buchanan, and Kristie Dotson. 2021. "Epistemic Exclusion: Scholar(Ly) Devaluation That Marginalizes Faculty of Color." *Journal of Diversity in Higher Education* 14 (4): 493–507.

Sharma, Sanjaym, and Jasbinder Nijjar. 2018. "The Racialized Surveillant Assemblage: Islam and the Fear of Terrorism." *Popular Communication* 16 (1): 72–85.

Silva Hope, M., A. L. Muñoz-Garcia, and L. Medina Morales. 2024. "Unmothering the Conversation on Gender in Academia." *Journal of Women and Gender in Higher Education* 17 (2): 79–99. https://doi.org/10.1080/26379112.2024.2308676.

Stengers, Isabelle. 2018. *Another Science Is Possible. A Manifesto for Slow Science*. Cambridge: Polity Press.

St. Pierre, Elizabeth. 2018. "Writing Post Qualitative Inquiry." *Qualitative Inquiry* 24 (9): 603–608.

St. Pierre, Elizabeth, and Alecia Jackson. 2014. "Qualitative Data Analysis After Coding." *Qualitative Inquiry* 20 (6): 715–19.

Tarducci, Mónica. 2010. "La profesora feminista como agente de transformación." In *Aproximaciones críticas a las prácticas teórico-políticas del feminismo latinoamericano*, edited by Yuderkys Espinosa Miñoso, 1st ed. Buenos Aires: En la Frontera.

Torlucci, Sandra, Verónica Cruz, and Vanesa Vasquez-Laba. 2023. "Género y universidades: ¿dónde nos encontramos?." In *RUGE. La formación de formadorxs en género en las universidades*, edited by Paula Torricella, María Flor Gianfrini, and Candela Luquet, 5–16. Buenos Aires: RUGE-CIN.

Trebisacce, Catalina, and Paloma Dulbecco. 2021. "Feminismos universitarios en la elaboración de los protocolos contra las violencias (2014–2019)." In *RUGE: El género en las Universidades*, edited by Ana Martin, 69–95. Ciudad Autónoma de Buenos Aires: RUGE-CIN.

Tuana, Nancy, and Shannon Sullivan. 2007. *Race and Epistemologies of Ignorance*. Albany, NY: State University of New York Press.

Valdés, Teresa. 2007. "Estudios de género: una mirada evaluativa desde el Cono Sur." In *Género, mujeres y saberes en América Latina: entre el movimiento social, la academia y el Estado*, edited by Luz Gabriela Arango and Yolanda Puyana. Bogotá: Universidad Nacional de Colombia.

Williams, Jamillah, Lisa Singh, and Naomi Mezey. 2019. "#MeToo as Catalyst: A Glimpse into 21st Century Activism." *University of Chicago Legal Forum* 22.

Ziga, Itziar. 2014. "¿El corto verano del transfeminismo?" In *Transfeminismos: Epistemes, fricciones y flujos*. Txalaparta.

Trans-Uranic Intimacies on a Queer(er) Planet

Daisy Atterbury

Abstract: This article explores the critical possibilities of queer aesthetic practice through the work of Diné artist DinéYazhi´, who interlaces queer/trans life with resistance to settler colonial structures and offers a bold critique of systemic violence and a vision for collective liberation. By situating queer existence and aesthetic practice within global anti-colonial struggle, the article considers how DinéYazhi´'s art and writing, including the long-form poem *An Infected Sunset* and sculpture *my ancestors will not let me forget this*, serve as capacious calls for alternative conceptions of space, institutional relations, and identity. **Keywords:** queer liberation, settler colonialism, decolonial aesthetics, nuclear-colonialism, queer aesthetics, Demian DinéYazhi´

The element's natural color is a dark silver gray, but most people think of uranium as yellow. When uranium is in a compound with oxygen, it forms a yellow oxide called uranyl peroxide. The peroxide group produces the color by causing a shift in the electronic structure of the uranium atom, affecting the way it interacts with light. The yellow of uranyl peroxide is produced through the absorption of certain wavelengths of light by the compound and the reflection of yellow light. The uranium atom in uranyl peroxide then has an oxidation state of +6, meaning it has lost six electrons from its natural state and is now highly reactive.

Demian DinéYazhi´'s sculpture *my ancestors will not let me forget this* (2019) is uranium yellow. Installed at the 2019 Honolulu Biennial, the sculpture is installed on a polished concrete floor against a corner, at 42 × 22 × 23 in., or about one-third body height. The back of the sculpture is visible for inspection, and the signage with lettering plugs simply into an outlet in the wall behind. In a large empty room, the sculpture glows in neon, itself a chemical element. The gaseous lettering illuminates this phrase: "EVERY / AMERICAN FLAG / IS A WARNING SIGN." The six-word statement originates from an ekphrastic prose poem titled *An Infected Sunset*, which is a book-length piece DinéYazhi´ wrote after the Pulse nightclub shooting in Orlando. Pulse exemplifies an American massacre of queer life, especially and most emphatically of BIPOC queer life, through what is nominally understood as an act of domestic "terrorism." Because it represents such a significant loss for the queer community, it remains a cultural touchstone for queer life in the contemporary moment and a tragedy exploited by mainstream culture and the media, what Eric Stanley (2021, 42) calls "yet another moment of heteronormativity's primitive accumulation." Through active writing and publication projects and an installation-based art practice, DinéYazhi´ tethers contemporary queer culture to concerns like the nuclear-colonial legacy that formed the backdrop for their coming-to-consciousness as a Diné artist. It is the intertwining of these social concerns that provokes me to answer to DinéYazhi´'s call to examine the critical possibilities of queer aesthetic practices that locate queer life within the U.S. settler colonial context. In *Transgender Studies Quarterly (TSQ)*'s first issue of 2024, which features *my ancestors will not let me forget this* on the cover in a radiant golden glow, editors Christopher Joseph Lee, Eric Stanley, Jemma DeCristo, and Ren-yo Hwang write that DinéYazhi´'s piece "offers not simply an alternative path for trans analysis and action but also one that confronts where we assume 'trans' properly lives" (Lee et al. 2024). As the photograph selected for the cover of the issue "Everything Must Go: Abolition, Anti-Imperialism, Anarchism," the image of DinéYazhi´'s neon sign in an empty room is a bold declaration for an issue on transgender theories, both a "reminder for us all that genocide is recursive" and a claim that "that colonialism's death symbolizes trans life as much as, if not more than, a pink and blue flag ever could." This provocation suggests that queer/trans life always already exists within and is determined by the settler colonial context, and such existence can be agitated to engage in wider global struggles against those colonial structures that necessarily construct queer life. For the editors, DinéYazhi´'s "queer" comes to signify something particular: a life constructed in, through, and explicitly resistant to the structuring forces of colonialism.

In the spring of 2024, just after *TSQ*'s "Everything Must Go" issue was released, DinéYazhi´ presented a new neon sculpture in the Whitney

Biennial. The sculpture visually echoed *my ancestors will not let me forget this*, but the Whitney Biennial submission was met with immediate controversy and media attention. The sculpture appeared to have slipped a hidden message past potential censors and directly to its audience. On first read, the neon and aluminum lettering spells out the phrase "we must stop imagining apocalypse / genocide + we must imagine liberation," a statement measured and galvanizing in the abstract, but universally applicable. But the flickering words, still installed in the white walls of the gallery, reveal a hidden, simultaneous message: "Free Palestine." The sculpture is installed facing outward, toward a window, and toward the sea.

DinéYazhi´ has a long relationship with the Whitney. On April 20, 2018, they performed a reading from their poem *An Infected Sunset* in conjunction with a group show, *Between the Waters*, which featured artists like Carolina Caycedo, Ginger Dunnill, Lena Henke, and Erin Jane Nelson. The show featured works responding to environmental crisis and took a personal, interdisciplinary, and "nondocumentary" approach. One piece addressed city planner Robert Moses's mid-twentieth-century intervention into the New York landscape as a form of institutionalized colonialism. DinéYazhi´'s contribution, a performance, was a reading from their long-form poem, which tethered the politics of queer life to environmental injustice and colonial dynamics. The poem, *An Infected Sunset*, is what DinéYazhi´ calls the "liberated poem," an offering to Indigenous communities and landscapes "striving for a decolonial and sovereign future" (DinéYazhi´ 2018). This poem, and the subsequent piece emerging from it, is where I'd like to focus my attention. How to read these works not only as unruly antagonists, but as capacious messages: the visioning of queer liberation as a project of aligning with global anti-colonial projects? How to collapse the binary between agitating and visioning, to the degree that collapse is sutured to possibility? Queer liberatory movements have always led the way.

The sculptural intervention *my ancestors will not let me forget this* (figure 1) was exhibited in Honolulu just one year after DinéYazhi´'s 2018 performance at the Whiney. The sculpture demands that its viewers consider the potentiality of queer aesthetic practice as a project of global anti-colonial struggle. The sculpture bathes the gallery in the warm neon glow of the "infected sunset," a "uranium yellow" color that signifies as legibly as the neon lettering illuminating the phrase "EVERY / AMERICAN FLAG / IS A WARNING SIGN." To signal the "American flag" on formerly sovereign territory like the island of Hawai'i is to insert a politically charged signifier.

Figure 1. Demian DinéYazhi´, *my ancestors will not let me forget this*, 2019. Mixed media sculpture, 42 × 22 × 23 in. Image courtesy of the artist.

The flag is a sign informed by its surround, the suppressed, violent history of colonial occupation and forcible erasure of Indigenous peoples and culture on the island. In a state biennial, reference to a flag signifies doubly as a gauntlet-laying move against state and nation. Identifying the flag as a "warning sign," DinéYazhi´ signals the unspeakable in American discourse. They whisper in plain sight that as long as the flag flies, the land remains forcibly occupied. The flag is a constructed signifier, one that embeds a reminder of its origins. It also serves as a reminder that these territories remain contestable.

For an installation artist, choice of material is of consequence. With neon, any chemical dangers are nonexistent, and the reactivity of the gas is not an issue. The element is stable. But its critical evocations are not. Neon is both *Americana*—"the nostalgia of driving along Route 66"—and *America*, in the sense that DinéYazhi´ writes, "to this day, when you're on the route ⌊66⌋—which passes through my hometown, Gallup, N.M.—you can see neon signs in the windows of white-owned businesses that read 'Indian jewelry' and 'Indian rugs'" (Rutter and Youngquist 2021). These racist formulations of Indigenous life are quintessentially American. The piece thus alights with decolonial longing and intergenerational warnings.

How to make sense of DinéYazhi´'s insistence, amid the constellation of signifiers and inflections that constitutes a body of work, on the intertwining of nuclear history, settler colonial dynamics, and *queer* aesthetic practice? Is it all one political project that keeps asking after the material forces that condition queer life in the present?

The rush and wayward energy of DinéYazhi´'s poetry in the printed book *An Infected Sunset* (2018) is exemplified by long phrases, sentence fragments, stream-of-consciousness writing, and the weaving together of scenes, persons, and contexts like #NODAPL and nuclear history. On the cover, also golden yellow, DinéYazhi´ writes, "This performance poem is a reflection on queer sex, survival/death politics, indigenous identity, settler and heteronormative romanticism, environmental injustice, and the importance of honoring community." The poems rush and bleed, amassing the urgency of a cry in the totality of their vision. Printed in limited edition risograph (400 copies), staple bound, in loose leaves, the tactility of the book lends a punk, DIY quality to the work, grounding the later gallery installations in zine culture and offering a handmade chapbook aesthetic that evokes pre-internet queer anarchist publication practices.

The energy of the chapbook is somehow reiterated in the multilayered signification of the gallery installations when the books, sculptures, and installation pieces are conceived together as a series rather than as discrete works. DinéYazhi´'s punk ethos is never lost in the white walls of the gallery for those who know where to look. Where individually, the installations offer brief, declarative statements in neon, or, as in other works, in vinyl wall text or window decal, when conceived together as linked projects, they function as dizzying signifiers bursting with fast intimacy, an intervention into conceptual art practices that typically employ more minimalist aesthetics. For DinéYazhi´, art-historical references to conceptualism, minimalism, and even Western feminist interventions—and the explicit rejection of these references in favor of others—I argue are as much an indication of lineage as they are an expansion of the more overt critique of heteronormative settler institutions. Visual aesthetics referencing Western art-historical conversations appear at times as mere propellants, fueling the smoldering project of tethering queer liberation to global anti-colonial struggle.

Drawing upon feminist figures in Western conceptual art practice like Jenny Holzer, Barbara Kruger, and the Guerilla Girls, DinéYazhi´ offers condensed and multiple proclamations in block lettering and a text-based manifesto that add up to a carefully curated cacophony of feeling-invoking interventions. Unlike Holzer and the Guerilla Girls, however, DinéYazhi´

explicitly ties critical issues of marginalization and social hierarchy to U.S. colonial genocidal practices against Indigenous peoples, putting the work in the realm of international artists who resist categorical terminology and methodological rationality. These contemporaries align their work in uneasy relation to Western art-historical references. Through visual and thematic congruencies, DinéYazhi´'s body of work appears, rather, to situate itself in relation to contemporary and emerging artists with practices similarly addressing colonial structures, queer life, and nuclear history. Mateo Galindo, Ryan Dennison, and Claudia X. Valdés come to mind as artists working at the peripheries of the current U.S. art market, turning out performances and conceptual projects visioning specifically decolonial futures.

Claudia X. Valdés, an artist born in Santiago, Chile, and based in the United States most of her life, spent years researching nuclear arms for her installation *For the Future, With Love* (2015). The installation features a hoisted flag designed in a pattern of black and yellow radiation warning symbols and refers to a U.S. Department of Energy report titled "Marking the [Nuclear] Waste Isolation Pilot Plant for 10,000 Years." Valdés's nuclear-informed artwork was exhibited as a flagpole installation at SITE Santa Fe and appeared in the traveling exhibition *Hot Spots: Radioactivity and the Landscape* (2015). The piece is featured in "A People's Atlas of the Nuclear United States," a digital public humanities project that "documents and interprets the relational geographies of nuclear materials used by the United States military" (Kanouse 2024). The artists mentioned in the project draw upon contemporary art references, conceptual framings, and the techniques of institutional critique, but also work with affect, community references, and a sense of locality. Claudia X. Valdés's piece considers what is brought into focus when aesthetic practice no longer remains cordoned off from the colonial circumstances of its own production and reception. In *For the Future, With Love* (figure 2), the form and function of nuclear colonialism takes center stage.

In *A Nation Is a Massacre* (vinyl on windows, 2019), another of DinéYazhi´'s contemporary works that references canonical Western feminist conceptual art and turns the critical lens back at its predecessors, the artist reformulates and recirculates queer artist Zoe Leonard's 1992 flyer with the manifesto "I want a dyke for president." The original piece, written to celebrate the poet Eileen Myles's "openly female" presidential bid the year then-governor Bill Clinton ran against independent businessman Ross Perot and incumbent president George H. W. Bush, was circulated at

Figure 2. Claudia X. Valdes, *For the Future, With Love* (installation view), 2015. Mixed media. Image courtesy of the artist.

the time among a queer underground community of artist-protestors in a viral firestorm of photocopying before internet virality. In 2018, Leonard's piece resurfaced in a series of one hundred prints produced by Hauser & Wirth after the U.S. midterm elections, marking a moment of protest similar to Leonard's 1992 critique of the paucity of viable governing entities representing women and marginalized people. "I want a dyke for president" launched in 2018 through Hauser & Wirth, which charged $1,000 per print, and the prints were created in aid of Treatment Action Group, which supports treatment for patients with HIV, tuberculosis, and hepatitis C.

DinéYazhi´'s piece simply states, "We don't want a president" (2018) (figure 3).

Trans-Uranic Intimacies
Teaching from home in Albuquerque, New Mexico, during the smokiest fire season in memory, I read the golden lettering of DinéYazhi´'s work to distract from my immediate surroundings. I'm struck by the relationship of my body to the words in the installation. Born in American Samoa and raised in Shiprock, New Mexico, and later in Santa Fe, I came into language within a colonial framework that exists prior to any sense of myself as a queer

> We don't want a president. We don't want tribal presidents. We don't want a vice president or a congress or supreme court that does not seek consent or guidance from over 562 Indigenous tribes in this colonized country. We don't want a nation state or a man-made border that severs ancestral traditions of trade and migration, or imposes on the continued existence of flora and fauna. We don't want corporations or an economic value system based on european dominion. We don't want to be consumed, commodified, or held prisoner under the torturous, deathly grip of capitalism. We don't want a white academic critique of settler colonialism and genocide unless it centers Indigenous, Brown, & Black livelihood. We don't want a revolution unless it involves Indigenous Sovereignty, the destruction of extractive industries, and the dissolution of the concept of wealth associated with power, oppression, assimilation, slavery, or death. We don't want a relationship with the earth that doesn't give back whenever something is stolen, lost, or contaminated. We don't want a sexual and gender empowerment movement that does not take into account missing and murdered Indigenous women, girls, trans/gender-gradient/non-conforming, femmes, queers, and 2spirit kin since the founding fathers and their ancestors pillaged this land. We don't want to support a society that cannot function without the implementation of a ~~paramilitary~~ police state or the prison industrial complex. We don't want to be dependent on the western medical industrial complex in order to survive or live in harmony with our bodies. We don't want the continued exploitation of Indigenous, Brown, & Black labour. We don't want a white ~~future~~ savior. We want to die of natural causes and hold our loved ones knowing that heteropatriarchy has lost its own war against itself. We want to create on our own terms, in bodies of our own choosing. We want to restore our relationship with the cosmos/earth and move beyond the concept of western "truth". We want to be fearless. We want decolonization. We want to exist never having to comprehend the need to defend ourselves. To worship only the earth.
>
> Part of the exhibition A NATION IS A MASSACRE
> Demian DinéYazhi' & R.I.S.E.: Radical Indigenous Survivance & Empowerment

Figure 3. Demian DinéYazhi´, *We Don't Want a President*, 2018. Shown at exhibition *A Nation Is a Massacre* at Pioneer Works in Brooklyn, NY. Image courtesy of the artist.

scholar. The intimacies produced through DinéYazhi´'s aesthetics situate me in a discourse of colonial subjectivity that informs all other formulations, intersections, and articulations of difference. I have always been interested in the ways queer aesthetic practices can reference and refract the structuring forces of normativity produced through coloniality.

Nuclear colonialism in the Southwestern U.S. has longtime structural antecedents, but its introduction as a new form of devastation is notable for the purposes of understanding the colonial circumstances informing DinéYazhi´'s decolonial project. The Manhattan Project, originally termed "Project Y" under its classified designation, and its arrival to the Pajarito Plateau in what became Los Alamos, New Mexico, severely reordered social relations in the region in a way that affected the flourishing of life outside strict heteropatriarchal structures. As scholars like Myrriah Gómez and Jordan Biro Walters discuss, this reordering was initiated in the land grab by the federal government of formerly Indigenous and hispano lands for the construction of nuclear labs for the Manhattan Project (Gómez 2022; Biro Walters 2023). Both Gómez and Biro Walters enact queer readings of these colonial dynamics by "reject[ing] dominant cartographies" (Gopinath 2018, 5) and examining how the reordered social landscape of the Manhattan Project's nuclear program disrupted queer precolonial lifeways that originally flourished in local tradition and the self-governance of original peoples. Biro Walters discusses how, beyond the initial trauma of occupation and removal, the initiation of "Project Y" invited the infusion of U.S. federal agents to the region during a period of government surveillance of queer life and heavy enforcement of anti-sodomy legislation. The criminalization of homosexuality affected anyone who exhibited "queer tendencies," driving visible queer life and any non-heteronormative lifeways underground or into carceral channels. The settlement of the plateau in the name of nuclear production spurred the introduction of a legally enforced white, heteronormative nuclear family model to the region.

Nuclear scholar Kate Brown, researching nuclear cities like Richland, Washington, a city adjacent to the U.S. Department of Energy Hanford plutonium production site, and Ozersk, Russia, site of a then-Soviet plutonium plant in the southern Ural mountain region, terms these highly stratified, hierarchical nuclear cities "plutopias" (Brown 2013). Brown's book, *Plutopia: Nuclear Families, Atomic Cities, and the Great Soviet and American Plutonium Disasters*, suggests that one characteristic of the "plutopia" is its production of affluence, a "mirage" that serves to protect the health and well-being of the scientists in its inner circle, leaving its temporary workers, laboring classes, and surrounding communities exposed simultaneously to radiation and watchful criminalization. Under the Manhattan Project, as in other "plutopias" like Ozersk, not only did the mining of uranium take on new urgency for the development of nuclear weapons in the regions surrounding the labs—mostly Indigenous reservations and tribal territories—but it also disrupted existing social formations surrounding the labs and mines. The development of the city of Los Alamos itself facilitated the release of irradiated material and toxic waste throughout the area occupied by its displaced and dispersed working classes, those Hispanic ranchers and Indigenous miners that began suffering from a "mysterious" set of symptoms—fatigue, aches, anemia, rapid aging, cancer—eventually (much later) diagnosed as chronic radiation syndrome. According to the newly implemented white, heterosexual, and patriarchal family models in place in Los Alamos, the experiences of increasingly marginalized people were dismissed, according to Brown, as exhibiting illnesses "from radiophobia, heavy drinking or inbreeding" (Brady 2013). Simultaneously, queers and other "degenerates" were incarcerated or forced into hiding.

The phenomenon of social restructuring under the nuclear project compels me to reclaim the term *trans-uranic*, originally "transuranic." In scientific verbiage utilized by the labs, "transuranic" at present describes chemical elements with an atomic number greater than 92, which is the atomic number of uranium. These elements are radioactively unstable and decay into other elements. Transuranic waste products left over from nuclear production processes are contaminated by low-level exposure to radioactive materials and are designated for disposal, which in the Southwestern U.S. means transportation to caverns like the Waste Isolation Pilot Plant, or WIPP Site, in Carlsbad, New Mexico. Such "waste disposal areas" are envisaged to contain hazardous materials for thousands of years in the underground salt caves they occupy.

The term *trans-uranic* might be introduced in this study of DinéYazhi´'s queer aesthetic project as an emphatically queer(ed) anti-colonial term, as it describes both the charged detritus of nuclear production processes and the remaindered life that is queer survival under a nuclear colonial regime, flourishing, as queer liberation movements do, in the margins. To reinforce the notion that "colonialism's death symbolizes trans life," the term *trans-uranic* conjures the anti-"plutopia." The term functions as if *trans* signified something akin to the * often used at the end of *trans**, the asterisk also known as a "wildcard in search lingo, a tool you can use to search for a batch of words that begin the same way" (Steinmetz 2018). The *trans** serves as a form of sticky inclusion: what adheres to all words that begins with the prefix, say, *transaction*, or *transience*—or, *trans-uranic*, what sticks to *uranium*, what or whom is conditioned and defined by its exposure to human life.

John Gery, in his book *Ways of Nothingness: Nuclear Annihilation and Contemporary American Poetry* (1996), describes an existential paradox the creation of the atomic bomb produces: "'the way of nothingness'—that individual sense of continuity coupled with a global sense of impending annihilation," which, he argues, has altered the state of American letters in the twentieth century. Gery goes on to argue that considering poetry and nuclear weapons together is unexpectedly prescient given that "our basic understanding of nuclear weapons is almost entirely symbolic." Gery, a leading nuclear poetics scholar, states that the fundamental danger of nuclear weapons is the danger of "mental self-immolation" (1996). What artists like DinéYazhi´, Claudia X. Valdés, and other contemporaries reveal is that nuclearism, coloniality, and queer life produce an uneasy intimacy that a critic beholden to the "plutopic mirage" might miss. That is, the lived consequences of nuclear colonialism for communities encountering the material processes of uranium mining, nuclear waste storage, and nuclear testing is a profound social and material reckoning that lives in the everyday. Though these artists deal in aesthetics, they understand that the intimacy produced by the nuclear industrial complex is not merely a symbolic experience nor a mental exercise, as in Gery's "way of nothingness." Nuclear weapons production touches communities on a global scale, materially altering settler and Indigenous communities in proximity. This reckoning takes place in material encounters between bodies and land.

As Kate Brown describes in *Plutopias*, the infiltration of nuclear detritus into the landscape surrounding the "plutopia" is near total. "Radioactive isotopes, so readily combining with biological forms, [have] no discrete boundaries" (184). Radiation is indiscrete, boundaryless. Radioactive isotopes are "no longer distinct from the local environment, from scientists' bodies, or from human evolution" (184). This level of contamination can itself be conceived as queer in its promiscuity; or at the least as an analogue to the potentiality of queer life. A queer frame introduced to these material conditions might reveal that in and surrounding the "plutopia," we're conditioned by the U.S. defense industry's material output and its heteronormative ideals, while at the same time we're affected by the emergence of queer life, pervasive and boundaryless in the detritus of the nuclear industry and colonial landscape. To conceive of space is to conceive of life as entangled materially and socially with the remaindered elements of colonial production. Meanwhile, queerness is both a phenomenon emerging from within these conditions and a frame we can use to describe the conditions themselves.

One response: chemical intimacy, firing and alighting in a quiet rage.

In her study *Wastelanding: Legacies of Uranium Mining in Navajo Country*, Traci Brynne Voyles (2015) argues that not only have Indigenous and rural working-class communities borne the burden of the research and development of nuclear weapons in their homelands since nuclear production ramped up during and after WWII, but these communities have also long experienced the material, social, and physiological effects of settler ideologies of space that designate most minority-populated areas as "wastelanded." In an analysis of nuclear imperialism published shortly afterwards, Roxanne Panchasi claims that French–Algerian relations in the twentieth century were directly impacted by nuclear colonialism, such that the colony of Algeria under French rule was at one moment called a "vital territory, where nuclear tests might be conducted far from the metropolitan French population" (Panchasi 2019, 91). In the essay "'No Hiroshima in Africa': The Algerian War and the Question of French Nuclear Tests in the Sahara," Panchasi goes on to note that the "distant" testing site was "one of many arguments against any [French] withdrawal from Algeria" (91). That is, on an international scale, examples of "wastelanding" (Voyles 2015) as an ideology are prevalent in the nationalist narratives of colonial states (Panchasi 2019). In another critical study, scholar Masahide Kato makes a list of all "nuclear warfare sites," most coded as "tests," which represent the start-to-finish detonation of nuclear weapons in the world. This military deployment of weapons, whether labeled as a "test" or a "strike," produces the effects of warfare unleashed upon the land it touches. It is against the "obliteration of the history of undeclared nuclear war" that Kato, hailing from Hiroshima, writes her article "Nuclear Globalism: Traversing Rockets, Satellites and Nuclear War via the Strategic Gaze," which observes a pattern: The political organization of radiation-impacted space is distributed according to colonial ideologies of center vs. periphery (Kato 1993, 339). Indeed, writing about nuclear colonialism and the U.S. Department of Defense, Karen

Barad cites Masahide Kato as noting that the "primary targets [of nuclear warfare] . . . have been invariably the sovereign nations of Fourth World and indigenous peoples" (Barad 2018). Barad notes that the targets of nuclear tests and extractive mining practices are the areas at the periphery of nuclear empires. Kato writes, "Such obliteration of the history of undeclared nuclear warfare by nuclear discourse does not merely posit the deficiency of the discourse. Rather, what it does reveal is the late capitalist form of domination, whereby an ongoing extermination process of the periphery is blocked from constituting itself as a historical fact" (339). These "nuclear warfare sites" where nuclear weapons have been tested and detonated can be said to include the Marshall Islands (66 times), French Polynesia (175 times), the Australian Aborigines (9 times), Newe Sogobia (the Western Shoshone Nation) (814 times), Christmas Island (24 times), Hawaii (Kalama Island, also known as Johnston Island) (12 times), the Republic of Kazakhstan (467 times), and Uighur (Xinjian Province, China) (36 times).

The distribution of detonation sites according to ideologies of space, a practice borne of the colonial legacy, recalls Elizabeth Povinelli's notions of "biosocial spacing" in her book *Empire of Love: Toward a Theory of Intimacy, Genealogy, and Carnality* (2006), or the geographical distribution of environmental harm. This uneven organization of harm, according to Povinelli, is informed by beliefs that produce spatial ideologies and map distributions of "ordinary and exceptional bodies" in space (2006, 32). In this schema, cancers caused by nuclear radiation distributed among Indigenous and white working-class mining communities in the U.S., for example, would be considered "ordinary" illnesses, without clear cause, rather than "extraordinary" illnesses, tied to a cause and therefore a solution.

Where Povinelli states, "Familiarity breeds this nervous system" (2006, 30), the artist might ask, what ideologies of space breed a different experiencing?

DinéYazhi´'s sculpture, *my ancestors will not let me forget this*, draws attention to itself as a material object. The sculpture is alive, not only in the way all matter is alive ("What makes us think that matter is lifeless to begin with?" [Barad 2015, 389]), but also in the way an electric current activates neon gas, exciting it into emitting a bright orange light. The work's electric hum is a reminder that the excitation of atoms is a material process, a response to energy coming in and stimulating what's already there. If its electroluminescence can signal the lively material casing for all the social and political activity brimming in the moment of its production, then the human nervous system must be a kind of reciprocal and reflective dynamic ordering.

In *Figuring*, a publication released by the University of Oregon's Center for Art Research, DinéYazhi´ writes that uranium's half-life was "formed within this universe" (2021, 37). The artist suggests that uranium is charged with tasks other than that of irradiating human life; as an independent element, it alights with other stories. In fact, when uranium is exposed to UV light, it absorbs energy and reemits this energy as visible light, giving off a greenish or bluish luminescence, which itself isn't radioactivity. While this light feels dangerous, it is the emission of particles from the nucleus of the unstable atom that is actually of concern, the aspect that can cause damage to human cells, DNA, and tissues, leading to radiation sickness and cancer in living beings. According to DinéYazhi´, material speaks. That's its nature. With Povinelli's (2002) call for scholars to engage in "radical interpretation," we might agree: The material has a story other than the one we've given it.

"What happened to the toxic matters after their employment?" asks Samia Henni, writing about France's nuclear program in the Sahara Desert. "Who is responsible and accountable for social reparation and environmental decontamination?" In the face of "partial or even truncated information" available to scholars and "the institutional obstruction of history-writing and the denial of social and environmental justice," Henni again asks, which institutions support not only reparations in this context, but also the immediate need to mitigate toxic fallout? A question about knowledge production emerges: "How to constitute alternative archives, sources, and evidence to narrate these [alternative] histories?" (Henni 2022, 18).

Of uranium, DinéYazhi´ writes, "i think this is how uranium speaks to me and I don't know what it's saying but i know that it's built into every single one of us and by US i mean Diné" (2021, 37). That the element has an unvoiced logic that "speaks" through material processes is neither an aesthetic claim nor a metaphoric turn, but is rather a landed material logic, that of DinéYazhi´'s project, born of colonial violence and other origins. The anthropocentric history of uranium is connected almost invariably to uranium extraction across the Navajo Nation, and those same circumstances produced structures that supplanted Indigenous knowledge systems with heteropatriarchal ideologies and governance. Yet DinéYazhi´'s writings convey a learning outside Western systems of knowledge and aside from human-centered impact. Their collective aesthetic project seems to voice a wish for a queer decolonial politics that includes but moves beyond institutional critique. *An Infected Sunset* brims with defiant tellings, as the sunset (noun) is "infected" (adjective modifier), but the artist knows that infection is a kind of relationship, the way uranium takes on the glow of reclamation as a landed chemical with its own intent: "we carry this sacred relationship with a radioactive sacred chemical that was formed within this universe and i don't know what it means" (37). In this way, DinéYazhi´ enacts "a practice and a doing, a reading strategy and viewing tactic, that allow us to see and sense differently" (Gopinath 2018, 21). The practice looks like one that *listens to uranium* and thus centers not only the human.

Of lightning, a "promiscuous" material prone to "errant wanderings" and "diverse forms of coupling and dis/connected alliance," Karen Barad writes, "no continuous path from sky to ground can satisfy its wild imaginings, its insistence on experimenting with different possible ways to connect" (2015, 387). If lightning is characterized, according to Barad's descriptions of quantum field theory, by its material errancy and inherently chaotic connection, then neon, according to these terms, is the alighting of atomic intimacy provoked by an outside intervention, a gas encountering a current. Its container inhabits the processes of its production, like a vacuum discharge tube, and a chemical element interacting with a current glowing red orange.

What, then, is uranium?

DinéYazhi´ grew up in Gallup, New Mexico, one hundred miles from Shiprock and less than twenty miles from Church Rock, the site of the largest radioactive nuclear spill in U.S. history. On July 16, 1979, over eleven hundred tons of acidic, radioactive tailings solution poured into Puerco River, spilling an estimated 1.36 short tons (1.23 t) of uranium and 46 curies of alpha contaminants across eighty miles downstream onto the Navajo Nation. The United Nuclear Corporation, which operated a uranium milling operation on land bordering Navajo Nation Tribal Trust lands, was responsible for the breach of its disposal area in Church Rock for ground waste containing radioactive rock and fluid, known as tailings. The radioactive spill had a severe impact on the environment and people in the area. The spill contaminated the groundwater and made the Puerco River unfit for use. The river's water, essential for drinking, irrigation, and livestock, became hazardous. The Governor of New Mexico denied the Navajo Nation's request to declare the site a federal disaster area and secure aid for affected residents, and residents were not informed of the toxic dangers posed by the spill for several days. The contamination event at Church Rock received less media coverage at the time than that of Three Mile Island, despite its comparatively disastrous effects.

Though Church Rock has faded in the collective memory, even among nuclear scholars, chemical contamination from nuclear production remains a threat, morphing into different disasters. In 2022, the unrestrained Cerro Pelado wildfire in New Mexico was about five miles from the back gate of the Los Alamos National Laboratory (LANL). A news release from LANL, Los Alamos County, the National Nuclear Security Administration's Los Alamos Field Office, and the Department of Energy Office of Environmental Management reported that the fire was, at the time, only 23 percent contained and covered 45,591 acres. The Laboratory and the County were alerted to the "set" stage of the evacuation command "ready, set, go." In the year 2000, just after the onset of Y2K and whispers of impending banking collapse, what became known famously as the Cerro Grande Fire came dangerously near the nuclear labs. The concern was the fire's proximity to LANL's Plutonium Facility and its Area G radioactive dump. Concerned Citizens for Nuclear Safety and the Nuclear Policy Project released a summary in December of that year of concerns in the fire's aftermath, noting specifically that dangers had been posed by the lab's disposal pits, burial grounds, and underground tanks: "hundreds of shafts filled with radioactive and hazardous wastes that have accumulated for more than a half century." Concerned Citizens for Nuclear Safety today claims that there are still over 2,120 potential radiation release sites at or near Los Alamos National Laboratory. Fires and winds pose a threat of releasing airborne contaminants, propelling increased contaminant-bearing sediment in watershed drainage feeding the Rio Grande River.

Any aesthetic practice that "rejects dominant cartographies" (Gopinath 2018, 4)—as we might describe DinéYazhi´'s projects' collection of seemingly disparate references like Palestine, Pulse, and Church Rock into the linked expression of queer anti-colonial practice—does more to combat the subjugation of queer and trans bodies when it names the ways in which the "normalizing logic of settler colonialism" produces a world of extractive social and material practices (Gopinath 2018, 5). The normalizing logic of extractivism is so sticky, and exerts itself with such staying power, that its violent moral imperatives like the regulating and policing of queer and

Indigenous bodies start to feel like an inevitability of modern life. From this perspective, queer aesthetic practice is not simply an expression, but an immeasurable social intervention and a matter of individual and collective survival.

I, and indeed many members of the queer community, remember where we were upon receiving news of the Pulse nightclub shooting of 2016. The colonial context aids in analyzing what Eric Stanley refers to, with reference to Pulse, as a "necropolitical site"; the rhetorical erasure of the nightclub shooting, a marker of brown queer grief and an emerging social struggle, which lingers long past the media focus. As Stanley describes, the massacre at Pulse, a gay nightclub attracting a predominately Latinx and Black crowd, was initially described as a targeted attack upon queer life by a presumed heterosexual attacker, but the story twisted and evolved as identifying details were filled in about the shooter's ethnicity and origins. Stanley notes: "Later, the event was recast as a terrorist attack by a 'radical Muslim'—the child of Afghan parents and husband of a Palestinian—against loyal 'Americans,' whose victims were LGBT by chance and whose race was assumed to be white" (2021, 42). The expressed connection between Pulse and the BIPOC queer community was de-emphasized in the media, supplanted by a narrative of the foreign terrorist on domestic soil killing "generically" (2021, 43), likely in protest of U.S. bombings in Iraq and Syria. These protests, and indeed the U.S. imperial context that makes such a protest conceivable as a possible explanation for a domestic mass shooting, are not unrelated to the concerns of a racialized and marginalized queer community on U.S. soil. Rather than think these contexts together (U.S. foreign policy in the Middle East, the bombings of Syria and Iraq, and the social and material insecurity that adheres to the marginalized lives of a queer BIPOC community in the U.S.), the media cut and pasted over the first story of queer targeting. Where "queerness also names the ways in which 'the normalizing logic of settler colonialism' produces sexually and gender non-normative bodies that are then subject to discipline, containment, and regulation" (Gopinath 2018, 5), the rendering of queer experiences as invisible serves a disciplinary and regulatory function. By calling back to Pulse as a cultural touchstone alongside other colonial contexts that condition queer life, DinéYazhi´ names queerness as a frame in which the normalizing logics, and, indeed, violent exterminating logics of settler colonialism are made visible. It's a trail that's impossible not to trace once it's unfurled.

In discussing the "queer lens," Gayatri Gopinath writes that queer aesthetic practice "teaches us how to read: it schools us as viewers in a queer mode and method of reading that is as attuned to ongoing processes of racialization and colonial dispossession" (2018, 5). Against the backdrop of the extermination of queer Black and brown bodies, and of trans bodies in particular, the specificity of the targeting of BIPOC LGBTQ+ individuals at Pulse underscores that any aesthetic practice of queer imagining, where attuned to dispossession and colonial dynamics, holds the possibility of infiltrating disciplinary and institutional containers in order to render visible and viable queer life inside colonial structures. Gopinath argues that queer works can produce a critical lens and "optic," one that "refuses to situate these formations in a hierarchical, equivalent, or binary relation to each other" (2018, 5). Much in this way, DinéYazhi´'s language instructs us to read in a way that allows any given piece of work to exceed its containers, to eschew hierarchical relationality, and to resist its own institutionalization. Crucially, DinéYazhi´ deconstructs orientations to space that reproduce normative experiencing, furthering lifeways that flourish despite the prescriptions and violent fluencies of colonial structures.

In her essay "1492, a New Worldview," Sylvia Wynter (1995) argues that culture is a product of language. As she reflects upon the question of whether "1492," a threshold date constructed retroactively in multiple competing colonial and anti-colonial narratives, can really be re-narrated with any productive sense of its significance to history in the present, language becomes central. Writing is evidence of the human process of narrating the "still to be written history of how the human represents to itself to the life that it lives . . . ," and poetry that attends to ongoing structures of displacement opens up an arena for examining what Wynter, citing linguist Melvin Donald, calls "symbolic representational systems" (Wynter 1995, 8). These representational systems display how "our species-specific cognitive mechanism (the mechanism to which we give the name *mind*) has been instituted, transformed, and reformed" (38). The stories we tell ourselves about our own history, as artists like DinéYazhi´ know, inform how we live in the present. Thus, *my ancestors will not let me forget this*, and even *we must stop imagining apocalypse / genocide + we must imagine liberation (Free Palestine)*, for example, become calls that, beyond rendering visible colonial systems, enact and support the incorporation of new social and material practices.

"Fuck a flag," the editors of *TSQ*'s "Everything Must Go" issue write, citing Miss Major (Lee et al. 2024). "Before we had a pride flag, we carried the North Vietnamese flag as our pride flag," the editors write in another epigraph, a quote attributed to Leslie Feinberg. In DinéYazhi´'s poems, redemption has no narrative, and a flag has no ambiguity. "We don't want a president." But the narratives do demonstrate uneasy multiplicities. "It's been nearly two years since i began the poem AN INFECTED SUNSET," DinéYazhi´ writes in *Figuring* in 2021. "i feel like most of the poem is inspired by all of the events that occurred during the summer of 2016 . . . how the entire country could just feel something in america breaking or becoming more obvious transparent" (37). By dwelling in the materiality exemplified in DinéYazhi´'s queer methods, we learn how social, political, and material structures can be re-formed.

It's smoky outside, and the fires around me move between labs. The media circles through stories, looking for the right narrative to explain our structural present. With me are the remainders of inheritance, not of queer trauma only, but of the potential abundance of queer framings and the stories that exceed their containers. Under the regime of narratives of nation, all manner of queer life persists.

Daisy Atterbury (they/them) is a scholar whose work focuses on queer aesthetic practices in the context of U.S. settler coloniality/colonialism and its logics. A full-time lecturer in the Department of American Studies and Program for Women's, Gender and Sexuality Studies at the University of New Mexico, Atterbury also serves on the board of the Feminist Research Institute. Their hybrid-genre book, *The Kármán Line*, was published in the fall of 2024 and has been called "a new cosmology" (Lucy Lippard) and "a cerebral alter to the desert" (Raquel Gutiérrez). They can be reached at daisyatterbury@unm.edu.

Works Cited

Barad, Karen. 2015. "TransMaterialities: Trans*/Matter/Realities and Queer Political Imaginings." *GLQ* 21 (2/3): 387–422.

Barad, Karen. 2018. "Troubling Time/s and Ecologies of Nothingness: Re-Turning, Re-Membering, and Facing the Incalculable." *new formations* 92: 56–86.

Biro Walters, Jordan. 2023. *Wide-Open Desert: A Queer History of New Mexico*. University of Washington Press.

Brady, Mattison. 2013. "Plutopia: Nuclear Families, Atomic Cities, and the Great Soviet and American Plutonium Disasters." Kennan Institute, Woodrow Wilson International Center for Scholars, May 28. https://www.wilsoncenter.org/publication/

plutopia-nuclear-families-atomic-cities-and-the-great-soviet-and-american-plutonium.

Brown, Kate. 2013. *Plutopia: Nuclear Families, Atomic Cities, and the Great Soviet and American Plutonium Disasters.* Oxford University Press.

Concerned Citizens for Nuclear Safety and the Nuclear Policy Project. https://https://nuclearactive.org/.

DinéYazhi´, Demian. 2018. *An Infected Sunset.* Printed Matter.

DinéYazhi´, Demian. 2019. *my ancestors will not let me forget this.* Glass, neon, aluminum frame, 42 × 22 × 23 in. Displayed in the Honolulu Biennial.

DinéYazhi´, Demian. 2021. "Through Ancestral Lands, Reading *An Infected Sunset.*" In *Figuring*, edited by Ford Family Foundation Visual Arts Program. The University of Oregon, Center for Art Research.

Gery, John. 1996. *Ways of Nothingness: Nuclear Annihilation and Contemporary American Poetry.* University Press of Florida.

Gómez, Myrriah. 2022. *Nuclear Nuevo México: Colonialism and the Effects of the Nuclear Industrial Complex on Nuevomexicanos.* The University of Arizona Press.

Gopinath, Gayatri. 2018. *Unruly Visions: The Aesthetic Practices of Queer Diaspora.* Duke University Press.

Henni, Samia. 2022. "Against the Regime of Emptiness." In *Deserts Are Not Empty*, edited by Samia Henni. Columbia University Press.

Kanouse, Sarah. 2024. "A People's Atlas of the Nuclear United States." Lab for Digital Humanities and Computational Social Science, Northwestern University. https://cssh.northeastern.edu/nulab/a-peoples-atlas-of-the-nuclear-united-states/.

Kato, Masahide. 1993. "Nuclear Globalism: Traversing Rockets, Satellites, and Nuclear War via the Strategic Gaze." *Alternatives* 18 (3): 339–60.

Lee, Christopher Joseph, Eric A. Stanley, Jemma DeCristo, and Ren-yo Hwang. 2024. "Introduction: Enemies and Friends." *TSQ* 11 (1): 3–15.

Panchasi, Roxanne. 2019. "'No Hiroshima in Africa': The Algerian War and the Question of French Nuclear Tests in the Sahara," *History of the Present* 9, no. 1 (Spring 2019): 84–112.

Povinelli, Elizabeth. 2002. *The Cunning of Recognition: Indigenous Alterities and the Making of Australian Multiculturalism.* Duke University Press.

Povinelli, Elizabeth. 2006. *The Empire of Love: Toward a Theory of Intimacy, Genealogy, and Carnality.* Duke University Press.

Rutter, Samuel, and Caitlin Youngquist. 2021. "10 Queer Indigenous Artists on Where Their Inspirations Have Led Them." *New York Times*, April 23. https://www.nytimes.com/2021/04/23/t-magazine/queer-indigenous-artists.html.

Stanley, Eric. 2021. "Necrocapital: Blood's General Strike." *Atmospheres of Violence: Structuring Antagonism and the Trans/Queer Ungovernable.* Duke

University Press.
Steinmetz, Katy. 2018. "The Oxford English Dictionary Added 'Trans*.' Here's What the Label Means." *Time Magazine*, April 3. https://time.com/5211799/what-does-trans-asterisk-star-mean-dictionary/.
Voyles, Traci Brynne. 2015. *Wastelanding: Legacies of Uranium Mining in Navajo Country*. University of Minnesota Press.
Wynter, Sylvia. 1995. "1492, a New Worldview." In *Race, Discourse, and the Origin of the Americas: A New World View*, edited by V. L. Hyatt and R. Nettleford. Smithsonian Institute Press.

Anti-Colonial Dreams and Their Resonant Afterlives: Facing the Ends of Man in Han Kang's *The Vegetarian*

Sunhay You

Abstract: In 2016, Han Kang's English translated novel *The Vegetarian* won the International Man Booker Prize. As the first South Korean novel to win the award, the event marked a momentous occasion. At the same time, the novel's anti-colonial narrative stood in stark contrast to the award's namesake—James Man, the founder of a British sugar cooperative in 1783. The colonial roots of the award arguably undermined the novel's anti-colonial politics. Counteracting the award's colonial sensibilities that frame the novel's English distribution, this essay highlights the novel's critique of South Korea's national formation as a neocolony of U.S. empire. The novel clarifies how U.S. colonial-imperialism manifests through mechanisms of complicity and compliance, "inviting" colonized peoples into a liberal-humanist order of capitalism as the "welcome" reprieve from war. The protagonist's dream of becoming a tree rests on rejecting the human pleasures of capitalist consumption and accumulation that sustain colonial hierarchies. In South Korea, this coloniality of being manifests through histories and social practices surrounding meat consumption and how racial-sexual violence preconditions such appetites. As such, *The Vegetarian* stages the simultaneously unbearable and emancipatory process of divesting from colonial ontologies. At the site of the protagonist's burgeoning plant consciousness, the novel reconceives human life as expansive networks of relations and ideas that exceed distinctions between humans and other species. Most suggestive is how the pursuit of arboreality implicitly revives the anti-colonial commitments of postcolonial women across history, speaking to a resonant poesis of thought that expands on the creative potential of knowledge production. **Keywords**: colonial-imperialism, U.S. empire, complicity, posthumanism, reproductive sexuality

The Pains of Dreaming Otherwise

The English translation of Han Kang's *The Vegetarian* rose to international acclaim after receiving the Man Booker Prize in 2016. The South Korean novel's win implicitly signaled the award's efforts to distance itself from its colonial conception, given that the award had been limited to current and former subjects of the British Empire just three years prior ("A Surprise and a Risk" 2013). The Man Booker prize broke from tradition again when it honored the novel's English translator, Deborah Smith, alongside Han Kang. The monetary reward was divided evenly between the two writers in recognition of "translation work as a distinct, and equally important, form of literary production" (Gullander-Drolet 2023, 632). Despite these meaningful gestures, the award had yet to remove "Man" from its title. The name paid homage to the investment company Man Group, which took over the administration of the International Booker Prize from 2005 to 2019 (Booker Prize Foundation 2023). The firm began as a British sugar cooperative that was founded by James Man in 1783 (Man Group 2023). While the Booker Prize Foundation later ended its affiliation with Man, this Man's colonial roots in the Atlantic slave trade cannot be divorced from the reception of Kang's English-translated novel.

According to Sylvia Wynter, Man constitutes a genre of humanism that normalizes and universalizes the authority of "the rational political subject" rooted in colonial projects (Wynter 2003, 227). She argues that this genre develops throughout the colonial period to cement a "purely secular, biocentric, and overrepresented modality of being" that stands in contradistinction to the non-European "subrational Human Other" (317, 266). As a recipient of the Man Booker Prize, Kang's novel gets folded into the world of colonial Man as a commodity that circuits in racial feeling. The novel incites attempts to affirm the universal applicability of colonial or "Western" reason. Claire Gullander-Drolet observes that "Western responses" and critics "under the sign of world literature" overwhelmingly engage Kang's novel using "canonical Western theory and generic conventions" (Gullander-Drolet 2023, 654). Additionally, the Eurocentric market for world literature sustains standard appetites for narratives about postcolonial women overcoming patriarchal oppression (Wang 2018, 411). The Man Booker's decision to honor Smith alongside Kang can then be read as a self-congratulatory gesture regarding the award-granting institution's laudable gender politics, which is to stand in stark contrast to Kang's depiction of gender violence in South Korea.

These uses and effects of the novel restage colonial hierarchies of knowledge and power.

Unsettling the "coloniality of being," or Man, then, calls for "a redescription of the human outside the terms of our present descriptive statement of the human" (Wynter 2003, 268). Attending to this task, Katherine McKittrick claims that the intellectual struggle against Man involves drawing attention to "new stories of being human that challenge the profitable brutalities that attend the realization of Man-as-human" (Wynter and McKittrick 2015, 7). *The Vegetarian* offers one such story for propounding that one could prefer to be nonhuman even at the risk of death. The novel traces how Yeong-hye's nonhuman subjectivity induces a near-intolerable interruption of normality, or what Alexis Pauline Gumbs might call a "species-scale betrayal of our founding mythologies" (Gumbs 2020, x). In this manner, *The Vegetarian*, more than reifying the subhuman, evinces how turning strange and estranged from humanity can be experienced as a painful but irresistible impulse to wrest one's creative existence from the ontology of Man.

To demonstrate the above, this essay locates Kang's novel within its national and transnational contexts to foreground its anti-colonial[1] and feminist interventions, interrupting the colonial sensibilities that inform its English distribution. While there are other works that situate Kang's novel within South Korean politics of *han,* Confucianism, and globalized misogyny, this examination stresses the need to account for the history and economy of meat consumption in South Korea (Casey 2021; Choi 2013; Gullander-Drolet 2023). The social ritual of meat-eating and its biopolitical-capitalist implications present the key to understanding how colonial-imperial violence inflects the reproductive futurity of South Korea and its structures of gender violence. The close readings that follow further position Kang's novel in relation to a more expansive genealogy of anti-colonial knowledge production, lending shape to what I term a resonant poesis of thought.[2]

Binding Appetites

Han Kang's *The Vegetarian* consists of three novellas that move across the perspectives of Yeong-hye's husband, Mr. Cheong; brother-in-law (who remains nameless); and older sister, In-hye. They chronicle Yeong-hye's progressively deteriorating health and growing obsession with turning into a tree. Yeong-hye's voice often traverses the margins of the novel, which are set in blocks of slanted italic text. Her words are at a slant, or slanted, meaning that they stand in a divergent orientation to the straight or normal trajectory of the other characters' narratives. A slant also denotes a particular viewpoint that deviates from the center, slipping sideways to reveal something ordinarily out of sight. The slanted space of Yeong-hye's voice indexes what becomes legible from her increasingly nonhuman positionality and sideways orientation to Man.[3] This site of her transformation serves as a dense metaphor that collates South Korea's neocolonial formation, meat, and the heteronuclear family as impediments to the flourishing of human life.

The slanted space of Yeong-hye's interiority first interrupts Mr. Cheong's narrative. She offers a story about the dream most responsible for her sudden distaste for meat, which additionally serves as an allegory for South Korea's entanglements with U.S. empire. The dream opens in the *"dark woods. No people"* (Kang 2015, 19). The dream continues in fragments: *"The sharp-pointed leaves on the trees, my torn feet. This place, almost remembered, but I'm lost now. Frightened. Cold. Across the frozen ravine, a red barn-like building"* (19–20). While lost, Yeong-hye uses the demonstrative *"this"* to describe where she is, as if she were in familiar and knowable territory *"almost remembered."* The apprehension of having forgotten this place is what turns her sense of loss into the contents of a nightmare. Yeong-hye is suddenly without the assurances of belonging anywhere despite the vague familiarity of her surroundings.

The poetic space of this dream grounds the novel in the events that shaped South Korea after WWII, when the people of the Korean peninsula suddenly found themselves liberated from Japanese rule and yet divided along the thirty-eighth parallel. Yeong-hye's disoriented sense of place aptly describes the confusing state of Korea after liberation, when the peninsula people called home became subject to foreign oversight once again. The united Korean peninsula that preceded the war became a distant dream—almost remembered, but lost to its people. In the aftermath of the Korean War, the U.S. offered "guidance" in the form of military governance, foreign aid, and economic opportunities (Berry 2012, 39; Choi and Yoon 2016, 112). The U.S. had effectively "replaced the Japanese colonial government" to shape the South Korean government as a model nation in the likeness of America's own image (Lee et al. 2014, 657). Tracking these developments, Yeong-hye journeys across a *"frozen ravine"* as if to signal the frozen results of the Korean War that keep the peninsula divided at the thirty-eighth parallel, of a people's suspended self-determinacy (Kang 2016, 19). The *"cold"* environment of *"this place"* seems to further cement this reference to the Cold War.

The stream also marks a site of crossing. On the other side of the stream, Yeong-hye comes across a *"barn-like building"* (19). The building more accurately refers to the Korean word "헛간,"[4] a large open shed commonly used to store industrial grain and livestock (Kang 2016, 18–19). This symbol of agricultural industrialism anchors this other side of the stream, suggestive of South Korea's crossing from an agrarian to a industrial-capitalist nation after the Korean War and under U.S. imperial oversight. Yeong-hye moves toward this barn as if it were to guide her out of the wilderness and back toward the modern comforts of human civilization. What Yeong-hye finds inside this building, however, becomes representative of the collateral damage that followed South Korea's industrialization. Once she moves past the threshold of the building, Yeong-hye finds *"a long bamboo stick strung with great blood-red gashes of meat, blood still dripping down"* (Kang 2015, 20). She continues: *"Try to push past the meat, and no exit. Blood in my mouth, blood-soaked clothes onto my skin"* (20). The *"barn-like"* structure turns out to be a slaughterhouse, signaling how reassuring signs of economic modernity can cloak structures of violence.

Mr. Cheong's narrative later reveals that Yeong-hye's father is a celebrated war hero of the Vietnam War, offering additional historical context to the slaughterhouse. Indeed, South Korea secured its place in the "first world" after participating in the Vietnam War. The U.S. funded the South Korean military and its supporting industries such that South Korea became the second-largest army in Vietnam, next to that of the U.S. (Brazinsky 2005). The gains from the war catalyzed the growth of the South Korean economy, most evident in the way meat became a regular part of the Korean diet (Nam et al. 2010). The wide availability of meat was a sign of South Korea's rise as a global economic power, such that meat become symbolic of the nation's postcolonial redemption and future prosperity. The resulting social practice of eating meat at once naturalizes and obfuscates South Korea's complicity with and subordination to U.S. imperialism. South Korea remains the only neocolony of the U.S. to have amassed global economic influence, a standing testament to how U.S. freedom serves those who can reap the spoils of war.

Yeong-hye's dream stages how South Korea's active complicity with U.S. imperialism sets the conditions for South Korea's modernity in the aftermath of the Cold War. In the dream, Yeong-hye begins to express a sense of shame over this complicity. After facing the carnage at the barn house, she is consumed by guilt, which prevents her from leaving the wilderness. Soaked in blood, Yeong-hye narrates:

> *Somehow a way out. Running, running through the valley, then suddenly the woods open out. Trees thick with leaves, springtime's green light. Families picnicking, little children running about, and that smell, that delicious smell. Almost painfully vivid. . . . Barbecuing meat, the sounds of singing and happy laughter.* (Kang 2015, 20)

If the dream began in the frigid cold of winter, in a place "*almost remembered,*" Yeong-hye now approaches the warmth and vitality of spring, toward what is clearly and painfully familiar. The narrative move from the barn to the open field tracks the role industrial capitalism plays in ushering a period of economic prosperity in South Korea, indicative of the happy domestic scene of families enjoying barbecued meats. However, instead of relief, the sight makes her self-conscious of her "*clothes still wet with blood . . . [Her] bloody hands. [Her] bloody mouth*" (20). She suddenly realizes that she had eaten the pieces of meat hanging in her path out of the barn. She then recalls seeing her reflection in a pool of blood, "*the look in [her] eyes . . . [her] face, undoubtedly, but never seen before. Or no, not mine, but so familiar . . . nothing makes sense*" (20). Her reflection is and is not hers, in the same sense that her murderous appetite is at once familiar and unfamiliar. Yeong-hye wakes up to this feeling of being alien to herself.

Yeong-hye's estrangement distills how U.S. colonial-imperial interventions shaped not only South Korea's economy but the people's diet. Cultural historian Chungmoo Choi contends that after the Korean War, "the power of the US and its material representations were irresistibly seductive and at the same time repulsive to many South Koreans" (Choi 1998, 10). Spam, sausages, powdered milk, chocolate, and other imported American goods were "a sensuous signifier of colonialism . . . irresistible and burdensome" (11). Such gifts cultivated the South Korean people's appetites for U.S. culture and its symbols of power while under the country's neocolonial subjection. Yeong-hye later tries to explain to her brother-in-law that the murderous face of her nightmares, so alien from her sense of self, "'rose up inside [her] stomach'" (Kang 2015, 122). The imagery suggests the biopolitical and symbolic force of U.S. empire, most explicit as the narrative of "survival-through-ever-increasing-processes-of-consumption-and-accumulation," that impregnates its subjects to reproduce and reify its self-descriptive legitimacy (Wynter and McKittrick 2015, 11).

The slanted space of her dream begins to retreat from the latter parts of the novel as it turns Yeong-hye's waking world aslant. Waking from the dream, Yeong-hye immediately empties all the meat in her fridge as if she were allergic to its very presence. Her actions, absurd in the eyes of her husband, apprehend how the neocolonial dynamics between the U.S. and South Korea inform and normalize domestic consumptive practices. As such, Yeong-hye's vegetarianism uncovers how her family's most "natural" appetites paradoxically pay tribute to South Korea's neocolonial formation—restaging their colonial-imperial subjugation to the tenets of racial capitalism. Yeong-hye stops eating meat as if to wrest her appetites from this dynamic.

The Meat of Empire and Sex

The backlash to Yeong-hye's vegetarianism further reveals the sexual logics that undergird the meat of empire. For instance, Yeong-hye's father orders Yeong-hye to eat meat at a family gathering, insisting that he is looking out "for [her] own good" (Kang 2015, 46). He extends the colonial uses of sexual domination when he claims to know what is best for his daughter. Moreover, his claims of care fix Yeong-hye's refusal to mean something more than a simple dietary choice. In her analysis of the novel, Yoo Jin Choi argues that meat "exemplifies the ideology of Korean patriarchy" such that "the act of eating meat is analogous to succumbing to male supremacy" (Choi 2013, 215). Yeong-hye's persistent refusal to consume meat constitutes a direct affront against her father's authority as a patriarch and national war veteran who understands the necessities of personal and national survival.

The father's care, then, creates a situation that justifies his right to control Yeong-hye's body and its future. He senses no contradiction in this care, as his orders are implicitly supported by other "concerned" members of their family. Her sister-in-law "never would have guessed that going vegetarian could damage your body like that" (43). And her older sister, In-hye, implores that "everyone needs a certain amount of energy while they're alive" (44). The building consensus over Yeong-hye's deteriorating health more than justifies her father's disciplinary interventions, revealing the violence of care intended to extend a subject's life (Lee 2023). Norms around health, meat consumption, and familial care manifest as biopolitical and disciplinary regimes that restrict the bodily autonomy of women's bodies so that they remain productive for the family and the state. In a final act of dominance, the father slaps Yeong-hye across the face to loosen her jaw and force meat down her throat, exposing the existential stakes of this "caring" intervention. Yeong-hye's submission is necessary to preserve the redemptive meaning of her father's military service, her family's economic security, and South Korea's extended life as a neocolonial and sub-imperial state.

The father's reactions specify how the biopolitical enjoyment of meat relies on structures of sexual domination. After Yeong-hye announces her vegetarianism, her husband starts thinking of her "as a stranger, or no, as a sister, or even a maid, someone who puts food on the table and keeps the house in good order" (38). Having reduced her humanity to an economic function, he soon normalizes marital rape. Meanwhile, Yeong-hye's brother-in-law becomes consumed by images of having sex with Yeong-hye, their bodies painted in flowers (67). Spellbound by her life-defying vegetarianism, he wonders if he might not be "a normal human being," affirming Yeong-hye's later desires to be a plant (69). He explores this arboreal subjectivity with Yeong-hye, a mutually beneficial and pleasurable collaboration that later devolves into another instance of rape. The brother-in-law's admiration for Yeong-hye had merely cloaked his need to recover his masculinity from being "worn down by the vicissitudes of late capitalist society" (67). These patriarchal responses to Yeong-hye's vegetarianism insinuate that the enjoyment of meat demands strategies for subverting the degrading preconditions of its pleasures.

Given the ways South Korea remains invested in U.S. empire, women's sexuality becomes the redemptive grounds upon which the nation can reassert its dominance. This structural logic builds upon the biopolitical belief that population management depends on the sexual reproduction and nourishment of the human species, which also necessitates capitalist modes of accumulation and consumption. Therefore, Yeong-hye's distaste for meat registers as a refusal to reify this temporally reproductive framework through which South Korea might secure its future and redeem its past to catch up to Western colonial-imperial powers. Yeong-hye becomes subject to disciplinary sexual violence precisely for undermining the capitalist and nationalist uses of her reproductive body.

South Korea overcomes U.S. imperial hegemony by reasserting its patriarchal dominance over women. The emasculation of South Korea, most emblematic in histories of U.S. and Japanese military sexual violence, was overcome by nationalist efforts to restore the nation's masculine virility. An Army textbook, *The Dragon Rise of the Korean Nation*, celebrates South Korea's participation in the Vietnam War as a necessary endeavor to nurture South Korea's statehood (Republic of the Korean Army 1982). Demonstrating the nation's military might against "another feminized former colony" was framed as a "rite of passage to recuperate [Korea's] virility and join the ranks of the imperialistic order" heralded by the U.S. (Choi 1998, 18). However, Yeong-hye's sexual violation also marks the limit to the above narratives. South Korea's uses of colonial power simultaneously affirm the conditions of its neocolonial subordination, which must then be continuously denied through the reassertion of the nation's patriarchal dominance over Korean women.

These entanglements between U.S. colonial-imperial and South Korean patriarchal violence disorganizes the tenets of human intimacy. Intimacy conventionally assumes that subjects are in possession of their essential selves as "the privileged sign of liberal interiority or domesticity," which becomes available to be exchanged or owned by others in binding relationships of love or debt (Lowe 2015, 18). However, colonialism also produces a less personal economy of intimacies that reflect "the global processes and colonial connections that are the conditions of its production" (18). Intimacy circulates as a residual form of interest that explicitly and implicitly reinvests in colonial racial-sexual dynamics. Therefore, Yeong-hye's renunciation of meat goes beyond a mere dietary choice to concern appetites for racial-sexual conquest via capitalist consumption and accumulation, which indirectly and yet pervasively normalize sexual violence as the precondition for human relationality. Therefore, the father, husband, and brother-in-law's treatment of Yeong-hye marks the ways colonial-imperial violence leaves its traces in the most "natural" and "caring" relationships. For refusing her social obligations to affirm the pleasures of meat, Yeong-hye threatens the colonial-imperial conditions for life that undergird the narrative trajectory of postcolonial redemption and survival.

Yeong-hye later cuts her wrists in response to her father's abuse. Her brother-in-law recalls "hoping she would survive, but at the same time doubting just what that 'survival' would mean" (Kang 2015, 74). In her total disregard for self-preservation, Yeong-hye reframes the idea that the violence of conquest is necessary for the flourishing of life, asserting a different descriptive statement for human survival. She carves out the space for a new hunger to take root, one so powerful as to obviate concerns over death. Her burgeoning arboreal subjectivity acts as a counterhumanist force that unsettles the colonial-imperial order of Man and its futurity.

Arboreal Subjectivity: Reimagining Human Life
The Vegetarian articulates how postcolonial subjects like Yeong-hye are already estranged from themselves given their attachments to practices and narratives that perpetuate the injustices they seek to overcome. Turning strange against an already alienated self can then be experienced as a painful but worthwhile recovery of one's creative existence. In *The Vegetarian*, this impulse manifests through Yeong-hye's fantasies of turning into a plant. Refusing all forms of human food, Yeong-hye appears intent on dying for the sake of forging a nonhuman existence. Instead of postcolonial redemption as managed via biopolitics and reproductive futurity, Yeong-hye's life becomes legible through the space of death to suggest a different story of the human.

Yeong-hye's later rejection of all forms of human sustenance starves the colonial-imperial symbology rooted in her belly, moving against its reproductive and redemptive future. One of the first effects of this starvation is that Yeong-hye's breasts become an ambivalent object of attachment. While turning away from the world and her murderous appetites, Yeong-hye finds solace in her breasts, for "nothing can be killed by them" (41). However, this relief is soon overwrought with her worries that her breasts "keep on shrinking," incapable of nurturing life (41). She wonders if her edges are all sharpening, as if they were intent on doing harm (41). Her breasts emerge as an object of violence and nonviolence, bringing into disarray their typical associations with nourishment and reproductive life.

This ambivalent attitude seems to allow Yeong-hye to persist despite her growing estrangement from the conditions of her survival. In other words, her breasts allow her to persevere in a state of dread. According to Lauren Berlant, a subject of dread discovers that "nothing at the moment compels the drives or action toward cultivating anything, or even pretending to," which opens the space for fantasies that offer "consolation for living on while failing to provide a reliable cushion" (Berlant and Edelman 2014, 39). Such fantasies do not lead into escapism, denial, or maniacal positivity but allow the subject to endure the uncertainty and suspension of one's desires—of not knowing what is worth living or dying for. It is through dread that Yeong-hye might survive the pains of her undoing and learn to experience those pains as the productive grounds for other modes of being.

Dread ultimately enables a subject to transmute ambivalence into the ecstatic conditions for a creatively improvised life, such that her "willed arboreality" becomes legible as "inherently sensible" (Casey 2021, 35). Berlant additionally claims that dread forces "the impossible-to-distinguish relation between attaching and destroying and between building a world and annihilating what's inconvenient to it," including the subject of dread (50). Given these insights, the meaning of Yeong-hye's emaciated body and flattening chest ambiguously indexes her proximity to death *and* a new world of existence. Berlant continues that such ambivalence toward one's self-preservation "can be the source of an affective creativity that is not just a fantasmatic toupeé, but also the possibility of a recalibrated sensorium, . . . new capacities for bearing, and not repairing, ambivalence" (61). Along these lines of thought, the images of Yeong-hye's shrinking breasts set the scene for a new idiom of human relationality to emerge, addressing the aching need for alternative paradigms not only for shifting out of cruel attachments to colonial ontologies but for finding something worthwhile about that very painful process.

However, Berlant's theory lacks an explicit account of how race and the coloniality of being factor into such processes of destroying and building worlds. Yeong-hye's orientation to death can be said to additionally invoke that "zero degree of social conceptualization" and the eviscerated "flesh," the racial abasement of which spawns the discourses and metaphors that ground colonial-imperial ontologies in the aftermath of slavery (Spillers 1987, 445). Yeong-hye offers her own eviscerated flesh not as an object of abasement but as the hinge upon which she can break from that very colonial judgment. She remakes the meaning of her flesh, unsettling (colonial) "hierarchies of knowledge pertaining to the nature of reality" (Jackson 2015, 216). This nonhuman flesh does not seek to be redeemed back into humanity. As such, Yeong-hye's arboreal subjectivity demands that audiences reconsider the logic of Man and its founding mythologies around the human/subhuman hierarchy such that what remains disavowed and illegible "as the lack of the West's ontologically absolute self-description" becomes more sensible and available to be desired (Wynter 2003, 282).

A new idiom of relationality emerges from Yeong-hye's shrinking flesh and arboreal becoming, which critically unsettles the iterative tempo of a colonial-imperial world and its reproductive ethos. She habitually sits outside with "her gaunt collarbones, emaciated breasts and brown nipples completely exposed [as] sunbeams [bathe] her face and naked body" (Kang 2015, 59). She goes on to insist that *"leaves are growing out of [her] body, roots are sprouting out of [her] hands,"* and flowers will bloom from between her legs (133). In Yeong-hye's dreams of becoming nonhuman, she gives birth to flowers instead of babies. Her desire to live lands on the ever-sprawling activity of vegetal life as if she were to live through its many parts—leaf, root, and flower. Within the networked vitality of connected vegetal life forms, Yeong-hye's life seems to extend past the singularity of her eviscerated flesh.

This vegetal orientation to life stands in contrast to the sexually reproductive logic of human survival. Indeed, Yeong-hye's commitment to becoming a plant only desexualizes her body. In the second chapter of the novel, her brother-in-law comments that "her breasts . . . were slender and elongated like those of a young girl . . . It was a body from which all superfluity had gradually been whittled away" (94–95). In-hye makes similar observations after admitting Yeong-hye to a psychiatric hospital. In-hye begins to question, is her sister

> trying to turn herself back into a preadolescent? She hadn't had her period for a long time now, and now that her weight has dropped below thirty kilos, of course there's nothing left of her breasts. She lies there looking like a freakish overgrown child, devoid of any secondary sexual characteristics. (156)

The lack of breasts signals not just Yeong-hye's proximity to death but also her transformation from a woman to a "freakish" child who defies the biological inevitability of sexual maturation. Critically, this child cannot be said to stand for the sexual reproductive futurity of the family, the nation-state, and a global neoliberal order of colonial-imperial origins. Yeong-hye affects a paradoxical sense of a future within the image of the dying child, which inspires awe as much as grief.

Yeong-hye's transformation forces In-hye to confront her own entrapment in the colonial world of Man, which leads to a series of painful revelations. Yeong-hye's incomprehensible insistence that she is turning into a plant, awakens in In-hye the feeling that she had never really lived in this world . . . [S]he had done nothing but endure. She had believed in her own inherent goodness, her humanity, and lived accordingly, never causing anyone harm . . . [S]he would have gone on like that indefinitely. (167)

In-hye confronts the biopolitical norms of human survival that had justified and lent meaning to her own life and ambitions as a businesswoman and working mother. Her startling revelations gesture to death worlds that South Korea's postcolonial nationalism produces. According to Achille Mbembe, death worlds describe "new and unique forms of social existence in which vast populations are subjected to conditions of life conferring upon them the status of *living dead*" (Mbembe 2003, 40). Given that reason stands as "one of the most important elements of both the project of modernity and of the topos of sovereignty" and this reason articulates "what the good life is all about, how to achieve it, and, in the process, to become a fully moral agent," then the incontrovertible good of the family and nation reasons that postcolonial women seek moral value in their subjugated positions as productive and sexually reproductive human capital (13). Through such concessions, postcolonial women's moral agency becomes determined by their subjection, evacuating the very meaning of women's moral agency. This incapacity to know one's own moral goodness without also effacing one's agency presents the context within which In-hye can come to the shocking realization that "she had never really lived in this world."[5]

In-hye's response to Yeong-hye also facilitates a process for mourning this death world and her attachments to it. In-hye claims that "the role she had adopted . . . of the hard-working, self-sacrificing eldest daughter had been a sign not of maturity but of cowardice. It had been a survival tactic" (163). If Yeong-hye had also remained in her role as the "docile and naïve" younger sister, In-hye might not have ever known the ideas that kept her a prisoner in her own life (148). Yeong-hye's turn toward death invites a break from biopolitics and necropolitical death worlds. Her desire to be a plant shocks In-hye to confront a world to which she never belonged, where being human consists of an idea not of her own making, and that with mourning this idea, she can look forward to other worlds that have always already been within reach. The ends of a colonial-imperial world are only threatening to the degree that its stories of survival remain the metaphysical substance of human life.

A Resonant Poesis of Thought

Despite wanting to honor Yeong-hye's vision for an alternative way of being, In-hye later succumbs to mounting pressures from the hospital staff to force-feed Yeong-hye in the face of her imminent death. A crowd of doctors descend on Yeong-hye to push tubes down her throat until she begins to vomit blood. The doctors' authority and use of force become legible as forms of torture intent on reshaping Yeong-hye's body to better align with the biopolitical imperative to extend her life and the postcolonial redemption such extensions secure. And yet, for being so resistant to torture, including prior events of disciplinary sexual violence, Yeong-hye invokes a history of Korean women who risked their lives in search of other ways of being—inducing a resonant structure of anti-colonial thought.

In 1919, Yu Guan-sun played a critical role in organizing the March First Movement against the Japanese empire. She was later captured and tortured to death. According to literary critic Karen Lee, official historical accounts of Yu's resistance "emphasize torture to demonstrate Yu's feminine willingness to obliterate herself for a greater patriarchal-identified good," namely South Korea's postcolonial and neocolonial formation (Lee 2010, 68). However, Lee also elaborates that Theresa Hak Kyung Cha's rendering of Yu Guan-Sun's life in *Dicteé* offers an alternative feminist and Korean diasporic perspective on the same topic. According to Lee, Cha stresses Yu's spiritual and political fortitude in resisting the "psychologically and physically destructive goals of torture: isolation, indoctrination, and dehumanization" (68). Yu's daring stance against Japanese authorities evinces her fearlessness in the face of pain and death, which ruptures colonial ideologies about the biocentric body upon which torture is based. The effectiveness of torture and corporeal punishment depends on the degree to which a subject can be reduced to a mere body that can be transfigured to better affirm the torturer's reality (as does the effect of slavery upon the "zero degree of social conceptualization"). However, in the event torture fails to re-form its subjects, the subjects' disregard for pain and death powerfully evinces the existence of other modes of being as the meaning of the flesh gets remade.

Cha's Korean diasporic rendering of Yu extends beyond the Japanese colonial context to also touch U.S. imperialism. Korean American poet Cathy Park Hong mentions that Cha found the task of surviving "disgusting" compared to when she felt "freed ... and ... also ... naked" after having published *Dicteé* (Hong 2020, 152). Despite her having moved to the U.S. to flee an increasingly authoritarian South Korean government, Cha's disgust at her dependency on U.S. art institutions for her survival was an insult to the anti-colonial sensibilities that imbued her art. Her tragic and often forgotten death at the hands of a serial rapist only adds to the gravity of her discontent. Situated within these histories, Yeong-hye's turn to death charts the enduring life of anti-colonial dissent as a resonant poesis of thought.

The word *resonance* refers to the way a sound, idea, or story reverberates across different subjects and spaces. Like the vibration of sound, an idea or story can enter a body and have resounding effects, reorganizing its composition. An idea or impulse of even those long gone can nonetheless persist as an echo to impact those in the present, producing a more slanted orientation to linear industrial time and reproductive sexuality. Resonance also stands in proximate relation to recognition, which describes an encounter with something known but previously forgotten. To recognize means to know again, which amplifies the way resonance can also trigger remembrance. Positioning Yeong-hye in relation to Yu Guan Soon and Theresa Hak Kyung Cha fuels the possibility that individual dreams of otherwise worlds are manifestations of more collective dreams and impulses, awakened from states of dormancy like a seed coming to bloom after a cycle of rest and maturation.

Wynter gestures to this very potential in an interview about her field-defining critiques of Man. She explains that her ideas

> never came linearly. It tends to come the way a flower blooms. It comes unexpectedly; and it has nothing to do with "genius" . . . It's the idea of *poesis*, again; there is *a poesis of thought; a new poesis of being human.* These concepts don't come in a linear fashion. They build up. They build up, you know? (Wynter 2006, 34)

Wynter attends to the non–sexually reproductive and yet cyclical life of emancipatory knowledge, theories, and stories, which crescendo in a nonlinear manner. These stories are what hold the power to remake humanity. In her writing about the Blombos Cave in South Africa, Wynter suggests that the evolution of human consciousness relied on the representative power of cave paintings to foster a collective identity that could transcend individual biological distinctions (Wynter and McKittrick 2015, 68). Humanity metamorphosized into "a now fictively chartered and encoded, thereby hybrid, *bios/mythoi* autopoietic form of symbolic life" (68). This other scientific story of the origins of humanity stresses how the colonial justifications for Man's supremacy over nature—and, in extension, racialized subhuman beings—coalesce as a hegemonic narrative and symbology that can be undone. However, the resonant structure of Kang's novel as it aligns with other Korean women's writings and histories suggests that it may not be enough to claim that the red ochre in Blombos Cave merely enabled human collectivity. Those symbolic expressions may have realized a sense of interconnectedness that preexisted human cognition, as a dormant ontological reality of being.

It is no coincidence, then, that Yeong-hye's pursuit of kinship with plants additionally echoes the work of Black and queer feminist poet Alexis Pauline Gumbs, which reimagines the very limits of scientific taxonomy. Offering her own counterhumanist stories of relationality, Gumbs asserts that the lines distinguishing one species from another are as "debatable and discursively unstable as . . . the discursive construction of man" (Gumbs 2020, xii). She forges a kindred relationality with "speakers who have never been considered human . . . [including] whales, corals, barnacles, bacteria, and more" (xii). This interspecial imaginary promises to reframe the purpose of human relationality, not around the survival of the human species or postcolonial redemption but around realizing an ever-expansive interdependency that preconditions our very existence.

As the red ochre paint of Blombos Cave offers a symbol for menstrual blood and the shared origins of human life, a mountain appears at the conclusion of *The Vegetarian* as another scarlet symbol, one that threads together the destiny of humanity with that of other species. While holding onto her dying sister, In-hye notices the ambulance finally leaving the embrace of Ch'ukseong Mountain, named after its brilliant red hue in autumn (Kang 2015, 187). The scene gestures back to when Yeong-hye ran away from the hospital only to be found in the mountain's thick woods under the pouring spring rain (133). Yeong-hye explained that something had called her to the depths of Ch'ukseong Mountain (165). Yeong-hye was to become one of the trees that dressed the mountain red, "about to go down into the earth" (165). *The Vegetarian* reads as a parable of our times that warns of the painful but promising process of "waking up" from the collective dreams of Man and finding ourselves in relation to the soil in their place.

Sunhay You is an assistant professor of Asian/American literature and culture at the Rhode Island School of Design. She can be reached at syou@risd.edu.

Notes

1. It is important to acknowledge that neither *anti-colonial* nor *decolonial* adequately describe the work of *The Vegetarian*. The novel does not forward an anti-colonial critique that reinvests in the state or makes rights-based claims so that postcolonial subjects can aspire to be equal to their former oppressors. However, neither does the novel further decolonialism to advocate for the repatriation of Indigenous land and life or show how such repatriation would uproot U.S. imperialism in South Korea. My use of *anti-colonial*, then, describes perspectives, feelings, desires, and actions that facilitate a material and psychic break from colonial ontologies. For more on the uses of these terms, see Tuck and Yang (2012).
2. My use of the term *poesis* draws from an interview with Sylvia Wynter, which describes how "poetics or *poesis* is so important not as some narrow, literary affair but because it tends to signify all these repressed or stigmatized orders of cognition, ones which differ profoundly from our now orthodox, linear modes of thinking or theorizing" (Wynter 2006, 32).
3. There is much about *The Vegetarian* that reads as queer in its deviant politics and perspectives, which speak to discourses on "queer inhumanisms" (Luciano and Chen 2015).
4. While beyond the scope of this article, issues of translation in the novel have incited controversy. For more on the politics of translation, see Godley (2021) and Gullander-Drolet (2023).
5. *The Vegetarian* suggests that necropolitics, originally conceived to describe late modern colonial occupation, extends past colonial-imperial warfare to buttress postcolonial sovereignty.

Works Cited

Berlant, Lauren, and Lee Edelman. 2014. *Sex, or the Unbearable*. Duke University Press.
Berry, Mark P. 2012. "The U.S. and the 1945 Division of Korea: Managing the 'Big Decisions.'" *International Journal on World Peace* 29 (4): 37–59.
Booker Prize Foundation. 2023. "The International Booker Prize and Its History." *The Booker Prizes*. https://thebookerprizes.com/international-booker-prize/the-international-booker-prize-and-its-history.
Brazinsky, Gregg Andrew. 2005. "From Pupil to Model: South Korean and American Development Policy During the Early Park Chung Hee Era." *Diplomatic History* 29 (1): 83–115.
Casey, Rose. 2021. "Willed Arboreality: Feminist Worldmaking in Han Kang's *The Vegetarian*." *Critique: Studies in Contemporary Fiction* 62 (3): 347–60.

Choi, Chungmoo. 1998. "Nationalism and Construction of Gender in Korea." In *Dangerous Women: Gender and Korean Nationalism*, edited by by Elaine H. Kim and Chungmoo Choi, 9–32. Routledge.

Choi, Yoo Jin. 2013. "Male Violence and Female Body in Kang Han's 'Vegetarian.'" *Feminist Studies in English Literature* 21 (3): 205–35.

Choi, Young Back, and Yong J. Yoon. 2016. "Liberalism in Korea." *Econ Journal Watch* 13 (2): 100–28.

Godley, Min Young. 2021. "The Feminization of Translation: Gender Politics in the Translation Controversy over Han Kang's *The Vegetarian*." *Meridians: Feminism, Race, Transnationalism* 20 (1): 193–217.

Gullander-Drolet, Claire. 2023. "The Translation Politics of Han Kang's *The Vegetarian*; or, The Task of the Reader of the Work in (English) Translation." *PMLA* 138 (3): 652–65.

Gumbs, Alexis Pauline. 2020. *Dub: Finding Ceremony*. Duke University Press.

Hong, Cathy Park. 2020. *Minor Feelings*. One World Press.

Jackson, Zakiyyah Iman. 2015. "Outer Worlds: The Persistence of Race in Movement 'Beyond the Human.'" *GLQ* 21 (2–3): 215–18.

Kang, Han. 2015. *The Vegetarian*. Translated by Deborah Smith. Hogarth.

Kang, Han. 2016. 채식주의자 (*The Vegetarian*). Changbi Publishers.

Lee, Karen An-hwai. 2010. "From Female Self-Sacrifice to Korean Freedom Fighter: Yu Guan Soon in Theresa Cha's *Dicteé*." In *Transnationalism and the Asian American Heroine*, edited by by Lan Dong, 63–81. McFarland & Company.

Lee, Seul. 2023. "Enforced Conviviality and the Violence of Care in Han Kang's *The Vegetarian*." *Critique: Studies in Contemporary Fiction* 64 (3): 465–76.

Lee, Seung-Ook, Najeeb Jan, and Joel Wainwright. 2014. "Agamben, Postcoloniality, and Sovereignty in South Korea." *Antipode* 46 (3): 650–68.

Lowe, Lisa. 2015. *The Intimacies of Four Continents*. Duke University Press.

Luciano, Dana, and Mel Y. Chen, eds. 2015. "Queer Inhumanities." Special issue, *GLQ* 25 (2–3).

Man Group. 2023. "About Us." https://www.man.com/about-us.

Mbembe, Achille. 2003. "Necropolitics." Translated by Libby Meintjes. *Public Culture* 15 (1): 11–40.

Nam, Ki-Chang, Cheorun Jo, and Mooha Lee. 2010. "Meat Products and Consumption Culture in the East." *Meat Science* 86 (1): 95–102.

Republic of the Korean Army. 1982. 한민족의 용틀임 [*The Dragon Rise of the Korean Nation*]. Seoul: Korean Army Headquarters.

Spillers, Hortense. 1987. "Mama's Baby, Papa's Maybe: An American Grammar Book." *Diacritics* 17 (2): 64–81.

"'A Surprise and a Risk': Reaction to Booker Prize Upheaval." 2013. BBC News, September 18. https://www.bbc.com/news/entertainment-arts-24126882.

Tuck, Eve, and K. Wayne Yang. 2012. "Decolonization Is Not a Metaphor." *Decolonization: Indigeneity, Education & Society* 1 (1): 1–40.

Wang Medina, Jenny. 2018. "At the Gates of Babel: The Globalization of Korean Literature as World Literature." *Acta Koreana* 21 (2): 395–421.

Wynter, Sylvia. 2003. "Unsettling the Coloniality of Being/Power/Truth/Freedom: Towards the Human, After Man, Its Overrepresentation—An Argument." *New Centennial Review* 3 (3): 257–337.

Wynter, Sylvia. 2006. "ProudFlesh Inter/Views: Sylvia Wynter." *ProudFlesh: New Afrikan Journal of Culture, Politics and Consciousness*, no. 4, 1–35.

Wynter, Sylvia, and Katherine McKittrick. 2015. "Unparalleled Catastrophe for Our Species? or, To Give Humanness a Different Future: Conversations." In *Sylvia Wynter: On Being Human as Praxis,* edited by Katherine McKittrick, 9–89. Duke University Press.

Homes, Houses, and Shelters

Mónica Palma

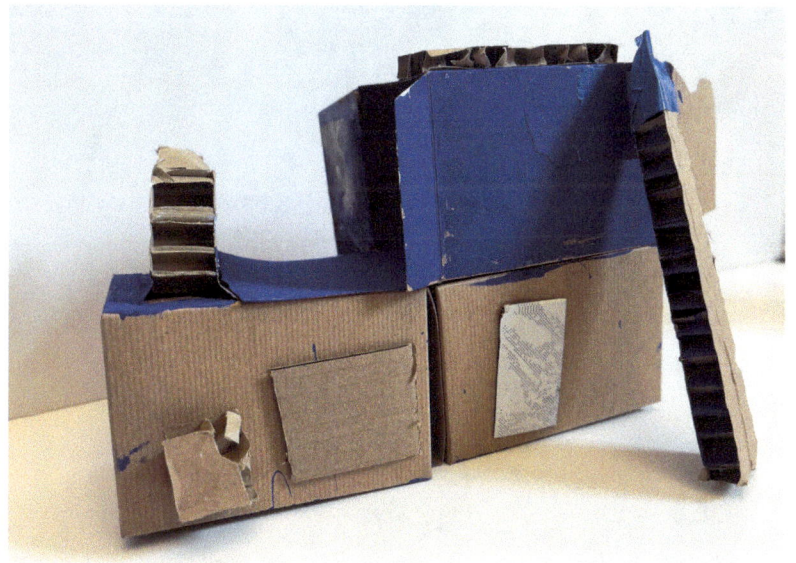

Casa y alberca (*House and Swimming Pool*), 2024. Photograph by Mónica Palma.

This is a house and a pool. It can be one or the other whenever it wants.

Besides cardboard and blue tempera paint, the duct tape did wonders while building the houses. The boy making this one was amazed to discover that some pieces of riveted cardboard functioned perfectly for stairs. He was in the zone, adding stairs in all directions, so when the house was done, he looked dizzy trying to find solid ground for the construction. He soon realized that in one position, the house was simply a house with some stairs, but in another one, the stairs flipped their position and took you to a big blue container. He exclaimed something like: It's also a pool! I can't recall the exact words.

198 Homes, Houses, and Shelters

En esta escuela están permitidos los gatos (*In This School Cats Are Welcome*), 2024. Photograph by Mónica Palma.

Although it's impossible to see it in this picture, the outside structure is covered with detailed squiggly drawings made with colored markers that look like fireworks and train tracks. After the maker of this building, a girl around eight years old, finished the outside, she moved to resolve the interior of the place. While painting everything blue, she told me that her favorite place was school, so she was going to make one where cats were allowed to visit. She waited some minutes for the paint to dry, then she added those white dots, which are the cat spoor; the tracks can be seen on top of the desk. Contrary to what one might think, the footprints were made slowly; I followed her hand, depositing the marks while she narrated that the cat was walking and recognizing the space, and getting closer to the final destination, which was the desk.

SECTION II. **POETRY**

Lessons on (from, for, to) a Free Press: My Path to the Newsroom

Jen Schneider

If not offered a curriculum of one's liking, curate, create, then churn one—

1. History; Wars of Words and Worlds

As a girl, I was neither expected nor permitted to study numbers. Not arithmetic. Not the War of 1812. Not the Wars of the Spanish or Austrian Succession. Not the American Independence. Domestic conflict was as intriguing as international relations. All objects proper nouns. I was gifted fifteen years of folding linens and laundry before graduating to a live-in governess position. With two years of passive language study, I learned the difference between consonants (not continents or continental divisions) and vowels (doweries distinct from destinies, I think). I actively consumed all portions of literary instruction (*seized* synonymous to *sensibility* for some). Each letter a layer of (y)earning with hidden earning possibilities—(l)earning skills, knowledge, and tools to do and become. I'd wrap my knobby fingers around my pen and dip its feathers in heavy blue ink, like the leaning tower of porcelain bowls in the metal basin, I'd think—if the history of a woman's way to words isn't something about which to write (and right), then how could things ever change?

2. Culinary Arts and Kitchen Chemistry

The kitchen was always a place and space of motion. Most mornings, I would pound chicken then help prep dough for the cookie press (noun)—a device that operated similarly to a syringe. Dough converted into delicacies for women and men. Mama often gifted me the chance to decide on the image that would grace the cookies' middle. Prime real estate. Perfectly situated. With a dash (a hyphen, of sorts) for emphasis. A pinch of pepper for pizzazz. Not unlike the comma's pause. As I'd pinch then press, I'd contemplate the device's potential to leave its mark. My word! Imprints of footsteps and thumbnails would form with each new push. In the kitchen I learned how to season my words. I'd invite hungry neighbors for tastings to satisfy their urge to consume. Punch lines flavored of sweet fruits and savory sauce. My ideas were regularly processed in a blender. Then sliced into individual portions—ready to serve. Not unlike a paper. As I'd dress the table and prep for the meal's headlines (remove excess traps, trim deep-seated beliefs), my thoughts would wander. Livers and onions were akin to layouts and comics funnies. Fried. Six degrees of separation from tried. And Muenster cheese. The oven dings timers on schedules similar to news alerts and press deadlines. Potato skins. The many layers of chips and cheese. Six-layer dip. Multiple ways, as the men say, to skin a cat. The news is like that. I'd brine (and prime) bylines and wonder in nineteen-point font—might a cookie press symbolize something greater?

3. Laundry Duty, a Daily Ritual

Laundry lingered in the small pockets of air between dawn and doing. The basket was always full. So different from opportunities. I'd press cottons, stitch hems, and sketch patterns. Bleach was as much a metric for diluted pigment as a solution. The chemical reaction would remove all stains and, in their place, form new ones. The subtle shadows of what used to be spun into a reminder of what we could become. Truth-telling. The steam from the kettle would remove wrinkles as new ones formed on the cheeks, jowls, brows of Mother and Father. The seasons always turned. The iron a press— as much a component of presentation (less one limb, plus one setting) as a pressure of sorts. The laundry line adopted a pattern. Its middle capable of holding multiple truths and both a concave and convex form. Each fabric appointed a communication—coarse wools, fine linens. A proper temperature (not unlike temperance) for textiles of all sorts. I'd learn. Temper as much a relative of temperature as temperance. Both noun and verb. Each pleat, a pressure point. Each stitch, a colon of sorts. The news an outlet for laundry and fabrics already worn. Also, a source of sustenance. I'd wear the stories untold as a robe, my corset a constriction like formal rules of construction—descriptive adjectives, adverbs to modify my words. Fury, frills, fabric. Gripes, grills, grammar. I toss consonants and vowels and wonder about states of being—To be. To become.

4. Mixers

The pear tree birthed odd, asymmetrical fruits. Mostly tart. Mostly unused. Unfit for daily household use. Not unlike the manual mixer Father bought one Sunday. He paid twenty cents. "A steal" of sorts. He set it down on the oak table in the middle of the shadow cast by the pear tree, its presence an always nearby reality. The squirrels had already nibbled the pear for thirty seconds longer than ideal. The hand crank mixer consumed the shade and all the fresh air us girls—one, two, three, more—were hoping for. We yearned for something new, something new to do, to learn, to earn. Our daily news much less fun than that our brother spun. Not all news is fit for print or consumption, Mother warned. Not all tools are fit for redemption or reduction, Father tooled. I listened, then mixed my own batter—a blend of sweet, sour, and another kitchen hour. The act of mixing ingredients to (re)create reality is not always easy nor should it be. Letters are, not surprisingly, refreshingly similar. *S* and *T*. *C* and *H*. *E* and *R*. Why not place "wo" before all men? Even the sweet pear is part ear. I learned to listen. To toil. To reimagine. Once mixed, "pear" becomes "reap." Swap an *R* for an *L*. An easy leap, I liked to think. Even as a young girl, decades before I'd become the first woman to run a newspaper, I'd mix afternoons with homemade mixers and handheld cranks. The music was always on. The news may not have always been right, like the consistency of the dough in the mixing bowl, but it became an always secure place to write. I'd wonder—might a press be a haven safer than home?

5. Measuring Cups and Magnifying Glasses

The relationship between magnification and unification remains interesting, even years after I first made the connection. I received my first pair of glasses when I was nearly fifteen. Suddenly, I could see much more than I ever before believed. Stains neatly spun. The world became less formidable, more malleable. Even a glass of water appeared, suddenly, somehow, different. I'd see stories waiting for moments to melt in the ice cube's wink. Now, I offer a glass before each interview, and as I write, I drink in measured intervals. Room temperature sliced and diced. To break the awkward silence is not unlike the undersized eggshells cracked on the side of an oversized mixing bowl. Tap once. Twice. Convert passive to active voice. Incorporate strong verbs—What more must women wait for?

> *It's our turn . . .*
> —Amelia Jenks Bloomer,
>   the first woman to edit, print,
>   and run a newspaper

Jennifer Schneider, JD, EdD, is an assistant professor at the Community College of Philadelphia. She can be reached at jschneider@ccp.edu.

Notes

This piece is modeled after Sejal Shah's *Curriculum* (2013), https://www.conjunctions.com/online/article/sejal-shah-02-26-2013.

    Amelia Jenks Bloomer (1818–1894) was a women's rights advocate, suffragist, and newspaper editor who took a socially informed and activist approach to all of her work. Born and raised in Homer, NY, she was an activist in all senses and tenses of the word. She remains an inspiration and source of important change—from fashion to fundamental freedoms. As the first woman to edit, print, and run a newspaper, she encountered unlikely audiences and unexpected celebrity. This poem provides a road map or pattern for Bloomer's path to the newsroom alongside her work to ensure freedoms, and a free press for all, including women. The poem tells only a few stitches or pages in Bloomer's larger story. Each section highlights a unique time in Bloomer's life and life work. Her aptitude for language and using language to inform, empower, and inspire change is celebrated through intentional wordplay. Bloomer spent much of her life in small spaces—the printing press was far from glamorous, yet she bloomed alongside the infamous bloomers. The words she printed would pen a movement and move a nation. She taught through daily print. This piece is a small attempt to amplify her voice, work, and vision on a larger stage and for a modern audience.

Women on horses

Virginia Gris

rarely discussed. Except distress.
Distressed. She rides alone until
his disguised gallops. She knows him by the smoke
of dimwit pre-rolls. She knows him by the way he yells
Te tengo.

       I got you. The beast below, the twisted
hemp in her hand whispering *men like these shouldn't see
the holy valleys, the sun-blushed fruit.* There was no fruit

left by the time I was born and she was
vacant in her chair
braiding acre-lengths of grays

waiting for death and then forgetting.

Both horses nicker as her whip draws a curve
to land his blindness.
                             Not a bad thing to know

of great-grandmothers
who knew nothing of side-saddles
everything of Themisian scales. Scales.
Scaled. I have
my sense of fairness
and a cold-bloodedness, I've heard
I have my love of horses that can't forgive the grope of human blood,
human blades, human bullets, bayonets.

Both horses split them away since, as it was,
there is no victory.
Back
in each of their homes nobody speaks of the matter.

Everything sold to women

Virginia Gris

absorbs.
Tampons and pads
Mops and sponges of all kinds
Reusable cotton squares
Handkerchiefs, dainty handkerchiefs with little
roses on the corners to remind us
if we poke below our surface we'll bleed
I got my grandma
leak proof underwear
Gigi, it's the best birthday gift
the best birthday gift. Ointments
and cologne just mold the shelves
Next day I had this urge to see to my gynecologist—she said
that *no, god no,* bleeding each month isn't necessary, it's just a planet
on our backs
that we got stuck with
I scheduled an IUD
because I have no doubts
because I have no doubts
for once I don't need to be the glorious creature consumed
Imagine being just a thing absorbing

Virginia Gris (often credited as Virginia Sánchez Navarro) is a Brooklyn-based multidisciplinary artist with a background in poetry, theatre, and film. She was born in the Dominican Republic to a family of mixed heritage—immigrants from Asturias, immigrants from Palestine, and native Dominicans. Now being an immigrant herself, this amalgam of cultures and nationalities has become a significant theme in her creative work—a constant search for a definite identity and home. Gris's film work has been part of the lineup at several international venues, such as the Austin Film Festival, Cinequest, Chelsea Film Festival, Festival Mix Mexico, and the Philadelphia Latino Film Festival. Her poetry has been accepted for publication in *Women's Studies Quarterly*, *Promethean*, *The Marbled Sigh*, and several Hispanic publications. She is currently completing a creative writing MFA at the City College of New York. She can be reached at virginia@virginia-gris.com.

surface tension

Elizabeth Sine

from around the corner, just outside the bathroom, peering in,
I see my mother bending over the counter to bring her face
closer to the mirror. inspecting, assessing, seeking out
the grooves and the drooping patches that most aligned
with all the remarks.
                        you look so tired.
   the words echoed
      like clouds of steam, filling the room.

      what's wrong?, some prodded.
                      you seem worried.
                                  I knew the way
she'd ruffle in response, as if her movements were a
dance sequence I could rehearse in my sleep. I'd memorized
how, in a single brushstroke, she'd adjust her posture, add a dollop
of conviction to her smile, raise her brow to add some brightness
to her eyes, then lift the beat of her voice into a nice, light "I do?,"
all with a slight chuckle she wished had the power to transform
their perceptions to butterflies that would flitter off to
who-knows-where.

but the comments would always make their way back. and I
delivered my share of them. I'd study the interplay of it all
like a science project, tracking actions and reactions, probing the
space between her sighs and her storyline, gathering metrics on
these mismatching puzzle pieces that never quite lined up no matter
how hard you jammed them together. in those narrow moments
when she was sure enough that no one was looking that she'd release
her top lid to rest on the bottom one, let her shoulders drop and her
cheeks sag and the lines on her forehead curve in the opposite way

like a rainbow turned upside down, my attention to other things could never be more than partial. I couldn't tell you why. I couldn't tell you what it was exactly that transfixed me about the whole thing. I couldn't tell you I needed to understand the way gravity acted on her like I needed to know my home town on a map. I couldn't tell you. she couldn't tell me. that's the thing about unspeakable things.

there were good reasons to be tired. I know that now. looking back at the memories, I'm able to see the anvils of history she dragged around and the stakes that pinned her wings to the ground. I can see the monsters that hovered around her, heckling. I see how they built her a tiny room and then held everything she cared about over the fire, threatening to drop it all should she dare to reach beyond the walls. I see how they lined that tiny room with mirrors, so that anytime she questioned how she got here in the first place all she could point to was herself. I see how she came to exist in a state of frenetic motion, racing to outrun the wolves that lashed at her heels, always on the brink of collapsing or being eaten alive. I see how she tried to wish it all away, padded her world with pleasantries, glass-half-full prophecies, and everything's-meant-to-be mythologies, hoping to dress it all up in enough layers the darkness couldn't seep through.

still leaning in for a close look at the face staring back at her, she raises two longing fingers to the place where her forehead meets her scalp, pulls back ever so slightly, imagining a satin curtain she could fluff and straighten, shrouding the grave in which she would bury the ghosts once and for all. a bit of slicing here, a bit of stitching there. is that all it takes to clean a slate? maybe. just maybe, she thinks, testing out a chipper smile with her promising new alignment. that might just do it.

and I shrink back from where I've been watching her. my knees crumble into my arms beside a coffee table made from the wood of a black walnut tree. I catch sight of how the light reflects off its smooth surface. I think of all the reminders over the years about using coasters, and how you don't set a drink right on the furniture because of the condensation that forms at the base of the glass, the mark it can leave. I think of how I've learned to fix a scratch, to sand and to varnish and apply polish when it was called for. I think of all the times I've witnessed someone's eyes burst and their spine bristle when I'd set my drink down, forgetting. and I wonder. I wonder about that black walnut tree. and I wonder about the place where it sank its roots and what stories its markings told and what storms it weathered and what storms the trees that came before it weathered too and how they held on. and I wonder about who rested in its shade and who built nests from its leaves and twigs and what lives it lived and what life it gave before it was reborn with four legs on the Persian-style rug that decorated our living room floor. and I sit there wishing, amid all this to-do about how to maintain the wood furniture's fine finish, for lessons in how to worship a forest.

Elizabeth Sine is a historian of race, labor, and social movements, as well as a community and cultural worker, writer, and poet. She currently teaches in the History Department at California Polytechnic State University, San Luis Obispo. She is the author of *Rebel Imaginaries: Race, Labor, and Culture in Depression Era California* (Duke University Press, 2021) and coeditor of *Another University Is Possible* (University Readers, 2010). She can be reached at esine@calpoly.edu.

Art and War (Homer's Art)

Onur Ayaz

POEM

Time to head to dead
Is what has been on
my mind—I starve when
people of Gaza
Starve as I watch with
Horror.
        Mosab writes
we listen, we Read.
—
Schools stay funny till
One Someone says "Pal"—
All eyes turn my way.
I stay silent for
A second. I hand
Them all *Homer's Art*
By Alice Notley.
we Read—we listen—
War is never fun.
—

Next you see students
Survey them with
The following—
What spaces are safest on campus?
Answers can vary but here is what
I receive
The Library, the Quad,
the Cafeteria, even
the hallways of some building
       on some floor—
These answers speak testament
To my failure—to our failure. I flourish
as others starve.

—

Preface

1863 Confederates sold clothing from yellow fever smallpox patients to Union troops, USA.
1675 German and French forces agree not
to use Poison Bullets.
1495 Spanish mix wine with blood of leprosy patients and sell
to their foes, Naples, Italy.
1155 Emperor Barbarossa poisons water wells
with human bodies—
History is the memory of time.

—

1488 First printed edition of Homer's Odyssey.
1616 Chapman's translations into English.
History full of war.

—

War and Art—*Homer's Art*, as Notley says
Is generated by war and men.

Alice Notley and *Homer's Art*—to tell a public story
Not in measure that makes
possible—though that would be nice—to tell a story
whose measure draws from the depth of poet
thought, feeling, sound, and memory,

I am neither man nor story
When faced with distant war—
I go Homer.

Prelude

1990 saw the publication of Alice Notley's *Homer's Art*
in "a curriculum of the soul" series
published for The Institute of Further Studies
by Glover Publishing in Canton NY.
I write this with a zeal for conceptual art and poetry—
To think, the possibilities, such a piece does
do to the reader. I write this not for you
to go out and read *Homer's Art*
1990
I write this because Homer's ART
Has always been a work about men
Published by men Told
by men Starring
men
Translated by men—and—
while Notley
Does not translate Homer she
Makes me wonder what
Art should and can be
As public storytelling.
—

Coda

In the month of Ramadan I fast and
I flourish—while those in Gaza
Fast and perish.

Onur Ayaz is a poet and doctoral candidate in the English department at the Graduate Center, CUNY. The Library of Congress Manuscript Division recently published his research guide on African American innovation, invention, and entrepreneurship. Ayaz can be reached at oayaz1@gradcenter.cuny.edu.

The Sea Is Not a Question of Power

Issis Palomo Sánchez

after Adrienne Rich's "Diving into the Wreck"

I.

No—the sea is power.
But what are words,
if not a means to power?
And what are purposes—
what their purpose?
What names are we to wear
who are otherwise faceless?

The wreck—
a stone quarried
far removed from her native place
harsh and blind it lies
open in your palm
the wind does not know her name
she stole the name of the sun,
once—
now she has forgotten her own.

For all things named
themselves
into existence:
a wind blew through
the worlds and everything
recalled what it will be once, remembered itself into being.

Even the Sahara
remembers the lakes rivers
streams that rolled through
this land
like Atete
holding her hands upwards
in a gesture of benediction
amid the spiraling faces
of the crescent-women:
oryx-woman
buffalo-woman
aurochs-woman
gazelle-woman

in that world where
the birds are the language,
not the thing itself—
the words are the means
and the maps,
the purpose but one—
the waters recede
the waters rise again.

If blood does not speak,
what can this borrowed
tongue say to make you
recognize the blood as your own?
You came
armored
with book camera knife,
predisposed to see to cut
to own. You came seeking
the origins of your own ruin
in the shadows
of our face.

The waters recede,
the waters rise again.
The elder ones
who once walked land
know us for brethren—
the sea awaits
the hour of our descent
and our return.

II.

Bearing instruments of death
you came seeking life
with knife camera
a book of names
robed and primed
the iron-forged tongue.

You who left the sea
seeking water,
seeking rain, lost
in the green-grey
columns of forests,
the labyrinths of memory,
the snarls of history.

Bearing the instruments
of death
you came to learn
the name of the voice
who first called fire
from stone, the dance
of those whose steps
traced constellations on the
nether vault, horned heads lifted
to figure meaning
in the upper heavens.

Bearing instruments of death
you come who claim
the first beginning
although last born.
These words are means,
and nothing else—
your purposed words an arrow
defacing what it seeks,
your map mistaken
for the lay of land.

The mind that asks
what the severed body knew
is no mind at all,
dispatching violent men
from pristine halls
to do in darkness
the things you cannot witness,
to twist in silence
the blade that you disown.

Words are the means
to call forth fire
from darkness,
to call forth thunder
from silence.
Words wound themselves
silver nets to catch
the fish of the sun
gleaming from
the black waters.
These words lie still,
signifying nothing.

You came bearing
the instruments
of death
camera book knife blade
sharpened on the keen edge
of your pale hungers,
your words a bright precision
whetted on the rock
of your desert thirst.

Issis Palomo Sánchez is an Afro-Cuban poet who immigrated with her family to the United States from La Habana when she was six years old. She holds an MFA in creative writing from the City College of New York and a bachelor of arts from Columbia University. She can be reached at ipalomo000@citymail.cuny.edu.

slick

Destiny Crockett

trouble followed me home on pale yellow paper called
a "help-needed" form
It was my introduction to a very American thing that is punishment
That loves the language of support
I almost always owned it, but on two occasions I tried to wring around my mother's wrath
She offered: "telling me the truth is the only way I can defend you up at that school."
If you lie to someone, a mother, they cannot have your back
If you lie out there it is protection
I am big by now but we become bisa butler's mobile madonna
meek, modern, vivid and velvet, my face is kept private

At one point, I enjoyed making pallets on the floor, pulling the comforter set
Off my bed
And arranging it on the hardwood, just so,
with another thick blanket underneath.
Seemingly without prompting,
My mother inserted "and you bet not go to that school saying you sleep on the floor."
I did not plan on doing that, nor did I know why I bet not say it, when it was the truth for just a few nights

Before we went to the doctor:
"If they ask you to rate your pain on a scale of one to ten, and your pain is really a five, tell them it's a ten."
The elder Black Lady friend of mine—a professor *and* smart—tells me there is never a reason to lie to a person who could have institutional backing to make decisions about your life

Even if you are afraid
Never a reason to lie period
And I know she knew different doctors than the ones we saw then
knew them differently than we did
At the dinner table—in a less warring way
The doctor I see now tells me that the institution in which he works,
Where I am his patient, primarily provides the kind of care that does not
worry me because they, unlike the last one I went to, serve the monied
and the somewhat monied, including Black middle-class people, like
spouses and children of physicians

But never a reason to lie, period?
There are women who tell their nieces
never let a man know how much money you have
Because if he doesn't steal from you
He will sort of magic you from your money
I have never been directly given this advice
I have only heard about this
I cannot know how many poor women
can stash enough money for secret savings
can get ovah[1] to get on

Mikki Kendall mentions that distrust[2] is taught, and is a skill, for Black girls
who grow up poor and working class
She says feminists discarded the women and girls who go without having
some of their basic needs met
Or pushed them to the margins
The margins influence the center
The center, in my early twenties, was/is Black feminism
And I was/am very romantic about it,
met us/myself at those margins
I attended the live virtual panel on intergenerational Black feminist
community
Where Demita Frazier asserted that academic Black feminist theory
abandoned the topic of poverty in the lives of Black women

There is often a compelling reason to appear more collaborative than I am
The state trooper asked me if I knew

That I was in the passing lane for too long
To just be passing
It's my first time on the highway, you can see that my license is new
wasn't a total lie. It was my first time on the highway *by myself*.
This highway was nearly empty, no one would hear me if I needed them to
And I have learned enough about disregard
to assume that even if any person, of any race or gender, were around to hear me scream, they might care that a Black woman is being hurt, but there is a good chance they would walk away
when they learn that actually, it is only a bitch with a bad attitude[3] who is being beaten
"ok you clearly don't know what you're doing, it'll just be a warning"
My hands shook so much I don't know how I got the license back in the green leather coach purse my best friend gifted me
I am driving from philly to baltimore, alone, and need this interaction to be as short as possible

The psychiatrist asks me how I was able to finish my PhD, "if" I was having a mental health crisis
I am annoyed by the question
Or suggestion
Clearly, not finishing would have been economically disastrous
I lament having gotten nothing done because of the pre-menstrual exacerbation of depression and fatigue
Ignoring the grocery errand I ran, the email I sent, the load of laundry I switched from the washer to the dryer, the paragraph I revised, the side hustle hours I racked up
"I guess I just know how to act in public"
It occurs to me that she may not pick up on the double meaning of the word "act" in Black English
And I do not like to stop what I am doing and explain Black English to anyone in real time
It sounds like I am telling her that I know how to deceive or perform
Which I do
But instead of that, I mean I can comport myself in such a way that does not immediately signal that I am in distress, not even to myself
without trying really
I have never not seen someone go to work during a crisis

My sister/friend and I stand in the line to enter the book of hov exhibit in the brooklyn library,
0.4 miles away from the entrance, in the rain, and I wore the mesh new balance.
We intend to go to the brooklyn museum after this to see the exhibit of tonya and spike lee's collection, and then to dinner, and she will drive back to new haven and I will drive back to philly
I did not take an edible to calm my ruminations because I knew I had the two-hour drive back.
We are grateful to break up our respective lonelinesses with sisterhood and Black art in a city neither of us lives in
Except

The reason I hate going to brooklyn is because I lived in bushwick for a little while
And when I sat in the graduate seminar the fall after I finished up my year in bushwick
I did not know what to ask about the statement "Black life is heartbreak"
No
I was too worried about doing a faux paus to ask three questions in a row
And I am having flashbacks, which I do not know are flashbacks, to
The very anti-Black disregard I experienced from a doctor in brooklyn
—a Southeast Asian male doctor and a Black woman nurse
"How do we who have been violated not say Black life is/wreckage?"
We just don't say it
I am so literal about my confusions that it probably comes off as caustic
During my ninth summer, I wrote a note
to my mother, saying I was going to go live somewhere else
and then ran "away" to another part of the south side
on foot of course
I was spotted by my auntie and a police officer.
My desperate mother called them, called my entire family, who did look for me.
Before I went to bed that night,
My mother told me that when asked if I left a runaway note, she answered no
Why lie? liars disgusted her
"If you say you running away, they will think you have a reason to run away, a real reason. They take kids, and wherever kids who get taken have to live,

they do not care what you like to eat, and they do not care if someone
there is hurting you. You wouldn't even have your own room"
In my neighborhood,
it was a privilege to carry on for nine colorful summers and be so green
She knew not firsthand but from paying attention what I would later
have language for by way of Dorothy Roberts:
It is exceptionally easy for the state to take poor Black women's children.
Help needed *is*
punishment rendered.
Sometimes the consequence for the truth is more dangerous than a lie

When my friend and I are walking from the museum to the Senegalese
restaurant, where we will have beef mafe and whole grilled branzino, I tell
her I am glad I moved to philly in July 2018

When I read Darlene Clark Hine's "Rape and the Inner Lives of Black
Women in the Middle West"
for the first time, no, the second time, I was appreciative.
Hine was not writing about dishonesty, rather, skillful withholding
I wonder if my elder relatives would have called the women about whom
Hine writes "slick"
No, slick is about being crafty
My friend once told me no one is slicker than Black americans, and I am
proud of us
We are reconsidering Black feminist textual fidelity,[4] but I must correct
myself here.
slick is stylish.
Dissemblance[5] is protective—
We are often both.

I grow irate when people who are home in time for goodnight moon with
their children tell me their lives are harder than mine
I do not like to compete with other women
When I was eight years old, and my mother worked late, I was trusted to
walk myself home from the bus stop, complete my homework in my mother's room, alone in front of the TV
go into my own bedroom to read or draw and to play with my Christy dolls
Prepare a meal for myself, bathe, slip on my pajamas, and put myself to bed

with every light in the house left on, knowing I would not see my mother again until the next morning, since she did not get off work caring for the elders until midnight.

I was to tell no one I spent those hours home alone.

I was not to answer the door, but if I did, and someone asked if I was in there by myself, I was

supposed

to lie

Destiny Crockett is a scholar, visual artist, and poet who is originally from St. Louis, Missouri. She is currently the inaugural Mellon Humanities Postdoctoral Fellow of Childhood Studies and Racial Justice at Rutgers University-Camden, where she is working on her first respective academic and poetry book monographs. She studies African American literature, Black feminisms, Black material culture, and archive theories. Right now, her poems are about materialisms, class, place, gender, and the Black art of concealment. Some of her poems can be found in *A Gathering Together*. Her visual art has been supported by the Colored Girls Museum in Philadelphia, and published in *Lesbians Are Magical* and *Aunt Chloe Magazine*, and featured in multiple local museums and exhibitions. Her academic writing has been published in multiple scholarly journals. She earned her PhD in English from the University of Pennsylvania and her BA from Princeton University. She can be reached at crockettdestiny@gmail.com.

Notes

1. Carolyn Rodgers, *How I Got Ovah: New and Selected Poems* (Anchor Press, 1975).
2. Mikki Kendall, *Hood Feminism: Notes from the Women That a Movement Forgot* (Viking, 2020).
3. Ntozake Shange, *for colored girls who have considered suicide when the rainbow is enuf* (Shameless Hussy Press, 1976).
4. Jennifer C. Nash, *Black Feminism Reimagined: After Intersectionality* (Duke University Press, 2019).
5. Darlene Clark Hine, "Rape and the Inner Lives of Black Women in the Middle West," *Signs: Journal of Women in Culture and Society* 14, no. 4 (1989): 912–20, https://doi.org/10.1086/494552.

SECTION III. **CREATIVE PROSE**

Indigenous Reflections on Poethood

Lois Beardslee

I never intended to be labeled as a poet. I was even less inclined to be labeled as an activist. So, I was surprised when, years ago, a scholar in the field of Native American literature told me I was known as an in-your-face feminist Native American poet-activist. I had just been minding my own business writing about the lives of my family and friends, indigenous people in contemporary times. I'd never intended to become a Native American writer, either. I was just a math nerd who fell into it. It's one of those low-paying, gig-based, default jobs that Native American women have always fallen into. Where I live, off-reservation unemployment for Native Americans is in excess of 99 percent, which, until recently, had been considerably worse than the unemployment rate for indigenous people in the Gaza Strip. Power brokers in northwest Lower Michigan don't even hire local Indians for unskilled labor, so now we've fallen into minority status even compared to the other minorities that are brought in by local businesses for that manual labor. Immigrants from El Salvador have a lower unemployment rate in the general community than indigenous Native Americans in Leelanau County. At the turn of the twenty-first century, the ethnic group with the highest number of college diplomas in Michigan was Native American women; and the ethnic group with the highest unemployment in the state was (and still is) Native American women, followed by Native American men. So, I guess that being a Native American poet is one of those uncredentialed fields that even a credentialed Indian woman can fall back on. It didn't come easy. I had to start out as an Indian "storyteller," staying close to America's myths about indigenous simplicity.

Ojibwe people make up the second largest tribe in North America, with families split up by an international border, and a lot of us don't live on reservations or belong to a local political entity known as "the tribe." So, our financial options don't necessarily include tribal benefits, although they inevitably include the downside that comes with socioeconomic apartheid and financial exclusion based upon traditional ethnic stereotypes and welfare myths. Among those stereotypes are notions of Native Americans as having a natural genetic propensity for creating arts and crafts for a pittance and telling cute stories about nature. Following forced school integration and the collapse of manufacturing in urban areas rimming the southern Great Lakes, the population of my home region swelled with non-Indians, and those old stereotypes became more firmly embedded than ever before. The intensifying cultural shift gave me a lot to write about, even if writing about the impact of white flight on rural Native Americans north of the Rust Belts of Detroit and Chicago wasn't necessarily marketable material in the new homelands overwhelmed by nonminority immigrants.

So, when people ask me what I do for a living, I sometimes twiddle my thumbs, look away, and mumble that "I'm a writer." When they ask what I write, I usually answer, "Nothing that most people read, just Indian stuff." Native American writers are our own category. We don't even fall into the same category as books about Native Americans. Most of those are written by non-Indians, for a non-Indian audience. They tend to concentrate on stuff like *The Fur Trade*, a socioeconomic phenomenon carefully packaged in non-Indian stereotypes that paint the original locals as dummies who couldn't exploit their resources properly and who fell all over themselves worshipping historic non-Indian heroes like that place-name-inspiring missionary, Pere Marquette. It's the kind of literature that my new neighbors consume voraciously in their attempts at being inclusive of the local Indian population, whose *Oneness with Nature* they hope to emulate while creating environment-altering exurbs. Other topics non-Indians who write about Indians like to fall back on are how-come stories about the specific traits of various mammals (short tails come to mind) as well as myths about Native American women who abandon their children, usually on the doorsteps of bars and mission churches, to superior white caretakers (Barbara Kingsolver and Carolyn Lewis come to mind). They are not the kinds of things I like to write about my friends and family. But sometimes I find myself utilizing stereotypes to draw in readers and listeners, so that I can slowly lead them to the well of genuine indigenous literature and try to let them have a little sip. It's a Sisyphean process, when one doesn't own the outlets by which literature that purports to represent people of color is disseminated in this country. Even after I became the first Native American to win a Michigan Notable Book Award, local bookstore owners refused to carry my books or even order them when customers asked them to, insisting that nobody buys books by Indians. But after the media blitz associated with the Dakota Access Pipeline, more people than usual started reading poetry by Native Americans.

That's where the whole poetry thing kind of falls into place. I've known for a long time that my prose often drifts into poetry. For years, I've been accused of bending genres. I'm more concerned with the message than adhering to a specific medium. So, I violate accepted formats and play with words. Sometimes I argue with younger, less experienced editors over a single comma, insisting that I need to slow down my readers, because my cadence is moving at a fast pace. Leave self-correcting computer programs to the writers of booklets on how to assemble a vacuum cleaner, I insist. Since bucking stereotypical ethnic content generates a fairly reluctant audience, I need to manipulate my media to keep a reader engaged long enough to make those serious points about how the promulgation of damaging ethnic stereotypes in faux Native American literature and children's books results in the promulgation of damage. And eventually, I want to be able to bring my audience within grasping distance of different notions than they're used to about the lethal connection between stereotypes and hate crimes. I live in a world of white-on-brown violence, and there are very few literary outlets that permit in-depth discussion of such a topic. But poetry is kind of a sneaky medium. One can broach difficult topics with poetry, through sheer manipulation of timing and resonance. Poetry can be visual or aural. It can be sterile when sterile is needed; and it can be staccato when staccato is important. Getting such poetry out to a broad audience is usually a greater challenge than composing the poetry itself. The market restrictions that serious Native American writers face are even tighter than those faced by James Baldwin in his day.

And that's where the whole Native American poetry as its own genre kind of thing falls into place, creating loopholes for getting America's attention. It doesn't matter if the genre is real or perceived, because it has been a reality in the marketplace. As someone who's become a part of that genre, I owe a lot to my predecessors, people like N. Scott Momaday and Joy Harjo, whose voices fell far enough out of the mainstream of American literature to create a genre of their own. I never read much of what other Native American writers have written, because I was always afraid that it might influence the way I wrote; and people were telling me that I was a pretty good writer. So, I only read enough of what a few other Indians wrote to convince myself that such a genre existed. Then I went off on my own.

And, really, that's where the whole poetry thing kind of falls into place (eventually). I hope I've managed to tell you, bending a medium to convey a message is a slow process—especially when the message is as big and as important as confronting the lethality of stereotypes and socioeconomic exclusion. At some point, I realized that there was a bigger market for warm and fuzzy nature-oriented poetry by Native American women than there was a market for prose about Indians as competent, contemporary, savvy people who've survived *The Fur Trade, Manifest Destiny, A Teaching Workforce That's 90 Percent White,* and a whole plethora of other *Socioeconomic Pitfalls*. I was already familiar with historic formats for writing within numerical syllabic limitations that had originated in corners of the world deemed more sophisticated than my own. It wasn't much different than the way I already wrote, confronted with limitations on content and academic stylistic expectations.

With the popularity of prose poetry and free-form poetry, I was in my comfort zone. I decided it was time for me to join the low-paying, intermittent, gig-based world of contemporary Native American poetry. Not only was I feeling liberated from academic restraints, but as a Native American female, I had the historic postcard-based stereotype of an indigenous woman with supple, heaving breasts straining against their buckskin restraints to draw in a potential audience. (Special thanks are due to Hulleah Tsinhnahjinnie for brandishing the absurdity of that image in America's face.) Fortunately, because my indigenous family was split up by that international border thing, I had grown up back and forth between rural northern Michigan and even more rural northern Ontario, thereby congealing a stereotypical mystic knowledge of the natural world with a gift for *Indian as Entertainment* (with words). I looked up a couple of successful white male poets, like Ted Kooser, I briefly scanned a few of their commercially successful hallowed words, and then I went off on my own.

I set out to write a book that was pure poetry. I included pieces that were user-friendly to cultural outsiders, celebrating the resilience and stoic nature of Anishinaabe women, and I created images that were dripping with descriptions of large mammals wafting through history while behaving in anthropomorphized manners. But as the book progressed, I realized that I don't just *want* to write about the lethal nature of apartheid and socioeconomic exclusion, I *need* to write about it. And no matter how hard I try to adjust to the marketplace, those things start sneaking into my poetry, as metaphors, as whispered thoughts, as wistful utterances . . . And all those attempts at falling into a genre controlled by outside forces started yielding to stronger internal forces. Creating rhythmic formats, controlling the speed at which readers move through my written words, providing resting places, and pirouetting with wordplay are easy. Dropping word bombs about our environmental and socioeconomic reality into peaceful stereotypes about myself and my loved ones has only recently become easy. As a Native American woman poet, giving myself permission to control content has always been the hardest part. These days, I plant my feet, lean in to the task, and unapologetically go off on my own.

Lois Beardslee (Ojibwe/Lacandon) is an award-winning illustrator and author of several books, including *Words Like Thunder: New and Used Anishinaabe Prayers* (Wayne State University Press, 2020). She was recently nominated for Michigan Poet Laureate.

Cartas a Fabián (Recién llegamos y ya nos queremos ir)

Carolina Suárez Latorre

16 de enero 2024. Houston, Texas

Mi Fabi, mi querido Fabi:

¿Cómo vas, amigo? ¿Cómo te trata la vida desde que me fui? Te extraño, Fabi.

¿Qué decirte de esta ciudad, Fabi? ¿Qué decir? Si Buenos Aires es la ciudad de la furia y Bogotá la de la niebla, Houston es la ciudad del vacío. No hay gente en las calles, Fabi, no hay nadie. Luego ya te metés al Walmart y, bum, un cojonal de gente escuchando a Marc Anthony, *voy a reir, voy a cantar, vivir la vida lalalalal*. Y todo ese cojonal atiborrados en el Walmart no camina, Fabi, esa gente no camina, se bajan de sus carros y se suben a otros minicarros y andan así. El privilegio de los pies no lo usan, Fabi, t e m o r í s.

Ciudad de Mierda, Fabi, con *M* mayúscula. Todo queda en la gran puta mierda y, si vos querés moverte de un lugar a otro, debes tomar un bus con dos o tres horas de anticipación, luego conectar con otros buses hasta llegar a donde vas. Y las calles solas, Fabi, solas, en la ciudad del vacío.

¿Te acordás del primer concierto de los Prisioneros al que fuimos en el Estadio Campín?, ¿te acordás?, llovía y los manes estos salieron y comenzaron: *son hermosos ruidos que salen de las tiendas atraviesan a la gente y les mueven los pies*. Vos me abrazaste y juramos ahí frente a los Prisioneros que nuestras flechas siempre marcarían al sur, que no nos iríamos nunca nunca nunca, *cause we are sudamerican rockers, nous sommes rockers sudamericaines*. ¿Qué? tendríamos si mucho dieciséis años, nuestro primer concierto, tu papá nos llevó, ¿te acordás? Todos punkeros gritando *no nos acompleja revolver los estilos mientras huelan a gringo y se puedan bailar*.

Fabi, si nosotros nos tiramos el rock, los gringos se tiraron el mundo.

Perdón, Fabi, perdón por traicionar nuestra promesa de no irnos nunca nunca nunca. En compensación a ello te tengo algo, t e m o r í s. Creo que encontré el vinilo de los Prisioneros, *La voz de los 80s*, aquí en la ciudad del vacío: Houston, autografiado por los manes, original, ¿te imaginás vos?

Al parecer lo tienen en una casa de discos que se llama Memo Records Shop, sólo música latina en español, "lo mejor de lo mejor" dice en un post en Instagram. El disco está en la gran puta mierda, te paso un screenshot del mapa. Pero, nada, iré por él.

Ya no se diga más, a llevarlo al sur, a llevarlo a Colombia: a casa.

Amigo, cómo te quiero.

Catalina.

Pd1: https://www.youtube.com/watch?v=NZB6KeU-6AM

Pd2:

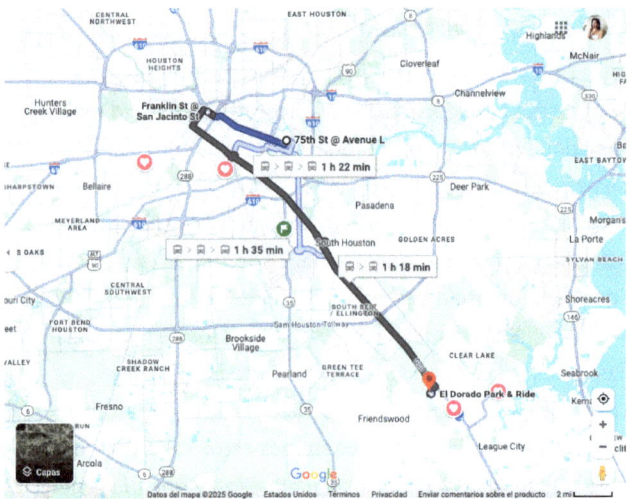

31 de enero 2024. La ciudad del vacío, Texas

Amigo, Fabi:

No, no he tenido tiempo de ver las noticias, vos que sos mi ventana a Colombia, vos que siempre me llevás a casa, gracias por contarme lo del presidente Petro, me hacés sentir allá pegadita al caos, pegadita a las montañas, pegadita a ti. Te quiero llevar el vinilo de los Prisioneros a vos. Un regalo.

Aunque conseguirlo está duro, bien duro, mi Fabi. Imagínate que, entonces, me fui ayer hasta el sitio este que te conté de vinilos, Memo Records Shop. Salí a eso de las doce y media del día a coger el bus, el puto bus pasó a la una y cuarenta, pero nada, me subí y ahí iba yo en la ruta 249 destino Downtown hasta Eastwood Transit Center. Me fui pensando en que necesitamos un tocadiscos, por ahí lo vi en Amazon, y en otros lados, ya veremos de dónde sacamos la plata, mi Fabi, ya veremos. En fin, llegué a Eastwood Transit Center y agarré la ruta 50, veinte paradas, amigo, v e i n t e, hasta Harrisburg Bulevar y desde ahí caminé como veinte minutos.

Fabi, aterricé en la entrada y el sudor me corría por las axilas y el bigote, la entrepierna me temblaba, sentía que me iba a orinar de lo emocionada que estaba. ¿Te acordás del perro de Ligia?, ¿que vos le ponías una mano encima y de los nervios se orinaba? Así, mi Fabi, así mismo me sentía yo, como el perro de Ligia, que me orinaba de imaginar el vinilo autografiado de los Prisioneros en mis manos.

Desde afuera el lugar se ve como un híbrido entre una bodega de zapatos y una casa colonial mexicana, las que a veces son amarillas y tienen los marcos de las ventanas rojas. Vos que viviste ahí la debes tener más clara. El lugar está todo pintado de notas musicales y retratos de cantantes, Vicente Fernández y otros tantos que no conozco, y arriba de la entrada un letrero neón color agua marina que dice Memo Record Shop.

Entré al lugar y el paraíso ante mis ojos: las cuatro paredes que encierran el espacio, que no es nada chiquito, están llenas de vinilos. Era la librería de los discos, aquí, en la ciudad del vacío. Yo entré así despacito y, pum, mi neurosis se activó, ya sabés, mi Fabi, ya sabés que me pongo loca cuando las cosas me gustan. Calculé atravesar el espacio de izquierda a derecha revisando primero por nombres o ¿por años?, ¿por bandas?, ¿álbumes? No estaba segura, pero quería el cálculo perfecto para encontrar a los Prisioneros. Me dije, te tenés que calmar, parcera, ¿qué tal otro gato esté buscando lo mismo?, avancé tranquila, como quien no quiere la cosa, ¿sabés?, manejando la respiración, aunque ya para ese entonces tenía las manos encharcadas de sudor.

Empecé a encontrar cositas interesantes, estaba el vinilo de *Pies descalzos* de Shakira, eso me dio confianza, en el nombre de la Shaki nada puede salir mal, me encomendé a ella y planeaba seguir mi búsqueda así cuando, pum, uno de los vendedores me atajó.

El man ese me dijo, buenas, ¿qué busca la señorita? Era grande y cuando te digo grande, Fabi, era quizás tres cabezas más arriba de la mía y unas dos veces y media mi cuerpo, el tipo era moreno, mechudo y traía el pelo agarrado en una cola hacia atrás y una chivera que se estaba consintiendo mientras me decía "señorita", iba todo vestido de negro y tenía sólo las uñas largas de los dedos gordos, intuyo yo que tocaba guitarra o hacía brujería. Yo así, como medio tranquila, le dije, no yo aquí buscando bandas de rock en español tipo ochentas, noventas, ¿sabés?, y él respondió, no mames, por aquí andan, y me llevó entre los recovecos de los estantes de vinilos hasta una esquina y completó, tenemos lo mejor de lo mejor: Caifanes, Café Tacuba, Molotov, La Lupita, déjame ver, por aquí está Maná. No había terminado de hablar cuando lo interrumpí, y creo que ahí estuvo el problema. ¿Lo mejor del rock en español? Aquí falta Soda Stereo, los Fabulosos, los Auténticos, Andrés Calamaro, Charly, Ekhymosis, Aterciopelados, qué sé yo, ¿Los Prisioneros?

Y ya sabés vos, mi Fabi, cómo arranca una pelea, ya sabés vos que de Soda y Caifanes nos fuimos a tu puta madre y a vos no sabés nada de rock y se escaló la cosa al punto de que terminé diciendo que le iba a partir la cara y el otro, JAJAJAJAJA, soltó esa carcajada que sonó por toda la caja de zapatos mexicana. Tanto que una pareja de gringos que estaba por ahí salió del lugar. Entonces otro señor, mucho más viejo pero parecido, se nos acercó y dijo, bueno, ya estuvo bueno de peleas con la boricua, salte a buscar vinilos a otro lado, ya vete de aquí.

¿Boricua? El tipo ese me dijo boricua. Sentí el peso de los 2218 kilómetros que separan a Houston de Bogotá. Sentí esa distancia enorme atravesar cada uno de mis nervios hasta parar con una punzada en el pecho. Para la gente que vive aquí el sur termina en Puerto Rico. Entonces escuché que mi corazón se fisuraba un poquito, así: crack, te lo juro, Fabi, que lo escuché.

No estamos en el mapa, mi Fabi. No existimos en el mapa.

El caso, no pude saber si el vinilo estaba o no en la tienda y ahora estoy vetada. Lloré como cuando iba perdiendo noveno en el colegio, que no quería ir a casa porque mi papá ya había alistado la correa y vos me dijiste que huyéramos a Buenos Aires, que nos fuéramos al concierto de los

Fabulosos y, mientras calibrábamos la brújula para irnos a pie, vos cantabas *por más que quieras sacarnos de nuestro lugar y pienses que sólo somos un puñado de idiotas no, no, podrás quitarnos lo que hicimos ya ahora somos más hermanos que antes.* Te acordás de nuestra canción, seguro que si estuvieras aquí, mi Fabi, le hubiéramos mostrado el sur en un mapa, le hubiéramos remarcado a Colombia en la cara.

Catalina.

Pd1: para que bailes toda la noche sin parar y para que me cubrás cuando vaya a llorar. https://www.youtube.com/watch?v=y5OdRh5lZOg

Pd2:

8 de febrero 2024. La ciudad del Ø, Texas

Mi amigo, mi amigo Fabi:

Gracias por la buena energía y la lista de vinilos que nos faltan y, sobre todo, gracias, parcerito, por los ahorros para el tocadiscos, yo también te quiero, te pienso y te llevo en el "cora" como dice Karol G.

Ya me siento mejor, pero me sigue emputando que el sur, desde la ciudad del vacío, solo alcance a llegar hasta Puerto Rico.

Tengo un plan para conseguir el vinilo, es macabro y sin precedentes luego te doy más detalles.

Catalina

Pd1: Casi no encuentro la bandera de Colombia.

15 de febrero 2024. Ø, Texas.

Fabi, mi Fabi, mi querido, Fabi:

Siento mucho que te haya dado gripa, parcerito, sé que te bajonea el ánimo, pero seguro con jengibre y miel todo, todo se supera todo se logra, así que vos pa' lante.

Esta vez, sólo buenas noticias para ti. El plan salió, cambiándole un poco el orden de las cosas, bien.

Lo que decidí hacer fue ir todos los días de la semana al lugar. La ciudad del vacío no tiene ni aceras para caminar ni árboles para esconderse, y, nada, yo me fui para allá en mis buses, los de las dos a tres horas, desde las diez de la mañana hasta las seis y media de la tarde. Yo tanteando el terreno, como siempre viendo a ver qué se podía hacer. Al frente de Memo Record Shop hay una cosa que llaman refresquería. ¿Qué venden? Jugos y como raspados, yo sin un peso, pero me sentaba ahí a esperar y mirar quién entraba y quién no. Por ahí como el miércoles, me puse a hablar con el dueño del Tampico (que es la refresquería) y, nada, ahí contándole que yo era colombiana, qué tales, que me gustaba el rock en español. En fin, contándole todo, y pues haciéndome amiga del man. El tipo, también mexicano, me contó que había estado en Bogotá en el 2004 cuando los Auténticos Decadentes, que en Colombia aún no llenaban estadios, se habían presentado en un centro de eventos pequeño y que por primera vez los había escuchado en vivo cantar, *yo no sé lo que me pasa cuando estoy con vos, me hipnotiza tu sonrisa, me desarma tu mirada y de mí no queda nada, me derrito como un hielo al sol.* ¿Te acordás de esa canción, Fabi? Vos y yo estábamos ese mismo día en ese mismo toque, viéndolos en vivo.

El caso es que ya era jueves y, yo así toda carismática, volví al sitio y, nada, me dije, sin mente como las barbies, y me senté frente al tipo y le dije, vení haceme un favor, uno grande, tengo cinco dólares, si querés te los doy. El dueño del Tampico se quedó mirándome como si le fuera a pedir que matara a alguien o que comprara drogas, todo timbrado. Y pues me arriesgué y le conté la historia de los Prisioneros, de Memo Records Shop y de vos, le conté de vos. Hasta le dije que en la caja de zapatos mexicana me habían dicho boricua. Solté la lengua y me encomendé a Shakira.

El señor me dijo, no mames, no más que cierre a las seis y treinta, vamos a rescatar a los Prisioneros. Se me hizo eterno y yo sin siquiera desayunar ahí espere y espere y espere, hasta que, por fin, el hombre se puso a cerrar y a despachar a su gente.

Cruzamos la calle y yo le dije, vení, te espero aquí detrás, el man respondió que ¿por qué? que no fuera pendeja, que entrara y yo le expliqué que no me iban a recibir. El dueño del Tampico se rio y se fue solo. No habían pasado, mi Fabi, ni cinco minutos y el man venía acompañado del mexicano de las tres cabezas más grande que yo y del que me había dicho boricua, yo iba a arrancar a correr y empieza el Tampico a decirme, espérate, colombiana, espérate que te tenemos un recado y yo, nada, ya, aquí me rompieron la cara.

En fin, me quedé quieta, como estatua, los tres se aproximaron, hice un cálculo rápido para gritar por si lo necesitaba. El Tampico habló, ya párale que él es mi primo y el señor aquí, mi tío. Bruta yo, pues eran familia, ya sabían desde ayer que yo andaba rondando y seguro, hoy, que era por los Prisioneros.

Nos quedamos los cuatro hablando un rato, el mexicano de las tres cabezas más grandes que yo seguía rayado, molesto, que como así que los Caifanes no pero que los Prisioneros sí, el Tampico sólo le decía que ya, que eso pasaba con la gente del sur, que se le regalaban a Argentina. No sé qué tanto sabía el Tampico, mi Fabi, de música o de geografía, porque los Prisioneros son chilenos.

Al final nos fuimos los cuatro a una oficina atrás de la tienda y el más viejo, el tío, el que me dijo boricua, se puso a hacer unas llamadas a San Antonio y a Austin a preguntar por los Prisioneros. El tío me contó que ellos habían mandado esos vinilos para allá, porque no les interesaban. Imagínate vos, la mierda de unos es el tesoro de otros. Pero, sea como sea, los mexicanos nos estaban ayudando, Fabi, a nosotros, los sudakas, lanzando su arsenal para que nos lleváramos el disco. Como a eso de las ocho me entregaron un papel:

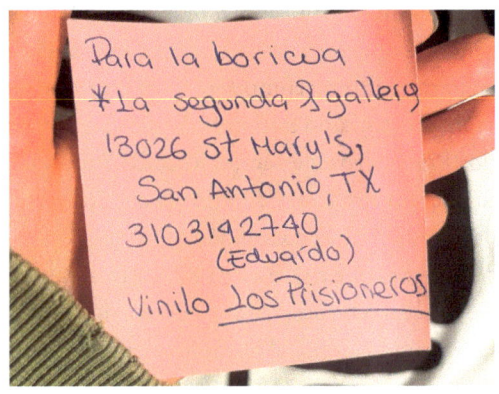

Siete y media en la mañana, mi asiento toca a la ventana, estación central, segundo carro del ferrocarril que me llevará al Sur ... Y no me digas pobre, por ir viajando así ¿No ves que estoy contento? ¿No ves que voy feliz? Viajando en este tren, en este tren al Sur.

Ahora sí, mi Fabi, ahora sí vamos al Sur, con S mayúscula, como antes, como siempre. Después de San Antonio, nos vamos al Sur.

Catalina.

Pd1: arranco el lunes para San Antonio, te paso el mapa.

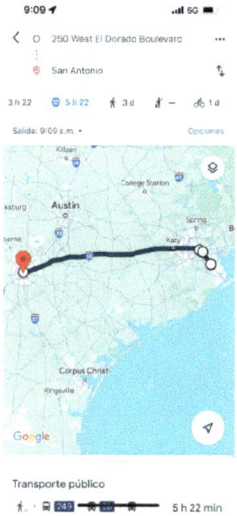

Pd2: https://www.youtube.com/watch?v=WRcCBI5rFfM

Carolina Suárez Latorre actualmente se encuentra en su segundo año de doctorado en escritura creativa de la Universidad de Houston, Texas. Su primer libro de cuentos, *Métale punk*, fue publicado en Bogotá, Colombia, por la editorial independiente Escarabajo en 2022; y durante su carrera ha publicado para diferentes medios impresos y digitales en Colombia y otros países. También fue la creadora del proyecto editorial *El Amor es Para Pobres* en 2017. Su email es dsuarezl@cougarnet.uh.edu.

Circle Home

Camille Goodison

ancestral bones. Riga Mountain, New York, Fall 2021. My teacher stands at the foot of the bowing mat. My fellow Zen students and I also stand behind our mats ready for morning service. For me, this feels like the beginning of a dance. Everyone's in their black robes. I, the newest monk, wear sweats and a pullover. We bow and chant. Outside, facing the Zendo (meditation hall), stands Riga Mountain, a witness to the fluid moves of the prostrating monks.

The kokyo (leader of the chants) announces the "Eihei Koso Hotsuganmon" ("Words for Arousing Vow")—a thirteenth-century sutra authored by Japanese Zen master Eihei Dogen. Immediately, I experience a powerful surge of emotion, coming from my gut. My eyes are moist. This all happens quickly. From the opening lines to the end, I sob quietly: ". . . Buddhas and ancestors of old were as we, we in the future shall be Buddhas and ancestors . . ." During my time as a monk, I will have many such moments. The rhythms and schedule of residential Zen life suit me fine: communal meals, study, kitchen practice, working in the garden, training in the ceremonies and forms. Communal temple living is not without challenges, yet I thrive.

A year later, on my last day, I offer incense at the ancestral altar. It holds a handsome, towering wooden statue of Kwan Yin, an embodiment of great compassion, alongside a framed portrait of San Francisco Zen Center founder Shunryu Suzuki Roshi. I follow the tanto (head of practice) into the Zendo for my monk leaving ceremony. As is custom, my teacher asks me what will I take with me to the marketplace (the world outside of the monastery). Incapable of a single answer, I list several things: the sentient beings I sat with (human and nonhuman), the sound of rushing stream water thawing in spring, the sound of gravel under feet by the entrance gate . . . Undoubtedly, the natural environment which surrounds me—starting with those grand, old mountains—lodges itself deep within the fascia of my muscles and the marrow of my bones.

ancestral fires. Brooklyn, Fall 2022. I return to my apartment in Brooklyn and try to resume my pre-monk life. I reestablish old friendships put on hold during my time away and soon realize I can't simply pick up where I left off. Too much has changed. The pandemic, remote work, the mountains. Old karmic habits return. Workaholism, busy-ism, news bingeing, disordered eating. Instead of sharing my struggles with those dearest to me, I retreat in shame. How to admit that my resumed work life feels like starting at zero? How to say, I need help with setting boundaries, prioritizing time for myself, getting proper nourishment, remembering to drink water, going outside, and reconnecting with family and friends? Winter is tough. Not enough water, exercise, or rest. I need help but can't let anyone know I'm struggling with old habits that didn't disappear with residential Zen practice but had merely been weakened by a supportive schedule and communal life.

While away, I gained helpful insights into old conditioning and I want to believe that's enough. Rather, I am now more sharply aware of these maladaptive habits and how entrenched they are. How do I ask for help? Am I not broken beyond repair? I keep practicing. Zen's my life. No turning back. After several miserable months, I remember. I've felt this way before. When I began sewing my rakusu (Buddha's robe) so I could formally receive the Buddhist precepts in a public ceremony announcing my lay ordination. What should have felt exciting and joyful instead felt very sobering as I contemplated a life of service, vow, and renunciation. It wasn't simply the idea of giving up material comforts—it wasn't that at all—but giving up old habits, old ways of being. In addition to being dressed in new clothes, I'd have a new name. I joked with my teacher that it's like reentering the world as a newborn baby. These old habits were as familiar and snug as an old shoe, and now I was making a promise to begin again and again, as often as it takes to return home to my true self, my buddha nature.

ancestral return. The Met Museum, Fall 2023. I meet with friends I haven't seen in a while. We gather at New York City's Metropolitan Museum. Three brothers are visiting from Plum Village, a Buddhist community founded by the late Vietnamese Zen master Thich Nhat Hanh. I agree to help show them around town while they are here. It is my first real outing since the COVID pandemic. I'd spent the time quarantining, in one form or another, in my apartment or in the mountains. What will it be like socializing with people I haven't seen in years? My body feels heavy and weird. I make it out the door, to the subway, and then I am traipsing around the museum enjoying the brothers' company. After my date, I walk around the city noting all the recent changes, the new shops and sights. The people feel different but look the same. It feels good walking with the crowd, the cool raindrops on my skin, my tired feet meeting the pavement. Later, when describing my day, a friend shares her favorite quote by Native scientist and author Robin Wall Kimmerer: "Action on behalf of life transforms. Because the relationship between self and the world is reciprocal, it is not a question of first getting enlightened or saved and then acting. As we work to heal the earth, the earth heals us."

I make plans to spend some quality time with my large, close-knit Jamaican family. Slowly we return to each other. Maternal aunts, uncles, cousins. My aunt's recent diagnosis for uterine cancer is the first family crisis I've had to face since my grandfather died of lung cancer forty years ago. I should say within my closest circle having lost two in-laws to COVID. Being around my relatives, I am softer and quieter now, and I more clearly recognize signs of trauma from generations of poverty and colonization. I see, too, all the resilience, humor, and liveliness. I see all these things that are also me. Amid the karmic fires of our historical inheritances, I find that I can risk intimacy with my messiness and that of others. Sure, I trust my decade-long Zen training, but, even more so, I am trusting my capacity to give and receive love. The more I share my time and careful attention with the land, nature and the sentient beings around me, the more I feel like my truest self and the more I heal. The more I heal, the more I can appreciate the love that surrounds me. It wasn't always so. Resting in this love, I am able to meet the world as it is and trust myself to respond appropriately.

I feel gratitude for authentic, wise relatives and friends who mirror and care for me. Before signing off on my daily check-ins with my aunt, I chant the song for well-being in Japanese, each syllable punctuated by my rhythmic drumming: "Kan Ze On Na Mu Butsu Yo Butsu U In Yo Butsu U En Bu Po So En Jo Raku Ga Jo Cho Nen Kan Ze On Bo Nen Kan Ze On Nen Nen Ju Shin Ki Nen Nen Fu Ri Shin." I enjoy these moments with my aunt, aware that I'm chanting for myself, too. My cousin, who struggles with panic attacks and Parkinson's, joins his mom on these visits. I chant with all my heart. Strong, deep, confident. This heart, these bones, and these songs return me to my formative years in Jamaica, the place that taught me how to be strong and tender. My aunt reminds me of this with her bright laugh—more of a cackle—and her family stories. This will soon be our last exchange—percussive chants for a storied legacy.

Camille Goodison, author of the story collection *Chance Wanderer and Other Tales of Hunger,* and coeditor of the anthology *Out of Many: Multiplicity and Divisions in America Today* (Cat In The Sun Books, part of Redux Consortium), has published writings in *Transition, Callaloo,* and *Guernica,* among other journals. She was a notable essayist mentioned by *The Best American Essays* in 2013. She lives and works in Brooklyn, New York, where she indulges her love for music, nature, and Zen. She can be reached at CGoodison@citytech.cuny.edu.

Watery Eyes

Saba Khan

The space between two flowing streams is called do-aab or do-aaba in Urdu and Punjabi. This was also a space my ancestors migrated to, from their parched land near the Afghanistan-Pakistan border to the watery space of Jalandhar, which is now part of India. My ancestors farmed near water, barrages, and canal colonies established by the statecraft of the British, who harnessed water to create a steady supply. Metaphorically, do-aaba also means to be teary-eyed, perhaps because it is like two eyes from which flow streams of water. Two streams of tears flowing down from eyes not visible to us.

South Asia, a region heavily dependent on rivers and glaciers for agriculture, has become one of the driest regions in the world, and with the most polluted cities (Shamim 2024). Punjab, one of the most fertile provinces, with five rivers, was annexed by the British Empire in the 1850s. Previously, it was ruled by the Sikh Maharaja's fierce widow, Rani Jindh Kaur, with her nine-year-old son as the king, who resisted the British Empire. The region of Punjab after its annexation became an "agrarian frontier" by laying down canal colonies that were linked to the rivers (Ali 2014, 5).

Rivers are natural frontiers that divide tribes, languages, and cultures, whereas modern dams are markers for claiming state borders and national sovereignty. Water is also a political push button to wind up lower riparian countries by blocking their waters (Haines 2018, 102). The winding continues in the shape of damming fresh water and letting factory effluents run into the neighboring country's dry riverbed (Lai 2022).

The British Empire's ambitious irrigation projects, beginning with canal colonies in the 1850s, continue in the form of dams. These infrastructures have created vast spaces for growing food but with the cost of extreme economic discrepancies (Ali 2014, 3). The region of Punjab is arid yet abundant with water; the rivers were an impetus for small urban societies that mushroomed around 4,000 BCE, forming the first organized towns, surviving through indentured labor and farming. Agriculture led to hierarchical societies where labor of reproduction was given to women to produce a labor force for farming (Thapar 2015, 60). Small communities of runaways began to retreat deep into the mountains or in deserts to get away from enslavement. In areas such as the Karakoram Mountains, women continue to farm and herd (Scott 2009, 189).

Access to water is determined by status, power, clout, and gender. Women are literally on the edge and at the periphery of water. Water decisions in Pakistan are made by men for other men. The head of the Water and Power Development Authority (WAPDA) is always a retired army general, and the bureaucracy has few to no women in key decision-making positions. The government glosses over these issues, using performative actions such as legislating laws to add women to the water committee in Sindh, which has had a minor impact on women on the ground (Genani 2021). At the same time, the majority of the labor force involved in harvesting, picking, and thrashing in fields in Pakistan are women. The herding and rearing of cattle and goats are also manned by women. According to the International Labour Organization, 63 percent of the women are in the workforce in agriculture, which contributes to 23 percent of the GDP of Pakistan (Janjua 2023). The burden of reproduction is also shouldered by women, who produce an endless supply of labor that enters the workforce as factory and domestic workers in urban centers.

How do we navigate the edge of water? Is it even a space to be entered? And who is allowed to go there? A space between two water bodies (do-aaba), the two weeping eyes, who can wander, watch, and witness water? Whose eye matters? The scientific eye of the British agent who comes to survey River Indus for a future annexation, or the indigenous inhabitant who has to protest or demand a separate nation for equal water rights. An area called "zomia," around the Himalayas; nomads and small communities retreated there so they could be shielded from the eye of the state. They remained illiterate to resist the bureaucracy (Scott 2009, 226).

In the 1980s, Zia ul Haq, the then military dictator, added misogynistic amendments to the Law of Evidence, which ruled that a woman's testimony was half of a man's (Kennedy 1988). "For all matters financial or future obligations," men are brought forth as witnesses. This not only infantilizes us women but also makes us doubt our own judgment.

Does this mean that whatever I witness is only half of what my male counterparts see? Is my witnessing and my word to become whole with that of another woman or another man? This law has gaslighted us forever, to second-guess our judgment. Since I have internalized my half-truths, I formed a collective, Pak Khawateen Painting Club (Nice/Pakistani Women's Painting Club) to travel to water bodies, to be seen as a whole, to have another eye to corroborate what I was witnessing, and to have safety in numbers.

Self-doubt and disbelief in one's own competency are reflected in the postcolonial modernity era, when white men from the Global North were imported for their expert advice. Decisions made by David Lilienthal of Tennessee Valley Authority (TVA), who superimposed his American expertise on the Indus Basin, reshaped our rivers forever (Gilmartin 2020, 214). The spacecraft-like lofty building of WAPDA, designed by Edward Durrell Stone along with many other official buildings, dominates the Charing Cross on the Mall Road in Lahore while dwarfing the parliament building next door. The WAPDA only has three women working there, one in the library and two in the PR department.

The water project and the self-doubt in one's own competency were further reinforced and continued by the former chief justice of Pakistan, who drumrolled a new era of dam-building in 2018, this time built with Chinese expertise and funding, as part of the "Belt and Road" project. He stated that the eye telling the truth about cutting of earth, damming of waterways, and pouring of concrete would be declared a traitor (Sheikh 2018).

Our pair of eyes fuse into one, like a cyborg, because of our half-witnessing. Six women's eyes, and witnessing turns into just three. Our new collective of women sets out to witness dams, documenting from the ones built during the modernization era of the 1960s, to the ones now being built by the Chinese experts; the first expedition covered six dams (figure 1). The second expedition traversed along the edge of the Indus River, going on seven barrages, from the first colonial barrage in Sukkur to the ones built after the Partition of India and Pakistan in 1947.

We remained safe by concealing ourselves under costumes or uniforms that resembled those of "girl guides" and transformed us into cyborgs. We defeminize ourselves, appropriating garbs and symbols of power and control, like badges, national flags, and the color green. The state has already

Figure 1. The Collective, the Pak Khawateen Painting Club, triggered by a new commission for Lahore Biennale 02 curated by Hoor Al Qasimi. Here we can be seen in front of a diorama of Tarbela Dam with the actual dam at the back, completed in 1976. Photo courtesy of Saba Khan.

appropriated uniforms and signifiers of the British Empire. But our uniforms are inspired by different vectors in history. In the first one, we copied the Girl Guides, organized and founded by Baden-Powell (founder of the Boy Scouts) and his sister to harden women and introduce them to a life lived in the colonies without the comforts of their sheltered homes. The uniforms dangle with shiny objects, badges, honors, and titles that rub and shine our egos. The second uniform was inspired by the French designer Pierre Cardin, who designed uniforms for the sleek, modern airlines, including Pakistan International Airlines (PIA), during the dam era of the 1960s (figure 2). It was a time to urgently modernize and chug along with developmental projects that plonked the country on the modernity bandwagon. PIA was also a brand ambassador for the newly formed country and advertized a progressive image, with air hostesses in Pierre Cardin's futuristic uniforms in front of snowy peaks. However, on the ground, women were left out of the modernity project and were projected as air hostesses serving others on flights.

The collective as genderless machine or naive girl guides was a prop to enter sensitive spaces within dam sites. We posed for the camera and pretended to make plein air paintings of dams and barrages for our ladies club or collected soil samples for "scientific work" (figure 3). Women artists

Saba Khan 255

Figure 2. The Collective's second uniform for the expedition to barrages built over the Indus River. Designed in collaboration with Zohra Rahman. Supported by the Graham Foundation and the Sharjah Art Foundation Production Program. Photo courtesy of Saba Khan.

Figure 3. The Collective pretending to paint in front of the foggy Taunsa Barrage built in 1958. Photo courtesy of Saba Khan.

Figure 4. The Collective, Natasha Malik, Emaan Shaikh, Saulat Ajmal, Amna Hashmi, and Malika Abbas, dining in Barseen Camp, which was set up by Chinese engineers for the building of Dasu Dam, currently under construction, 2019. Photo courtesy of Saba Khan.

are stereotyped as benign objects, a bourgeois class who like to discuss politics from the luxury of their drawing rooms. Our "innocent, pretty, and useless" hobby gave us access into basements of the dam turbines, inside the chairman's offices, official rest houses, and an adit tunnel carved out by Chinese engineers (figure 4).

Cutting, diverting, and allocating. The rivers were severed in sections by barrages to divert waters to the hinterland; what was considered barren wastelands were spaces for nomadic lives, for gathering and living off the ground. The vast irrigation engineering program also engineered societies, creating a new sedentary, agricultural class. This not only generated landlords who owned large tracts of land, but also gave rise to waterlords who oversaw water dispersal on the behalf of the colonial statecraft. These families continue to hold power and have retained a political clout in Pakistan (Gilmartin 2020, 126).

Deep inside Sindh, we drive on narrow, potted roads, crossing over several dry canals surrounded by dry tracts of land with dust blowing over bleached soil. This is the tail end of the canal command, where a trickle is reserved for farms owned by women. Small hamlets around the town of Badin, a belt, called "laar," is just above the coast. Their proximity to the sea has brought in sea intrusion and saline water. With less fresh water coming from the north, they must rely on saline groundwater for drinking and irrigation. They complain of health issues from a lack of access to potable water. Sometimes the crop goes to waste if the water is not released from upstream. A major share of the water is taken by the upper riparian provinces and then by powerful landlords (Kaleem 2019).

Here women own the land they farm. Men leave for urban centers like Karachi to look for menial jobs, for example, as laborers or domestic workers. The women farmers' water supply comes from the Sukkur barrage, built in the 1930s, one of the last ambitious "nation-building" colonial projects to lead "material progress" in the province of Sindh. The barrage is a long bridge cutting across the widest part of the Indus River, with sixty-six gates, and distributes water to areas deep inside Sindh (Haines 2011, 3).

The barrage also is near some islands, a small cluster holding holy architecture that is revered by different religions, a space that may come across as syncretic and has also been a site for communal clashes during the pre-Partition era.

We hop from island to island in our small wooden motorboat. The larger island holds the Hindu temple of Sad Belo. A tiny island holds a shrine of Khwaja Khizr, the green-robed water saint who reappears in several regions. He is the savior of those lost in waters and shows boaters and wayfarers the way.

Close by, there is another island, of graves of seven female friends who let the earth swallow them up to avoid rape or abduction by a king. It has become a space of healing for women, who make a pilgrimage for fertility and other health issues. It is not clear what the real origin of the story is or if it was just another story to rile up communal issues where the king was the prominent Hindu Raja Dahir, who was defeated by the Arabian Muslim conqueror Mohammed Bin Qasim. The women were also in a group or collective. Safety was in numbers, and maybe for their testimony to be whole, they had to be many.

Between these islands, a family of dolphins swim and wade through gray waters. They appear above the water for a split second to gasp for a breath of air. They now live in between two barrages, forever unable to mate with the ones across the barrage, leaving a stunted genetic pool. They were once spotted swimming as far up as Punjab, in the mid-1800s, by a colonial officer (Braulik et al. 2021, 31–32).

Is our half-witnessing making us blind like the eyes of the dolphin? The dolphin has evolutionarily adapted to the dark waters of the Indus and

Figure 5. The Diamer Bhasha dam reservoir site, which will inundate thousands of ancient petroglyphs. This is also a region of Kohistan that has resisted state governance for centuries. Photo courtesy of Saba Khan.

has lost its sight. It relies on sonar for communication and navigation. The muddy waters made its eyes useless.

The young, eroding Karakoram Mountains in the north continue to grow as the two tectonic plates push upwards. They rub and grind, adding silt to the Indus, making it dark and gritty. The silt made soil in the plains fertile, creating mud plains, which sprouted the first ancient, urban villages of Mohenjodaro that depended on farming. However, the barrages and dams now block the flow of the alluvial soil, resulting in dependence on artificial fertilizers, encouraged during the green revolution.

The mud plains around the delta are retreating because the river is no longer regurgitating silt at the sea. The sea is intruding and eating up the land (figure 5).

To witness, we perform and tread cautiously around water edges. While I perform in front of water infrastructure, pretending to be productive, pretending to paint or conduct "scientific tasks" such as soil collection, documentation, interviews, the government also takes performative measures. The Sindh government has blamed their own mismanagement and greed on climate change, claiming that the recent floods in 2022 were an act of God, and has brought the onus on polluting by Western countries. While there is weight in the argument, it does not take away their responsibility over citizens who are exasperated from neglect from the state.

How do we navigate without seeing, without our testimonies? The Indus River dolphin has let go of its eyes and its sensory function of seeing, because there was nothing visible in its dark waters. Women in Pakistan with their half-witnessing and half testimonies, as stated by the state law, will we begin to see less clearly, and will we lose our sight too? To witness and document the edges of water is important, to leave a testimony of what had happened on-site.

Saba Khan is a visual artist whose interdisciplinary practice stretches over the fields of art, ecology, performance, and colonial histories, which come together through expeditions, research, and fieldwork. The work explores the history and politics of water bodies, flow, fluidity—bodies blocking water and bodies moving along water. Her work weaves through the language of memorial, monument, and public projects, balancing grandeur, artifice, and satire in order to explore the cracks in the structures. She recently exhibited at Swiss Institute, USA; National Museums of Qatar, Doha, 2024; Sharjah Biennial 15, UAE; Sharjah Art Foundation, UAE, 2022; and Lahore Biennial 02, Pakistan, 2020. She can be reached at saba.khan@arts.ac.uk.

Works Cited

Ali, Imran. 2014. *The Punjab Under Imperialism, 1885–1947*. Princeton University Press.

Braulik, Gill T., Frederick I. Archer, Uzma Khan, et al. 2021. "Taxonomic Revision of the South Asian River Dolphins (Platanista): Indus and Ganges River Dolphins Are Separate Species." *Marine Mammal Science*, March. https://doi.org/10.1111/mms.12801.

Genani, Manoj. 2021. "Women in Pakistan's Sindh Win Historic Recognition to Manage Water." *Dialogue Earth,* January 20. https://www.thethirdpole.net/en/culture/women-in-pakistans-sindh-winhistoric-recognition-to-manage-water/.

Gilmartin, David. 2020. *Blood and Water: The Indus River Basin in Modern History*. University of California Press.

Haines, Daniel. 2011. *Building the Empire, Building the Nation*. PhD thesis, Royal Holloway College, University of London.

Haines, Daniel. 2018. *Indus Divided*. Random House India.

Janjua, Haroon. 2023. "Pakistan's Female Agriculture Workers Suffering Since 2022 Floods." *Al Jazeera*, March 31. https://www.aljazeera.com/news/2023/3/31/pakistans-female-agriculture-workers-suffering-since-2022-floods.

Kaleem, Moosa. 2019. "Why Badin Is Facing a Massive Canal Water Shortage." *Herald Magazine*, April 28. https://herald.dawn.com/news/1398870.

Kennedy, Charles. 1988. "In Pakistan, Islamic Laws Are Applied Without Political Control." *New York Times*, July 24, sec. Opinion. https://www.nytimes.com/1988/07/24/opinion/l-in-pakistan-islamic-laws-are-applied-without-political-control-017588.html.

Lai, Olivia. 2022. "Pakistan's Ravi Is Most Polluted River in the World from Pharmaceutical Pollution." *Earth*. May 11, 2022. https://earth.org/most-polluted-river-in-the-world-pharmaceutical-pollution/.

Scott, James C. 2009. *The Art of Not Being Governed*. Yale University Press.

Shamim, Sarah. 2024. "Why Does South Asia Have the World's Worst Air Pollution?" *Al Jazeera*, April 2. https://www.aljazeera.com/news/2024/4/2/why-does-south-asia-have-the-worst-air-pollution-in-the-world.

Sheikh, Wajih Ahmad. 2018. "CJP Hints at Charging Dam Opponents with Treason." *Dawn*, September 16. https://www.dawn.com/news/1433201.

Thapar, Romila. 2015. *The Penguin History of Early India: From the Origins to A. D. 1300*. Penguin Books.

La Vorágine en Cuerpo

Fátima Vélez

1. La posición

La imagen es la de José Eustasio Rivera escribiendo *La Vorágine* un día lluvioso de 1923, aproximadamente.[1] La posición de sus glúteos sobre la silla de cedro nogal, la vértebra sacra entumecida. El cuello doblado, la cervical rígida y abultada; lleva días mal durmiendo, las piernas con calambres, la mano (¿derecha, izquierda?) tiembla, va soltando calor en la tinta azul con que deletrea cada palabra.[2]

Regresa a la silla de cedro nogal, se acomoda los isquiones, endereza la espalda para volver a encorvarse de inmediato sobre el manuscrito. Empuña la pluma, la sumerge en tinta azul, y en ese momento se antoja de un cigarrillo, o de un trago, o de ambas cosas. Se sirve un vaso del whiskey finísimo que le trajo su amigo de Irlanda. Prende un tabaco. Inhala. Lee un párrafo en voz alta mientras exhala. Hay algo que no le cuadra. Apaga el cigarro. Quizás tiene frío. Trato de entrar en su temperatura. Una ruana aparece en su espalda. Quizás tiene hambre y el ruido es el de sus intestinos. Voy a su nervio auditivo, lo que ahí se almacena, resonancias de lo que escuchó durante su viaje como abogado representante de Colombia en la Comisión de Límites con Venezuela y Brasil, del que tomará la materia prima para elaborar otro viaje, el de Arturo Cova hacia el inframundo de lo verde.

¿Se excita y se manosea José Eustasio Rivera mientras imagina y escribe las fantasías de Arturo Cova con la manigua y las mujeres?[3] ¿Qué tan conectado siente su cuerpo con el de su personaje? ¿Cuánta autopercepción está puesta en la subjetividad del soberbio e impulsivo poeta citadino que emprende una huida sin retorno hacia la selva y cuyo corazón es robado por la violencia?

En coro escucho las palabras de otro personaje, Clemente Silva, quien dice: "La selva trastorna al hombre" (173). Entran en la escritura de *La Vorágine* las fiebres de la malaria que llevarán al escritor a la muerte, cinco años después, en Nueva York, la ciudad desde donde lo imagino, a los cuarenta años suyos, a los treinta y nueve míos; él tendido en un cuarto del Stuyvesant Polyclinic, el hospital en el East Village del que me separan cuarenta y tres minutos en tren. Mi deseo de atravesar tiempos, espacios, otredades, para conectar mi cuerpo de mujer, madre, inmigrante, trabajadora, estudiante, escritora, con el cuerpo de José Eustasio Rivera mientras escribe *La Vorágine*, me impulsa a darle una vuelta al hospital, a ver qué puede decirme el lugar donde murió el autor sobre su cuerpo de escritor. ¿Y qué ganaría tomando tres trenes en llegar hasta allá? Más bien guardo mi energía, me quedo aquí, sentada en la silla blanca de plástico, el sacro adolorido, los omoplatos contracturados, la muñeca con artrosis temprana, los dedos dermatíticos de uñas descascaradas sobre el teclado. Observo mi cuerpo vivo imaginando el proceso de embalsamiento del cuerpo en rigor mortis de José Eustasio Rivera. Imagino el viaje por mar y tierra del embalsamado. Las miradas de asombro y curiosidad sobre el cuerpo del hombre que tuvo adentro la selva; el cuerpo del hombre que logró volver esa posesión una novela y luego fue devorado por la peste que producen los insectos protectores de los árboles.

2. El cuerpo del escritor

En mi época como estudiante de pregrado de literatura las preguntas y especulaciones sobre el cuerpo que escribe no eran permitidas. Habrían sido una vergüenza, por no ser yo lo suficientemente rigurosa. "Nada que se salga del texto, el texto no es un pretexto", creo que decían mis profesorxs. Mencionar el cuerpo del escritor[4] dentro de un ensayo crítico no era una posibilidad.

El vacío del cuerpo del escritor en los estudios literarios me dio vueltas por años. Gracias al feminismo me di cuenta de que, como escritora, me es imposible esquivar la pregunta por el cuerpo que escribe cuando leo un libro. ¿Es legítimo explorar el cuerpo escribiendo *La Vorágine* de José Eustasio Rivera como detonante de una lectura crítica de una de las obras colombianas que más lecturas críticas ha generado?

Rastreo datos comunes sobre la novela en Google, Wikipedia, X, algunos artículos en Academia y Jstore, anécdotas; elementos materiales que me conecten con ese cuerpo.

Es de notar que los procesos físicos de los escritores varones, esos que han producido casi la totalidad de la literatura, están muy poco documentados. La falta de documentación de los procesos físicos de la escritura es una oportunidad para el asombro. La imaginación para dar cuenta de que los libros de tres mil páginas sobre lo humano y lo divino son posibles gracias a un cuerpo, con órganos y contracturas y sueños y cansancio y deseos sexuales. Tampoco olvidar que para que muchos de esos cuerpos puedan escribir las tres mil páginas de lo humano y lo divino, una serie de otros cuerpos, por lo general cuerpos de mujeres, han estado alimentando, limpiando, criando, cuidando.

3. El cuerpo del personaje

Dicen que José Eustasio Rivera escribió *La Vorágine* en cuatro meses. Debió haber sido un asunto caudaloso, de entrega corporal, y al mismo tiempo, un ejercicio milimétrico de memoria y carpintería lingüística. Se nota que José Eustasio lo dio todo, hasta su vida.[5]

A su personaje Arturo Cova le tomó menos escribir las memorias/diarios/cartas que constituyen el manuscrito de Cova dentro de la novela de Rivera. Cova escribe desde el campamento de su amante, la madona Zoraida Ayram, mientras espera con ansias el retorno de Clemente Silva. Me da la impresión de que Cova escribe sus aventuras como si no tuviera cuerpo. Y es que si una se fija no hay ninguna descripción física del personaje. No hay ningún momento en que se mire al espejo. No hay espejos en esta selva.

Como Arturo Cova no tiene más cuerpo que el lenguaje con el que describe, desde su subjetividad, el mundo que lo rodea, uso lo que tengo a mi alcance para hacerle uno: la fotografía de José Eustasio Rivera de la edición crítica de Monserrat Ordóñez de *La Vorágine*. De smoking negro, muy serio, así imagino a Arturo Cova antes de internarse en la selva que se lo devoró. Cuando estoy editando este ensayo una amiga me manda una foto de Rivera, de 1923, no la había visto antes, no la encuentro en Internet. Es el escritor con un traje blanco, abotonado hasta el cuello; me hace pensar en un general de la guerra civil estadounidense. Mi amiga dice que hasta se ve guapo. Me parece que sí. Que ahora Arturo Cova también puede tener un traje blanco de botones hasta el cuello, sentado en una silla con el pelo desordenado, en la mano lo que parece un trébol, o un cigarro; a pesar de lo borrosa que resulta la imagen se intuyen nidos de hormigas tombochas en la mirada.

En mi fantasía Arturo Cova sale de Bogotá vestido, a veces con ese smoking, a veces con el traje blanco; Alicia engarzada del brazo. En mi fantasía, Cova se quita prenda por prenda a medida que cambian los pisos térmicos y la vegetación excede lo humano. Cuando Arturo y su combo, con todo y la promesa redentora de su linaje, llegan al "solemne cerro cuya base lame el río Curicuriarí" (320) del final del viaje, cuando ya ni siquiera tiene pellejo, ni un pedacito del pantalón de lino del smoking, en otro lugar geográfico aparece un manuscrito como prueba de la experiencia vivida por un cuerpo, cuyo destino, se intuye, es volverse materia orgánica.

Busco otras formas de invocar la imagen física de Arturo Cova. Para esto me valgo de la voz de Mauco, el brujo que cura las gusaneras, el que dice: "Cuando el reclutamiento de la guerra grande me vinieron a cogé, y me les convertí en mata de plátano. Una vez me apañaron antes de acabá el rezo y me encerraron en una pieza, con doble yave; pero me volví hormiga y me picurié... Yo tuve listo pa evaporarme, cuando entraran, y taparlos a tóos con mi neblina. Apenas supe que usté taba herío, le recé la oración del 'sana que sana' y la hemorragia se contuvo" (77).

El rezo que el brujo Mauco hace sobre la herida de Arturo Cova me despierta un impulso transfigurador, en el que no es necesaria una imagen humana para dar con el cuerpo de Cova; puedo tomar algunas de sus descripciones sintomáticas para hacerle un cuerpo, por ejemplo, la escena del ataque de beriberi en el que se convierte en árbol de caucho y su pierna en raíz: "Hablaba, hablaba, me oía la voz y era oído, pero me sentía sembrado en el suelo, y, por mi pierna, hinchada, fofa y deforme como las raíces de ciertas palmeras, ascendía una savia caliente, petrificante. Quise moverme y la tierra no me soltaba. ¡Un grito de espanto! ¡Vacilé! ¡Caí!" (112).

En este momento en que el cuerpo de Cova es excedido por la fuerza del árbol, por la savia de su devastación, ante la inexistente imagen física humana, la imagen de Arturo Cova que se forma en mi cabeza es la de un hombre que empieza como la fotografía de José Eustasio Rivera y en un viaje por ríos, pantanos y raíces, va perdiendo el traje y el cuerpo capitalino y va deviniendo Hevea brasiliensis, árbol de caucho, shiringa o seringueira, de la familia de las euforbiáceas, de 20, 30, excepcionalmente 45 metros de altura. Arturo Cova va deviniendo árbol de caucho con toda la violencia sobre él impartida.

Arturo Cova, cuya imagen física queda en el plano de la especulación, tal como el cuerpo de José Eustasio Rivera mientras escribe *La Vorágine*; Arturo Cova, en cuyas memorias no habla en ningún momento de cómo se hace popó y chichi en la selva, ni del embarazo ni del parto de Alicia, al mismo tiempo, es quien narra la fisicalidad de la selva, la exuberancia de la corriente de los ríos, la fuerza del comején y las tombochas, el intestino de El Cayeno extraído y desenrollado por los perros Martel y Dólar; la muerte de Barrera, descuartizado por las pirañas del Orinoco, llamadas "caribes", como los indígenas presuntamente devoradores de carne humana, tan temidos por los conquistadores españoles.

Da la impresión de que los personajes de *La Vorágine* sólo existen físicamente al devenir selva o al ser violentados.

4. La foto

No hay espejos en la selva, pero hay papel y tinta y una cámara fotográfica, una Kodak, de *Mosiú*, que es como Clemente Silva llama al fotógrafo francés del que se hace amigo, el fotógrafo del que se dice que es explorador y naturalista, patrocinado por los amos gamonales para retratar las caucheras. Cuando *Mosiú* empieza a observar a través de su lente los maltratos físicos contra los trabajadores esclavizados, decide usar sus fotos como forma de mostrarle al mundo los abusos cometidos por los gamonales del caucho, tanto en el cuerpo de los trabajadores esclavizados, la mayoría indígenas, como en el de los árboles gangrenados por la demanda desaforada de la industria automovilística.

En la foto, que quiero imaginar revelada, enmarcada y exhibida en algún museo en Londres, aparece la espalda cubierta de heridas de Clemente Silva junto a un árbol de caucho lleno de cortes para desangrarlo y extraerle la goma lechosa. Dice Clemente Silva: "Momentos después, el árbol y yo perpetuamos en la kodak nuestras heridas, que vertieron para igual amo distintos jugos: siringa y sangre" (195). En la fotografía, ese proceso material en el que se pueden fijar imágenes con luz y así dar cuenta de la existencia material de algo o de alguien, queda el registro de la herida común: la destrucción del cuerpo humano y del cuerpo árbol en manos de la extracción desmedida.

5. El cuerpo de Alicia

El contraste entre la falta de fisicalidad del personaje de Arturo Cova y la elaboración física del paisaje y las escenas de violencia me hace detenerme en Alicia, que en la subjetividad de Cova aparece como la odiada y amada y binaria Alicia.

Me pregunto si Alicia lleva también un diario. No, diría Arturo Cova, Alicia no escribe. Ella cose y enseña a coser. La mantiene entretenida practicar lo que aprendió en el colegio, le dice Cova a la niña Griselda. Alicia no sólo no escribe. Alicia no tiene voz más que la que le presta Aruto Cova, el tipo con el que se fugó, y se la presta como cuatro veces apenas en toda la novela. Me llama la atención que Alicia no tiene cuerpo, pero está embarazada. Alicia da a luz sin ninguna descripción física del parto ni de la lactancia ni de lo que implica tener un bebé y transportarlo por la selva, Alicia y su bebé en vez de cuerpos parecen ser de aire.

Arturo Cova tiene la escritura para hacerse árbol, una escritura que le permite tener cuerpo, ir más allá de lo humano para tener un cuerpo. La fisicalidad de Alicia, en cambio, aparece de vez en cuando y radica en algunas descripciones que dependen del estado de ánimo de Cova. Así, Alicia varía, adjetivizada, entre los cielos de pureza angelical; la ígnea amada malvada; la mujer guerrera que practica la autodefensa cuando Barrera intenta sobrepasarse con ella, como se lo cuenta la niña Griselda a Cova; y finalmente, tenemos a Alicia embarazada, cuyo cuerpo es sustituido por el de la promesa redentora del vientre que alberga al progenitor Cova.

Llama la atención el primer síntoma del embarazo de Alicia. En la escena, al principio del viaje, están don Rafael, Arturo y Alicia en una "laguneta de aguas amarillosas . . . cubierta de hojarascas" (25). Aparece una boa "que a mis tiros de revólver se hundió removiendo el pantano y rebasándonolo en las orillas" (25), dice Cova. Esta situación hace que Alicia, en vez de escuchar a la serpiente y comer del fruto de la sabiduría, quede "Presa de pánico . . . se reclinó temblorosa bajo el mosquitero. Tuvo vahídos, pero la cerveza le aplacó las náuseas. Con espanto no menor comprendí lo que le pasaba, y, sin saber cómo, abrazando a la futura madre, lloré todas mis desventuras" (26). En ese momento, Cova se aparta con don Rafael, mientras Alicia yace desmayada, y coinciden en que "No convenía, durante el viaje, advertirla del estado en que estaba, pero debía rodearla de todos los cuidados posibles" (26). El hecho de que Arturo Cova y don Rafael se den cuenta del embarazo de Alicia, pero decidan ocultárselo, hace que el cuerpo de Alicia se trate de un asunto de especulación entre dos hombres.

Más adelante, cuando Alicia y la niña Griselda se pierden en la selva, y Arturo Cova lleva meses sin saber de ella, es más, ya poco piensa en Alicia ni en su presunto embarazo, cuando Cova escucha que Alicia de hecho sí está embarazada, se riega en verso sobre cómo la maternidad "la santificó" y cómo "desde el vientre materno, mi hijo la ampara" (315). Y en el momento en que Alicia reaparece, al final de la novela, Cova se olvida por completo de ella, la amada deja de ser Eurídice, después de haber emprendido semejante viaje a los infiernos para rescatarla, y es reemplazada por la promesa de futuro que lleva en el vientre "En tal momento me había olvidado de buscar a Alicia. La niña Griselda la tenía abrazada al cuello y yo me detuve sin saludarla: ¡sólo quería mirarle el vientre" (321).

6. El diario de Alicia
Imagino el diario de Alicia sobre el viaje paralelo que emprende con la niña Griselda bajo el yugo de Barrera. También fantaseo con el diario de la niña Griselda, con el de la madama Zorayda. Sueño con los cantos de la indiecita Mapiripana. No será en este texto donde se escribirán estas ficciones. Lo más fácil es pensar que el diario de Alicia es sobre su pena de amor con Arturo Cova. Tal vez aparezca ahí una descripción física del personaje. Arturo es un idiota, me imagino que dice, Huele a chivo, es violento, no me lo aguanto. Me gusta pensar que la indiferencia de Alicia, de la que Cova se queja varias veces en la novela, está movida no sólo por su embarazo, sino porque Cova le parece un tonto y se da cuenta de que cometió un gran error al escaparse con él. Pero no va a quejarse, tampoco quiere hacerse una carga para nadie. Y así, imagino que Alicia se interesa por la botánica y las plantas medicinales y las recolecta en una libreta que le cambia a Barrera por un anillo que tiene muy bien guardado y del que Arturo Cova no sabe.

Es una lástima que el tratado botánico de Alicia, en el que recoge cada una de las especies medicinales usadas por las diferentes comunidades indígenas que se encuentra en el camino, sea devorado por la manigua, al igual que ella, su hijo y la gente que la acompañaba.

Pero también, podría pensarse en otra posibilidad: que Alicia logre escapar con su hijo de las tombochas gracias a la palmera de cananguche, "que, según la leyenda, describe la trayectoria del astro diurno, a la manera del girasol" (232); la misma palmera cananguche que, "encumbrada en aquel destierro como un índice hacia el azul" (232), le indicó el camino a Clemente Silva, cuando se perdió con los siringueros brasileros. Alicia, con su hijo en brazos, guiada por los árboles burlones, se va a vivir a una ciudad al norte de Brasil, cultiva plantas medicinales amazónicas y practica el culto a Iemanja. Su hijo nace con unas ramitas de caucho en los omoplatos y no se parece en nada a Arturo Cova.

Fátima Vélez nació en tierra volcánica. Es escritora, profesora, productora cultural, estudiante y mamá. Le gustan los procesos colectivos de escritura. Hace parte de *Como un lugar*, un colectivo de poetas latinoamericanxs que desde Nueva York hacemos fiestas, libros y encuentros. Ha publicado los libros de poesía *Casa Paterna*, *Del Porno y Las Babosas*, *Diseño de Interiores*, y las novelas *Galápagos* y *Jardín en Tierra Fría*. Vive en Nueva York. Su email es fvelez@gradcenter.cuny.edu.

Notas

1. Para la escritura de este ensayo usé la edición crítica de *La Vorágine* de Monserrat Ordóñez, publicado por Cátedra en el 2006.
2. Dice Nelson Freddy Padilla, cuando en el 2010 puede ver y tocar las páginas de los cuadernos originales de *La Vorágine* recién clasificados por la Biblioteca Nacional de Colombia: "La caligrafía en tinta azul es hermosa, alterada por enérgicas enmendaduras y anotaciones al margen, siempre en busca del término más cadencioso. Palabras sobre palabras, pasadas luego a la máquina de escribir antes de lograr la versión definitiva". Tomado del artículo *Los manuscritos de la Vorágine*, publicado en El Espectador el 6 de febrero de 2010.
3. Me fascina pensar en ese canal que hay entre la imaginación, la escritura y el deseo sexual.
4. En masculino, porque poco leíamos escritoras.
5. Siempre me han llamado la atención las coincidencias entre el final de una novela y el final de la vida de un escritor. Es inevitable invocar la fantasía de que la obra lleva al escritor a la muerte. Supongo que la historia de la indiecita mapiripana que aparece en *La Vorágine* puede leerse, entre otras posibles lecturas, como una metáfora de la escritura como selva vampira que devora al hombre que se atreve a sobrepasar límites.

SECTION IV. CLASSICS REVISITED

Cartas y recados de una militancia por la paz: Olga Poblete y Gabriela Mistral

Javiera Manzi A.

Retomar la pregunta por los horizontes de paz como feministas socialistas en América Latina nos lleva a una larga historia que se asienta en la lucha de quienes, desde los años treinta, supieron estrechar la emancipación política, económica y biológica de las mujeres con la lucha contra el fascismo y la guerra. En 1950, Gabriela Mistral escribió uno de sus textos más célebres por fuera de la reconocida obra poética que la llevó a ser la primera mujer en recibir el premio Nobel de Literatura en América Latina. Es un ensayo corto, un *recado,* tal como ella misma nombraba este género suyo titulado "La Palabra Maldita". Allí Mistral hace alusión a la urgencia de retomar el compromiso con el vocablo "paz" y a la vez encarar la paz como un problema. No teme criticar la indiferencia del campo político y literario e incluso la impotencia de instituciones supranacionales como las Naciones Unidas, incapaces de evitar conflictos armados y en particular, aunque no lo mencione directamente, el flagelo de la guerra nuclear. Al final de este breve pero elocuente escrito declara con dureza y sin concesiones: "el pacifismo no es la jalea dulzona que algunos creen; el coraje lo pone en nosotros una convicción impetuosa que no puede quedársenos estática" (Mistral 1950). Gabriela escribe estas líneas sin un atisbo de ingenuidad. Muy por el contrario, su trayectoria como intelectual pública, en especial como diplomática desde la década de los treinta (fue la primera mujer chilena en desempeñar una labor consular en Chile), la llevó a conocer de cerca la amenaza que supuso la avanzada del fascismo en Europa. Uno de sus primeros encuentros fue precisamente en Italia, donde había sido nombrada cónsul, pero no llegó a ejercer sus funciones por declararse antifascista, a lo que se sumó que, para entonces, Mussolini no aceptaba a mujeres diplomáticas. En texto, Mistral insiste en que se trata de repetir esta palabra en toda circunstancia, pero en especial de garantizar las condiciones para su posibilidad. No bastaba con la denuncia, la paz debía ser una tarea política: "Digámosla cada día en donde estemos, por donde vayamos, hasta que tome cuerpo y cree una *militancia de la paz* la cual llene el aire denso y sucio y vaya purificándolo" (Mistral 1950). Hay algo muy bello e incluso esperanzador en aquella imagen atmosférica donde alude al sopor que se respira en aquellos años y que solo puede ser interrumpido por la acción colectiva, organizada y valiente de lo que ella anuncia como una militancia de la paz.

Unos meses después, en abril de 1951, la historiadora Olga Poblete, integrante del Movimiento por la Emancipación de las Mujeres de Chile (MEMCH)[1], y también del Movimiento de Partidarios de la Paz, le escribe una carta a Mistral llena de entusiasmo. Lo primero que señala es que desea que sus palabras lleguen a todos los rincones del país, en especial a las mujeres del pueblo a quienes Gabriela "interpreta tan hondamente" (Poblete 1951). Pero no solo eso, Poblete hace suya la idea de una militancia de la paz que según le escribe, ya ha comenzado a constituirse: "Dura es la lucha que vendrá, pero la causa es grande y el anhelo de la paz nos está hermanando con los millones de Europa, de Asia, de África.... Ella está llevando al primer plano una conciencia universal, que ninguna técnica, ningún mecanismo internacional, ninguna diplomacia lograron antes despertar. Es la *militancia de la paz* que usted reclama y ya comienza a tomar forma" (Poblete 1951). Ahí queda en evidencia algo más que el entusiasmo por las palabras de la poeta; está en ciernes una articulación de "esta hermosa solidaridad hemisférica" (Poblete 1951) que anuncia una alianza desde el Tercer Mundo contra las "máquinas administrativas que ya están montadas para acallar toda voz, donde sea que aparezca" (Poblete 1951). Para Poblete, Mistral había logrado darle nombre a aquella actividad que, cargada de urgencia, la había llevado a recorrer el mundo guiada por la imperiosa necesidad de acabar con las guerras coloniales en pleno siglo XX.

La militancia por la paz de Poblete contaba con varias ramificaciones, incluyendo la influencia que tuvo (junto a otras figuras como Marta Vergara y Elena Caffarena) en hacer que ésta fuese una de las principales causas del movimiento feminista chileno. De hecho, en 1937 "la defensa del régimen democrático y de la paz" (Movimiento Pro Emancipación de las Mujeres de Chile 1938) fue reconocida como una de las cinco grandes aspiraciones del MEMCH durante su Primer Congreso. Para Poblete esta preocupación se vio intensificada por su estadía en Nueva York a mediados de los cuarenta cuando estudiaba un Magíster en Educación en la Universidad de Columbia.

Según su propio relato, el bombardeo atómico a las ciudades de Hiroshima y Nagasaki en 1945 por parte de Estados Unidos fue lo que terminó de hacer germinar su sentimiento antiimperialista. No es casual que, a su regreso a Chile, el MEMCH se sumara al Comité Femenino Anti Armamentista y a las campañas de presión al gobierno para evitar la firma del Pacto Militar de Ayuda Mutua con Estados Unidos. En 1950 fue una de las principales promotoras del Primer Congreso Nacional del Movimiento de Partidarios de la Paz en Santiago y presidió en 1951 la Delegación Chilena al II Congreso Mundial de la Paz en Varsovia del que luego realizó un informe titulado "¡La paz no se espera, se conquista!" (Poblete 1952). En este contundente y sentido informe, comparte con el Movimiento en Chile su experiencia y los principales acuerdos de esta instancia: la férrea denuncia de las condiciones de dominación colonial y dependencia económica de los países subdesarrollados, la amenaza de gobiernos fascistas en la región y la importancia de oponerse a los planes armamentistas en escalada planetaria. Era, tal como señalaba Mistral, una militancia sostenida tanto en la urgencia como en la insistencia de luchar por la paz en todos los espacios que tuviera disponibles.

En agosto de 1951, no será solo una carta personal a Mistral, sino una respuesta conjunta firmada por Olga Poblete (Secretaria General), Guillermo del Pedregal (Presidente) y Santiago Aguirre (Secretario de Relaciones) desde el Movimiento Nacional de Partidarios de la Paz. En esta oportunidad, la misiva comienza refiriéndose a ella como *Querida amiga*, dando cuenta del progresivo y afectivo acercamiento que se ha producido entre las partes. En la carta agradecen a Mistral por haberles escrito en medio de un contexto donde si bien la lucha por la paz "se intensifica y crece a través de toda la tierra" (Poblete, del Pedregal y Aguirre 1951), también ha sido blanco de "la más odiosa propaganda dirigida a sembrar desconfianza y a separar a los individuos por las cortinas del temor y la mentira" (Poblete, del Pedregal y Aguirre, Carta a Gabriela Mistral 1951). ¿Quiénes eran los responsables y quiénes los blancos de esa propaganda, tanto en lo local como a nivel internacional? En plena Guerra Fría, las expresiones públicamente organizadas de un movimiento internacional fueron objeto de vigilancia, persecución y estigmatización. La campaña anticomunista hábilmente expandida por los Estados Unidos en América Latina a través de la Doctrina Truman, tuvo un fuerte correlato en Chile bajo el gobierno de Gabriel González Videla, quien promovió en el Congreso en 1949 la Ley de defensa permanente de la democracia, popularmente conocida como la Ley Maldita, que declaró la ilegalidad del Partido Comunista, cuyos militantes fueron borrados de los registros electorales, despojados de sus cargos de representación popular e incluso detenidos en calidad de prisioneros políticos en el campo de concentración ubicado en Pisagua. De hecho, el entonces presidente de Chile llegó a identificar "la reunión pacifista como una maniobra del comunismo internacional contra el mundo libre" (Poblete 1991, 26) (algo bastante similar a lo que pasó con la criminalización de las movilizaciones que se multiplicaron en todo el mundo en solidaridad con Palestina). Seguramente la odiosidad de la propaganda en contra de este Movimiento provenía también de quienes buscaban asociarlo a un instrumento de la órbita soviética en un contexto donde hacerlo implicaba un riesgo vital para sus adherentes. En un artículo escrito por Poblete para el periódico El Siglo, también responsabilizó de esa hostilidad creciente a las mentiras difundidas por los medios de comunicación, el "instrumento informativo monopolizado por intereses económicos" (Poblete 1961), y expresó su confianza en que la verdad se abriría paso, y que la solidaridad internacional atravesaría "las distancias geográficas, raciales, ideológicas y culturales" (Poblete 1961). En la carta enviada a Mistral está muy presente la preocupación y reconoce que "sobre los destinos de su pueblo se juegan poderosos intereses que propugnan la guerra" (Poblete 1952), pero advierte que "la voluntad popular está claramente consciente de este deber, nuestros esfuerzos se dirigen a vigorizar dicha voluntad y mantenerla alerta" (Poblete 1952). El apoyo abierto de Mistral fue también demostración de que el Movimiento y su causa convocaban a sectores humanistas de diversas sensibilidades políticas.

Esta serie de intercambios, entre recados y epístolas, son parte de una trama mucho más amplia que durante la década de los cincuenta y sesenta avanzó en construir una concepción compartida del "vocablo maldito". Lejos de una idea abstracta y ahistórica de la paz, esta fue concebida, tanto por Poblete como por Mistral, como el principal problema y desafío político de su tiempo. Para Poblete, su conquista solo era posible a través de la acción organizada e internacionalmente coordinada desde los pueblos del Tercer Mundo que debían articular una alianza abiertamente antifascista y antiimperialista que se opusiera al dominio y las condiciones de dependencia con las potencias centrales. En plena guerra fría, ambas coincidían en que el resguardo de la autonomía y la soberanía nacional eran requisitos esenciales de la paz, al igual que las condiciones de desarrollo económico y social de cada pueblo. Lo que sí enfrentaban, y esto es algo que ambas anunciaron innumerables veces, es el hostigamiento e incluso la estigmatización mediática a quienes se opusieran a la política armamentista. Casi treinta años después, Olga publicó el libro *La guerra, la paz, los pueblos* donde reconstruye su trayectoria como militante de la paz desde el movimiento en Chile y su itinerario de presentaciones en distintas instancias internacionales. Es ahí donde condensa con mayor claridad su principal tesis sobre los tres asuntos sustantivos para la comprensión del problema de la paz luego de la Segunda Guerra Mundial. Las denominó como "las tres D de la paz: descolonización, desarrollo y desarme" (Poblete 1991). Para Poblete no era posible separar la conquista de la paz de estas cuestiones que apremiaban la subsistencia de pueblos sometidos al intervencionismo neocolonial, y por eso señaló con tanta fuerza hasta el final de sus días que "la tarea descolonizadora es monumental: montar el aparato Estatal, construir una economía que lleve a un desarrollo efectivo, integrar una nación y rescatar su identidad cultural" (Poblete 1991).

Ni una jalea dulzona, ni un alto al fuego. La militancia de la paz supuso la lucha por su conquista efectiva. Esto es: abogar por el desarme nuclear al mismo que tiempo que acompañar las luchas de liberación nacional y por el desarrollo de las condiciones materiales que hacen posible una vida libre para pueblos empobrecidos. En un presente de guerras incesantes en el Congo y Sudán, con el genocidio en curso en Palestina, es indispensable volver a historizar y politizar la militancia de la paz como condición de existencia y futuro. Una militancia que, al decir de Mistral, vaya purificando ese aire denso y sucio que nos impide pensar sin dejarnos abrumar por los entramados de mentiras y las oleadas de desinformación. Pero también, y especialmente para el campo intelectual, de una política de silencio y omisión que se ha impuesto en espacios académicos, políticos y culturales. Pienso en las preocupaciones que rondaban a Mistral al decidirse a escribir sobre aquella palabra maldita y sus consecuencias, tenía claro que hacerlo suponía una toma de posición no exenta de riesgos ni costos incluso con todo el reconocimiento internacional que tenía. Cuánta falta hace hoy la valentía de intelectuales como Mistral y su determinación por escribir sobre temas controversiales y la de Poblete y su responsabilidad por asumir la tarea política de articular una respuesta organizada contra la guerra.

Ante las elecciones de Estados Unidos, hay quienes señalaron que la política proteccionista de Trump podría llevarlo a alejarse del intervencionismo belicista de gobiernos anteriores, pero lo que en realidad sostiene es que el fin de la guerra no es más que la aniquilación total (y final) de poblaciones completas que hoy viven bajo ataque permanente con el patrocinio norteamericano. Una política antimilitarista no surgirá del cálculo de magnates que acceden al mando de potencias mundiales. Hoy es urgente, diría que indispensable, retomar aquel ímpetu internacionalista y la imaginación política de estas dos amigas, intelectuales y pacifistas, que a mediados del siglo XX ampliaron los horizontes de emancipación feminista con una concepción materialista y antiimperialista de la paz.

Javiera Manzi A. is a sociologist and archivist (Universidad de Chile), educator, and independent researcher. In her work, she focuses on the intersections between art, politics, and social movements. She is coauthor of the book *Resistencia Gráfica. Dictadura en Chile* (Graphic Resistance: Dictatorship in Chile), published by LOM in 2016. She can be reached at javiera.manzi@gmail.com.

Nota
1. Fundado en 1935 y activo hasta 1954, el MEMCH fue una organización feminista amplia y diversa que tuvo un alcance nacional y que se propuso luchar por la autonomía política, económica y biológica de las mujeres. Participó activamente en la lucha por el sufragio universal y el reconocimiento de los derechos sexuales y reproductivos. Sostuvieron Congresos Nacionales y llegaron a tener una revista propia, La Mujer Nueva donde hacían públicos sus debates, campañas y reflexiones. Si bien muchas de sus integrantes eran militantes de izquierda, sostuvieron su autonomía de los partidos políticos y declararon su posición abiertamente antifascista y antimilitarita.

Trabajos citados
MEMCH. 1938. *¿Qué es el MEMCH? ¿Qué ha hecho el MEMCH?* Santiago: Antares.
Mistral, Gabriela. 1978. *La palabra maldita*. En *Recados para America: Textos de Gabriela Mistral*, ed. Mario Céspedes. Santiago: Revista Pluma y Pincel/ Instituto de Ciencias Alejandro Lipschutz.
Poblete, Olga. 1983. "Prólogo." En *MEMCH: Antología para una historia del movimiento femenino en Chile*. Santiago: MEMCH.
Poblete, Olga. 1951. Carta a Gabriela Mistral, April 21.
Poblete, Olga. 1952. Carta a Gabriela Mistral, May 30.
Poblete, Olga. 1961. "Problemas chilenos están ligados íntimamente con la paz mundial." *El Siglo*, January 21.

Poblete, Olga. 1991. *La guerra, la paz y los pueblos*. Santiago: Tacora.
Riobó Pezoa, Enrique. 2021. "Humanismo, nación y antiguedades griegas e indígenas en Juan Gómez Millas, Roberto Prudencio, Yolanda Bedregal y Olga Poblete 1932–1964." PhD diss., Universidad de Chile.

Letters and Recados of a Militancy for Peace: Olga Poblete and Gabriela Mistral

Javiera Manzi A.
Translated by Camila Valle

Returning to the question of the horizons of peace as socialist feminists in Latin America brings us to a long history based on the struggle of those who, since the 1930s, have been able to link the political, economic, and biological emancipation of women with the fight against fascism and war. In 1950, Gabriela Mistral wrote one of her most famous texts outside of the renowned poetic work that made her the first woman to receive the Nobel Prize for Literature in Latin America. It is a short essay—a *recado* (message, note), as she herself called this genre of hers—entitled "La Palabra Maldita," or "The Cursed Word." In it, Mistral alludes to the urgency of recommitting to the word *peace* while also facing peace as a problem. Mistral is not afraid to criticize the indifference of the political and literary field, and even the impotence of supranational institutions like the United Nations, incapable of avoiding armed conflicts and, though not explicitly mentioned, the scourge of nuclear war. At the end of this brief but eloquent text, she declares harshly and uncompromisingly: "Pacifism is not the sweet jelly that some believe it to be; courage places it in us an impetuous conviction that cannot remain static." Gabriela writes these lines without a hint of naivety. On the contrary, her trajectory as a public intellectual, especially as a diplomat since the 1930s (she was the first Chilean woman to act in a consular role in Chile), led her to experience firsthand the threat posed by the advance of fascism in Europe. One of her first encounters was in Italy, where she had been named consul, though she ultimately did not carry out her duties because of her self-declaration as antifascist, in addition to the fact that, at the time, Benito Mussolini did not accept female diplomats. In "The Cursed Word," Mistral insists that it is about repeating the word in every circumstance, but especially about guaranteeing the conditions for its possibility. Denunciation was not enough; peace had to be a political task: "Let us say it every day wherever we are, wherever we go, until it takes shape and creates *a militancy for peace* that fills the dense and dirty air and purifies it." There is something very beautiful, even hopeful, in that atmospheric image, which alludes to the lethargy breathed in those years that can only be interrupted by the collective, organized, and courageous action of what she declares as a militancy for peace.

A few months later, in April 1951, the historian Olga Poblete, a member of the Movement for the Emancipation of Women of Chile (MEMCH)[1] and the Movement of Supporters of Peace, wrote Mistral an enthusiastic letter (Poblete 1951). The first thing she noted was how she wanted her words to reach every corner of the country, especially the working-class women whom Gabriela "understood so deeply." But not only that, Poblete adopted the idea of a militancy for peace, which, she wrote, had already begun to constitute itself: "The struggle that is to come is hard, but the cause is great and the desire for peace is uniting us with the millions in Europe, Asia, Africa.... She is bringing to the forefront a universal conscience that no technique, no international mechanism, no diplomacy had managed to awaken before. It is the *militancy for peace* that you demand and is already beginning to take shape." There is evidence of something more than enthusiasm for the poetess's words; there is the budding confidence in a force that is starting to articulate itself, "this beautiful hemispheric solidarity" that announces an alliance from the Third World against the "administrative machines that are already set up to silence every voice, wherever it appears." For Poblete, Mistral had managed to give name to that activity that, charged with urgency, had led her to travel the world guided by the imperative to end colonial wars in the twentieth century.

Poblete's activism for peace had several ramifications, including her influence (along with that of other figures such as Marta Vergara and Elena Caffarena) in making it one of the main causes championed by the Chilean feminist movement. In fact, in 1937, "the defense of the democratic regime and of peace" was recognized as one of the five great aspirations of the MEMCH during its First Congress (MEMCH 1938). For Poblete, this concern was intensified by her stay in New York in the mid-1940s, when she was getting a master's in education at Columbia University. According to her own account, the atomic bombings of Hiroshima and Nagasaki in 1945 by the United States caused her anti-imperialist sentiment to fully flourish. It is no coincidence that, upon her return to Chile, the MEMCH joined the Women's Anti-Armaments Committee and the campaigns to pressure the government against signing the Military Pact of Mutual Aid with the United States. In 1950, she was one of the main promoters of the First National Congress of the Movement of Supporters of Peace in Santiago and, in 1951, presided over the Chilean Delegation to the Second World Peace Congress in Warsaw, later producing a report entitled "Peace Is Not Awaited, It Is Won!" In this powerful and heartfelt report, she shared with the Movement in Chile her experience of and the main agreements come to during the event: the staunch denunciation of the conditions of colonial domination and economic dependence of developing countries, the threat of fascist governments in the region, and the importance of opposing the arms plans on the rise worldwide. It was, as Mistral pointed out, a militancy sustained both by the urgency and the insistence of fighting for peace in all every available space.

In August 1951, it was not just a personal letter to Mistral, but a joint response signed by Olga Poblete (Secretary General), Guillermo del Pedregal (President), and Santiago Aguirre (Secretary of Relations) from the National Movement of Supporters of Peace (Poblete 1952). On this occasion, the missive begins by referring to her as *Dear friend*, to note the progressive and affective rapprochement that had unfolded between the two parties. In the letter, they thank Mistral for having written to them in a context where, although the struggle for peace "intensifies and grows throughout the entire land," it has been the target of "the most hateful propaganda aimed at sowing distrust and separating individuals by the curtains of fear and lies." Who was responsible for this propaganda and who were the targets, both locally and internationally? As the Cold War raged, publicly organized expressions of an international movement were subject to surveillance, persecution, and stigmatization. The anti-communist campaign skillfully expanded by the United States in Latin America through the Truman Doctrine had a strong correlative in Chile under the government of Gabriel González Videla, who in Congress in 1949 promoted the Law for the Permanent Defense of Democracy, popularly known as the Cursed Law, which made the Communist Party illegal, erased its members from the electoral registers, stripped them of their positions of popular representation, and even detained them as political prisoners in the concentration camp located in Pisagua. In fact, the then-president of Chile came to identify "the pacifist meeting as a maneuver of international communism against the free world" (something quite similar to what happens today with the criminalization of the mobilizations multiplying throughout the world in solidarity with Palestine) (Poblete 1991, 26). Surely the odiousness of the propaganda against the movement also came from those who sought to categorize it as a Soviet tool in a context where this implied a fatal risk for its adherents. In an article written by Poblete for the newspaper *El Siglo* in 1961, she also blamed this growing hostility on the lies spread by the media, the "informational instrument monopolized by economic interests," and expressed confidence that the truth would emerge and international solidarity would cross "geographical, racial, ideological, and cultural distances" (Poblete 1961). The letter sent to Mistral is very concerned with and recognizes that "the destiny of your people is at stake in powerful interests that advocate war," but warns that "the popular will is clearly aware of this duty, our efforts are directed toward strengthening said will and keeping it alert" (Poblete 1952). Mistral's open support was also a demonstration that the movement and its cause called on humanist sectors of diverse political sensibilities.

This series of exchanges, from recados to letters, are part of a much broader story that in the 1950s and '60s advanced the construction of a shared understanding of the "cursed word." Far from being an abstract and ahistorical idea, peace was conceived by both Poblete and Mistral as the principal political issue and challenge of their time. For Poblete, its achievement was only possible through organized and internationally coordinated action from the peoples of the Third World, who had to create an openly antifascist and anti-imperialist alliance that opposed the domination of and conditions of dependence on the central powers. In the midst of the Cold War, both agreed that the protection of autonomy and national sovereignty were essential requirements for peace, as were the conditions of economic and social development of each people. What they did face, which they both expressed countless times, was the harassment and even media stigmatization of those who opposed armament policies. Almost thirty years later, Olga published the book *War, Peace, Peoples*, where she reconstructs her journey as a peace activist from the movement in Chile and her series of presentations to different international bodies. It is there that she most clearly condenses her main thesis on the three substantive issues for understanding the problem of peace after the Second World War. She called them "the three *D*s of peace: decolonization, development, and disarmament" (Poblete 1991). For Poblete, it was not possible to separate the achievement of peace from these issues that threatened the survival of peoples subjected to neocolonial interventionism, which is why she so strongly pointed out until the end of her days that "the decolonizing task is monumental: setting up the state apparatus, building an economy that leads to effective development, integrating a nation, and rescuing its cultural identity" (Poblete 1991).

Neither a sweet jelly nor a ceasefire. Peace activism means fighting for its victory. That is: advocating for nuclear disarmament while simultaneously supporting national liberation struggles and the development of material conditions that make a free life possible for impoverished peoples. In a present of incessant wars in Congo and Sudan, of the ongoing genocide in Palestine, it is essential to rehistoricize and repoliticize the militancy for peace as a condition of existence and futurity. An activism that, in the words of Mistral, purifies that dense and dirty air that prevents us from thinking without becoming overwhelmed by the web of lies and waves of misinformation. And, especially for the intellectual field, counters a politics of silence and omission that has been imposed on and haunts academic, political, and cultural spaces. I think of the issues preoccupying Mistral when she decided to write about that cursed word and its consequences. She was clear that doing so meant taking a position not free of risks or costs, even with all her international renown. We are sorely missing today much of the courage of intellectuals like Mistral, with her determination to write about controversial subjects, and Poblete, with her sense of duty in taking on the political task of articulating an organized response against the war.

In light of the U.S. elections, there are those who noted that Donald Trump's protectionist policy could lead him to distance himself from the bellicose interventionism of previous governments, but what he really maintains is that the end of war is nothing more than the total (and final) annihilation of entire populations that today live under permanent attack, sponsored by the United States. An antimilitarist politics will not emerge from the calculations of magnates who accede to the command of world powers. Today it is urgent, indispensable, to reclaim that internationalist impetus and political imagination of these two friends, intellectuals, and peace activists, who in the mid-twentieth century strengthened the horizons of feminist emancipation with a materialist and anti-imperialist conception of peace.

Javiera Manzi A. is a sociologist and archivist (Universidad de Chile), educator, and independent researcher. In her work, she focuses on the intersections between art, politics, and social movements. She is coauthor of the book *Resistencia Gráfica. Dictadura en Chile* (Graphic Resistance: Dictatorship in Chile), published by LOM in 2016. She can be reached at javiera.manzi@gmail.com.

Note

1. Founded in 1935 and active until 1954, the MEMCH was a broad and diverse feminist organization that had a national reach and fought for the political, economic, and biological autonomy of women. It actively participated in the struggle for universal suffrage and the recognition of sexual and reproductive rights. They held National Congresses and even had their own magazine, *La Mujer Nueva*, where they published their debates, campaigns, and reflections. Although many of its members were left-wing activists, they maintained their autonomy from political parties and declared their openly antifascist and anti-militarist position.

Works Cited

MEMCH. 1938. *¿Qué es el MEMCH? ¿Qué ha hecho el MEMCH?* Santiago: Antares.

Mistral, Gabriela. 1978. "La palabra maldita." In *Recados para America: Textos de Gabriela Mistral*, edited by Mario Céspedes. Santiago: Revista Pluma and Pincel/Instituto de Ciencias Alejandro Lipschutz.

Poblete, Olga. 1951. Letter to Gabriela Mistral, April 21.

Poblete, Olga. 1952. Letter to Gabriela Mistral, May 30.

Poblete, Olga. 1961. "Problemas chilenos están ligados íntimamente con la paz mundial." *El Siglo*, January 21.

Poblete, Olga. 1983. "Prólogo." In *MEMCH: Antología para una historia del movimiento femenino en Chile*. Santiago: MEMCH.

Poblete, Olga. 1991. *La guerra, la paz y los pueblos*. Santiago: Tacora.

Riobó Pezoa, Enrique. 2021. "Humanismo, nación y antiguedades griegas e indígenas en Juan Gómez Millas, Roberto Prudencio, Yolanda Bedregal y Olga Poblete 1932–1964." PhD diss., University of Chile.

SECTION V. **BOOK REVIEWS**

On Healing Our Selves and the Injured History of Our Homeland

Ghina Abi-Ghannam

Lara Sheehi and Stephen Sheehi's *Psychoanalysis Under Occupation: Practicing Resistance in Palestine*, New York: Routledge, 2022

To begin where *Psychoanalysis Under Occupation* concludes, in the book's epilogue, Lara Sheehi and Stephen Sheehi cite a *New York Times* article written by Danny Danon, Israel's ambassador to the United Nations. In his piece, Danon urges Palestinians to commit what he crudely terms as "national suicide," matter-of-factly asking: "What's wrong with surrender when staying the course proves costlier than submission?"

Danon's overbearing proposition brings forth a formula that the authors of this book excavate from the history and present of the Israeli occupation, a formula that required coordinated operations to ensure that the Palestinian struggle for national liberation is reliably always "costlier than submission." In the concrete, Lara and Stephen Sheehi observe that this doctrine had materialized in a necropolitical system that deliberately and continuously aggravates the cost of Palestinian refusal to surrender to colonial ambitions: a system planted in a "settler-colonial logic of elimination" that impresses a multitude of violent vectors against the Palestinian people, targeting Palestinian bodies, geographies, institutions, and—most relevant to this book, Palestinian selves.

We revisit *Psychoanalysis Under Occupation* over a year into the ongoing magnified genocide in Gaza—with inconceivable scales of destruction and injury that are ever so undermined by the statistics of the tens of thousands of Palestinian martyrs killed and the hundreds of thousands wounded, starved, and displaced. In the wake of growing atrocities, the book at hand offers to clarify the thrusts of strategic devastation that the Israeli occupation has exacted onto the besieged people of Gaza, its military operations physically demonstrating the immeasurable cost of resistance for Palestinians, while sardonically waving—in the rubble of catastrophic conditions—a proposal for submission, for national suicide.

Lara and Stephen Sheehi's writing is an accolade to resistance as *practice* through their book engaging a textual exercise that provides the language and the methodology to locate where psychoanalysis lives in the wars against the Palestinian people past, current, and forthcoming. This book patiently lays bare the colonial logics embedded in Danon's "radical truth" and the Israeli system of violence that banks on its atrocities forcefully breaking the will of the Palestinian people into capitulation.

Broadly, *Psychoanalysis Under Occupation: Practicing Resistance in Palestine* interweaves three porous threads. First, the book interrogates the role of psychoanalysis as an institution of colonialism and positions itself contentiously toward the weaponization of psychoanalysis as an additional technology of violence in the arsenal of Israel's necropolitical doctrine. Second, it methodically leans on psychoanalysis to uncover systemic violence that targets the Palestinian self. And third, stimulated by decolonial and queer feminist psychoanalytic modalities of inquiry that are relational and dynamic in their fabric and ethics, the authors draw on their conversations with clinicians practicing in Palestine to elevate stories of Palestinian willfulness, in addition to the intactness and coherence that resistance grants the Palestinian self living under occupation, in the clinical space and outside of its doors.

Reading the Room: Psychoanalysis as a Technology of Israeli Violence

In tracing the institution-building of the Zionist state, Lara Sheehi and Stephen Sheehi examine the process through which institutions have historically scaffolded the establishment and maintenance of settler colonialism in Palestine. This infrastructure constitutes institutions of armed forces, knowledge production, labor formations, carceral structures, and *psychoanalysis*. Here, the role of psychoanalysis is identified as an agent of *reality bending*, or the systematic effort to distort the historical-material condition, creating in its stead a reality that allows for settler-colonial logics and operations to go unchallenged.

The book is attentive to how psychoanalysis and psychological institutions promote an etiology that locates sociopolitical issues exclusively within the psychic realm—permitting and even requiring the disavowal of material reality and of settler-colonial history. A generated by-product of this etiology is "ideological misattunement": the inability to comprehend the complexities of the self living under occupation, subsequently manufacturing a Palestinian who is deprived of an "interior world," allowed to exist only as an overaccumulation of aggregated symptoms. In this terrain, the misattuned psychoanalyst is able to read the Palestinian exclusively through their symptoms, reserving criminality and pathology as the only "codes of legibility" that equip the observing psychoanalyst to make a diagnosis.

Anchored in psychoanalytic innocence, psychoanalysis fortifies settler colonialism and its longevity through graphing Palestinian subjects that are ridden with a negated interiority, that float as a comorbidity of symptoms to be diagnosed and repaired into *healthy* subjects well acclimated to the necropolitical system asphyxiating them.

This book takes the clinical room as its unit of analysis, with a poignant premise dictating that when the clinic exists within a space that is under occupation, the topographical structures of the occupation—the checkpoints, the apartheid wall, the blockade, the warplanes, the prison—all enter the room. To the authors, the stories and musings of Palestinian clinicians probe the urgent task to overwrite the boundaries of psychoanalytic space to one that is cognizant of the history and materiality of the land it exists on, and that allows the clinical space to become a "breathing room" for those entering it instead of an additional site of occupied space that reproduces technologies of violence and asphyxiation.

In keeping with their own refusal to absolve the violence of colonization, the authors conjure Frantz Fanon's concept of sociogenesis, which steps away from the psychoanalytic tendency to atomize and isolate the internal world from the external vectors acting on it. With that, *Psychoanalysis Under Occupation* is a project that is first and foremost concerned with (1) naming the violence that enters the clinical room, (2) dispelling the use of the room as a space for dialogue and negotiation that disempowers the subject through governing politics of appeal and recognition, and (3) gesturing toward a capacity to imagine a clinical space *otherwise*—one that declines to integrate the occupation as "another stressor" but that insists on psychic healing being contingent on liberation.

"The Occupation Always Enters the Room"

In one conversation with Yoa'd, a Palestinian clinician, she identifies violence as a technical fixture in the therapy room:

> It always enters the room. One way or another, the occupation always enters the room... Most people who come in for therapy don't explicitly say "Help me Doctor, the Occupation is making me crazy." They come to talk about their marriages, their families, their own insecurities and fears, frustrations, and stressors. Just like anyone else.... But when you know that they are coming from a camp, their father or husband is in jail, settlers—with the help of the state—are trying to take their house in the Old City, how can you ignore the presence of the Occupation? We work through these parallels to identify deflection so that we do not contribute to the "splitting" that the Occupation forces on us. (56)

In outlining the landscape of life under occupation, Lara and Stephen Sheehi carefully chart the multidimensional sites and operations that host Israeli technologies of violence. In their illustration, we see how vectors of necropolitics facilitate processes of death, imprisonment, humiliation, dismemberment, and asphyxiation. Listening to dispatches from the clinical space, the authors discern the penetrating character of these vectors infiltrating the body and invading psychic territory, reminded by Dr. Samah Jabr that the worst effect of occupation is "the internalization of oppression and the undermining of Palestinian's collective self-concept."

From here, the book takes seriously an appreciation of psychic wounding away from the practice of reading the Palestinian through marking manualized defects, longitudinally scaling symptomatic surges, to ultimately land on the appropriate diagnosis. Safeguarded by psychoanalytic innocence, diagnosis superimposes pathology on top of the Palestinian to make them legible and to facilitate a process of repair that requires acclimation, demanding a performance of normalcy under abnormal conditions of occupation and violence. Here, diagnosis becomes "a blockage (a checkpoint, *hajiz*) to accessing the language of the patient. Diagnosis increases alienation."

Diagnosis is designated as a technology of violence precisely because it demands and enables a process of *splitting* where the self embraces the *colonial introject*: the split away from "the 'bad Palestinian' [who] refuses to be 'reasonable,' remains covetous, tends to violence, is stuck in the 'ideology of their identity,' and a turn towards the colonial introject who enacts otherness, internalizes and 'takes in' the colonial self as an ego-ideal in a bid to defend against the violence that is anticipated." Instead, this book urges the analyst to listen to the symptom as an affirmation of life, as a signal vindicating the intactness of the ego, as a resistance to splitting and a practice of sumud (steadfastness) that confronts dismemberment and tightly embeds the individual with the collective, all through the self's unbending refusal to normalize relations with abnormal conditions.

The Negotiation Room

The misattuned psychoanalyst enters the room to manage, and not to care for, the Palestinian. Moved by the colonial impulse to preserve the system of suffering inscribed by the occupation, the analyst takes on the role of a mediator imploring the Palestinian patient to dissociate from their lived reality and concede to a prescription of victimhood and trauma that they must internalize as their own and then reciprocally grant to their perpetrator, the settler.

Here, the Palestinian is vended the politics of appeal and mutual recognition as a normative trajectory to "heal." Palestinian subjectivity is pinned as a battlefront to achieve psychically what the Zionist project is yet to achieve militarily—the expulsion of a national liberation struggle from consciousness, or to return to Danon's literary device, national suicide. Coming up against refusal, the misattuned psychoanalyst sifts through the (diagnostic) manual for codes of legibility to detect the defect, the subterranean pathology, brewing the diagnosis that they can then bring to the negotiations table.

Dynamics of negotiation in the clinical space replicate the deployment of "dialogue initiatives" in their communicated objectives of disarming Palestinians of their refusal and personifying the occupation as a "partner in peace," thus securing settler futurity. The misattuned psychoanalyst occupies the role of the mediator, saturated with foreclosures that invite the Palestinian patient to "move beyond violence," actuating a process of *psychic inversion*—where the willful subject, and not the occupation, becomes the agent of violence, with an adjacent procedural prerequisite that encourages the willful subject to consent to surgically ostracizing the psychic world that does not cohere with the provisions of dialogue.

The book primarily demonstrates this diplomatic procedure through the dynamics that emerge between Palestinian clinicians and their Israeli supervisors. Supervision in this context is grounded in a framework that is mainly invested in stabilizing the crisis of settler-colonial society, one that "pathologizes the wounded power of Palestinians as an impediment to 'recognizing the other' rather than understanding willfulness and resistance as a means of maintaining psychological and subjective coherence and cohesion."

At this turn, we see negotiation as the negation of the self, a treaty for the

Palestinian to receive conditional recognition in exchange for dissociating from the self, the community, and lived reality. When refusing to contort reality, the defiant, willful subjects become unintelligible. Their refusal to mirror misattunement and their desires for liberation are then designated as symptoms of a *paranoid-schizoid functioning*.

A Breathing Room

In the final section of the book, we sit in on conversations between the authors and Palestinian clinicians that interrupt a psychoanalysis that works to erode and further dissect the Palestinian self. What grounds this conversation is an appreciation of the Palestinian self as the primary site for "life, willfulness, and resistance," with resounding statements asserting that "resistance keeps us [Palestinians] sane." This brings us to a psychoanalysis that commits itself to the "restructuration" and the survival of Palestinian subjectivity, that abandons its post as a technology of violence and aligns itself as a countertechnology of liberation.

Here, the clinicians recognize that the occupation had ruptured Palestinian land and history and that this rupture created a life in crisis, an abnormal condition that registers as the presenting symptom. While the misattuned psychoanalyst aspires to diagnose and eradicate the symptom, further asphyxiating and closing in on the self to fortify the occupation, this book ushers us to instead consider national liberation as psychoanalytic objective, a liberation that hinges on identity-building in as much as it requires institution-building.

This conviction entrusts the patient and the clinician, both living under occupation and wounded by its vectors, to cocreate an autonomous space for mutual recognition, away from the surveillance of Israeli institutions and the regulations of the donors in the human rights industry. This generates a plane of a shared language and shared grammar that allows the self to breathe under a system of necropolitics and asphyxiation, opening up the space to "surpass its wrecking effects":

> What we learn from our conversations with clinicians is that if we understand the goal of psychology as working to alleviate personal suffering, the history and reality of Zionist colonial violence is the chief source of collective and individual pain and suffering inflicted collectively upon the Palestinian people. (91)

The book's proposal urges us to interrupt and reject the splitting between a Palestinian self that is defiant and resistant, cohered with *sumud*, and another Palestinian self that is wounded and fractured by the weight of Israeli violence. An attuned psychoanalysis becomes a promising instrument to re-member social and intersubjective relations among Palestinians isolated from one another by means of colonial sentencing. To borrow from Samah Jabr's words, it is this psychoanalysis that "will heal us as individuals and help us to heal the injured history of our homeland." This psychoanalysis wages a war on reality-bending through an unbending conviction that the move "beyond violence" and beyond disalienation and beyond psychic pain is contingent on profound structural changes. Reminding us, always, that the precondition is liberation.

Ghina Abi-Ghannam is a writer and researcher currently completing her PhD in critical social psychology at The Graduate Center, City University of New York. Her work broadly involves the political psychology of violence and the sociology of science. Some of her previous contributions include publishing on the social psychological study of violence in Palestine, the exile of Frantz Fanon from the field of social psychology, and the psychology of land dispossession. She can be reached at gabighannam@gradcenter.cuny.edu.

Review of *The Home as Laboratory*

César Barros Arteaga

Lucía Cavallero and Verónica Gago's *The Home as Laboratory. Finance, Housing, and Feminist Struggle* (translated by Liz Mason-Deese), Philadelphia: Common Notions, 2024

There is no question that, for at least the last decade, feminisms have been the most powerful, productive, and uniting dissident force in Latin America. Feminists have won important ground, from growing visibility and legislation around femicide, gender violence, and reproductive rights, to the transformation of traditional spaces for leftist politics and confrontation of the divisions of space (private/public) and labor (reproductive/productive) in national and international heteropatriarchal-racial-capitalist systems. The feminist strike, in particular, has shown everyone who wants to see and hear how all of these issues intersect and redefine the places of enunciation and meaning of social justice. It is no surprise, then, that the right wing and its current popular fascist manifestation have chosen feminisms, and what they call "gender ideology," as their preferred target.

Contemporary feminisms, of course, are not traditional political movements with innovative ideas. Rather—and this is one of the reasons they have grown so much and have, at times, become massive—they are a spring of political methodologies: strictly horizontal, assembly-based, thinking and theorizing collectively from below and from political praxis, never abandoning political imagination to mere electoral politics. Luci Cavallero and Verónica Gago, both independently and as a team, have been tireless participants in this feminist work as militants of the Ni Una Menos collective and the Feminist Intervention and Research Group (GIIF). They have been intervening and theorizing in Argentina and building a "feminist international" (the English title of one of Gago's books), and not only, or even mainly, by publishing books but also by working and intervening in every space necessary.

One of their most important contributions as a team is their work on debt and financialization as a central tool of patriarchal exploitation and extraction. In book form (again, their interventions are not at all limited to books), this work starts with *Una lectura feminista de la deuda ¡Vivas, libres y desendeudadas nos queremos!* (Tinta Limón, 2021), translated by Liz Mason-Deese the same year as *A Feminist Reading of Debt* (Pluto Press); *¿Quién le debe a quién? Ensayos transnacionales de desobediencia financiera* (Who Owes Who? Transnational Essays on Financial Disobedience) (Tinta Limón, 2021), which they edited alongside Silvia Federici; and *La casa como laboratorio: Finanzas, vivienda y trabajo esencial* (Tinta Limón, 2022), recently translated as an extended edition with Mason-Deese as translator and coauthor.

In *A Feminist Reading of Debt*, Cavallero and Gago open a rich theoretical-political path by, in their words, "taking debt out of the closet." One of their crucial propositions in this "coming out" is that financialization cannot be analyzed and criticized as an abstraction (which would mimic how finance presents itself), but instead needs to be analyzed in the ways it territorializes. Nowadays, debt *lands* in particular communities (those experiencing the most precarity), and affects in distinct ways specific bodies—those of women, lesbians, travestis, trans, and nonbinary people. *The Home as Laboratory* continues this work by focusing specifically on la casa—the home, the house, the household—as a lab for finance, and its real estate arm, during the pandemic and its aftermath. In their own words, the book "summarizes and condenses the questions that emerged in our political practice during the pandemic and, at the same time, continues our research on the impacts of public and private debt in the everyday lives of women, lesbians, travestis, and trans persons that we have carried out as the [GIIF]" (4). The book is based on the work Cavallero and Gago as members of these groups have done with the feminist assemblies of the Villas 31 and Villa 31 Bis (the oldest and largest urban popular settlements in Buenos Aires, which are located on what speculators now consider prime real estate) and the national collective Inquilinos Agrupados (which fights for the rights of tenants).

The home, the authors argue, was a laboratory during the pandemic, and the dynamics unleashed then are the trend and the rule now. The book explores this territory of experimentation in two main dimensions. On the one hand, there is the home as a space of reproductive unpaid labor, a traditionally feminized space that during the pandemic, given the directives to stay at home, was transformed in both its functions and its ways of visibility. As the authors argue, "everyday spaces of the home have become financial 'terminals' (to which financial apparatuses of debt, the mediation of incomes and consumption, and the capture of rent are directed), but they are also intensified as spaces of the production of value (reproductive labor, telework, and new modes of home work) that are exploited by different speculative circuits" (29). On the other hand, there is the dimension of the home as a piece of real estate and a financial asset, which creates dynamics of forced displacement mediated by familial mandates that end up affecting nonnormative people and forms of kinship the most. Debt is, again, one of the main instruments of displacement. As the authors tellingly contextualize, "while the civilian-military dictatorship (1976–1983) failed in its plan to evict the villa [31 tenants] through direct violence, now we see that this eviction occurs through other means, through the violence of debt" (33).

The first part of the book is dedicated to analyzing the home in the first dimension. There is both a complex and succinct theorization and revision of feminist ideas around crucial notions tied to the home, such as reproductive labor, essential labor, domestic territories, the notion of value tied to the former, the factory-home, primitive accumulation, and, of course, debt and finance as violent apparatuses of capture and transformation in the context of the pandemic and its aftermath. The authors cover a lot of ground in this part, and I would like to single out just two issues that illuminate both the matter of (non)valorization of reproductive labor and of the dynamics of indebtedness that the authors trace so vividly.

The Argentinean National Division of Economy, Equality and Gender—a division of the Ministry of Economy that would have not existed without the force of the feminist movement and that has now unfortunately and very tellingly disappeared under current President Milei's rule—published a study in August 2020 in which they measured unpaid domestic and care work (TDCNR) and its contribution to the country's GDP. The study concluded that TDCNR contributed at that point with 15.9 percent of the GDP, more than the top two usually measured sectors, industry (13.2 percent) and commerce (13 percent). Domestic and care work's invisible and uncompensated status shows the amount of pressure mostly feminized laborers must endure (75.7 percent of TDCNR is done by women), and how indebtedness becomes one of the only ways of survival. This unpaid work also enables the authors to think about how "domestic territories" go beyond the enclosure of the house and extend networks in the neighborhood and beyond. The authors argue: "Recognizing that domestic labor must be unpaid as a condition of possibility for capitalist profit displaces the question about value production: it is not a matter of whether or not value is produced (given that of course it is), but rather why it is necessary to deny that and force that labor to go unpaid. Ultimately, it is a matter of identifying the political apparatus that guarantees those conditions each time and, later, the strategies for its recognition, remuneration, and, above all, its reorganization" (16). The closure of a governmental division that worked to give visibility to this production of value is a direct and vicious attack on women, lesbians, travestis, and trans people, and shows how and why fascism and financial capital go hand in hand against transfeminist movements.

Another issue analyzed in the book shows the scale of pressure that households have had to endure during and after the pandemic. It has to do with the articulation between governmental assistance programs and dynamics of indebtedness. The most important assistance program during the pandemic was the IFE (Emergency Family Income). First, to access that aid, people needed a bank account. That meant that "two million people opened a bank account for the first time to be able to receive the payment," further adding to the bankification that in this context mostly enables debt capture. Another important program, the Universal Child Allowance, has deteriorated so much given austerity measures and the state's debt payments (another dimension of debt that directly affects households) that it is now used by households mostly as collateral for credit. This is one of the clearest examples of how deepening precarity is articulated in the context of debt extraction.

The dynamic of displacement that debt enables sheds light on the other dimension that the authors illuminate in this work. Through legal and illegal rent hikes, structures of titling (enabled by the state), plus a growing indebtedness, the real estate arm of financial capitalism is swiftly colonizing spaces like the Villas 31 and 31 Bis, and women and LGBTQ households are the most likely victims of this displacement (and at the same time the most organized). The authors explain the heteropatriarchal compulsive mandates enforced by the state and market (Melinda Cooper's *Family Values* comes to mind) that make this "property violence" possible.

The English edition gives the reader privileged access to two new sections absent in the original Spanish edition: "Counter-Cartographies of Domestic Territories" and "Postscript on the Emergency Society." The first section further explores the theorization of domestic territories and networks of resistance. The second, a clear reference to Deleuze's classic text on the advent of the society of control, thinks about the context of the pandemic as a laboratory for a new paradigm of social experimentation. In its final subsection, titled "Program," the authors argue that feminist interventions in labor, especially the space of the union, are crucial in this context.

Overall, this book is, like other works by the authors, a must-read for anyone interested in better understanding the dynamics of financialization and feminist interventions. Cavallero and Gago offer a complex feminist intervention that never abandons the streets, homes, and neighborhoods from which it springs.

César Barros Arteaga is associate professor of Spanish and director of the Latin America, Caribbean and Latinx Studies Program at SUNY New Paltz. His work focuses on the intersections of political economy, historical memory, performance, and visual culture. He is a member of the somoslacélula video collective.

Review of *Set Fear on Fire* and *Against Ageism*

Claudia Cabello Hutt

LASTESIS's *Set Fear on Fire: The Feminist Call That Set the Americas Ablaze* (translated by Camila Valle), New York: Verso Books, 2023
Simon(e) van Sarloos's *Against Ageism: A Queer Manifesto*, Vancouver: Emily Carr University Press, 2023

Set Fear on Fire: The Feminist Call That Set the Americas Ablaze and *Against Ageism: A Queer Manifesto* are examples of the power of slim, affordable volumes of essays and mixed-genre texts that reach beyond the market of academic books. Each of them can be read as an intersectional transfeminist manifesto; their lighter format and affordability align with their political project as a radical collective refusal of oppressive power structures. Manifestos and essays on polemic and radical ideas published in this format are a phenomenon coming mostly out of independent publishers such as Verso and AK Press, and more recently, the trend has reached university presses, many of whom are struggling financially and looking to increase sales. There are evident advantages to this publishing format: more open to thinkers and activists outside academia, faster response to current conversations, accessibility due to price, and a less academic, more flexible format. In many cases, such as the ones included here, published essays bring to print bold ideas that are being tested (*ensayadas*) and mobilized in current radical feminist, decolonial, abolitionist, and queer movements—ideas that are pushing boundaries and challenging reformist politics at a time of extreme social, political, and environmental crisis. It goes without saying that this format, as well as its provocative topics, can be easily co-opted and depoliticized if disconnected from its activist grassroots or constrained by academic standards.

Set Fear on Fire: The Feminist Call That Set the Americas Ablaze, by Chilean feminist art collective LASTESIS, is written, just as their performances are conceptualized, from the expansive solidarity of speaking as *us*. "Most likely, violence is the starting point for all of us" (76), they say, as the anger and pain of age-old violence against women and girls is turning into powerful and highly visible feminist movements across Latin America. #NiUnaMenos (Not One Less) against femicide, the Green Wave for legal and safe abortion, and countless other local and transnational campaigns emerging from collective solidarity are delivering not only groundbreaking reforms but a profound cultural change in the face of unrelenting violence against women and LGBTQ+ people. Combining mostly prose with song lyrics and poetry, this book is a fearless and sharp rallying cry that spares no one in its unmasking of systems and ideologies that alienate women and queer people from themselves and their freedom.

The English translation of this book by Camila Valle allows readers in the Global North to engage with the ideas, sentiments, and methodologies of LASTESIS, a feminist practice that draws its power from embodied knowledge, feminist theory, and local histories of political resistance that don't rely on institutions, states, or nongovernmental organizations (NGOs) to create the change and collective healing they seek. LASTESIS's performance of "A Rapist in Your Path," a protest song and choreography that went viral in 2019 and was performed across the world, gained them international attention. They reject the notion of success, however, and instead prefer to focus on the social effect of their art-activist work.

Set Fear on Fire starts from a position of epistemic justice—the belief that women and all who defy heteronormativity and the binary sex/gender system under patriarchy and capitalism have knowledge and experience essential to fight against this system. From there, the book reads as a collective consciousness-raising effort that connects individual pain to community action and care. LASTESIS recognizes the contributions of feminist thinkers but includes only a few direct references, as proof that ideas can circulate in many ways and that academic language, especially coming to the South from the Global North, can be used to exclude and invalidate embodied experiences and other feminist expressions. There is a brief section of conceptual notes that include short definitions for words such as *women*, *cisgender*, and *hegemony*, a resource that allows for participation and understanding and only comes after the first chapter, titled "Us." LASTESIS's work—this book, their performances and workshops—are all aligned with a practice of denouncing oppression and building resistance in the most inclusive and horizontal way possible, a model and inspiration for transnational feminists.

It is remarkable how this slim volume manages to touch on most of the issues at the heart of the feminist struggle today: care as work, the nuclear heterosexual family, romantic love, rape and sexual violence, parenthood and abortion, economic exploitation, state and police violence, migration, racism, pleasure, and strategies of resistance. This makes it an exceptional point of entry to transnational feminisms and gender studies for students in addition to activists and general readers.

The group's concept of *us* does not suggest homogeneity, and the text dedicates many pages to visibilize and embrace the fact that the feminist struggle is intersectional and therefore includes a variety of contexts, identities, desires that need to be acknowledged to make the movement stronger. "Together" is the title of the poem that closes this book. Each verse in this poem begins with "Together we set fire…" and goes on to call out oppressive systems, institutions, and ideas that are inseparable from each other, stemming from patriarchy, capitalism, and colonialism, and that all us "juntas" can set on fire.

"As a category, age is coercive," affirms Simon(e) van Saarloos in their latest book *Against Ageism: A Queer Manifesto*. A manifesto that opposes ageism as the naturalized arbitrary correlation between age and generalized qualities, such as innocence, maturity, and vulnerability, that results in protections, expectations, violence, and exclusions. Ageism appears intrinsically linked to the violence and injustice perpetuated by structural racism, ableism, heteronormativity, and coloniality. Consequently, van Saarloos refuses arguments against ageism that are grounded on ableist assumptions of speed and ability or capitalistic notions of economic value and productivity. "Age obstructs mutuality, mutation and mutiny" (116), and it is precisely its opacity, its deceptive power, that van Saarloos exposes and resists through a queer, abolitionist, crip, and decolonial approach.

The book consists of seven chapters; an unnumbered section that reproduces Aristotle's *Rhetoric*, book 2, chapter 12, "On the Character of the Young"; two paintings by Samantha Nye that play with eroticism, queerness, and age; two of Adrian Piper's performance art "calling cards"; a photograph of Miss Major and her partner; and a poem by Cheryl Clarke. The collection that conforms the manifesto provokes us to question why the anti-ageist movement is not yet part of anti-oppression resistance. Van Saarloos suggests a couple of possible reasons: aging is seen as a privilege resulting from individual actions, and therefore its obstacles, under a neoliberal individualistic logic, are unique to each of us and should be solved accordingly. This manifesto calls instead for collective resistance.

Colonial, white supremacist, ableist, and heteronormative ideas of time in its relation to age are questioned and examined through discussions of criminalization: Black teenagers treated like adults while white youth are infantilized; racism: youth as less racist, and old as more; age difference: the misreading or erasure of intergenerational intimacies; voting rights: "the belief that adulthood coincides with sensible, logical decision-making has racist, sexist and ableist origins" (135); and disciplining of bodies: time as a mechanism to categorize disability as well as normative ability. These are only some points of entry to van Saarloos's arguments against ageism.

Mutuality emerges in this book by rejecting ageist categories of similarity and by instead creating solidarity through consensual connection and collective thinking and feeling. In their account of sexual abuse as an experience of their childhood, the framework of restorative justice serves the author as a tool for integration between harm and self that affirms agency while rejecting discourses of victimhood (not the existence of victims) "that serve patriarchal fantasies of protection." Van Saarloos warns against "reducing collective knowledge to an individual trauma that hinders personal success" (23), an individualization that conceals the epidemic and epistemic nature of patriarchy.

"To break down ageism, the gender binary needs to be dismantled as well" (128), argues van Saarloos when looking into the gendered and racialized roles imposed on (white) girls and boys and their subsequent transition into adult women and men. Queer intimacies, life trajectories, and families implode some of the pillars of straight, colonial, reproductive, and linear time, thus installing queer time as a denaturalizing force of what is imposed as logical, respectable, and productive. The chapter on crip time further engages the disruption of naturalized temporalities that sustain injustice and exclusion. Van Saarloos rejects arguments that condition the value of life according to function, potential, productivity, or belonging to a group, such as the young, to push instead for the full recognition of life.

Against Ageism provokes us then to recognize the inherent value of life, not conditioned by age, function, or normative time. What happens when we see ourselves, first and foremost, in relationship with our own body, subjectivity, desire, and community with others? This book does not provide the answers, but it demonstrates, by revealing the intertwined oppressive structures at play, that abolishing age categories would transform society and our relations. Finally, van Saarloos is a philosopher and artist who pushes boundaries in ways most are reluctant to. This feels urgent now, when books and ideas are easily considered too radical and dangerous. When white supremacy, patriarchy, transphobia, and capitalist war machines kill, and create unlivable conditions for the majority.

Claudia Cabello Hutt is associate professor in the Women and Gender Studies Program and the Department of Philosophy at George Mason University. Her research focuses on Latin American and feminist queer thought and history, decolonial theory, and queer archives. She is the author of *Artesana de sí misma: Gabriela Mistral, una intelectual en cuerpo y palabra* (Artisan of Herself: Gabriela Mistral, an Intellectual in Body and Words) (Purdue University Press, 2018).

Review of *Between Shadows and Noise*

Kimberly Juanita Brown

Amber Jamilla Musser's *Between Shadows and Noise: Sensation, Situatedness, and the Undisciplined*, Durham: Duke University Press, 2024

Amber Jamilla Musser is one of our more incandescent thinkers, melding the sensorial with visual and sonic reverberations in fluid prose meant to embolden her line of argumentation while also enchanting the reader. Her newest work, *Between Shadows and Noise: Sensation, Situatedness, and the Undisciplined*, does not disappoint. Buoyed by a vibrant archive of texts and artistic gestures and imbricated through Musser's own mind-body instantiation of form, the literary critic and queer theorist begins by engaging "situatedness as an analytic rooted in amplifying the politics of difference and corporeality" (9). She follows this amplification as an embodied practice accentuating the interstices between, the sliver of space separating concept from materiality. Musser's investment is in both, and as such, her attention to purposeful indecipherability sets the tone for the book. *Between Shadows and Noise* pulls us toward the uncanny to reveal the world beneath. This world, as Musser engages it, is inflected through the prism of anti-imperialist movement and Black feminist praxis.

Musser's readings throughout the chapters of *Between Shadows and Noise* include Jordan Peele's film *Us*, Katherine Dunham's *Shango*, Titus Kaphar's *A Pillow for Fragile Fictions*, Teresita Fernández's *Puerto Rico (Burned) 6*, and Samita Sinha's *This ember state*. Each chapter emphasizes artistic expansions from "the threat of Black femininity," to "spectacles of the spirit," "the critical encounter," and "making racialized labor visible." The chapters, then, reinvigorate already-present discourses on sensation so that Musser, as author, as agent, also experiences them. Along with her facility with aesthetic interventions and inflections, Musser returns to memory and her scaffolded interiority to situate the reader in time. "This place between memory and embodiment," she writes of the arc of possession in Katherine Dunham's *Shango*, "is also the location of the gesture—movement traces that convey constellations of selfhoods and orientations toward the world that belong to historical and imagined encounters" (53). She is a part of this world in *Between Shadows and Noise*, and as such, the book navigates a circular terrain that keeps the reader in sync with the writer and thinker who has opened new habituated imaginaries for us all. Beginning with her introduction ("Body Work") and ending with the conclusion ("Inflammation: Notes from the Front"), we are immersed in the fleshy sorority of corporeality that binds us together and the resistant anarchisms that engender creativity.

Woven throughout *Between Shadows and Noise* is the hovering specter of bodily vulnerability—be it Musser's, with her recent cancer diagnosis, or the frailty embedded in contemporary art forms and performances—so the reader is ever-cognizant of this as it is rendered, as method. This makes for some remarkable observations and provocations, and Musser is at her most fluid—both shadow and noise—in offering a series of unexpected discursive connections that may never have occurred had she not been on the way to writing another book when her body demanded her attention.

Kimberly Juanita Brown is the inaugural director of the Institute for Black Intellectual and Cultural Life at Dartmouth College, where she is also an associate professor in the Department of English and Creative Writing. She is an interdisciplinary scholar working at the intersection of contemporary literatures of the Black diaspora and visual culture studies. She is the author of *The Repeating Body: Slavery's Visual Resonance in the Contemporary* (Duke University Press, 2015), and *Mortevivum: Photography and the Politics of the Visual* (MIT Press, 2024). Brown's third book, *Black Elegies*, is forthcoming from MIT Press in early 2025. *Black Elegies* concerns the art of mourning in contemporary art and literature. She is the founder and convener of the Dark Room: Race and Visual Culture Studies Seminar. The Dark Room is a working group of women of color scholars, artists, and curators whose work examines critical race theory and visual culture studies. Brown can be reached at kimberly.juanita.brown@dartmouth.edu.

Review of *Disappearing Rooms*

Anne McNevin

Michelle Castañeda's *Disappearing Rooms: The Hidden Theaters of Immigration Law* (with illustrations by Molly Crabapple), Durham: Duke University Press, 2023

Book reviews are often written from a position of distance—flying in over the top, as it were, to assess the strengths and weaknesses of an author's work on the basis of shared knowledge within the general field. In this case, however, my starting point is a deep sense of respect and humility in the face of a work of scholarship the insights and profundity of which has stopped me in my tracks—not once but each of the three times I've now read this book since I first saw a draft of the manuscript shared by its author, who spoke to a class I was teaching on the politics of sanctuary. I have been working in the general field of citizenship, migration, and border studies for close to twenty years. Michelle Castañeda's *Disappearing Rooms* is one of only a handful of works over that time that has presented material known to me in a technical or abstract way—specifically, the interconnection between humanitarian recognition and racialized colonial violence in the context of immigration proceedings affecting migrants and asylum seekers—with such originality, raw force, and poetic clarity as to make me feel changed after reading it, politically and intellectually. It is a book that conveys brilliantly what I could not have known otherwise, precisely because it documents a social movement that attempts to center "the *autonomy* of mobility" (17)—the will to freedom of movement—amongst those who are up against the violent force of laws designed to welcome some kinds of bodies and repel and immobilize others.

This social movement takes many forms across a world whose border regime enforces a global color line in ways that defy crude geographic bearings between Global North and South. Most of the attention focuses on border policing at the points where those worlds meet: the Mediterranean Sea and the U.S.–Mexico border, in particular. But much border policing happens within the interiors of states, including the United States, terrorizing those already present, often performing essential labor but rendered permanently deportable. The laws and legal rituals that enable this condition are Castañeda's object of critique. But hers is not a standard account. Castañeda undertakes a "scenographic" analysis (14). As a scholar of performance studies, Castañeda is concerned with how the law "put[s] on a show" (15). She shows the subtle details, the routines and gestures, the "mise-en-scène" (9) in and through which a person judged guilty by the law is already cast as deserving of their fate by the strange cruelties enacted in the drama of the courtroom well before the formal judgment. The book includes a series of illustrations by journalist and artist Molly Crabapple, which add powerfully to the stories being told. Castañeda includes an account of the process by which she and Crabapple worked to capture the courtroom scene from different perspectives. Resonating with the revelatory quality of the finest kinds of prison literature, the results convey, on one hand, the absurdity of the law and, on the other, its failure to subsume all that happens within the courtroom scene, including forms of quiet indignation that sometimes change what unfolds.

Castañeda draws on her own extensive experience working in New York and Texas with the New Sanctuary Coalition—a recent rearticulation of the 1980s Sanctuary movement—and in particular, with the practice of accompaniment developed by undocumented people within the coalition. Drawing on traditions within liberation theology in the South American context, accompaniment is designed to bear witness to the violence of the law—*walking with* those at risk of deportation, including being present for legal proceedings—in ways that respect their autonomy. This means resisting the activist's impulse to intervene, to assume to know the right course of action, or to assert one's privileged status, as citizen for instance, even for strategic reasons. Castañeda allows the reader to walk with *her* as she accompanies friends at risk of deportation into the "ninth floor" and "removal room"—the Orwellian names for locations in which immigration proceedings are held in a building in downtown Manhattan, and from which a person can be spontaneously deported should the court rule against them. The stakes could not be higher, and yet accompaniment is premised on staying silent—not because of acquiescence to the law but because the impulse to speak, to help, to do at least *something*, so often does more harm than good, reflecting the activist's own emotional needs and the fact that they are shielded from the adverse if also unintended impacts of their actions, unlike the potential deportee. Castañeda shares her own sense of frustration, awkwardness, and impotence as she takes part in this scene, as well as the vexed internal politics that ultimately undermine the coalition's viability. There is something inherently feminist about Castañeda's approach, revealing her own vulnerability as a political gesture and a form of normative insight, and something inherently queer about the analysis that follows, emerging in a grounded way from the practice of accompaniment itself. What emerges is an extraordinary account of an organized political refusal of the binary categories according to which immigration law is enforced: citizen/alien, good/bad migrants, innocent/guilty parties.

The title of the book, *Disappearing Rooms*, refers to rooms from which a person can literally disappear, removed for deportation. But it also refers to a larger process of violent expulsion erased from view, in the sense of being an object of denial, of legal and bureaucratic obfuscation, and of political rationalization. Castañeda shows through her own experience—at once both personal and political—that there are no positions of innocence with respect to a form of law premised upon the state's right to arbitrate a distinction between citizen and alien. She shows through painful example that even the legal strategies pursued to resist state imperatives participate in what they seek to change, arguing the case for this or that migrant whose exceptional qualities—as refugee, family member, skilled or integratable—work to cast others as justifiably excludable: criminal, costly, or deviant. Where Castañeda and her companions attempt to use asylum law in favor of two particular people, Ana and Yesenia, they induct Ana into "the parameters of a humanitarian legal system in which [her autonomy] has no place" (79) and "drag" Yesenia into a form of "self-disclosure she [ultimately] refused" (86). Castañeda challenges even the most sympathetic and strategic of readers to confront the forms of denial that make one able to imagine themselves on any right side of this equation. In the process, she develops a rich theorization of what it means to accompany under conditions that do not permit redemption either for the migrant who faces impossible options before a law that excludes them, or for the person who accompanies, whose own legal status is at once the condition that allows them to witness and that which makes them implicated in the ongoing fact of exclusion.

The honesty and complexity of this interrogation makes Castañeda's book stand out amongst the growing literature grappling with the question of what can be done in the face of violent border controls including but well beyond the United States. It is a bleak account, in many ways, but also a profoundly disruptive one that challenges liberal and multicultural fantasies of progress, as if the routine violence of immigration law were somehow an exception. Castañeda's confrontation with her own and others' implication in that violence represents the starting point of a horizon that might be different—not a redemptive horizon but a genuinely political one that opens onto more than a more humane version of the status quo. In this she joins forthcoming work by Miriam Ticktin on the political value of abandoning narratives of innocence, as well as a scholarly and activist milieu that, in its most challenging formulations, pursues a highly self-reflexive practice of border abolition. Perhaps most strikingly of all, Castañeda shows us how attunement to the scene in and through which cumulative acts of violence occur in the form of a disappearance can inform abolitionist practice. Drawing on the "experimental sensibility" (14) that performance artists bring to the space of rehearsal, as well as the forms of improvisation that characterize accompaniment, Castañeda shows the "plasticity" (9) of that which otherwise seems like a foregone conclusion, including the intransigence of the current border regime. For anyone concerned to find new ways to contemplate such changes, *Disappearing Rooms* is one of the most compelling and confronting places to begin.

Anne McNevin is associate professor of politics at The New School. She can be reached at mcnevina@newschool.edu.

Work Cited

Ticktin, Miriam. Forthcoming. *Against Innocence: Undoing and Remaking the World*. University of Chicago Press.

On the Threshold of Humanity: Maternal Influence and the Scientific Construction of Fetal Life in *Of Human Born*

Googie Karrass

Caroline Arni's *Of Human Born: Fetal Lives, 1800–1950* (translated by Kate Sturge), Princeton, NJ: Zone Books, 2024

At a time when debates about the boundary between the pregnant person and the unborn carry profound consequences, Caroline Arni's *Of Human Born: Fetal Lives, 1800–1950* offers a timely exploration of how fetal life was conceptualized in the life sciences. Drawing on writings from the nineteenth and early twentieth centuries in physiology, pediatrics, and psychology, Arni examines how the emergence of the fetus as a biological object was intertwined with theories of maternal influence, revealing an overlooked history of maternal-fetal relationality. Empirical investigations into fetal life, she argues, far from resolving its status, embedded a "profound ontological indeterminacy" within the sciences as the question of when and how life became recognizably human persisted (246). Arni's work, though grounded in historical contingency, opens pathways for understanding the enduring ambiguities surrounding the unborn in contemporary debates on reproduction, science, and ethics.

The guiding thread of Arni's study is French scientist Charles Féré's 1880s hypothesis that maternal emotional shock brought about by the terrifying events surrounding the 1871 Siege of Paris inflicted lasting "developmental disturbances" on children conceived during this crisis. Exploring how Féré and his contemporaries linked maternal trauma to "physical and mental deformities," Arni seeks to understand "the object of a curiosity that made childhood anomaly in the present point to fetal life in the past" (16, 20). Arni uses this case to explore fetal life not as an empirical object but as an "epistemic space" where scientific curiosity configured the prenatal in such a way that maternal trauma and heritable pathology could be interwoven within the child.

With the curious case of the enfants du Siège as its focal point, *Of Human Born* unfolds "concentric circles" across four sections (29). This nonchronological structure, while at times challenging for the reader, allows Arni to trace the "genesis of scientific facts" (29) that contributed to the constitution of fetal life. Expanding outward from the 1880s, her analysis spans disciplines and geographies—drawing from primarily French but also German and English sources—to examine how theories like the distinctions of maternal and fetal blood or the fetus's sensitivity to pain emerged. Complementing this structure, Arni's historiographic approach illuminates an assemblage of continuity and discontinuity, resisting portrayals of the nineteenth century as a neutral period of knowledge acquisition. This framework also rejects framing this period's constitution of fetal life as a "prehistory of the present" or as part of a transhistorical inquiry into life in utero (23, 52).

The opening chapters situate the children of the siege within a broader history of "the unborn" and introduce Arni's central interventions. Drawing from the history of science, anthropology, and historical ontology, she argues that the nineteenth-century constitution of the unborn as an empirical object did not resolve the enduring question of what makes a human being. In chapter 3, she elaborates on a "historical ontology of the unborn," demonstrating how embryonic development was framed as an epistemological response to this ontological question—one that remained incomplete. Ultimately, this scientific framework produced "a conception of the human being becoming no less peculiar than the conceptions by medievalists and ethnologists when they tell of moments of animation and transmigration of the soul" (48).

Arni contextualizes this indeterminacy in a paradox endemic to the eighteenth-century "science of man." Once understood metaphysically as the union of earthly body and immortal soul, man was redefined as an organism on a continuum with nonhuman beings yet definitively separate from them. Within this paradoxical distinction, the unborn emerged as liminal creatures, "on the threshold of no longer and not yet human" (247). Physiological investigations into the unborn, now viewed through a developmental lens, grappled with this persistent uncertainty about the timing of the subject's arrival. "The unborn," she writes, "was already human inasmuch as it was a human organism, and it was not yet human inasmuch as it still needed to achieve subjectivity" (46).

In part 2, "Living Beings," Arni explores nineteenth-century physiological inquiries into how the unborn lives, feeds, breathes, and moves. She explains how fetal life, previously framed topographically within the uterine environment, became understood temporally through developmental processes. In a fascinating overview, she traces the shift from premodern ideas of preformation (that organisms develop from miniature versions of themselves) and ensoulment (that personhood begins with fetal movement) to successive changes in fetal form. While existing historiography emphasizes the emergence of the fetus as a discrete entity, Arni inventively highlights its enmeshment within the maternal organism. Through dense but compelling descriptions of physiology, she reveals how scientists' investigations into placental function, fetal blood circulation, and sensory experiences were rooted in curiosity about the connection between fetus and mother. While scientists invented novel—and sometimes violent—strategies to investigate this relationality, dissecting living animals and testing newborn reflexes, they were simultaneously thwarted by it as the fetal organism was fundamentally obscured by the maternal body. These unresolved questions shaped Féré's novel account of hereditary transmission, which framed certain "developmental disturbances" as the result of maternal pathogenic influences.

In part 3, "Inner Life," Arni turns to the psychological sciences, examining maternal imagination, emotional impact, and the unborn's psychological interiority. She deftly traces the evolution of beliefs that maternal thoughts and feelings could affect fetal development, an idea that gained renewed life in the nineteenth and twentieth centuries. As the psyche came to be seen both as an organic function and as the marker of subjectivity, scientists sought to determine when its development began. This trajectory encompasses Féré's focus on psychical influence, early psychoanalytic debates on birth trauma, and the rise of endocrinology, which linked maternal stress to physical outcomes in offspring, reframing the maternal–fetal relationship in hormonal terms.

In part 4, "Politics of the Unborn," Arni situates the children of the siege in post-Commune France. As concepts like population, evolution, and heredity took hold, she argues, historical events became explainable through the life sciences while biological processes were reinterpreted as historical phenomena (230). These pathologized children thus became symbols of generational connection, embodying debates over national character and social continuity in the aftermath of disaster.

The book concludes with a meditation on the challenges of investigating fetal life as both an epistemic object entangled with the maternal environment and a being on the threshold of humanity. Arni argues that while the fetus was redefined as a biological object during this period, this transformation did little to resolve the ambiguity of its status as not-yet-human being. This incompleteness is revealed in the tension of recognition for the investigators at the heart of her study. Confronted by the maternal body as both an impediment to positivist knowledge and an inextricable part of their work, investigators also faced the unborn's paradoxical demand to be recognized as one of their own. The more they uncovered the mechanics of fetal life, the more elusive its boundaries became, leaving unresolved the question of where and when humanity begins.

Arni's *Of Human Born* offers a masterful exploration of the historical constitution of fetal life with implications for contemporary debates. Indeed, Féré's hypothesis, linking maternal trauma during the 1871 Siege of Paris to childhood "developmental disturbances," may strike some readers as an uncanny reflection of prenatal medicine's current focus on maternal behavior and the potentially gene-altering effects of trauma emphasized by the epigenetic turn. A major strength of Arni's work, however, is her ability to acknowledge these resonances while resisting a teleological framing of this history as a precursor to the current fetishization of fetal life. Artfully navigating an interplay of continuity and rupture, Arni is able to connect Féré's ideas to ancient concepts of maternal impression, twentieth-century hormonal theories, and epigenetics while preserving the historical specificity of the enfants du Siège.

Amid this intricate web of historical, scientific, and cultural contingencies, *Of Human Born* offers a profound insight into the enduring ontological uncertainty surrounding the unborn, positioning the book as an essential resource for interdisciplinary feminist scholars, historians of science, and researchers in reproductive ethics and science and technology studies. While its complex scientific language and detailed accounts of physiology may limit its accessibility to broader audiences, Arni's nuanced exploration of maternal–fetal relationality provides critical insights into ongoing debates about humans-in-the-making, rewarding the dedicated reader. This evocative history challenges us to reconsider how the boundaries of human life have been and continue to be constructed, inviting reflection on the ethical and political stakes of these questions today.

Googie Karrass (she/her) is a doctoral candidate in cultural anthropology at the Graduate Center, CUNY, where she also earned an MA in women's and gender studies. Her research examines new reproductive technologies, eugenics, and natalism in the United States. She teaches at Baruch College and can be reached at gkarrass@gradcenter.cuny.edu.

Homes, Houses, and Shelters

Mónica Palma

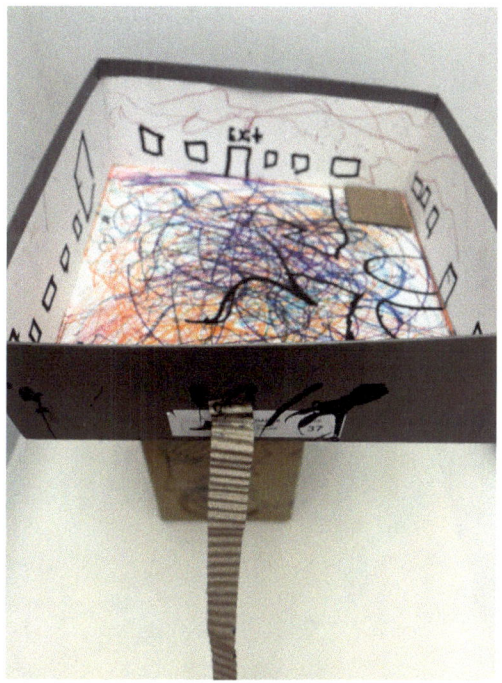

Museo de arte, entre (*Art Museum, Please Enter*), 2024. Photograph by Mónica Palma.

This is an art museum on top of a tall building. To get to the museum, the maker, a ten-year-old, attached the longest floating stairs, reminding me of Rapunzel's braid. He wanted to hang as many paintings as possible on the wall, but also, his plan was to make the floor an art project. Some children find meaning in their houses after they are done, letting the materials and shapes speak for themselves, while others know from the beginning what they will make, just like this child. The museum is constructed using a shoebox. Many families come intermittently to the clinic, but this child's family has been present every Thursday for months; we know that the dad is an artist who used to be an art teacher in Colombia.

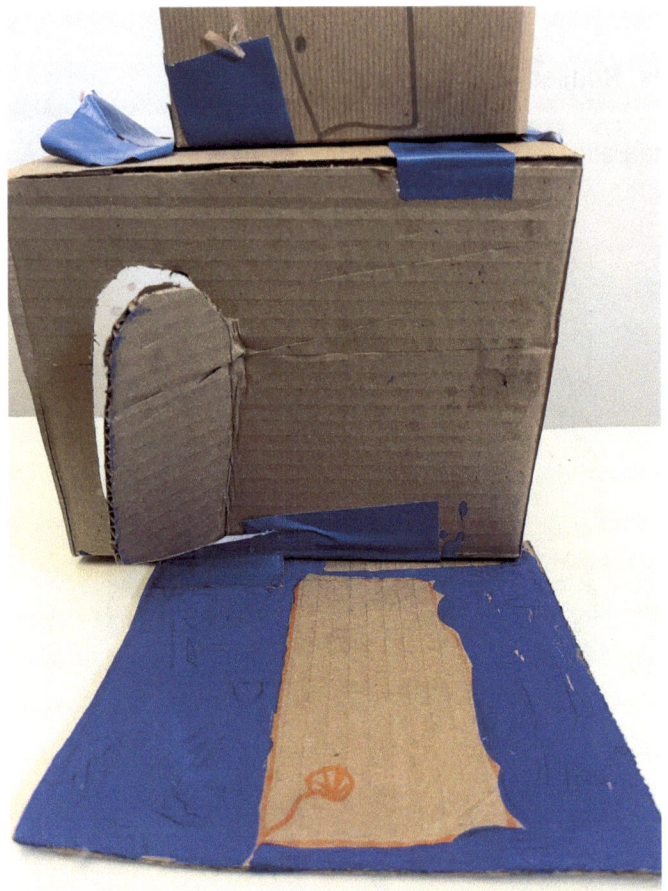

Una panadería con patio trasero (*A Baker's Shop with a Back Patio*), 2024. Photograph by Mónica Palma.

In this house, we see two levels: the bottom floor is a panadería, a baking shop; the top part is the family bedroom. The boy who made it quietly narrated the different kinds of bread he made in Ecuador with his dad before coming to the U.S. While building the oven and the table, he was eager to get through the back door; he urged me to help him get there, so we carved a door using a box cutter and added an extension to make a patio. The high importance of the patio for him was clear; his eyes were sparkling when he drew a pila (a concrete water basin) using a marker and a hose. This hose was perhaps the detail that mattered most to him. It is easy to picture him playing in that patio, sneaking out from his baking duties to get a sprinkle from the water hose.

SECTION VI. ALERTS AND PROVOCATIONS

Através da lente dos Orixás: Repensando solidaridades feministas globais

Djamila Ribeiro

Recentemente, participei do Festival de Literatura em Lviv, na Ucrânia. Com o país ainda em guerra após a invasão da Rússia, que segue deixando um rastro de morte e destruição, minha participação foi online, junto a companheiras feministas de diversos países. O moderador nos fez uma pergunta comum, que nos desafiava a comparar a situação em nossos países de origem com a realidade colonial enfrentada pelos ucranianos naquele momento. Tive a sorte de ser uma das últimas a responder, o que me deu tempo para refletir com mais cuidado. O maior desafio foi a minha falta de informações sobre a história da Ucrânia, algo que poderia se tornar uma armadilha caso eu me aventurasse a falar sobre o que não conhecia profundamente. No entanto, foi ao pensar a partir dos orixás que encontrei o caminho para minha contribuição.

Sou uma mulher negra nascida no Brasil, o país que mais recebeu pessoas escravizadas ao longo dos séculos. Dados do "The Transatlantic Slave Trade Database" estimam que mais de quatro milhões de pessoas foram trazidas do continente africano para as plantações e cidades brasileiras, submetidas a todos os horrores do regime escravista no país, que também foi o último país das Américas e do Caribe a abolir oficialmente a escravidão, em 1888.

Contudo, essa abolição foi em grande parte simbólica, pois não foi acompanhada de políticas de inserção da população negra na sociedade. Pelo contrário, negros e negras foram relegados às favelas, enquanto o Estado brasileiro incentivava a imigração europeia, financiando o traslado e concedendo terras aos recém-chegados. Essas políticas faziam parte do projeto de "branqueamento" racial, liderado por intelectuais europeus como Arthur de Gobineau e James Watson e, no Brasil, defendido por figuras como Nina

Rodrigues. Esse projeto, baseado no racismo científico, sustentava a ideia de uma suposta "inferioridade natural" da população negra, que deveria ser eliminada, seja através da imigração em massa, seja pelo incentivo à miscigenação, originando a mestiçagem no país entre outras medidas perversas.

No século seguinte, a população negra continuou a ser o principal alvo da violência policial, das campanhas de esterilização forçada e dos mais altos índices de desumanização, como mortalidade materna, desnutrição e desemprego. As políticas racistas, na expressão de Ibram X. Kendi, são reinventadas até hoje e cicatrizes do passado escravocrata se mantêm vivas, exigindo de nós, mulheres negras, resistência e luta constante para superar essas injustiças históricas. Como disse Lélia González, grande intelectual e referência do feminismo negro brasileiro, nosso legado é de dor, mas também de resistência.

Nesse sentido, podemos dizer que o grande fiasco do projeto de branqueamento se deve à luta da população negra. Segundo dados do Instituto Brasileiro de Geografia e Estatística (IBGE) de 2023, a população negra representa 55 por cento da população brasileira, o que evidencia a dimensão desse fracasso. A população preta, como é categorizada aquela de pele retinta, constitui 8 por cento da população brasileira. São números como esses em uma nação de mais de 200 milhões de habitantes que fazem do Brasil a nação negra fora da África.

Evidentemente, o projeto de branqueamento deixou suas marcas, a começar pelo projeto de miscigenação estar fundado na violência sexual sistemática contra mulheres negras. O objetivo do branqueamento criou uma categorização de pessoas negras a partir do tom de pele, sendo um tom mais claro mais tolerado. Em argumento que resume essa relação dialética entre opressão e resistência, a feminista negra Alessandra Devulsky (2019) afirma:

> A mestiçagem, de origem violenta, fez parte de um projeto colonial que pretendia diluir a negritude até o ponto em que ela desaparecesse. Não foi o que aconteceu. Graças à resistência indomável dos descendentes dos primeiros africanos que foram trazidos para o país sob a condição da escravidão, criaram-se variadas estratégias de sobrevivência cultural da identidade negra. Os quilombos, as músicas, as danças, as religiosidades, entre tantos outros aspectos da cultura negra que superaram o castigo, o cárcere e mesmo a morte de tantos negros não permitiram que as hierarquizações raciais fossem capazes de obliterar a negritude no Brasil. Contudo, a força coerciva dos códigos culturais e as imposições de políticas públicas de

branqueamento fizeram com que o colorismo também fosse adotado dentro das comunidades negras. (17–18)

Faço essa contextualização por escrever em uma revista estrangeira. Geralmente, quando digo para pessoas do Norte Global que sou do Brasil, associam-me ao samba, a biquinis e carnaval. Uma estereotipação ridícula, que encontra reflexo em meios intelectuais e feministas. Há alguns anos venho fazendo parte de um movimento de publicação de intelectuais negras brasileiras, enfrentando, em seguida, as barreiras coloniais de tradução no Norte Global. Temos tido algum sucesso, sobretudo na França, onde, em parceria com Paula Anacaona, mais de uma dezena de obras escritas por mulheres negras brasileiras foram publicadas. Nos Estados Unidos, porém, onde publico esse texto, foi somente em 2024 que consegui a primeira tradução, anos depois que traduções para o francês, alemão, italiano, e espanhol foram publicadas. Chad Post (2017), um editor independente estadunidense, traz um dado que reflete bem o argumento desta necessária contextualização, bem como o argumento que lançarei em seguida sobre uma necessária explicação básica do que é pensar a partir dos orixás: apenas 3 por cento dos livros publicados nos Estados Unidos são traduções; 97 por cento correspondem ao mercado interno. Desses 3 por cento, uma parcela ínfima é de língua portuguesa, e uma fatia ainda menor corresponde a livros publicados no Brasil.

Essas barreiras podem ser vistas de diversas formas. Ao considerarmos que também fiz parte de um movimento de tradução de escritoras negras estadunidenses no Brasil desde 2015, podemos compreender quando é dito que se trata de uma relação sem troca. Se eu, uma brasileira, tive de ser best-seller no meu próprio país por anos, como também precisei ser laureada em inúmeros países para somente então conseguir minha primeira tradução ao inglês, o acesso ao mercado editorial por estrangeiras não é tão exigente. São diversas as mulheres negras não ficcionistas publicadas no Brasil—tanto as cânones do pensamento feminista negro do Norte Global, como também jovens e pessoas que estão no seu primeiro livro. Essa relação fica ainda mais desigual quando olhamos para o fato de o mercado editorial brasileiro ser consideravelmente menor em comparação com o mercado estadunidense, tanto em número de leitores, quanto em número de editoras.

E mesmo nesse mercado menor, é de se ressaltar que a mobilização editorial ainda enfrenta o ambiente interno. Uma pesquisa da Universidade de Brasília desnudou o oligopólio editorial no país que sufoca vozes da diáspora ao revelar que, entre 1964 e 2014, 90 por cento dos livros publicados no país foram escritos por pessoas brancas. Destes, 70 por cento por homens brancos. Mulheres negras representam a menor fatia entre os 10 por cento, sendo que dessas são contabilizadas, ainda, traduções (Massuela 2018).

A reedição da lógica imperialista no pensamento feminista prejudica toda formulação de um pensamento feminista apto a entender uma sociedade multicultural. De um lado, impede que pensadoras brilhantes como Lélia González, Sueli Carneiro, Carla Akotirene, entre muitas e muitas outras, possam ver suas reflexões ampliadas ou até mesmo devidamente referenciadas. De outro, torna reflexões sobre feminismos incompleta, como uma forma de reificar uma espécie de epistemologia da ignorância, sobre a qual recentemente pude ler trabalhos de Linda Alcoff e que também se vê refletido no trabalho de Charles Mills (1997).

A epistemologia da ignorância, segundo Mills, é um fenômeno no qual certos conhecimentos são ativamente ocultados ou ignorados, particularmente aqueles que dizem respeito às realidades do racismo e das injustiças estruturais. Ele aponta que essa ignorância não é passiva, mas é mantida por práticas e instituições que beneficiam as classes dominantes. Essa perspectiva ajuda a compreender como as sociedades podem perpetuar desigualdades e discriminação ao mesmo tempo que desenvolvem narrativas que ocultam essas realidades. Mills sugere que a ignorância é uma ferramenta política que sustenta o poder ao garantir que certas populações, especialmente as pessoas brancas em contextos de supremacia racial, permaneçam inconscientes das condições de opressão enfrentadas por outros grupos. Dessa forma, a epistemologia da ignorância não só revela o racismo como um fenômeno visível, mas também como algo que é estrategicamente ocultado na estrutura social. Importo essa análise para voltar à reflexão sobre lógicas imperialistas no debate de gênero, em especial, na troca desequilibrada entre saberes produzidos no Norte e no Sul Global. Um exemplo de epistemologia da ignorância, nesse caso, seria no sentido de autoras do Norte serem cientes dessa realidade, mas ao mesmo tempo não se importarem em, de fato, construir pontes que estabelecem uma relação que seja mais justa.

Questionamos, como fez Lélia González nos anos oitenta, uma visão limitada do que é a "Black America," e vamos além para questionar o que é a América. Essa é uma provocação necessária que venho fazendo em encontros como o que inaugurou o texto, inspirada na conceituação por Lélia da categoria política da *Amefricanidade*. Para a pensadora brasileira, a

Amefricanidade destaca que a experiência africana no continente americano transcende fronteiras nacionais e aponta para uma identidade comum que é construída a partir da resistência ao colonialismo, ao racismo, e à dominação. Ela enfatiza como essa identidade está vinculada ao idioma, à religião, às práticas culturais e à luta por direitos, destacando que as culturas africanas nas Américas foram e são criativas, resistentes, e moldadas em contextos de opressão, sendo um espaço de construção contínua de pertencimento, solidariedade, e transformação política. A *Amefricanidade* é, portanto, uma proposta de leitura do mundo a partir das experiências de afrodescendentes, que conecta as lutas das Américas e do Caribe, com uma visão mais ampla de diáspora e resistência global:

> Os termos "afro-american" (afro-americano) e "african-american" (africano-americano) nos remetem a uma primeira reflexão: a de que só existiriam negros nos Estados Unidos, e não em todo o continente. E a uma outra, que aponta para a reprodução inconsciente da posição imperialista dos Estados Unidos, e não em todo continente. E a uma outra, que aponta para a reprodução inconsciente da posição imperialista dos Estados Unidos, que afirmam ser "A América". Afinal, o que dizer dos outros países da "América" do Sul, Central, Insular e do Norte? Por que considerar o Caribe como algo separado, se foi ali, justamente, que se iniciou a história dessa "América"?
> ... As implicações políticas e culturais da categoria de amefricanidade (*Amefricanity*) são, de fato, democráticas; exatamente porque o próprio termo nos permite ultrapassar as limitações de caráter territorial, linguístico e ideológico, abrindo novas perspectivas para um entendimento mais profundo dessa parte do mundo onde ela se manifesta: a «América» como um todo (Sul, Central, Norte e Insular). Para além do seu caráter puramente geográfico, a categoria de amefricanidade incorpora todo um processo histórico de intensa dinâmica cultural (adaptação, resistência, reinterpretação e criação de novas formas) que é afrocentrada, isto é, referenciada em modelos como: a Jamaica e o akan, seu modelo dominante; o Brasil e seus modelos iorubá, banto e ewe-fon. Em consequência, ela nos encaminha no sentido da construção de toda uma identidade étnica. Desnecessário dizer que a categoria de amefricanidade está intimamente relacionada áquelas de *pan-africanismo, négritude, afrocentricity* etc. (Gonzalez 2020, 134–5)

Com isso em mente, quando digo que encontrei um caminho para refletir sobre aquela mesa na Ucrânia a partir dos orixás, estou me referindo à epistemologia amefricana, particularmente dos povos de candomblé e umbanda e, por que não, da *santería* em países como Cuba, Haiti, e Colômbia, entre outros onde se cultuam os orixás. Como mulher de candomblé, minha visão de mundo é profundamente influenciada pelos povos de terreiro. Os terreiros são comunidades onde se vive e onde são cultuado os orixás, divindades trazidas ao Brasil com os povos escravizados e reelaboradas em solo brasileiro. No Brasil, há diferentes nações de candomblé, e a perspectiva que trago aqui é baseada nos princípios nagôs, em particular da nação Ketu. Os orixás são divindades associadas aos fenômenos da natureza: o mar é um orixá, assim como o rio, o trovão, a névoa, e assim por diante. Cada orixá tem suas passagens míticas, ou itãs, que narram suas existências na Terra. A reflexão sobre os fenômenos naturais, os itãs e a sabedoria ancestral transmitida de geração em geração constrói uma imagem arquetípica de cada orixá. Os orixás masculinos são conhecidos como Oboró, enquanto as orixás femininas são as Yabás.

Podemos começar a vislumbrar conexões entre a realidade da Ucrânia e a do Brasil, entre realidades de mulheres negras dos Estados Unidos e da Índia, pois, a partir da lógica dos orixás, é possível fazer associações teóricas já que a natureza se manifesta em todos os lugares. Oxum, por exemplo, é uma divindade no candomblé representada pela cachoeira. Seu arquétipo está associado ao autoamor, à fertilidade, à beleza, e à prosperidade, mas também à resistência e à força feminina. Um itã relata que, nos tempos primordiais, os Oborós começaram a decidir o destino da humanidade sem consultar nenhuma Yabá. Ressentida por ter sido excluída, Oxum se vingou dos orixás masculinos, condenando todas as mulheres à esterilidade e fazendo com que qualquer tentativa masculina de fertilidade falhasse. As águas secaram, e a terra tornou-se estéril. Alarmados, os homens consultaram Olodumare, o deus supremo, que revelou que Oxum havia sido excluída. Ele os aconselhou a convidá-la, bem como as outras mulheres, pois, sem Oxum e seu poder sobre a fertilidade, nada poderia progredir. Seguindo a sabedoria de Olodumare, eles a convidaram, e a vida na Terra voltou a florescer. Este itã fala sobre o poder das mulheres quando suas vozes são silenciadas. Ele desafia a expectativa de submissão feminina e destaca uma reflexão sobre o quão longe a sociedade patriarcal pode ir antes que a natureza entre em colapso, deixando os homens implorando por um riacho.

De forma semelhante, Iansã, também conhecida como Oyá, governa os ventos. Um de seus itãs conta como ela guardava um poder secreto para se transformar em búfalo. Ogum, encantado por sua força, roubou sua pele de búfalo, tentando controlá-la ao casar-se com ela. No entanto, ela redescobriu seu poder, liberou sua fúria e garantiu que seus filhos tivessem ferramentas para chamar por sua proteção. Essas histórias das Yabás desafiam as noções patriarcais sobre as mulheres, apresentando-as como figuras sábias, criativas, protetoras e poderosas.

Os ensinamentos dos orixás não apenas oferecem ferramentas para entender as experiências humanas, mas também guiam reflexões sobre nossa relação com a natureza. Iemanjá, a orixá do mar, nos ensina sobre a paciência e a resiliência do oceano. Uma vez, como conta um itã sobre ela, Iemanjá não conseguiu mais suportar o desrespeito que enfrentava e começou a se elevar cada vez mais, assustando todos ao seu redor. Como sabemos na comunidade de terreiro, sua paciência não é infinita, e a atual degradação dos ecossistemas marinhos serve como um lembrete contundente das consequências das ações humanas.

A guerra na Ucrânia, por exemplo, levou ao uso indiscriminado de tecnologia sonar, causando danos significativos à vida marinha, especialmente aos golfinhos. Essas mortes nos lembram da interconexão entre o sofrimento humano e ambiental. Assim como os mitos de Iemanjá revelam a necessidade de equilíbrio e respeito pelo mundo natural, essas tragédias nos convocam a refletir sobre como a violência da guerra se estende além das fronteiras humanas, afetando os próprios ecossistemas que sustentam a vida.

Ao entrelaçar a sabedoria ancestral com crises contemporâneas, as epistemologias Amefricanas oferecem um arcabouço para compreender os desafios globais de maneiras que enfatizam o respeito, a solidariedade e a necessidade urgente de ação transformadora. Essa visão de mundo interconectada pode nos inspirar a reimaginar soluções que honrem tanto o bem-estar humano quanto o ecológico. Assim, a epistemologia Amefricana e o culto aos orixás fornecem ferramentas para entender o mundo de maneira conectada, respeitando diferenças e destacando semelhanças nas experiências humanas. Essas narrativas nos lembram da importância de valorizar a sabedoria ancestral e fomentar a solidariedade global diante dos desafios.

Djamila Ribeiro é professora convidada na New York University e na Pontífica Universidade Católica de São Paulo. Ela tem Mestrado em Filosofia Política da Universidade Federal de São Paulo. Publicações incluem *Lugar de Fala*.

Referências bibliográficas

Barreto, Raquel. 2024. "Pensar o Brasil com Suas Festas: O que Lélia nos Ensina." Prefácio em *Festas Populares No Brasil*, de Lélia Gonzalez, 23-45. Boitempo.

Devulsky, Alessandra. 2019. *Colorismo*. Jandaira.

Gonzalez, Lélia. 2020. "A categoria político-cultural Amefricanidade." Em *Por um feminismo afrolatinoamericano: ensaios, intervenções e diálogos*, organizado por Flávia Rios e Márcia Lima. São Paulo: Zahar.

Massuela, Amanda. 2018. "Quem é e sobre o que escreve o autor brasileiro." *Cult*, 5 de fevereiro. https://revistacult.uol.com.br/home/quem-e-e-sobre-o-que-escreve-o-autor-brasileiro/.

Mills, Charles W. 1997. *The Racial Contract*. Cornell University Press.

Prandi, Reginaldo. 2013. *Mitologia Dos Orixás*. Companhia Das Letras.

Post, Chad. 2017. "The Three Percent 10 Years Later: An Interview With Chad Post." Entrevista por Maria Eliades. *Ploughshares,* 30 de janeiro. https://pshares.org/blog/the-three-percent-10-years-later-an-interview-with-chad-post/.

Through the Lens of the Orixás: Rethinking Feminist and Global Solidarities

Djamila Ribeiro

Recently, I participated in the Lviv Literary Festival in Ukraine. With the country still at war following Russia's invasion, which continues to leave a trail of death and destruction, my participation was online, alongside feminist companions from various countries. The moderator posed a common question, challenging us to compare the situation in our home countries with the colonial reality faced by Ukrainians at that moment. I was fortunate to be one of the last to respond, which gave me time to reflect more carefully. The greatest challenge was my lack of knowledge about Ukraine's history, something that could have become a trap had I ventured to speak on what I did not deeply understand. However, it was by reflecting through the perspective of the orixás that I found the path to my contribution.

I am a Black woman born in Brazil, the country that received the largest number of enslaved people over the centuries. Data from the Transatlantic Slave Trade Database estimate that over four million people were brought from the African continent to plantations and cities in Brazil, subjected to all the horrors of the slavery regime in a country that was also the last in the Americas and the Caribbean to officially abolish slavery in 1888.

However, this abolition was largely symbolic, as it was not accompanied by policies to integrate the Black population into society. On the contrary, Black men and women were relegated to favelas while the Brazilian state encouraged European immigration, funding their transportation and granting land to new arrivals. These policies were part of a racial "whitening" project championed by European intellectuals such as Arthur de Gobineau and James Watson, and in Brazil, advocated by figures like Nina Rodrigues. This project, rooted in scientific racism, upheld the notion of a supposed "natural inferiority" of the Black population, which was to be eliminated either through mass immigration or by promoting miscegenation, among other pernicious measures, resulting in the country's mestizaje.

In the following century, the Black population continued to be the primary target of police violence, forced sterilization campaigns, and the highest rates of dehumanization, such as maternal mortality, malnutrition, and unemployment. Racist policies, in the words of Ibram X. Kendi, are continually reinvented, and the scars of the slaveholding past remain alive, demanding of us, Black women, relentless resistance and struggle to overcome these historical injustices. As Lélia Gonzalez, a great intellectual and a cornerstone of Black Brazilian feminism, once said, our legacy is one of pain, but also of resistance (Gonzalez 2020).

In this sense, we can say that the major failure of the whitening project is due to the resistance of the Black population (*população negra* in Portuguese).[1] According to data from the Brazilian Institute of Geography and Statistics (IBGE) in 2023, the Black population represents 55 percent of the Brazilian population, underscoring the resilience and impact of Black resistance in Brazil. The Black population with darker skin, categorized as *preta* (a term used in Brazil to describe individuals with darker skin within the Black population), makes up 8 percent of the Brazilian population. These figures, in a nation of over 200 million inhabitants, make Brazil the largest Black nation outside Africa.

Evidently, the whitening project left its marks, beginning with the systematic sexual violence against Black women that underpinned the project of mestizage.[2] The goal of whitening created a categorization of Black individuals based on skin tone, with lighter skin tones being more tolerated. Summarizing this dialectical relationship between oppression and resistance, Black feminist Alessandra Devulsky (2019) argues:

> The mestizage, rooted in violence, was part of a colonial project aimed at diluting Blackness to the point of disappearance. That is not what happened. Thanks to the indomitable resistance of the descendants of the first Africans brought to the country under the condition of slavery, various strategies for the cultural survival of Black identity were created. The quilombos, the music, the dances, the religions, and so many other aspects of Black culture that withstood punishment, imprisonment, and even the deaths of so many Black people, ensured that racial hierarchies could not obliterate Blackness in Brazil. However, the coercive force of cultural codes and the imposition

of public whitening policies led to the adoption of colorism within Black communities as well. (17–18)

I provide this context because I am writing for a magazine foreign to Brazil. Usually, when I tell people from the Global North that I am from Brazil, they associate me with samba, bikinis, and Carnival—a ridiculous stereotype that is also reflected in intellectual and feminist circles. For several years, I have been part of a movement to publish Black Brazilian intellectuals, who face colonial barriers to translation in the Global North. We have had notable success, especially in France, where, in partnership with Paula Anacaona, several works by Black Brazilian women writers have been published. In the United States, however, where I am publishing this text, it was only in 2024 that I achieved my first translation—years after translations into French, German, Italian, and Spanish were already available.

Chad Post, an independent U.S. publisher, provides a statistic that aptly underscores the necessity of contextualization, as well as the need for a basic explanation of what it means to think through the lens of the *orixás*: Only 3 percent of books published in the United States are translations (Post 2017). The remaining 97 percent are from the domestic market. Of that 3 percent, an even smaller fraction comes from Portuguese-language works, and an even tinier portion represents books published in Brazil.

These barriers can be viewed in various ways. Considering that I have also been part of a movement to translate Black American women writers into Portuguese since 2015, it becomes clear why this is often described as a one-sided relationship. If I, a Brazilian, had to be a bestseller in my own country for years and earn numerous accolades in other countries before securing my first English translation, it is evident that access to the Brazilian publishing market is not as demanding for foreign authors. In Brazil, many Black women nonfiction writers are published—not only the canonical thinkers of Black feminist thought from the Global North but also younger authors and those releasing their first books. This inequality becomes even starker when we consider that the Brazilian publishing market is considerably smaller compared to the U.S. market, both in terms of readership and the number of publishing houses.

And even within this smaller market, it is worth highlighting that editorial mobilization also faces internal challenges. A study conducted by the University of Brasília exposed the publishing oligopoly in the country, which stifles voices from the diaspora, by revealing that between 1964 and 2014, 90 percent of books published in Brazil were written by white people, 70 percent of them by white men. Black women represent the smallest share of the remaining 10 percent, and even among those, translations are included (Massuela 2018).

The reassertion of imperialist logic within feminist thought harms the development of a feminist framework capable of understanding a multicultural society. On the one hand, it prevents brilliant thinkers like Lélia Gonzalez, Sueli Carneiro, Carla Akotirene, and many others from having their reflections amplified or even properly referenced. On the other hand, it renders reflections on feminism incomplete, reinforcing a kind of "epistemology of ignorance," as explored by Charles Mills (1997) and, more recently, in works by Linda Alcoff, which I have had the opportunity to read.

According to Mills, the epistemology of ignorance is a phenomenon in which certain forms of knowledge, particularly those concerning the realities of racism and structural injustices, are actively concealed or ignored. He argues that this ignorance is not passive but is maintained by practices and institutions that benefit dominant classes. This perspective helps us understand how societies perpetuate inequality and discrimination while simultaneously developing narratives that obscure these realities.

Mills suggests that ignorance is a political tool that sustains power by ensuring that certain populations, particularly white people in contexts of racial supremacy, remain unaware of the conditions of oppression faced by other groups. Thus, the epistemology of ignorance reveals racism not only as a visible phenomenon but also as something strategically concealed within the social structure.

I bring this analysis to reflect on imperialist logic in gender debates, particularly the unbalanced exchange of knowledge produced in the Global North and South. An example of epistemology of ignorance in this context would be authors from the Global North being aware of this reality but at the same time failing to genuinely build bridges that establish more equitable relationships.

We question, as Lélia Gonzalez did in the 1980s, the limited view of what constitutes "Black America," and we go further to challenge the very notion of what "America" is. This is a necessary provocation that I have been making in discussions like the one that opened this text, inspired by Gonzalez's conceptualization of the political category of *Amefricanity*. For the Brazilian thinker, *Amefricanity* highlights that the African experience on the American continent transcends national borders and points to a shared identity built on resistance to colonialism, racism, and domination. She emphasizes how this identity is tied to language, religion, cultural practices, and the fight for rights, underscoring that African cultures in the Americas have been and continue to be creative, resilient, and shaped by contexts of oppression, serving as a continuous space for belonging, solidarity, and political transformation.

Amefricanity is therefore a proposal for understanding the world through the experiences of African descendants, connecting the struggles of the Americas and the Caribbean with a broader vision of diaspora and global resistance.

> The terms "Afro-American" and "African-American" lead us to an initial reflection: that Black people would only exist in the United States and not across the entire continent. And to another, which points to the unconscious reproduction of the imperialist position of the United States, which claims to be "America." After all, what about the other countries in South, Central, Insular, and North America? Why consider the Caribbean as something separate, when it was precisely there that the history of this America began?... The political and cultural implications of the category of "Amefricanity" are, in fact, democratic; precisely because the term itself allows us to go beyond territorial, linguistic, and ideological limitations, opening new perspectives for a deeper understanding of this part of the world where it manifests: America as a whole (South, Central, North, and Insular). Beyond its purely geographical character, the category of Amefricanity incorporates an entire historical process of intense cultural dynamics (adaptation, resistance, reinterpretation, and the creation of new forms) that is Afro-centered, that is, referenced in models such as: Jamaica and the Akan, its dominant model; Brazil and its Yoruba, Bantu, and Ewe-Fon models. Consequently, it guides us towards the construction of an entire ethnic identity. Needless to say, the category of Amefricanity is closely linked to those of Pan-Africanism, Negritude, Afrocentricity, etc. (Gonzalez 2020, 134–5)

With this in mind, when I say that I found a way to reflect on that panel in Ukraine through the orixás, I am referring to the Amefrican epistemology, particularly of the peoples of candomblé and umbanda, and, why not, of santería in countries like Cuba, Haiti, and Colombia, among others where the orixás are worshipped. As a woman of candomblé, my worldview is profoundly influenced by the terreiros[3] and its epistemology.[4] In Brazil, there are different nations of candomblé, and the perspective I bring here is based on nagô principles, particularly from the Ketu nation.

The orixás are deities associated with natural phenomena: The sea is an orixá, as is the river, thunder, mist, and so on. Each orixá has mythical stories, or itãs, that narrate their existence on Earth. Male orixás are known as Oboró, while female orixás are the Yabás.

We can begin to glimpse connections between the realities of Ukraine and Brazil, between the experiences of Black women in the United States and India, because through the logic of the orixás, theoretical associations become possible since nature manifests everywhere. Oxum, for instance, is a deity in candomblé represented by waterfalls. Her archetype is associated with self-love, fertility, beauty, and prosperity, but also with resistance and feminine strength.

An itã recounts that in the early times, the Oborós began deciding the course of humanity without consulting any Yabás. Resentful at being excluded, Oxum took revenge on the male orixás by condemning all women to sterility, making any male attempts at fertility fail. The waters dried up, and the land became barren. Alarmed, the men consulted Olodumare, the supreme god, who revealed that Oxum had been excluded. He advised them to invite her and the other women to decide the course of humanity, for without Oxum and her power over fertility, nothing could progress. Following Olodumare's wisdom, they invited her, and life on Earth flourished once again.

This itã speaks to the power of women when their voices are silenced. It challenges the expectation of women's compliance and highlights the reflection on how far patriarchal society can go before nature collapses, leaving men begging for a stream.

Similarly, Iansã, also known as Oyá, governs the winds. One of her itãs tells how she guarded a secret power to transform into a buffalo. Ogum, enchanted by her strength, stole her buffalo skin, attempting to control her by marrying her. However, she rediscovered her power, unleashed her fury, and ensured her children had tools to call for her protection. These stories of the Yabás challenge patriarchal notions of women, showcasing them as wise, creative, protective, and powerful figures.

The teachings of the orixás not only offer tools for understanding human experiences but also guide reflections on our relationship with nature. Iemanjá, the orixá of the sea, teaches us about the patience and resilience of the ocean. Once, as an itã about her tells us, she could no longer bear the disrespect she faced and began to rise higher and higher, frightening everyone around her. As we in the terreiro community know, her patience is not infinite, and the current degradation of marine ecosystems serves as a stark reminder of the consequences of human actions.

The war in Ukraine, for example, has led to the indiscriminate use of sonar technology, which has caused significant harm to marine life, particularly dolphins (Kroger 2023). These deaths remind us of the interconnectedness of human and environmental suffering. Just as the myths of Iemanjá reveal the necessity of balance and respect for the natural world, these tragedies call on us to reflect on how the violence of war extends beyond human borders, affecting the very ecosystems that sustain life.

By weaving together ancestral wisdom with contemporary crises, the Amefrican epistemologies offer a framework for understanding global challenges in ways that emphasize respect, solidarity, and the urgent need for transformative action. This interconnected worldview can inspire us to reimagine solutions that honor both human and ecological well-being.

Thus, Amefrican epistemology and the worship of the orixás provide tools to understand the world in a connected way, respecting differences and highlighting similarities in human experience. These narratives remind us of the importance of valuing ancestral wisdom and fostering global solidarity in the face of challenges.

Djamila Ribeiro is a guest professor at New York University and at the Pontifical Catholic University of São Paulo. She holds a degree and a master's in political philosophy from the Federal University of São Paulo. As a writer, her works include *Where We Stand* (Yale University Press, 2024). She can be reached at contatodjamilaribeiro@gmail.com.

Notes

1. In Brazil, the terms *negro* and *preto* are used in different contexts to refer to the Black population, but they carry distinct nuances. *Negro* is a broader sociopolitical term that encompasses individuals of African descent, including those categorized as preto (dark-skinned) and pardo (mixed-race) according to official data classifications. *Preto*, on the other hand, refers specifically to individuals with darker skin tones within the Black community. For the purposes of this text, the term *Black* will be used as a synonym for negro, reflecting the broader, collective identity of African-descendant populations in Brazil.

2. The term *mestizage* refers to the process of racial mixing that occurred throughout Latin America during the colonial and postcolonial periods. Derived from the Spanish *mestizaje* and the Portuguese *mestiçagem*, it historically described the blending of Indigenous, African, and European ancestries. In Brazil, mestizage was not merely a demographic phenomenon but a deliberate colonial strategy tied to ideologies of "whitening" (branqueamento). Unlike the English term *miscegenation*, which is commonly associated with laws regulating interracial marriage, *mestizage* carries a broader cultural and historical connotation, encompassing the social and political projects that framed racial mixing as both a tool of oppression and a marker of national identity. The term is particularly significant in discussions about the enduring legacies of colonial violence and the resistance of marginalized communities to cultural and racial erasure. For further discussion on these topics, see Gloria Anzaldúa, *Borderlands/La Frontera: The New Mestiza* (1987) and Alessandra Devulsky, *Colorismo* (2019).
3. Terreiros are sacred spaces and communities central to Afro-Brazilian religions like candomblé and umbanda. These spaces serve as places of worship, cultural preservation, and communal living, where spiritual practices and rituals are conducted to honor the orixás—deities associated with natural forces and human experiences. Terreiros also function as social and cultural hubs, preserving ancestral knowledge, oral traditions, and rituals brought to Brazil by enslaved Africans and adapted to the Brazilian context. Each terreiro is typically led by a spiritual leader, such as a yalorixá (a female priest) or a babalorixá (a male priest), who guides the community in spiritual matters. The structure of terreiros reflects African traditions of hierarchy and collective living, with members often participating in roles that support the spiritual and material needs of the community. Beyond their religious role, terreiros have historically been spaces of resistance and solidarity, offering refuge and cultural identity for Afro-Brazilian communities in the face of systemic racism and oppression. They remain vital to understanding the spiritual, social, and cultural dynamics of Afro-Brazilian traditions. See Sidnei Barreto Nogueira, *Intolerância Religiosa* (2019).
4. Thinking in an epistemology of terreiros is one example of Amefrican epistemology and emphasizes the unique ways of knowing, understanding, and interpreting the world that emerge from these sacred spaces. This epistemology is grounded in the lived experiences of spiritual practices, communal care, and ancestral wisdom cultivated in terreiros. It highlights a relational, embodied, and cyclical approach to knowledge, contrasting with dominant Western frameworks that prioritize linearity, individualism, and abstraction. The term underscores how terreiros generate and sustain

knowledge systems that resist colonial erasure and offer alternative ways of understanding identity, nature, and human relationships. See Sidnei Barreto Nogueira, *Intolerância Religiosa* (2019).

Works Cited

Anzaldúa, Gloria. 1987. *Borderlands/La Frontera: The New Mestiza*. San Francisco: Aunt Lute Books.

Barreto, Raquel. 2024. Preface to *Festas Populares no Brasil*, by Lélia Gonzalez. São Paulo: Boitempo.

Devulsky, Alessandra. 2019. *Colorismo*. São Paulo: Jandaira.

Gonzalez, Lélia. 2020. "A categoria político-cultural Amefricanidade." In *Por um feminismo afrolatinoamericano: ensaios, intervenções e diálogos*, compiled by Flávia Rios and Márcia Lima. São Paulo: Zahar.

Hollanda, Heloisa Buarque de, comp. 2020. *Pensamento feminista hoje: perspectivas decoloniais*. Rio de Janeiro: Bazar do Tempo.

Kroger, Alix. 2023. "How the War in Ukraine Is Killing Marine Mammals." *BBC*, January 4. https://www.bbc.com/future/article/20221222-how-the-war-in-ukraine-is-killing-marine-mammals.

Massuela, Amanda. 2018. "Quem é e sobre o que escreve o autor brasileiro." *Cult*, February 5. https://revistacult.uol.com.br/home/quem-e-e-sobre-o-que-escreve-o-autor-brasileiro/.

Mills, Charles W. 1997. *The Racial Contract*. Ithaca: Cornell University Press.

Nogueira, Sidnei Barreto. 2019. *Intolerância Religiosa*. São Paulo: Jandaíra.

Post, Chad. 2017. "The Three Percent 10 Years Later: An Interview with Chad Post." Interview by Maria Eliades. *Ploughshares,* January 30. https://pshares.org/blog/the-three-percent-10-years-later-an-interview-with-chad-post/.

Prandi, Reginaldo. 2013. *Mitologia dos Orixás*. São Paulo: Companhia das Letras.